Advances in Statistical Simulation and Computing

Advances in Statistical Simulation and Computing

Guest Editors

Francisco Novoa-Muñoz
Bernardo M. Lagos-Álvarez

MDPI

Basel • Beijing • Wuhan • Barcelona • Belgrade • Novi Sad • Cluj • Manchester

Guest Editors
Francisco Novoa-Muñoz
Department of Nursing
University of Bío-Bío
Chillán
Chile

Bernardo M. Lagos-Álvarez
Statistics Department
Concepción University
Concepción
Chile

Editorial Office
MDPI AG
Grosspeteranlage 5
4052 Basel, Switzerland

This is a reprint of the Special Issue, published open access by the journal *Axioms* (ISSN 2075-1680), freely accessible at: https://www.mdpi.com/journal/axioms/special_issues/9A9BMR2T71.

For citation purposes, cite each article independently as indicated on the article page online and as indicated below:

Lastname, A.A.; Lastname, B.B. Article Title. *Journal Name* **Year**, *Volume Number*, Page Range.

ISBN 978-3-7258-6844-5 (Hbk)
ISBN 978-3-7258-6845-2 (PDF)
https://doi.org/10.3390/books978-3-7258-6845-2

Contents

About the Editors

Francisco Novoa-Muñoz

Francisco Eduardo Novoa Muñoz is with the Departamento de Enfermería, Facultad de Ciencias de la Salud y de los Alimentos, Universidad del Bío-Bío, Chile. His research interests focus on goodness of fit, applied statistics, time series analysis, and statistical modeling, with particular emphasis on simulation based methods and their applications in health sciences and interdisciplinary contexts. He holds a doctoral degree in Mathematics with specialization in Statistics and Operations Research and has more than thirty years of academic experience in teaching, research, and graduate supervision. He has directed undergraduate and graduate theses, participated in national and international scientific conferences, and published research articles in peer reviewed journals indexed in major international databases. He is the author of a specialized monograph on goodness of fit methods and has contributed to the development and execution of institutional research projects both as principal investigator and coinvestigator, as well as to externally funded research initiatives. His academic activity includes active participation in research groups and membership in the academic boards of master's and doctoral programs. He also serves regularly as a reviewer for scientific journals, contributing to the evaluation of methodological and applied research in statistics. His work is characterized by the integration of statistical theory, computational techniques, and simulation based approaches aimed at addressing complex inferential problems and supporting reproducible and rigorous scientific research.

Bernardo M. Lagos-Álvarez

Bernardo Moisés Lagos-Álvarez obtained his PhD in Science with a specialization in Statistics from the University of São Paulo, Brazil. His doctoral dissertation focused on Bartlett correction in ARMA models. He is currently a faculty member of the Department of Statistics at the University of Concepción, Chile, where he teaches undergraduate and graduate courses, including Geostatistics, Bayesian Analysis, Statistical Computing, Generalized Linear Models, and related subjects. His research interests and thesis supervision activities at both undergraduate and graduate levels include time series analysis, statistical methods, space–time statistics, and Bayesian statistics. He has taught the course Space–Time Statistical Models on two occasions within the University's Summer School program. In addition, he collaborates as a faculty member in doctoral programs and research centers from other academic units, both within and outside his home university.

Dr. Lagos-Álvarez has been a visiting researcher at McMaster University, Colorado School of Mines, Universitat Jaume I, the University of Seville, and the Institute of Mathematics and Computer Science of the University of São Paulo. He has also participated in the organization of several scientific conferences and specialized sessions. His main academic interest lies in the quantitative understanding of real-world phenomena through stochastic methods, aiming to model, describe, control, predict, and forecast uncertainty.

axioms MDPI

Editorial

Advances in Statistical Simulation and Computing

Francisco Novoa-Muñoz [1,*] and Bernardo M. Lagos-Álvarez [2]

[1] Department of Nursing, Faculty of Health and Food Sciences, University of Bío-Bío, Chillán 3800708, Chile
[2] Statistics Department, Faculty of Physical Sciences and Mathematics, Concepción University, Concepción 4030000, Chile; bla@udec.cl
* Correspondence: fnovoa@ubiobio.cl

1. Introduction

In this Editorial, we are pleased to introduce the Special Issue of the journal Axioms entitled "Advances in Statistical Simulation and Computing".

Statistical simulation and computational methods play a central role in addressing complex problems across a wide range of scientific disciplines. Simulation-based techniques, particularly those relying on stochastic sampling, provide indispensable tools for exploring probabilistic and statistical models that are analytically intractable. At the same time, the rapid growth in computational power and the development of advanced algorithms have significantly reduced computational costs, enabling more sophisticated analyses and large-scale studies.

The aim of this Special Issue is to bring together recent theoretical and applied contributions that advance simulation methodologies, computational techniques, and their applications in statistics and related fields. The published articles address novel probability models, robust and flexible inferential methods, efficient algorithms for large and complex datasets, and simulation-based assessments of statistical procedures. Collectively, these contributions reflect current trends and future directions in statistical simulation and computing.

2. Overview of the Published Papers

This Special Issue comprises eight peer-reviewed contributions, each addressing methodological, computational, or applied challenges in modern statistical simulation and computing.

In Contribution 1, Caamaño-Carrillo, Bevilacqua, Zamudio-Monserratt, and Contreras-Reyes develop a novel bivariate distribution constructed via the Appell hypergeometric function, with Pareto–Feller marginals derived from independent gamma random variables. The proposed model extends classical bivariate beta-type distributions and accommodates heavy-tailed behavior, a key feature in many applied settings. The authors provide a comprehensive analytical treatment, deriving distributional functions, moment-based characteristics, and information-theoretic measures, and they support their theoretical results with numerical illustrations.

In Contribution 2, Chocotea-Poca, Nicolis, and Ibacache-Pulgar focus on flexible modeling of binomial response data through the introduction of a skew-t link function. By incorporating both asymmetry and heavy tails, the proposed model enhances robustness and adaptability in regression settings characterized by complex data structures. A penalized likelihood estimation strategy is adopted to stabilize inference, and extensive simulation studies, together with real-data applications, demonstrate clear improvements over traditional symmetric and skewed link models.

In Contribution 3, Novoa-Muñoz and Aguirre-González address a long-standing gap in goodness-of-fit assessment for the bivariate negative binomial distribution. They propose a computationally efficient test based on a Cramér–von Mises-type statistic, combined with a reparameterization via the probability generating function. The null distribution is approximated using a parametric bootstrap scheme accelerated through parallel computing. Simulation results confirm accurate size control and satisfactory power, while real-data applications highlight the practical feasibility of the proposed approach.

In Contribution 4, Liu, Zhao, Xu, and Wang examine nonparametric specification testing for nonlinear regression models in the context of large-scale data. To overcome computational limitations, the authors employ a divide-and-conquer strategy and study the role of smoothing parameter selection in ensuring optimal test performance. By adopting a penalty-based method, they obtain a scalable test with an asymptotic normal null distribution and adaptive properties, as confirmed through numerical simulations.

In Contribution 5, Reyes, Arnold, Gómez, Venegas, and Gómez propose a new family of distributions designed to model non-negative bimodal data with an excess of small values. The model is constructed by modifying the exponential distribution through a polynomial adjustment, yielding greater flexibility in capturing complex distributional shapes. The authors investigate analytical properties, perform simulation-based maximum likelihood estimation, and demonstrate superior empirical performance in real-data applications when compared to existing bimodal exponential models.

In Contribution 6, Almulhim, Alamari, Laksaci, and Kaid introduce a nonparametric estimator for conditional mode estimation with functional covariates. The proposed method combines local linear smoothing with L1-robust techniques and formulates modal regression through the minimization of a quantile derivative. Theoretical results establish almost complete consistency and convergence rates consistent with those found in functional data analysis. Simulation experiments and real-data studies illustrate the estimator's effectiveness in high-dimensional prediction contexts.

In Contribution 7, Jiang, Chen, and Yan develop a robust adaptive lasso methodology for autoregressive models, motivated by the need for robustness and sparsity in the presence of outliers and heavy-tailed innovations. By leveraging partial autocorrelation coefficients as adaptive penalty weights and a robust autocorrelation estimator based on the FQn statistic, the proposed approach improves parameter estimation and variable selection. Its performance is supported by simulation studies and applications to real datasets.

Finally, Contribution 8 by Phoophiwfa, Busababodhin, Volodin, and Suraphee presents a closed-form expression for the asymptotic variance of the coefficient of variation estimator under a reparameterized Birnbaum–Saunders distribution. Using moment-based estimation and the delta method, the authors derive compact analytical results that facilitate practical implementation. Monte Carlo simulations confirm favorable finite-sample properties, and an application to environmental data illustrates the relevance of the proposed methodology in applied statistical analysis.

3. Concluding Remarks

The contributions collected in this Special Issue reflect the growing importance of statistical simulation and computationally driven methodologies in modern statistical research. Across diverse contexts—ranging from distribution theory and regression modeling to time series analysis and functional data—the published papers emphasize robustness, computational efficiency, and practical applicability. Together, they illustrate how simulation-based approaches and advanced computational strategies can effectively address complex data structures and emerging challenges. We hope that this Special Issue will stimulate further

https://doi.org/10.3390/axioms15010062

methodological developments and foster continued research at the intersection of statistics, simulation, and computing.

Conflicts of Interest: The authors declare no conflict of interest.

List of Contributions:

1. Caamaño-Carrillo, C.; Bevilacqua, M.; Zamudio-Monserratt, M.; Contreras-Reyes, J.E. Bivariate Pareto–Feller Distribution Based on Appell Hypergeometric Function. *Axioms* **2024**, *13*, 701. https://doi.org/10.3390/axioms13100701.
2. Chocotea-Poca, O.; Nicolis, O.; Ibacache-Pulgar, G. Maximum Penalized Likelihood Estimation of the Skew-*t* Link Model for Binomial Response Data. *Axioms* **2024**, *13*, 749. https://doi.org/10.3390/axioms13110749.
3. Novoa-Muñoz, F.; Aguirre-González, J.P. Goodness-of-Fit Test for the Bivariate Negative Binomial Distribution. *Axioms* **2025**, *14*, 54. https://doi.org/10.3390/axioms14010054.
4. Liu, P.; Zhao, Y.; Xu, L.; Wang, T. Optimal Minimax Rate of Smoothing Parameter in Distributed Nonparametric Specification Test. *Axioms* **2025**, *14*, 228. https://doi.org/10.3390/axioms14030228.
5. Reyes, J.; Arnold, B.C.; Gómez, Y.M.; Venegas, O.; Gómez, H.W. Modified Bimodal Exponential Distribution with Applications. *Axioms* **2025**, *14*, 461. https://doi.org/10.3390/axioms14060461.
6. Almulhim, F.A.; Alamari, M.B.; Laksaci, A.; Kaid, Z. Modal Regression Estimation by Local Linear Approach in High-Dimensional Data Case. *Axioms* **2025**, *14*, 537. https://doi.org/10.3390/axioms14070537.
7. Jiang, Y.; Chen, F.; Yan, X. Robust Adaptive Lasso via Robust Sample Autocorrelation Coefficient for the Autoregressive Models. *Axioms* **2025**, *14*, 701. https://doi.org/10.3390/axioms14090701.
8. Phoophiwfa, T.; Busababodhin, P.; Volodin, A.; Suraphee, S. Derivation of a Closed-Form Asymptotic Variance for the Coefficient of Variation Under the Reparameterized Birnbaum–Saunders Distribution. *Axioms* **2025**, *14*, 792. https://doi.org/10.3390/axioms14110792.

https://doi.org/10.3390/axioms15010062

axioms

MDPI

Article

Bivariate Pareto–Feller Distribution Based on Appell Hypergeometric Function

Christian Caamaño-Carrillo [1], Moreno Bevilacqua [2,3], Michael Zamudio-Monserratt [4] and Javier E. Contreras-Reyes [5,*]

1 Departamento de Estadística, Facultad de Ciencias, Universidad del Bío-Bío, Concepción 4081112, Chile; chcaaman@ubiobio.cl
2 Facultad de Ingeniería y Ciencia, Universidad Adolfo Ibañez, Viña del Mar 2580335, Chile; moreno.bevilacqua@uai.cl
3 Dipartimento di Scienze Ambientali, Informatica e Statistica, Ca' Foscari University of Venice, 30172 Venice, Italy
4 NCT/Odisseia-Observatory of Socio-Environmental Dynamics (UnB), Universidade de Brasilia, Brasilia 70910-900, Brazil; michael.zamudio@postgrado.uv.cl
5 Instituto de Matemática, Física y Estadística, Facultad de Ingeniería y Negocios, Universidad de Las Américas, Sede Viña del Mar, 7 Norte 1348, Viña del Mar 2531098, Chile
* Correspondence: jecontrr@uc.cl; Tel.: +56-9-7960-8218

Abstract: The Pareto–Feller distribution has been widely used across various disciplines to model "heavy-tailed" phenomena, where extreme events such as high incomes or large losses are of interest. In this paper, we present a new bivariate distribution based on the Appell hypergeometric function with marginal Pareto–Feller distributions obtained from two independent gamma random variables. The proposed distribution has the beta prime marginal distributions as special case, which were obtained using a Kibble-type bivariate gamma distribution, and the stochastic representation was obtained by the quotient of a scale mixture of two gamma random variables. This result can be viewed as a generalization of the standard bivariate beta I (or inverted bivariate beta distribution). Moreover, the obtained bivariate density is based on two confluent hypergeometric functions. Then, we derive the probability distribution function, the cumulative distribution function, the moment-generating function, the characteristic function, the approximated differential entropy, and the approximated mutual information index. Based on numerical examples, the exact and approximated expressions are shown.

Keywords: generalized gamma distribution; beta prime marginal distributions; generalized hypergeometric function; moment generation function; entropy

MSC: 60E05; 62H10; 33C65

1. Introduction

The Pareto distribution has been a key tool in economics and for modeling wealth distribution, as well as in other areas like insurance and finance, where capturing extreme events is crucial [1]. However, real-world data often exhibit more complex structures than those described by the classical Pareto distribution [2]. In this context, Feller (1971) [3] proposed an extension called the Pareto–Feller distribution which includes an additional shape parameter, allowing the distribution to better fit a wider range of phenomena with thicker or heavy tails as needed [1].

The Pareto–Feller distribution has been widely used across various disciplines to model "heavy-tailed" phenomena, where extreme events such as high incomes or large losses are of interest. The Pareto–Feller distribution emerged from the need for a distribution that offers greater flexibility in data modeling by introducing an additional parameter to control the tail shape and skewness, thus providing a more accurate description of empirical data compared with the standard Pareto distribution [2]. This distribution has found applications in various fields such as risk theory, river flow modeling, and natural disaster analysis due to its ability to represent both heavy tails and asymmetric distributions. The additional flexibility provided by this distribution is especially valuable in situations where conventional distributions, like the classical Pareto distribution, fail to capture the observed variability and extreme behavior in the data. Notable variants include Pareto type I, used in wealth analysis [1], the generalized Pareto distribution for modeling extreme events [4], and the Lomax or Pareto type II distribution, which is applied in survival analysis [5]. Other important variants are Pareto type IV, which offers greater flexibility in tail shapes [6], and the truncated Pareto distribution, which is used in scenarios with physical upper limits [7]. Additionally, the log-logistic distribution, which is employed in contexts similar to the Pareto distribution but with greater flexibility in the tails, is used in survival analysis and system failure studies [8].

The Pareto–Feller distribution can be constructed as a location-scale transformation of the ratio of two independent gamma-distributed random variables. This method allows the distribution to capture a wide range of tail behaviors and offers flexibility in modeling heavy-tailed phenomena. The use of gamma distributions for generating such models is well documented in the statistical literature. Specifically, more flexible models can be obtained through an appropriate transformation of a bivariate gamma distribution or independent copies of it. This approach is appealing because the correlation of the transformed bivariate gamma distribution is directly tied to the correlation of the original bivariate gamma distribution. Such constructions are commonly used in spatial data modeling. Examples include $t-$distributed spatial models [9], Weibull spatial models [10], and Poisson spatial models [11]. On the other hand, Kotz et al. (2004) [12] described similar methods for transforming distributions via ratios of gamma variables which are widely applicable in reliability and survival analysis contexts [12].

Since the construction of the Pareto–Feller distribution is related to the gamma distribution, it is necessary to first define the bivariate gamma distribution to develop the bivariate case of the Pareto–Feller distribution. Thus, we start by defining a sequence of independent normal random variables and show how these lead to a gamma distribution as follows. Let Z_{ik}, $i = 1, \ldots, \nu$ with $\nu > 2$ be a sequence of independent standardized normal random variables whose correlation function is given by $Corr(Z_{ik}, Z_{jk}) = \rho, i \neq j$, and let

$$W_k = \sum_{i=1}^{\nu} \frac{Z_{ik}^2}{\alpha}, \quad \alpha > 0, \;\; k = 1, 2. \tag{1}$$

Then, W_k is a random variable with a gamma marginal distribution (i.e., $W_k \sim Gamma(\nu/2, \alpha/2)$, where $\nu/2$ represents the shape parameter and $\alpha/2$ represents the rate parameter), with the probability density function (pdf) being given by

$$f_{W_k} = \frac{\alpha^{\nu/2}}{2^{\nu/2}\Gamma(\nu/2)} w_k^{\nu/2-1} e^{-\alpha w_k/2},$$

where $\mathbb{E}[W_k] = \nu/\alpha$ and $Var(W_k) = 2\nu/\alpha^2$ [10].

The construction of a bivariate Pareto–Feller distribution is derived from the ratio of two bivariate gamma distributions as shown in Section 2. We consider the bivariate vector $\mathbf{W} = (W_1, W_2)^\top$, where the stochastic representation of W_k, $k = 1, 2$ is given in Equation (1). Vere-Jones [13] showed that the distribution of $\mathbf{W}$ has a correlated bivariate gamma distribution with the parameters $\nu > 0$ and $\gamma > 0$, while the pdf is given by

$$f_{\mathbf{W}}(\mathbf{w}) = \frac{2^{-\nu}\gamma^{\nu}(w_1 w_2)^{\nu/2-1} e^{-\frac{\gamma(w_1+w_2)}{2(1-\rho^2)}}}{\Gamma(\frac{\nu}{2})(1-\rho^2)^{\nu/2}} \left(\frac{\gamma\sqrt{\rho^2 w_1 w_2}}{2(1-\rho^2)}\right)^{1-\nu/2} I_{\nu/2-1}\left(\frac{\gamma\sqrt{\rho^2 w_1 w_2}}{(1-\rho^2)}\right), \tag{2}$$

where $I_\alpha(\cdot)$ is the usual modified Bessel function of the γ-order of the first kind. Gamma variables can be used as building blocks for the construction of flexible non-Gaussian variables. Henceforth, we will call $\mathbf{W}$ a gamma random vector with an underlying correlation ρ [14,15] such that the correlation of the gamma bivariate is $\rho_{\mathbf{W}} = \rho^2$. Moreover, when

$\rho = 0$, Equation (2) can be written as the product of two independent gamma random variables (i.e., $W_k \sim Gamma(\nu/2, \alpha/2), k = 1, 2$). Thus, zero pairwise correlation implies pairwise independence, as in the Gaussian case. The pdf $f_{\mathbf{W}}$ was first discussed in [16], and its properties were studied in [17,18].

The bivariate Pareto–Feller distribution represents a less commonly discussed extension in the statistical literature. It builds upon the principles established by the univariate Pareto distribution. The authors of [19] addressed extreme value distributions and included discussions which may be relevant to bivariate generalizations. Additionally, the authors of [20] provided further insights into bivariate distributions, enriching the understanding of Pareto–Feller distributions. These references offer both theoretical and practical frameworks for researching and applying Pareto–Feller distributions in bivariate contexts. The latter works motivated this paper, which presented a bivariate Pareto–Feller distribution built from an Appell hypergeometric function.

This paper is organized as follows. Section 2 presents the bivariate Pareto–Feller distribution. In particular, the pdf, cumulative distribution function (cdf), joint moment-generating function (mgf), characteristic functions, cross-product moment function, mean, variance, covariance, and correlation function are presented. In Section 3, some approximations of the differential entropy and, consequently, the mutual information index are presented. Finally, some discussions and conclusions are presented in Section 4. All simulations included special hypergeometric functions such as the Appell hypergeometric one, and all were implemented in `R` 4.4.1. software [21] using the `zipfR` and `hypergeo` packages. All proofs of theorems and propositions can be found in the Appendix A.

2. Bivariate Pareto–Feller Distribution

Let us define a random variable V with support on the positive real line, defined as a scale mixture of two gamma random variables:

$$V = \frac{W}{R}, \tag{3}$$

where $W \sim Gamma(\alpha/2, 1), \alpha > 0$ and $R \sim Gamma(\nu/2, 1), \nu > 0$. Then, V is a random variable with a marginal distribution of the beta I type or beta prime [12,22] and denoted by $V \sim Be'(\nu/2, \alpha/2)$, with the pdf given by

$$f_V(v) = \frac{\Gamma(\frac{\nu+\alpha}{2})}{\Gamma(\frac{\nu}{2})\Gamma(\frac{\alpha}{2})} v^{\nu/2-1}(v+1)^{-(\nu+\alpha)/2}.$$

The beta prime distribution is anchored to a shape parameter of the gamma distributions. This construction was previously proposed in [23–25].

Based on the stochastic representation in Equation (3), we consider the bivariate vector of $\mathbf{V} = (V_1, V_2)^\top$, where

$$V_i = \frac{W_i}{R_i}, \quad i = 1, 2; \tag{4}$$

Here, $\mathbf{W} = (W_1, W_2)^\top$ and $\mathbf{R} = (R_1, R_2)^\top$ are two correlated bivariate gamma distributions with correlations $\rho_W = \rho_R = \rho^2$, where $W_i \sim Gamma(\alpha/2, 1)$, $\alpha > 0$ and $R_i \sim Gamma(\nu/2, 1), \nu > 0, R_i \perp W_j, \forall i, j, i, j = 1, 2$. Thus, $V_i \sim Be'(\nu/2, \alpha/2), i = 1, 2$.

A new bivariate distribution with a beta prime marginal distribution obtained from the Kibble-type bivariate gamma distribution given in Equation (2) is presented in the following theorem. This result can be viewed as a generalization of the standard bivariate beta I distribution (or inverted bivariate beta distribution) [26].

Theorem 1. *Let W and R be two independent gamma random variables, and let $V = WR^{-1}$. Then, the pdf of $\mathbf{V} = (V_1, V_2)^\top \in \mathbb{R}_+ \times \mathbb{R}_+$ is given by*

$$
\begin{aligned}
f_{\mathbf{V}}(\mathbf{v}) &= \frac{(v_1v_2)^{\nu/2-1}\Gamma^2\left(\frac{\nu+\alpha}{2}\right)[(v_1+1)(v_2+1)]^{-(\nu+\alpha)/2}}{\Gamma^2\left(\frac{\nu}{2}\right)\Gamma^2\left(\frac{\alpha}{2}\right)(1-\rho^2)^{-(\nu+\alpha)/2}} \\
&\quad \times F_4\left(\frac{\nu+\alpha}{2}, \frac{\nu+\alpha}{2}; \frac{\nu}{2}, \frac{\alpha}{2}; \frac{\rho^2 v_1 v_2}{(v_1+1)(v_2+1)}, \frac{\rho^2}{(v_1+1)(v_2+1)}\right),
\end{aligned} \tag{5}
$$

where F_4 is an Appell hypergeometric function of the fourth kind, defined as

$$
F_4(a,b;c,c';w,z) = \sum_{k=0}^{\infty}\sum_{m=0}^{\infty} \frac{(a)_{k+m}(b)_{k+m}w^k z^m}{k!m!(c)_k(c')_m}, \quad |\sqrt{w}| + |\sqrt{z}| < 1.
$$

The special functions F_4 and the Gaussian hypergeometric function ${}_2F_1$ are related through the identity

$$
F_4(a,b;c,c';w,z) = \sum_{k=0}^{\infty} \frac{(a)_k(b)_k z^k}{k!(c')_k} {}_2F_1(a+k, b+k; c; w), \quad |\sqrt{w}| + |\sqrt{z}| < 1.
$$

where $(a)_k := \Gamma(a+k)/\Gamma(a)$, for which $k \in \mathbb{N} \cup \{0\}$ is the Pochhammer symbol. The Gaussian hypergeometric function is a special case of more general power series, where the generalized hypergeometric function is defined for $p, q = 0, 1, 2, \ldots$ as

$$
{}_pF_q(a_1, a_2, \ldots, a_p; b_1, b_2, \ldots, b_q; x) := \sum_{k=0}^{\infty} \frac{(a_1)_k, (a_2)_k, \ldots, (a_p)_k}{(b_1)_k, (b_2)_k, \ldots, (b_q)_k} \frac{x^k}{k!}
$$

When $\rho = 0$, the pdf in Theorem 1 involves the product of two independent beta prime random variables $Be' \sim (\nu/2, \alpha/2)$.

We now consider a new random variable Y, defined as

$$
Y := \mu + \frac{q}{c} V^{1/p}, \tag{6}
$$

where $Y \geq \mu \geq 0$, $c = \frac{\Gamma\left(\frac{\nu}{2}+\frac{1}{p}\right)\Gamma\left(\frac{\alpha}{2}-\frac{1}{p}\right)}{\Gamma\left(\frac{\nu}{2}\right)\Gamma\left(\frac{\alpha}{2}\right)}$, $q > 0$, and $p > 0$. This random variable is a marginal Pareto–Feller distribution. Specifically, using the notation of [20], we marginally have $Y \sim PF(\mu, q/c, 1/p, \nu/2, \alpha/2)$ with a density defined by

$$
f_Y(y) = \frac{\frac{(cp)}{q}\left(\frac{c(y-\mu)}{q}\right)^{p\nu/2-1}\Gamma\left(\frac{\nu+\alpha}{2}\right)}{\Gamma\left(\frac{\nu}{2}\right)\Gamma\left(\frac{\alpha}{2}\right)}\left[\left(\frac{c(y-\mu)}{q}\right)^p + 1\right]^{-(\nu+\alpha)/2}, \quad y > \mu,
$$

and a mean and variance given by

$$
\begin{aligned}
\mathbb{E}[Y] &= \mu + q, \\
Var(Y) &= q^2\left[\frac{\Gamma\left(\frac{\nu}{2}+\frac{2}{p}\right)\Gamma\left(\frac{\alpha}{2}-\frac{2}{p}\right)}{c\Gamma\left(\frac{\nu}{2}+\frac{1}{p}\right)\Gamma\left(\frac{\alpha}{2}-\frac{1}{p}\right)} - 1\right],
\end{aligned}
$$

respectively, with $\alpha p > 4$ [3].

The Pareto–Feller distribution includes as special cases different types of Pareto random variables definitions (type I, II, III, and IV; see [20]) and the so-called beta prime one. If we consider $\mu = 0$, then $Y \sim PF(0, q/c, 1/p, \nu/2, \alpha/2)$, and $\mathbf{Y} = (Y_1, Y_2)^\top$ is a random vector with a marginal Pareto–Feller distribution. A new bivariate distribution based on marginal Pareto–Feller distributions is presented in the following theorem.

Theorem 2. *Let $\mathbf{Y} = (Y_1, Y_2)^\top$, where $Y_i := \frac{q_i}{c} V_i^{1/p}$, $i = 1, 2$. The pdf of $\mathbf{Y}$ is given by*

$$f_{\mathbf{Y}}(\mathbf{y}) = \frac{\frac{(cp)^2}{q_1q_2}\left(\frac{c^2y_1y_2}{q_1q_2}\right)^{pv/2-1}\Gamma^2\left(\frac{v+\alpha}{2}\right)}{\Gamma^2\left(\frac{v}{2}\right)\Gamma^2\left(\frac{\alpha}{2}\right)(1-\rho^2)^{-(v+\alpha)/2}}\left[\left(\left(\frac{cy_1}{q_1}\right)^p+1\right)\left(\left(\frac{cy_2}{q2}\right)^p+1\right)\right]^{-(v+\alpha)/2} \times$$
$$F_4\left(\frac{v+\alpha}{2},\frac{v+\alpha}{2};\frac{v}{2},\frac{\alpha}{2};\frac{\rho^2(c^2y_1y_2)^p(q_1q_2)^{-p}}{\left(\left(\frac{cy_1}{q_1}\right)^p+1\right)\left(\left(\frac{cy_2}{q_2}\right)^p+1\right)},\frac{\rho^2}{\left(\left(\frac{cy_1}{q_1}\right)^p+1\right)\left(\left(\frac{cy_2}{q_2}\right)^p+1\right)}\right). \quad (7)$$

The pdf in Theorem 2 considers an Appell hypergeometric function F_4. We can write this as a series of hypergeometric functions ${}_2F_1$.

Figure 1 illustrates the pdf of Equation (7) for some parameters. When ρ increases, the largest values of y_1 and y_2 in the pdf are produced. However, these values depend on the other parameters. Independent of the ρ value, the pdf is close at the origin $(y_1, y_2) \approx (0,0)$ with a positive bias, and it decays exponentially for the smallest values ($v = 4$, $\alpha = 4$, $q_1 = 4$, $q_2 = 4$, and $p = 4$). When $\rho = 0.9$ and $v, \alpha = 8$ or 12, for example, the pdf has more symmetry and variability but less bias. Note that the pdf of $\mathbf{Y}$, given in Equation (5), is symmetric for negative values of ρ. Specifically, the same representations hold for $\rho = -0.25, -0.5, -0.9$ from Figure 1 while keeping the other parameters fixed.

Theorem 3. *The joint cdf of* $\mathbf{Y} = (Y_1, Y_2)^\top$ *in Equation (7) can be expressed as*

$$F_{\mathbf{Y}}(Y_1 \le t_1, Y_2 \le t_2) = \frac{\left(\frac{c^2t_1t_2}{q_1q_2}\right)^{pv/2}\Gamma^2\left(\frac{v+\alpha}{2}\right)}{\Gamma^2\left(\frac{v}{2}\right)\Gamma^2\left(\frac{\alpha}{2}\right)(1-\rho^2)^{-(v+\alpha)/2}}$$
$$\times\sum_{k=0}^{\infty}\sum_{m=0}^{\infty}\frac{\left(\frac{v+\alpha}{2}\right)^2_{k+m}\rho^{2k+2m}}{k!m!\left(\frac{v}{2}\right)_k\left(\frac{\alpha}{2}\right)_m(v/2+k)^2}\left(\frac{c^2t_1t_2}{q_1q_2}\right)^{pk}$$
$$\times{}_2F_1\left(\frac{v+\alpha}{2}+k+m,\frac{v}{2}+k;\frac{v}{2}+k+1;-\left(\frac{ct_1}{q_1}\right)^p\right)$$
$$\times{}_2F_1\left(\frac{v+\alpha}{2}+k+m,\frac{v}{2}+k;\frac{v}{2}+k+1;-\left(\frac{ct_2}{q_2}\right)^p\right). \quad (8)$$

Proposition 1. *The joint mgf and characteristic functions of* $\mathbf{Y} = (Y_1, Y_2)^\top$ *given in Equation (7) are*

$$(a)\ M_{\mathbf{Y}}(t_1,t_2) = \frac{\frac{(cp)^2}{q_1q_2}\Gamma^2\left(\frac{v+\alpha}{2}\right)}{\Gamma^2\left(\frac{v}{2}\right)\Gamma^2\left(\frac{\alpha}{2}\right)(1-\rho^2)^{-(v+\alpha)/2}}$$
$$\times\sum_{k=0}^{\infty}\sum_{m=0}^{\infty}\frac{\left(\frac{v+\alpha}{2}\right)_{k+m}\left(\frac{v+\alpha}{2}\right)_{k+m}}{\left(\frac{v}{2}\right)_k\left(\frac{\alpha}{2}\right)_m k!m!}\rho^{4km}(c^2/q_1q_2)^{(pv/2+pk-1)}$$
$$\times\left[\frac{1}{p}\left(\frac{q}{c}\right)^{p(v/2+k)}\frac{\Gamma(v/2+k)\Gamma(k+m+((v+\alpha)/2))}{\Gamma(m+((v+\alpha)/2)+v/2)}\right]^2$$
$$\left[-\frac{(t_1)^2-1}{(t_1)^4}\right]\left[-\frac{(t_2)^2-1}{(t_2)^4}\right], \quad (9)$$

with $t < 0$ *and*

$$(b)\ \phi_{\mathbf{Y}}(t_1,t_2) = \frac{\frac{(cp)^2}{q_1q_2}\Gamma^2\left(\frac{v+\alpha}{2}\right)}{\Gamma^2\left(\frac{v}{2}\right)\Gamma^2\left(\frac{\alpha}{2}\right)(1-\rho^2)^{-(v+\alpha)/2}}$$
$$\times\sum_{k=0}^{\infty}\sum_{m=0}^{\infty}\frac{\left(\frac{v+\alpha}{2}\right)_{k+m}\left(\frac{v+\alpha}{2}\right)_{k+m}}{\left(\frac{v}{2}\right)_k\left(\frac{\alpha}{2}\right)_m k!m!}\rho^{4km}(c^2/q_1q_2)^{(pv/2+pk-1)}$$

$$\times \left[\frac{1}{p} \left(\frac{q}{c} \right)^{p(\nu/2+k)} \frac{\Gamma(\nu/2+k)\Gamma(k+m+((\nu+\alpha)/2))}{\Gamma(m+((\nu+\alpha)/2)+\nu/2)} \right]^2$$
$$\times \left[-\frac{(it_1)^2 - 1}{(it_1)^4} \right] \left[-\frac{(it_2)^2 - 1}{(it_2)^4} \right]. \tag{10}$$

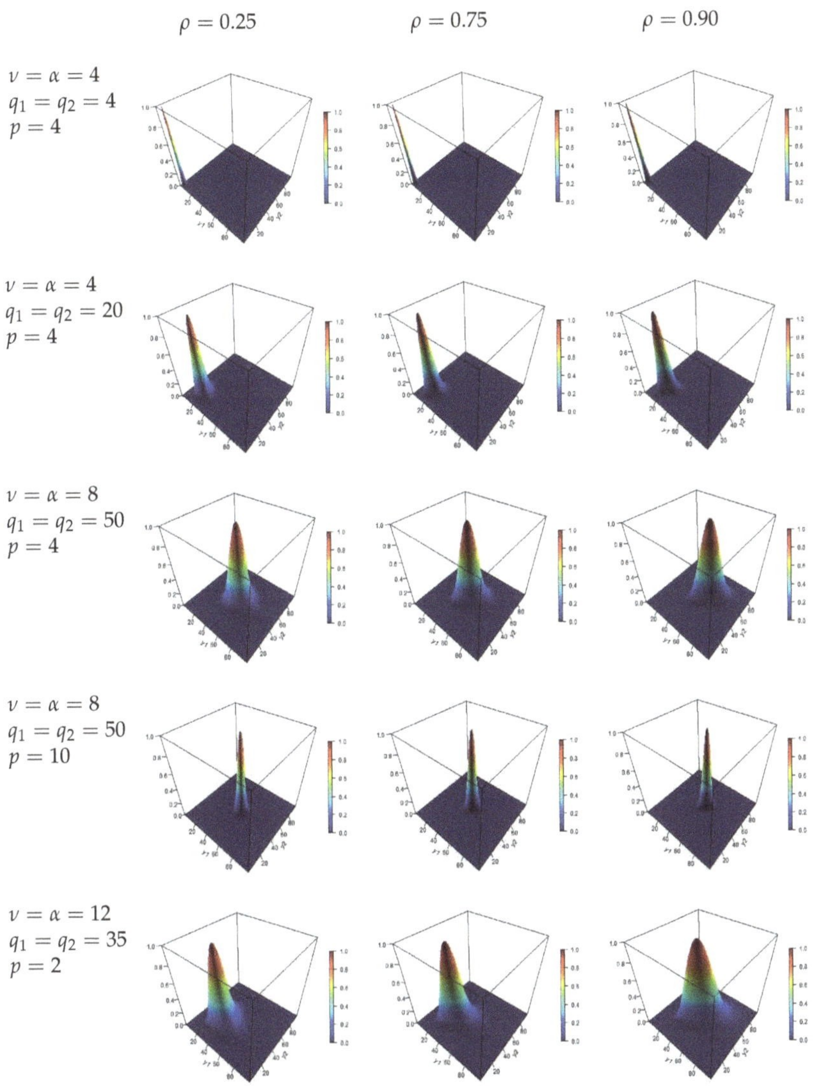

Figure 1. Bivariate pdf of Equation (7) for some parameter combinations.

Proposition 2. *The cross-product moment of* $\mathbf{Y} = (Y_1, Y_2)^\top$ *in Equation (7) can be expressed as*

$$\begin{aligned}\mathbb{E}[Y_1^a Y_2^b] &= \frac{q_1^a q_2^b \Gamma\left(\frac{\alpha}{2} - \frac{a}{p}\right)\Gamma\left(\frac{\alpha}{2} - \frac{b}{p}\right)\Gamma\left(\frac{\nu}{2} + \frac{a}{p}\right)\Gamma\left(\frac{\nu}{2} + \frac{b}{p}\right)}{c^{a+b}\Gamma^2\left(\frac{\nu}{2}\right)\Gamma^2\left(\frac{\alpha}{2}\right)} \\ &\quad \times {}_2F_1\left(-\frac{a}{p}, -\frac{b}{p}; \frac{\nu}{2}; \rho^2\right){}_2F_1\left(\frac{a}{p}, \frac{b}{p}; \frac{\alpha}{2}; \rho^2\right). \end{aligned} \tag{11}$$

Proposition 2 illustrates that the cross-product moment is the product of two Gaussian hypergeometric functions. Corollary 1 is straightforward from Proposition 2, where the expected value and variance of a marginal Pareto–Feller random variable Y_k are presented as well as the covariance and correlation between two marginal Pareto–Feller random variables (Y_1 and Y_2).

Corollary 1. *If* $\mathbf{Y} = (Y_1, Y_2)^\top$*, then it has a pdf according to Equation (7). According to Proposition 2, we have the following:*

1. $\mathbb{E}[Y_i] = q_i, \ i = 1, 2.$
2. $Var(Y_i) = q_i^2 \left[\frac{\Gamma\left(\frac{\nu}{2} + \frac{2}{p}\right)\Gamma\left(\frac{\alpha}{2} - \frac{2}{p}\right)}{c\Gamma\left(\frac{\nu}{2} + \frac{1}{p}\right)\Gamma\left(\frac{\alpha}{2} - \frac{1}{p}\right)} - 1\right]$ *if* $\alpha p > 4$ *for* $i = 1, 2.$
3.

$$\begin{aligned} Cov(Y_1, Y_2) &= \frac{q^i 2\Gamma\left(\frac{\alpha}{2} - \frac{1}{p}\right)\Gamma\left(\frac{\alpha}{2} - \frac{1}{p}\right)\Gamma\left(\frac{\nu}{2} + \frac{1}{p}\right)\Gamma\left(\frac{\nu}{2} + \frac{1}{p}\right)}{c^2\Gamma^2\left(\frac{\nu}{2}\right)\Gamma^2\left(\frac{\alpha}{2}\right)} \\ &\quad \times {}_2F_1\left(-\frac{1}{p}, -\frac{1}{p}; \frac{\nu}{2}; \rho^2\right){}_2F_1\left(\frac{1}{p}, \frac{1}{p}; \frac{\alpha}{2}; \rho^2\right). \end{aligned} \tag{12}$$

4. *Let* $\rho_Y \equiv Corr(Y_1, Y_2)$*. Thus, we have*

$$\begin{aligned} \rho_Y &= \frac{\Gamma^2\left(\frac{\nu}{2} + \frac{1}{p}\right)\Gamma^2\left(\frac{\alpha}{2} - \frac{1}{p}\right)}{\Gamma\left(\frac{\nu}{2}\right)\Gamma\left(\frac{\alpha}{2}\right)\Gamma\left(\frac{\nu}{2} + \frac{2}{p}\right)\Gamma\left(\frac{\alpha}{2} - \frac{2}{p}\right) - \Gamma^2\left(\frac{\nu}{2} + \frac{1}{p}\right)\Gamma^2\left(\frac{\alpha}{2} - \frac{1}{p}\right)} \\ &\quad \times \left[{}_2F_1\left(-\frac{1}{p}, -\frac{1}{p}; \frac{\nu}{2}; \rho^2\right){}_2F_1\left(\frac{1}{p}, \frac{1}{p}; \frac{\alpha}{2}; \rho^2\right) - 1\right]. \end{aligned} \tag{13}$$

Figure 2 shows the correlation ρ_Y for some density parameters. When ν and α increase, ρ_Y increases. More specifically, when p increases, the correlation ρ_Y increases with small-to-large values of ν and α. When ρ increases, ρ_Y increases, as does its maximum value (from 0.05 to 0.80). Nevertheless, Corollary 1(4) illustrates that the correlation ρ_Y does not depend on either q or c.

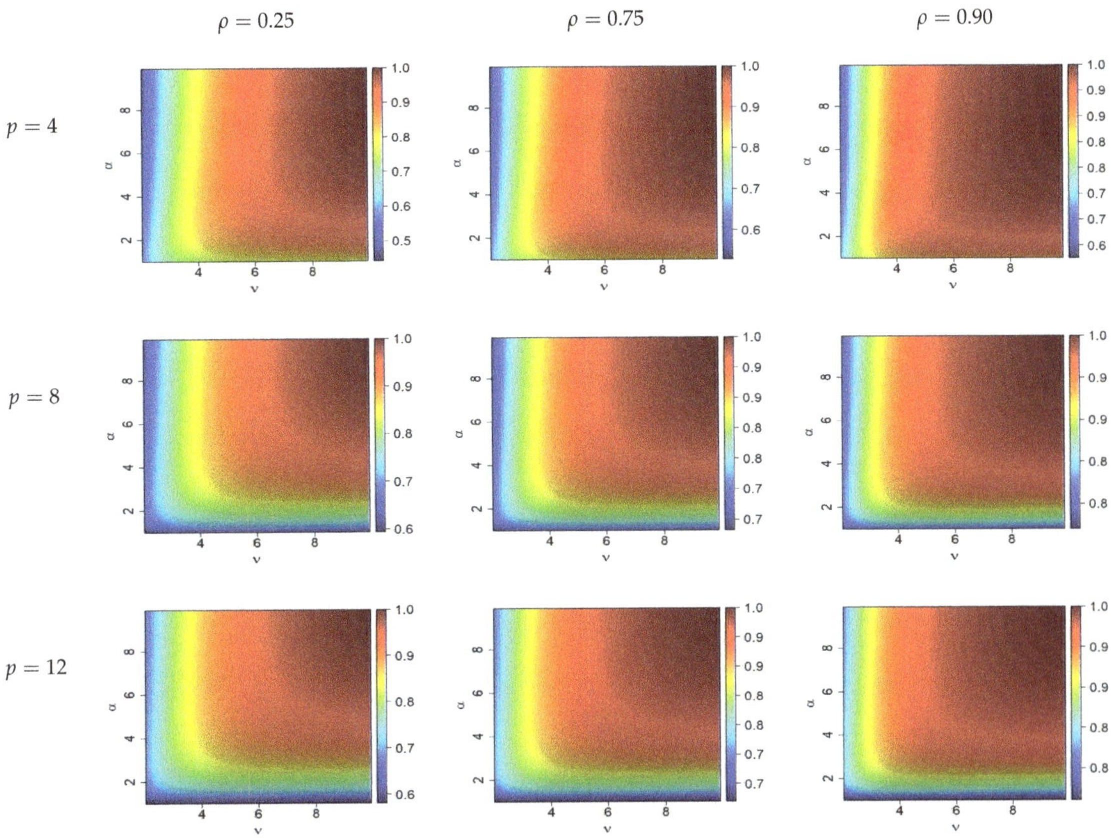

Figure 2. Correlation ρ_Y of Corollary 1(4) for some parameter combinations.

3. Differential Entropy and Mutual Information Index

The differential entropy of $\mathbf{Y}$ is an information uncertainty measure [27]. The differential entropy of $\mathbf{Y} = (Y_1, Y_2)^\top$ with a pdf $f_{\mathbf{Y}}(\mathbf{y})$ is

$$\begin{aligned} \mathcal{H}(\mathbf{Y}) &= -\mathbb{E}_{\mathbf{Y}}[\log\{f_{\mathbf{Y}}(\mathbf{Y})\}] \\ &= -\int_0^\infty \int_0^\infty f_{\mathbf{Y}}(\mathbf{y}) \log f_{\mathbf{Y}}(\mathbf{y}) dy_1 dy_2, \end{aligned} \quad (14)$$

and measures the contained information in $\mathbf{Y}$ based on its pdf's parameters.

On the other hand, the mutual information index (MII) [28] between Y_1 and Y_2 under a dependence assumption ($\rho \neq 0$) is

$$\begin{aligned} \mathcal{M}(\mathbf{Y}) &= \mathbb{E}\left[\log\left\{\frac{f_{\mathbf{Y}}(y_1, y_2)}{f_{Y_1}(y_1) f_{Y_2}(y_2)}\right\}\right] \\ &= \int_0^\infty \int_0^\infty f_{\mathbf{Y}}(y_1, y_2) \log\left\{\frac{f_{\mathbf{Y}}(y_1, y_2)}{f_{Y_1}(y_1) f_{Y_2}(y_2)}\right\} dy_1 dy_2. \end{aligned} \quad (15)$$

Proposition 3 ([29])**.** *Let $Y_i \sim PF(\mu, q_i/c, 1/p, \nu/2, \alpha/2)$. The entropy of Y_i $(i = 1, 2)$ is*

$$\mathcal{H}(Y_i) = \log\left[\frac{cp}{q_i} \frac{\Gamma(\frac{\nu+\alpha}{2})\Gamma(\frac{\alpha}{2})}{\Gamma(\frac{\nu}{2})}\right] + \left(\frac{1}{p} - \frac{\alpha}{2}\right)\left[\psi\left(\frac{\alpha}{2}\right) - \psi\left(\frac{\nu}{2}\right)\right] + \left(\frac{\nu+\alpha}{2}\right)\left[\psi\left(\frac{\nu+\alpha}{2}\right) - \psi\left(\frac{\nu}{2}\right)\right],$$

where $\psi(X) = \frac{d\log\Gamma(x)}{dx}$ *is the digamma function.*

Proposition 4 ([30]). *Let* $x = u/n$. *We have that*

$$\log(1+x) = x + \mathcal{O}(n^{-2}),$$

as $n \to \infty$.

Proposition 5. *If* $\mathbf{Y} = (Y_1, Y_2)^\top$ *has the pdf given in Equation (7), then the following are true:*

(a) $\mathbb{E}_{\mathbf{Y}}[Y_i^p] = \frac{q_i^p \Gamma(\frac{\nu}{2}+1)\Gamma(\frac{\alpha}{2}-1)}{c^p \Gamma(\frac{\nu}{2})\Gamma(\frac{\alpha}{2})}$.

(b) $\mathbb{E}_{\mathbf{Y}}[\log(Y_i)] = \frac{1}{p(1-\rho^2)^{-(\nu+\alpha)/2}} \sum_{k=0}^{\infty}\sum_{m=0}^{\infty} \frac{(\frac{\nu}{2})_k(\frac{\alpha}{2})_m \rho^{2k+2m}}{k!m!} \left\{\psi(\frac{\nu}{2}+k) - \psi(\frac{\alpha}{2}+m) - \log\left(\frac{c}{q_i}\right)^p\right\}$.

Proposition 6. *An approximation of the differential entropy of* $\mathbf{Y} = (Y_1, Y_2)^\top$ *is*

$$\begin{aligned} \mathcal{H}(\mathbf{Y}) \approx & -\log\left[\frac{\frac{(cp)^2}{q_1q_2}\Gamma^2(\frac{\nu+\alpha}{2})}{\Gamma^2(\frac{\nu}{2})\Gamma^2(\frac{\alpha}{2})(1-\rho^2)^{-(\nu+\alpha)/2}}\right] \\ & + \left(1 - \frac{p\nu}{2}\right)\left\{\log\left(\frac{c^2}{q_1q_2}\right) + \mathbb{E}_{\mathbf{Y}}[\log Y_1] + \mathbb{E}_{\mathbf{Y}}[\log Y_2]\right\} \\ & + c^p\left(\frac{\nu+\alpha}{2}\right)\left\{\frac{\mathbb{E}_{\mathbf{Y}}[Y_1^p]}{q_1^p} + \frac{\mathbb{E}_{\mathbf{Y}}[Y_2^p]}{q_2^p}\right\}, \end{aligned}$$

where $\mathbb{E}_{\mathbf{Y}}[Y_i^p]$ *and* $\mathbb{E}_{\mathbf{Y}}[\log Y_i]$, $i = 1,2$ *are obtained from parts (a) and (b) of Proposition 5, respectively.*

From Equation (15), an MII between Y_1 and Y_2 is expressed in terms of the marginal and joint differential entropies [28,31]. Then, using Propositions 3 and 6, the MII between Y_1 and Y_2 can be approximated as follows:

$$\begin{aligned} \mathcal{M}(\mathbf{Y}) &= \mathcal{H}(Y_1) + \mathcal{H}(Y_2) - \mathcal{H}(\mathbf{Y}) \\ &\approx 2\log\left[cp\frac{\Gamma(\frac{\nu+\alpha}{2})\Gamma(\frac{\alpha}{2})}{\Gamma(\frac{\nu}{2})}\right] - \log(q_1q_2) + \log\left[\frac{\frac{(cp)^2}{q_1q_2}\Gamma^2(\frac{\nu+\alpha}{2})}{\Gamma^2(\frac{\nu}{2})\Gamma^2(\frac{\alpha}{2})(1-\rho^2)^{-(\nu+\alpha)/2}}\right] \\ & -\left(1 - \frac{p\nu}{2}\right)\left\{\log\left(\frac{c^2}{q_1q_2}\right) + \mathbb{E}_{\mathbf{Y}}[\log Y_1] + \mathbb{E}_{\mathbf{Y}}[\log Y_2]\right\} \\ & -c^p\left(\frac{\nu+\alpha}{2}\right)\left\{\frac{\mathbb{E}[Y_1^p]}{q_1^p} + \frac{\mathbb{E}[Y_2^p]}{q_2^p}\right\} + \left(\frac{2}{p} - \alpha\right)\left[\psi\left(\frac{\alpha}{2}\right) - \psi\left(\frac{\nu}{2}\right)\right] \\ & +(\nu+\alpha)\left[\psi\left(\frac{\nu+\alpha}{2}\right) - \psi\left(\frac{\nu}{2}\right)\right]. \end{aligned}$$

One particular case is when $p = 1$. Thus, using Corollary 1(1), we have

$$\begin{aligned} \mathcal{M}(\mathbf{Y}) \approx & \left(1 + \frac{\nu}{2}\right)\log\left(\frac{c^2}{q_1q_2}\right) + 2\log\left[\frac{\Gamma^2(\frac{\nu+\alpha}{2})}{\Gamma^2(\frac{\nu}{2})}\right] \\ & -\left(\frac{\nu+\alpha}{2}\right)\log(1-\rho^2) + (2-\alpha)\left[\psi\left(\frac{\alpha}{2}\right) - \psi\left(\frac{\nu}{2}\right)\right] \\ & +(\nu+\alpha)\left[\psi\left(\frac{\nu+\alpha}{2}\right) - \psi\left(\frac{\nu}{2}\right) - c\right] \\ & -\left(1 - \frac{\nu}{2}\right)\{\mathbb{E}_{\mathbf{Y}}[\log Y_1] + \mathbb{E}_{\mathbf{Y}}[\log Y_2]\}. \end{aligned} \quad (16)$$

Figure 3 illustrates the behavior of the approximated MII obtained in Equation (16) while assuming several values for $\mathbf{Y}$ and $p = 1$. We observed that $\mathcal{M}(\mathbf{Y}) > 0$ and increased for $q_i \to 0$. As in the correlation function case (Figure 2), the MII increased when the correlation parameter ρ increased.

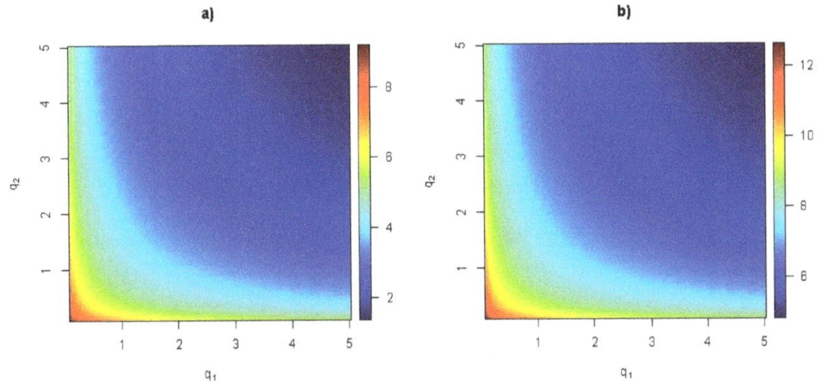

Figure 3. Approximated mutual information index of Pareto–Feller distribution assuming $p = 1$, $\alpha = 5, \nu = 4$, (**a**) $\rho = 0.25$, and (**b**) $\rho = 0.75$.

4. Concluding Remarks

We presented a representation of the Pareto–Feller distribution with a scale mixture of two gamma random variables. The respective stochastic representation was obtained by the quotient of a scale mixture of two gamma random variables. Then, the resulting bivariate density considered the products of two confluent hypergeometric functions. In particular, the probability distribution function, cumulative distribution function, moment generation function, covariance function, correlation function, cross-product moments, and approximations for the differential entropy and, as a consequence, the mutual information index were derived. Some numerical examples illustrated the behavior of the provided expressions.

Some inferential aspects can be addressed in a future work, such as (1) a numerical approach for optimization of the log-likelihood function; (2) the pseudo-likelihood method, considering the optimization of an objective function which depends on a bivariate pdf; (3) the model's identifiability; (4) a Bayesian approach; and (5) an extention to the multivariate case. We also encourage researching the consideration of a Pareto–Feller distribution in modeling nonnegative bivariate data.

Author Contributions: C.C.-C., M.B., M.Z.-M., and J.E.C.-R. wrote the paper and contributed the reagents, analysis, and materials; M.Z.-M. and J.E.C.-R. conceived, designed, and performed the experiments. All authors have read and agreed to the published version of the manuscript.

Funding: C. Caamaño-Carrillo was partially supported by grant FONDECYT 11220066 from the Chilean government and DIUBB 2120538 IF/R from the University of Bío-Bío. M. Bevilacqua acknowledges financial support from grants FONDECYT 1200068 and ANID/PIA/ANILLOS ACT210096 from the Chilean government. J. Contreras-Reyes's research was supported by FONDECYT (Chile) grant No. 11190116.

Data Availability Statement: No new data were created or analyzed in this study. Data sharing is not applicable.

Acknowledgments: The authors thank the editor and three anonymous referees for their helpful comments and suggestions.

Conflicts of Interest: The authors declare that there are no conflicts of interest in the publication of this paper.

Appendix A

Proof of Theorem 1. Following [10], note that the bivariate distribution of the gamma random vector can be rewritten in terms of the hypergeometric function using the identity ${}_0F_1(;b;x) = \Gamma(b)x^{(1-b)/2}I_{b-1}(2\sqrt{x})$, given by

$$f_{\mathbf{H}}(\mathbf{h}) = \frac{(h_1h_2)^{\delta/2-1}e^{-\frac{(h_1+h_2)}{(1-\rho^2)}}}{\Gamma^2\left(\frac{\delta}{2}\right)(1-\rho^2)^{\delta/2}}{}_0F_1\left(\frac{\delta}{2};\frac{\rho^2h_1h_2}{(1-\rho^2)^2}\right) \tag{A1}$$

Under the transformations $w_1 = v_1r_1$ and $w_2 = v_2r_2$ in Equation (A1) with the Jacobian $J((w_1,w_2) \to (v_1,v_2)) = r_1r_2$, and by using series expansion of the hypergeometric function ${}_0F_1$, we have

$$\begin{aligned}
f_{\mathbf{V}}(\mathbf{v}) &= \int_{\mathbb{R}^2_+} f_{\mathbf{W}|\mathbf{R}}(\mathbf{w}|\mathbf{r})f_{\mathbf{R}}(\mathbf{r})Jd\mathbf{r} \\
&= \int_{\mathbb{R}^2_+} \frac{(v_1v_2)^{\nu/2-1}(r_1r_2)^{(\nu+\alpha)/2-1}e^{-\frac{(v_1r_1+v_2r_2)}{(1-\rho^2)}}e^{-\frac{(r_1+r_2)}{(1-\rho^2)}}}{\Gamma^2\left(\frac{\nu}{2}\right)\Gamma^2\left(\frac{\alpha}{2}\right)(1-\rho^2)^{(\nu+\alpha)/2}} \\
&\quad \times {}_0F_1\left(\frac{\nu}{2};\frac{\rho^2v_1v_2r_1r_2}{(1-\rho^2)^2}\right){}_0F_1\left(\frac{\alpha}{2};\frac{\rho^2r_1r_2}{(1-\rho^2)^2}\right)d\mathbf{r} \\
&= \sum_{k=0}^{\infty}\sum_{m=0}^{\infty}\int_{\mathbb{R}^2_+} \frac{(v_1v_2)^{\nu/2-1}(r_1r_2)^{(\nu+\alpha)/2-1}e^{-\frac{(v_1+1)r_1}{(1-\rho^2)}}e^{-\frac{(v_2+1)r_2}{(1-\rho^2)}}}{\Gamma^2\left(\frac{\nu}{2}\right)\Gamma^2\left(\frac{\alpha}{2}\right)(1-\rho^2)^{(\nu+\alpha)/2}k!m!\left(\frac{\nu}{2}\right)_k\left(\frac{\alpha}{2}\right)_m} \\
&\quad \times \left(\frac{\rho^2(\mathbf{m}h)v_1v_2r_1r_2}{(1-\rho^2)^2}\right)^k\left(\frac{\rho^2r_1r_2}{(1-\rho^2)^2}\right)^m d\mathbf{r} \\
&= \frac{(v_1v_2)^{\nu/2-1}}{\Gamma^2\left(\frac{\nu}{2}\right)\Gamma^2\left(\frac{\alpha}{2}\right)(1-\rho^2)^{(\nu+\alpha)/2}} \\
&\quad \times \sum_{k=0}^{\infty}\sum_{m=0}^{\infty}\frac{I(k,m)}{k!m!\left(\frac{\nu}{2}\right)_k\left(\frac{\alpha}{2}\right)_m}\left(\frac{\rho^2v_1v_2}{(1-\rho^2)^2}\right)^k\left(\frac{\rho^2}{(1-\rho^2)^2}\right)^m,
\end{aligned} \tag{A2}$$

where, using Fubini's theorem and Equation (3.381.4) in [32], we obtain

$$\begin{aligned}
I(k,m) &= \int_{\mathbb{R}_+} r_1^{(\nu+\alpha)/2+k+m-1}e^{-\frac{(v_1+1)r_1}{(1-\rho^2)}}dr_i \int_{\mathbb{R}_+} r_2^{(\nu+\alpha)/2+k+m-1}e^{-\frac{(v_2+1)r_2}{(1-\rho^2)}}dr_2 \\
&= \Gamma^2\left(\frac{\nu+\alpha}{2}+k+m\right)\left[\frac{(1-\rho^2)}{v_1+1}\right]^{\frac{\nu+\alpha}{2}+k+m}\left[\frac{(1-\rho^2)}{v_2+1}\right]^{\frac{\nu+\alpha}{2}+k+m}
\end{aligned} \tag{A3}$$

In addition, by combining Equations (A3) and (A2), we obtain

$$\begin{aligned}
f_{\mathbf{V}_{12}}(\mathbf{v}_{12}) &= \frac{(v_1v_2)^{\nu/2-1}\Gamma^2\left(\frac{\nu+\alpha}{2}\right)[(v_1+1)(v_2+1)]^{-(\nu+\alpha)/2}}{\Gamma^2\left(\frac{\nu}{2}\right)\Gamma^2\left(\frac{\alpha}{2}\right)(1-\rho^2)^{-(\nu+\alpha)/2}} \\
&\quad \times \sum_{k=0}^{\infty}\sum_{m=0}^{\infty}\frac{\left(\frac{\nu+\alpha}{2}\right)^2_{k+m}}{k!m!\left(\frac{\nu}{2}\right)_k\left(\frac{\alpha}{2}\right)_m}\left(\frac{\rho^2v_1v_2}{(v_1+1)(v_2+1)}\right)^k\left(\frac{\rho^2}{(v_1+1)(v_2+1)}\right)^m \\
&= \frac{(v_1v_2)^{\nu/2-1}\Gamma^2\left(\frac{\nu+\alpha}{2}\right)[(v_1+1)(v_2+1)]^{-(\nu+\alpha)/2}}{\Gamma^2\left(\frac{\nu}{2}\right)\Gamma^2\left(\frac{\alpha}{2}\right)(1-\rho^2)^{-(\nu+\alpha)/2}} \\
&\quad \times F_4\left(\frac{\nu+\alpha}{2},\frac{\nu+\alpha}{2};\frac{\nu}{2},\frac{\alpha}{2};\frac{\rho^2v_1v_2}{(v_1+1)(v_2+1)},\frac{\rho^2}{(v_1+1)(v_2+1)}\right)
\end{aligned}$$

□

Proof of Theorem 2. Under the transformations $v_1 = (y_1/q_1)^p$ and $v_2 = (y_2/q_2)^p$ in Equation (5) with a Jacobian $J((v_1;v_2) \to (y_1;y_2)) = (p/q)^2(y_1y_2/(q_1q_2))^{p-1}$, the pdf of $\mathbf{Y}$ is given by Equation (7). $\square$

Proof of Theorem 3. Using series expansion of the Appell hypergeometric function, we obtain

$$\begin{aligned}
&F_{\mathbf{Y}}(Y_1 \le t_1, Y_2 \le t_2)\\
=\;& \frac{p^2c^{p\nu}(q_1q_2)^{-p\nu/2}\Gamma^2\left(\frac{\nu+\alpha}{2}\right)}{\Gamma^2\left(\frac{\nu}{2}\right)\Gamma^2\left(\frac{\alpha}{2}\right)(1-\rho^2)^{-(\nu+\alpha)/2}}\int_0^{t_1}\int_0^{t_2}(y_1y_2)^{p\nu/2-1}\left[\left(\left(\frac{cy_1}{q_1}\right)^p+1\right)\left(\left(\frac{cy_2}{q_2}\right)^p+1\right)\right]^{-\frac{(\nu+\alpha)}{2}}\\
\times\;& F_4\left(\frac{\nu+\alpha}{2},\frac{\nu+\alpha}{2};\frac{\nu}{2},\frac{\alpha}{2};\frac{\rho^2(c^2y_1y_2)^p(q_1q_2)^{-p}}{\left(\left(\frac{cy_1}{q_1}\right)^p+1\right)\left(\left(\frac{cy_2}{q_2}\right)^p+1\right)},\frac{\rho^2}{\left(\left(\frac{cy_1}{q_1}\right)^p+1\right)\left(\left(\frac{cy_2}{q_2}\right)^p+1\right)}\right)d\mathbf{y}\\
=\;& \frac{p^2c^{p\nu}(q_1q_2)^{-p\nu/2}\Gamma^2\left(\frac{\nu+\alpha}{2}\right)}{\Gamma^2\left(\frac{\nu}{2}\right)\Gamma^2\left(\frac{\alpha}{2}\right)(1-\rho^2)^{-(\nu+\alpha)/2}}\int_0^{t_1}\int_0^{t_2}(y_1y_2)^{p\nu/2-1}\left[\left(\left(\frac{cy_1}{q_1}\right)^p+1\right)\left(\left(\frac{cy_2}{q_2}\right)^p+1\right)\right]^{-\frac{(\nu+\alpha)}{2}}\\
&\times\sum_{k=0}^{\infty}\sum_{m=0}^{\infty}\frac{\left(\frac{\nu+\alpha}{2}\right)^2_{k+m}}{k!m!\left(\frac{\nu}{2}\right)_k\left(\frac{\alpha}{2}\right)_m}\\
&\times\left(\frac{\rho^2(c^2y_1y_2)^p(q_1q_2)^{-p}}{\left(\left(\frac{cy_1}{q_1}\right)^p+1\right)\left(\left(\frac{cy_2}{q_2}\right)^p+1\right)}\right)^k\left(\frac{\rho^2}{\left(\left(\frac{cy_1}{q_1}\right)^p+1\right)\left(\left(\frac{cy_2}{q_2}\right)^p+1\right)}\right)^m d\mathbf{y}\\
=\;& \frac{p^2c^{p\nu}(q_1q_2)^{-p\nu/2}\Gamma^2\left(\frac{\nu+\alpha}{2}\right)}{\Gamma^2\left(\frac{\nu}{2}\right)\Gamma^2\left(\frac{\alpha}{2}\right)(1-\rho^2)^{-(\nu+\alpha)/2}}\sum_{k=0}^{\infty}\sum_{m=0}^{\infty}\frac{\left(\frac{\nu+\alpha}{2}\right)^2_{k+m}\rho^{2m}I(k,m)}{k!m!\left(\frac{\nu}{2}\right)_k\left(\frac{\alpha}{2}\right)_m}\left(\frac{c^{2p}\rho^2}{(q_1q_2)^p}\right)^k
\end{aligned} \tag{A4}$$

Let $z_1 = y_1^p$ and $z_2 = y_2^p$ be transformations in Equation (A4), where $0 < z_i < t_i^p$, $i = 1,2$. Using Fubini's theorem and Equation (3.1941.1) in [32], we obtain

$$\begin{aligned}
I(k,m) &= \frac{1}{p^2}\int_0^{t_1^p} z_1^{\nu/2+k-1}\left[\left(\frac{c}{q_1}\right)^p z_1+1\right]^{-\left(\frac{\nu+\alpha}{2}+k+m\right)}dz_1\\
&\quad\times\int_0^{t_2^p} z_2^{\nu/2+k-1}\left[\left(\frac{c}{q_2}\right)^p z_2+1\right]^{-\left(\frac{\nu+\alpha}{2}+k+m\right)}dz_2\\
&= \frac{(t_1t_2)^{p\nu/2+pk}}{p^2(\nu/2+k)^2}\,{}_2F_1\left(\frac{\nu+\alpha}{2}+k+m,\frac{\nu}{2}+k;\frac{\nu}{2}+k+1;-\left(\frac{ct_1}{q_1}\right)^p\right)\\
&\quad{}_2F_1\left(\frac{\nu+\alpha}{2}+k+m,\frac{\nu}{2}+k;\frac{\nu}{2}+k+1;-\left(\frac{ct_2}{q_2}\right)^p\right)
\end{aligned} \tag{A5}$$

In addition, by combining Equations (A4) and (A5), we obtain Equation (8). $\square$

Proof of Proposition 1. For part (a), by using the definition of the mgf and series expansion of the Appell hypergeometric function, we obtain

$$\begin{aligned}
&M_{\mathbf{Y}}(t_1,t_2)\\
=\;& \frac{p^2c^{p\nu}(q_1q_2)^{-p\nu/2}\Gamma^2\left(\frac{\nu+\alpha}{2}\right)}{\Gamma^2\left(\frac{\nu}{2}\right)\Gamma^2\left(\frac{\alpha}{2}\right)(1-\rho^2)^{-(\nu+\alpha)/2}}\\
&\times\int_{\mathbb{R}^2_+} e^{t_1y_1+t_2y_2}y_1^{p\nu/2-1}y_2^{p\nu/2-1}\left[\left(\left(\frac{cy_1}{q_1}\right)^p+1\right)\left(\left(\frac{cy_2}{q_2}\right)^p+1\right)\right]^{-\frac{(\nu+\alpha)}{2}}
\end{aligned}$$

$$\times \sum_{k=0}^{\infty}\sum_{m=0}^{\infty} \frac{\left(\frac{\nu+\alpha}{2}\right)^2_{k+m}}{k!m!\left(\frac{\nu}{2}\right)_k\left(\frac{\alpha}{2}\right)_m}$$

$$\times \left(\frac{\rho^2(c^2y_1y_2)^p(q_1q_2)^{-p}}{\left(\left(\frac{cy_1}{q_1}\right)^p+1\right)\left(\left(\frac{cy_2}{q_2}\right)^p+1\right)}\right)^k \left(\frac{\rho^2}{\left(\left(\frac{cy_1}{q_1}\right)^p+1\right)\left(\left(\frac{cy_2}{q_2}\right)^p+1\right)}\right)^m d\mathbf{y}$$

$$= \frac{p^2c^{p\nu}(q_1q_2)^{-p\nu/2}\Gamma^2\left(\frac{\nu+\alpha}{2}\right)}{\Gamma^2\left(\frac{\nu}{2}\right)\Gamma^2\left(\frac{\alpha}{2}\right)(1-\rho^2)^{-(\nu+\alpha)/2}} \times \sum_{k=0}^{\infty}\sum_{m=0}^{\infty} \frac{\left(\frac{\nu+\alpha}{2}\right)^2_{k+m}\rho^{2m}I(k,m)}{k!m!\left(\frac{\nu}{2}\right)_k\left(\frac{\alpha}{2}\right)_m}\left(\frac{c^{2p}\rho^2}{(q_1q_2)^p}\right)^k. \quad \text{(A6)}$$

Using Fubini's theorem in Equation (A6), we obtain

$$\begin{aligned} I(k,m) &= \int_0^{\infty} e^{t_1y_1} y_1^{(p\nu/2)+pk-1}\left[\left(\frac{cy_1}{q_1}\right)^p+1\right]^{-\left(\frac{(\nu+\alpha)}{2}+k+m\right)} dy_1 \\ &\quad \times \int_0^{\infty} e^{t_2y_2} y_2^{(p\nu/2)+pk-1}\left[\left(\frac{cy_2}{q_2}\right)^p+1\right]^{-\left(\frac{(\nu+\alpha)}{2}+k+m\right)} dy_2 \\ &= \left[\frac{1}{p}\left(\frac{q}{c}\right)^{p(\nu/2+k)}\frac{\Gamma(\nu/2+k)\Gamma(k+m+((\nu+\alpha)/2))}{\Gamma(m+((\nu+\alpha)/2)+\nu/2)}\right]\left[e^{(t_1y_1)}-\frac{1}{(t_1)^2}\right]\Bigg|_{y_1=0}^{y_1=\infty} \\ &\quad \times \left[\frac{1}{p}\left(\frac{q}{c}\right)^{p(\nu/2+k)}\frac{\Gamma(\nu/2+k)\Gamma(k+m+((\nu+\alpha)/2))}{\Gamma(m+((\nu+\alpha)/2)+\nu/2)}\right]\left[e^{(t_2y_2)}-\frac{1}{(t_2)^2}\right]\Bigg|_{y_2=0}^{y_2=\infty} \\ &= \left[\frac{1}{p}\left(\frac{q}{c}\right)^{p(\nu/2+k)}\frac{\Gamma(\nu/2+k)\Gamma(k+m+((\nu+\alpha)/2))}{\Gamma(m+((\nu+\alpha)/2)+\nu/2)}\right]^2\left[-\frac{1}{(t_i)^2}\right]\left[1-\frac{1}{(t_i)^2}\right]. \end{aligned} \quad \text{(A7)}$$

Note that if $f(y) = e^{t_iy_i}$ and

$$g(y) = (y_i)^{(p\nu/2)+pk-1}\left[\left(\frac{c}{q_i}\right)^p(y_i)^p+1\right]^{-(k+m+(\nu+\alpha)/2)} dy_i,$$

then we can apply integration by substitution for $\int_0^{\infty} f(y)g(y)dy$. With the change in variables $u_i = e^{t_iy_i} \Rightarrow du_i = t_ie^{t_iy_i}$, and by letting

$$dv_i = (y_i)^{(p\nu/2)+pk-1}\left[\left(\frac{c}{q_i}\right)^p(y_i)^p+1\right]^{-(k+m+(\nu+\alpha)/2)} dy_i,$$

then $v_i = \int_0^{\infty} dv_i$, where Equation (3.241.4.11) in [32] was used with $t_i < 0$, $i = 1,2$. By combining Equations (A6) and (A7), we obtain

$$\begin{aligned} M_{\mathbf{Y}}(t_1,t_2) &= \frac{\frac{(cp)^2}{q_1q_2}\Gamma^2\left(\frac{\nu+\alpha}{2}\right)}{\Gamma^2\left(\frac{\nu}{2}\right)\Gamma^2\left(\frac{\alpha}{2}\right)(1-\rho^2)^{-(\nu+\alpha)/2}} \\ &\quad \times \sum_{k=0}^{\infty}\sum_{m=0}^{\infty}\frac{\left(\frac{\nu+\alpha}{2}\right)_{k+m}\left(\frac{\nu+\alpha}{2}\right)_{k+m}}{\left(\frac{\nu}{2}\right)_k\left(\frac{\alpha}{2}\right)_m k!m!}\rho^{4km}(c^2/q_1q_2)^{(p\nu/2+pk-1)} \\ &\quad \times \left[\frac{1}{p}\left(\frac{q}{c}\right)^{p(\nu/2+k)}\frac{\Gamma(\nu/2+k)\Gamma(k+m+((\nu+\alpha)/2))}{\Gamma(m+((\nu+\alpha)/2)+\nu/2)}\right]^2 \\ &\quad \times \left[-\frac{(t_1)^2-1}{(t_1)^4}\right]\left[-\frac{(t_2)^2-1}{(t_2)^4}\right]. \end{aligned}$$

For part (b), and by following the proof of part (a), the proof of the characteristic function of $\mathbf{Y}$ is straightforward. □

Proof of Proposition 2. By the definition of cross-product moment, and using series expansion of the Appell hypergeometric function of the fourth kind, we obtain

$$
\begin{aligned}
&\mathbb{E}(Y_1^a Y_2^b) \\
= &\ \frac{p^2 c^{p\nu}(q_1q_2)^{-p\nu/2}\Gamma^2\left(\frac{\nu+\alpha}{2}\right)}{\Gamma^2\left(\frac{\nu}{2}\right)\Gamma^2\left(\frac{\alpha}{2}\right)(1-\rho^2)^{-(\nu+\alpha)/2}} \\
&\int_{\mathbb{R}_+^2} y_1^{p\nu/2+a-1} y_2^{p\nu/2+b-1}\left[\left(\left(\frac{cy_1}{q_1}\right)^p+1\right)\left(\left(\frac{cy_2}{q_2}\right)^p+1\right)\right]^{-\frac{(\nu+\alpha)}{2}} \\
\times &\ F_4\left(\frac{\nu+\alpha}{2},\frac{\nu+\alpha}{2};\frac{\nu}{2},\frac{\alpha}{2};\frac{\rho^2(c^2y_1y_2)^p(q_1q_2)^{-p}}{\left(\left(\frac{cy_1}{q_1}\right)^p+1\right)\left(\left(\frac{cy_2}{q_2}\right)^p+1\right)},\frac{\rho^2}{\left(\left(\frac{cy_1}{q_1}\right)^p+1\right)\left(\left(\frac{cy_2}{q_2}\right)^p+1\right)}\right)d\mathbf{y} \\
= &\ \frac{p^2 c^{p\nu}(q_1q_2)^{-p\nu/2}\Gamma^2\left(\frac{\nu+\alpha}{2}\right)}{\Gamma^2\left(\frac{\nu}{2}\right)\Gamma^2\left(\frac{\alpha}{2}\right)(1-\rho^2)^{-(\nu+\alpha)/2}} \\
&\times\int_{\mathbb{R}_+^2} y_1^{p\nu/2+a-1} y_2^{p\nu/2+b-1}\left[\left(\left(\frac{cy_1}{q_1}\right)^p+1\right)\left(\left(\frac{cy_2}{q_2}\right)^p+1\right)\right]^{-\frac{(\nu+\alpha)}{2}} \\
\times &\ \sum_{k=0}^{\infty}\sum_{m=0}^{\infty}\frac{\left(\frac{\nu+\alpha}{2}\right)_{k+m}^2}{k!m!\left(\frac{\nu}{2}\right)_k\left(\frac{\alpha}{2}\right)_m} \\
&\times\left(\frac{\rho^2(c^2y_1y_2)^p(q_1q_2)^{-p}}{\left(\left(\frac{cy_1}{q_1}\right)^p+1\right)\left(\left(\frac{cy_2}{q_2}\right)^p+1\right)}\right)^k\left(\frac{\rho^2}{\left(\left(\frac{cy_1}{q_1}\right)^p+1\right)\left(\left(\frac{cy_2}{q_2}\right)^p+1\right)}\right)^m d\mathbf{y} \\
= &\ \frac{p^2 c^{p\nu}(q_1q_2)^{-p\nu/2}\Gamma^2\left(\frac{\nu+\alpha}{2}\right)}{\Gamma^2\left(\frac{\nu}{2}\right)\Gamma^2\left(\frac{\alpha}{2}\right)(1-\rho^2)^{-(\nu+\alpha)/2}}\sum_{k=0}^{\infty}\sum_{m=0}^{\infty}\frac{\left(\frac{\nu+\alpha}{2}\right)_{k+m}^2\rho^{2m}I(k,m)}{k!m!\left(\frac{\nu}{2}\right)_k\left(\frac{\alpha}{2}\right)_m}\left(\frac{c^{2p}\rho^2}{(q_1q_2)^p}\right)^k,
\end{aligned}
\tag{A8}
$$

Using Fubini's theorem and Equation (3.241.411) from [32] in Equation (A8), we obtain

$$
\begin{aligned}
I(k,m) &= \int_{\mathbb{R}_+} y_1^{p\nu/2+a+pk-1}\left[\left(\frac{cy_1}{q_1}\right)^p+1\right]^{-\left(\frac{\nu+\alpha}{2}+k+m\right)}dy_1 \\
&\quad\times\int_{\mathbb{R}_+} y_2^{p\nu/2+b+pk-1}\left[\left(\frac{cy_2}{q_2}\right)^p+1\right]^{-\left(\frac{\nu+\alpha}{2}+k+m\right)}dy_2 \\
&= \frac{\Gamma\left(\frac{\nu}{2}+\frac{a}{p}+k\right)\Gamma\left(\frac{\alpha}{2}-\frac{a}{p}+m\right)\Gamma\left(\frac{\nu}{2}+\frac{b}{p}+k\right)\Gamma\left(\frac{\alpha}{2}-\frac{b}{p}+m\right)}{p^2\Gamma^2\left(\frac{\nu+\alpha}{2}+k+m\right)} \\
&\quad\times\left(\frac{q_1}{c}\right)^{\frac{p\nu}{2}+a+pk}\left(\frac{q_2}{c}\right)^{\frac{p\nu}{2}+b+pk}.
\end{aligned}
\tag{A9}
$$

By combining Equations (A8) and (A9), we obtain

$$
\begin{aligned}
\mathbb{E}(Y_1^aY_2^b) &= \frac{q_1^aq_2^b\Gamma\left(\frac{\nu}{2}+\frac{a}{p}\right)\Gamma\left(\frac{\nu}{2}+\frac{b}{p}\right)\Gamma\left(\frac{\alpha}{2}-\frac{a}{p}\right)\Gamma\left(\frac{\alpha}{2}-\frac{b}{p}\right)}{c^{a+b}\Gamma^2\left(\frac{\nu}{2}\right)\Gamma^2\left(\frac{\alpha}{2}\right)(1-\rho^2)^{-\frac{\nu+\alpha}{2}}} \\
&\quad\times\sum_{k=0}^{\infty}\sum_{m=0}^{\infty}\frac{\left(\frac{\nu}{2}+\frac{a}{p}\right)_k\left(\frac{\nu}{2}+\frac{b}{p}\right)_k\left(\frac{\alpha}{2}-\frac{a}{p}\right)_m\left(\frac{\alpha}{2}-\frac{b}{p}\right)_m}{k!m!\left(\frac{\nu}{2}\right)_k\left(\frac{\alpha}{2}\right)_k}\rho^{2(k+m)} \\
&= \frac{q_1^aq_2^b\Gamma\left(\frac{\nu}{2}+\frac{a}{p}\right)\Gamma\left(\frac{\nu}{2}+\frac{b}{p}\right)\Gamma\left(\frac{\alpha}{2}-\frac{a}{p}\right)\Gamma\left(\frac{\alpha}{2}-\frac{b}{p}\right)}{c^{a+b}\Gamma^2\left(\frac{\nu}{2}\right)\Gamma^2\left(\frac{\alpha}{2}\right)(1-\rho^2)^{-\frac{\nu+\alpha}{2}}} \\
&\quad\times{}_2F_1\left(\frac{\nu}{2}+\frac{a}{p},\frac{\nu}{2}+\frac{b}{p};\frac{\nu}{2};\rho^2\right){}_2F_1\left(\frac{\alpha}{2}-\frac{a}{p},\frac{\alpha}{2}-\frac{b}{p};\frac{\alpha}{2};\rho^2\right)
\end{aligned}
$$

Finally, using a Euler transformation, we have Equation (11). □

Proof of Proposition 5. For part (a), we have

$$\begin{aligned}\mathbb{E}_{\mathbf{Y}}(Y_i^p) &= \frac{p^2 c^{p\nu}(q_iq_j)^{-p\nu/2}\Gamma^2\left(\frac{\nu+\alpha}{2}\right)}{\Gamma^2\left(\frac{\nu}{2}\right)\Gamma^2\left(\frac{\alpha}{2}\right)(1-\rho^2)^{-(\nu+\alpha)/2}} \\ &\quad\times\sum_{k=0}^{\infty}\sum_{m=0}^{\infty}\frac{\left(\frac{\nu+\alpha}{2}\right)^2_{k+m}\rho^{2m}I(k,m)}{k!m!\left(\frac{\nu}{2}\right)_k\left(\frac{\alpha}{2}\right)_m}\left(\frac{c^{2p}\rho^2}{(q_iq_j)^p}\right)^k. \end{aligned} \tag{A10}$$

By using Fubini's theorem and Equation (3.241.411) from [32] in Equation (A10), we obtain

$$\begin{aligned} I(k,m) &= \int_{\mathbb{R}_+} y_i^{p\nu/2+pk+p-1}\left[\left(\frac{cy_i}{q_i}\right)^p+1\right]^{-\left(\frac{\nu+\alpha}{2}+k+m\right)}dy_i \\ &\quad\times\int_{\mathbb{R}_+} y_j^{p\nu/2+pk-1}\left[\left(\frac{cy_j}{q_j}\right)^p+1\right]^{-\left(\frac{\nu+\alpha}{2}+k+m\right)}dy_j \\ &= \frac{\Gamma\left(\frac{\nu}{2}+k+1\right)\Gamma\left(\frac{\alpha}{2}+m-1\right)\Gamma\left(\frac{\nu}{2}+k\right)\Gamma\left(\frac{\alpha}{2}+m\right)}{p^2\Gamma^2\left(\frac{\nu+\alpha}{2}+k+m\right)}\left(\frac{q_i}{c}\right)^{\frac{p\nu}{2}+pk+p}\left(\frac{q_j}{c}\right)^{\frac{p\nu}{2}+pk}. \end{aligned} \tag{A11}$$

By combining Equations (A10) and (A11), we obtain

$$\begin{aligned}\mathbb{E}_{\mathbf{Y}}(Y_i^p) &= \frac{q_i^p\Gamma\left(\frac{\nu}{2}+1\right)\Gamma\left(\frac{\alpha}{2}-1\right)}{c^p\Gamma\left(\frac{\nu}{2}\right)\Gamma\left(\frac{\alpha}{2}\right)(1-\rho^2)^{-\frac{\nu+\alpha}{2}}} \\ &\quad\times\sum_{k=0}^{\infty}\sum_{m=0}^{\infty}\frac{\left(\frac{\nu}{2}+1\right)_k\left(\frac{\nu}{2}\right)_k\left(\frac{\alpha}{2}-1\right)_m\left(\frac{\alpha}{2}\right)_m}{k!m!\left(\frac{\nu}{2}\right)_k\left(\frac{\alpha}{2}\right)_k}\rho^{2(k+m)} \\ &= \frac{q_i^p\Gamma\left(\frac{\nu}{2}+1\right)\Gamma\left(\frac{\alpha}{2}-1\right)}{c^p\Gamma\left(\frac{\nu}{2}\right)\Gamma\left(\frac{\alpha}{2}\right)(1-\rho^2)^{-\frac{\nu+\alpha}{2}}}\,{}_2F_1\left(\frac{\nu}{2}+1,\frac{\nu}{2};\frac{\nu}{2};\rho^2\right){}_2F_1\left(\frac{\alpha}{2}-1,\frac{\alpha}{2};\frac{\alpha}{2};\rho^2\right). \end{aligned}$$

Using the identity ${}_2F_1(a,b;b;x)=(1-x)^{-a}$ in the last equality, we obtain

$$\mathbb{E}_{\mathbf{Y}}(Y_i^p)=\frac{q_i^p\Gamma\left(\frac{\nu}{2}+1\right)\Gamma\left(\frac{\alpha}{2}-1\right)}{c^p\Gamma\left(\frac{\nu}{2}\right)\Gamma\left(\frac{\alpha}{2}\right)}.$$

For part (b), we have

$$\begin{aligned}\mathbb{E}_{\mathbf{Y}}(\log Y_i) &= \frac{p^2 c^{p\nu}(q_iq_j)^{-p\nu/2}\Gamma^2\left(\frac{\nu+\alpha}{2}\right)}{\Gamma^2\left(\frac{\nu}{2}\right)\Gamma^2\left(\frac{\alpha}{2}\right)(1-\rho^2)^{-(\nu+\alpha)/2}} \\ &\quad\times\sum_{k=0}^{\infty}\sum_{m=0}^{\infty}\frac{\left(\frac{\nu+\alpha}{2}\right)^2_{k+m}\rho^{2m}I(k,m)}{k!m!\left(\frac{\nu}{2}\right)_k\left(\frac{\alpha}{2}\right)_m}\left(\frac{c^{2p}\rho^2}{(q_iq_j)^p}\right)^k. \end{aligned} \tag{A12}$$

Using Fubini's theorem and Equation (3.241.411) from [32] in Equation (A12), we obtain

$$\begin{aligned} I(k,m) &= \int_{\mathbb{R}_+} \log(y_i)y_i^{p\nu/2+pk-1}\left[\left(\frac{cy_i}{q_i}\right)^p+1\right]^{-\left(\frac{\nu+\alpha}{2}+k+m\right)}dy_i \\ &\quad\times\int_{\mathbb{R}_+} y_j^{p\nu/2+pk-1}\left[\left(\frac{cy_j}{q_j}\right)^p+1\right]^{-\left(\frac{\nu+\alpha}{2}+k+m\right)}dy_j \\ &= \frac{\Gamma^2\left(\frac{\nu}{2}+k\right)\Gamma^2\left(\frac{\alpha}{2}+m\right)}{p^3\Gamma^2\left(\frac{\nu+\alpha}{2}+k+m\right)}\left(\frac{q_i}{c}\right)^{\frac{p\nu}{2}+pk}\left(\frac{q_j}{c}\right)^{\frac{p\nu}{2}+pk} \end{aligned}$$

$$\times\left\{\psi\left(\frac{\nu}{2}+k\right)-\psi\left(\frac{\alpha}{2}+m\right)-\log\left(\frac{c}{q_i}\right)^p\right\}. \tag{A13}$$

By combining Equations (A12) and (A13), we obtain

$$\begin{aligned}\mathbb{E}_{\mathbf{Y}}(\log Y_i) &= \frac{1}{p(1-\rho^2)^{-(\nu+\alpha)/2}}\\ &\times\sum_{k=0}^{\infty}\sum_{m=0}^{\infty}\frac{\left(\frac{\nu}{2}\right)_k\left(\frac{\alpha}{2}\right)_m\rho^{2k+2m}}{k!m!}\left\{\psi\left(\frac{\nu}{2}+k\right)-\psi\left(\frac{\alpha}{2}+m\right)-\log\left(\frac{c}{q_i}\right)^p\right\}.\end{aligned}$$

□

Proof of Proposition 6. In evaluating the density of Theorem 2 in Equation (14), we have

$$\begin{aligned}&\mathcal{H}(\mathbf{Y})\\ &=-\log\left[\frac{\frac{(cp)^2}{q_1q_2}\Gamma^2\left(\frac{\nu+\alpha}{2}\right)}{\Gamma^2\left(\frac{\nu}{2}\right)\Gamma^2\left(\frac{\alpha}{2}\right)(1-\rho^2)^{-(\nu+\alpha)/2}}\right]-\left(\frac{p\nu}{2}-1\right)\left[\log\left(\frac{c^2}{q_1q_2}\right)+\mathbb{E}_{\mathbf{Y}}[\log Y_1]+\mathbb{E}_{\mathbf{Y}}[\log Y_2]\right]\\ &+\left(\frac{\nu+\alpha}{2}\right)\left\{\mathbb{E}_{\mathbf{Y}}\left[\log\left(\left(\frac{cy_1}{q_1}\right)^p+1\right)\right]+\mathbb{E}_{\mathbf{Y}}\left[\log\left(\left(\frac{cy_2}{q_2}\right)^p+1\right)\right]\right\}\\ &-\mathbb{E}_{\mathbf{Y}}\left[\log F_4\left(\frac{\nu+\alpha}{2},\frac{\nu+\alpha}{2};\frac{\nu}{2},\frac{\alpha}{2};\frac{\rho^2(c^2y_1y_2)^p(q_1q_2)^{-p}}{\left(\left(\frac{cy_1}{q_1}\right)^p+1\right)\left(\left(\frac{cy_2}{q_2}\right)^p+1\right)},\frac{\rho^2}{\left(\left(\frac{cy_1}{q_1}\right)^p+1\right)\left(\left(\frac{cy_2}{q_2}\right)^p+1\right)}\right)\right].\end{aligned}$$

By assuming in the last Appell hypergeometric function that its sum converges at the first term (i.e., when $k=m=0$) [14], we have that $\mathbb{E}_{\mathbf{Y}}[\log F_4(\cdot)]\approx 0$. Aside from this, considering Proposition 4, we have that

$$\mathbb{E}_{\mathbf{Y}}\left[\log\left(\left(\frac{cY_i}{q_i}\right)^p+1\right)\right]\approx\left(\frac{c}{q_i}\right)^p\mathbb{E}_{\mathbf{Y}}[Y_i^p],\quad i=1,2.$$

Then, the differential entropy of $\mathbf{Y}$ can be approximated by

$$\begin{aligned}\mathcal{H}(\mathbf{Y})\approx&-\log\left[\frac{\frac{(cp)^2}{q_1q_2}\Gamma^2\left(\frac{\nu+\alpha}{2}\right)}{\Gamma^2\left(\frac{\nu}{2}\right)\Gamma^2\left(\frac{\alpha}{2}\right)(1-\rho^2)^{-(\nu+\alpha)/2}}\right]\\ &-\left(\frac{p\nu}{2}-1\right)\left[\log\left(\frac{c^2}{q_1q_2}\right)+\mathbb{E}_{\mathbf{Y}}[\log Y_1]+\mathbb{E}_{\mathbf{Y}}[\log Y_2]\right]\\ &+c^p\left(\frac{\nu+\alpha}{2}\right)\left\{\frac{\mathbb{E}_{\mathbf{Y}}[Y_1^p]}{q_1^p}+\frac{\mathbb{E}_{\mathbf{Y}}[Y_2^p]}{q_2^p}\right\}.\end{aligned}$$

This concludes the proof. □

References

1. Johnson, N.; Kotz, S.; Balakrishnan, N. *Continuous Univariate Distributions*, 2nd ed.; John Wiley & Sons Ltd.: New York, NY, USA, 1994; Volume 1.
2. Arnold, B. *Pareto Distributions*, 2nd ed.; Chapman and Hall/CRC: Boca Raton, FL, USA, 2015.
3. Feller, W. *An Introduction to Probability Theory and Its Applications*, 2nd ed.; John Wiley & Sons: Hoboken, NJ, USA, 1971; Volume 2.
4. Pickands, J. Statistical Inference Using Extreme Order Statistics. *Ann. Stat.* **1975**, *3*, 119–131.
5. Lomax, K.S. Business failures: Another example of the analysis of failure data. *J. Am. Stat. Assoc.* **1954**, *49*, 847–852. [CrossRef]
6. Arnold, B. *Pareto Distributions*; International Cooperative Publishing House: Fairland, MD, USA, 1983.
7. Cohen, C.A. *Truncated and Censored Samples: Theory and Applications*, 1st ed.; CRC Press: Boca Raton, FL, USA, 1991.
8. Gupta, R.C.; Akman, O.; Lvin, S. A study of log—Logistic model in survival analysis. *Biometrical J.* **1999**, *41*, 431–443. [CrossRef]
9. Bevilacqua, M.; Caamaño-Carrillo, C.; Arellano-Valle, R.B.; Morales-Oñate, V. Non-Gaussian geostatistical modeling using (skew) T processes. *Scand. J. Stat.* **2021**, *48*, 212–245. [CrossRef]

10. Bevilacqua, M.; Caamaño-Carrillo, C.; Gaetan, C. On modeling positive continuous data with spatiotemporal dependence. *Environmetrics* **2020**, *31*, e2632. [CrossRef]
11. Morales-Navarrete, D.; Bevilacqua, M.; Caamaño-Carrillo, C.; Castro, L.M. Modeling point referenced spatial count data: A Poisson process approach. *J. Am. Stat. Assoc.* **2022**, *119*, 1–14. [CrossRef]
12. Kotz, S.; Balakrishnan, N.; Johnson, N.L. *Continuous Multivariate Distributions, Volume 1: Models and Applications*; John Wiley & Sons: Hoboken, NJ, USA, 2004.
13. Vere-Jones, D. Ergodic properties of nonnegative matrices. I. *Pac. J. Math.* **1967**, *22*, 361–386. [CrossRef]
14. Caamaño-Carrillo, C.; Contreras-Reyes, J.E. A generalization of the bivariate gamma distribution based on generalized hypergeometric functions. *Mathematics* **2022**, *10*, 1502. [CrossRef]
15. Caamano-Carrillo, C.; Contreras-Reyes, J.E.; González-Navarrete, M.; Sánchez, E. Bivariate superstatistics based on generalized gamma distribution. *Eur. Phys. J. B* **2020**, *93*, 43. [CrossRef]
16. Krishnamoorthy, A.S.; Parthasarthy, M.D. A multivariate gamma-type distribution. *Ann. Math. Stat.* **1951**, *22*, 549–557. [CrossRef]
17. Krishnaiah, P.R.; Rao, M.M. Remarks on a multivariate gamma distribution. *Math. Assoc. Am.* **1961**, *68*, 342–346. [CrossRef]
18. Royen, T. Integral representations and approximations for multivariate gamma distributions. *Ann. Inst. Stat. Math.* **2004**, *59*, 499–513. [CrossRef]
19. Kotz, S.; Nadarajah, S. *Extreme Value Distributions: Theory and Applications*; Imperial College Press: London, UK, 2004.
20. Arnold, B. Univariate and multivariate pareto models. *J. Stat. Distrib. Appl.* **2014**, *1*, 1–16. [CrossRef]
21. R Core Team. *A Language and Environment for Statistical Computing*; R Foundation for Statistical Computing: Vienna, Austria, 2023; ISBN 3-900051-07-0. Available online: http://www.R-project.org (accessed on 24 July 2024).
22. Dubey, S.D. Compound gamma, beta and F distributions. *Metrika* **1970**, *16*, 27–31. [CrossRef]
23. Bowman, K.O.; Shenton, L.R.; Gailey, P.C. Distribution of the ratio of gamma variates. Commun. *Stat. Simul. Comput.* **1998**, *27*, 1–19. [CrossRef]
24. Pham-Gia, T.; Duong, Q.P. The Generalized Beta- and F-distributions in statistical modelling. *Math. Comput. Model.* **1989**, *12*, 1613–1625. [CrossRef]
25. Crooks, G. *Field Guide to Continuous Probability Distributions. V1.0.0*; Berkeley Institute for Theoretical Sciences: Berkeley, CA, USA, 2006.
26. Tiao, G.; Guttman, I. The multivariate inverted beta distribution with applications. *J. Am. Stat. Assoc.* **1965**, *60*, 793–805. [CrossRef]
27. Cover, T.M.; Thomas, J.A. *Elements of Information Theory*; Wiley & Son, Inc.: New York, NY, USA, 2006.
28. Contreras-Reyes, J.E. Mutual information matrix based on Rényi entropy and application. *Nonlinear Dyn.* **2022**, *110*, 623–633. [CrossRef]
29. Tahmasebi, S.; Behboodian, J. Shannon entropy for the Feller-Pareto (FP) family and order statistics of FP subfamilies. *Appl. Math. Sci.* **2010**, *4*, 495–504.
30. Contreras-Reyes, J.E. Asymptotic form of the Kullback—Leibler divergence for multivariate asymmetric heavy-tailed distributions. *Physica A* **2014**, *395*, 200–208. [CrossRef]
31. Contreras-Reyes, J.E. Mutual information matrix based on asymmetric Shannon entropy for nonlinear interactions of time series. *Nonlinear Dyn.* **2021**, *104*, 3913–3924. [CrossRef]
32. Gradshteyn, I.; Ryzhik, I. *Table of Integrals, Series, and Products*, 7th ed.; Academic Press: New York, NY, USA, 2007.

axioms

MDPI

Article

Maximum Penalized Likelihood Estimation of the Skew–t Link Model for Binomial Response Data

Omar Chocotea-Poca [1,2,*,†], Orietta Nicolis [3,*,†] and Germán Ibacache-Pulgar [2,4,*,†]

1 Department of Mathematics and Computer Science, Universidad de Santiago de Chile, Avenida Libertador Bernardo O'Higgins 3363, Santiago 9170022, Chile
2 Statistical Institute, Universidad de Valparaíso, Avenida Gran Bretaña 1111, Valparaíso 2360102, Chile
3 Engineering Faculty, Universidad Andres Bello, Calle Quillota 980, Viña del Mar 2520000, Chile
4 Centro de Estudios Atmosféricos y Cambio Climático, Universidad de Valparaíso, Avenida Gran Bretaña 644, Valparaíso 2360102, Chile
* Correspondence: omar.chocotea@usach.cl (O.C.-P.); orietta.nicolis@unab.cl (O.N.); german.ibacache@uv.cl (G.I.-P.)
† These authors contributed equally to this work.

Abstract: A critical aspect of modeling binomial response data is selecting an appropriate link function, as an improper choice can significantly affect model precision. This paper introduces the skew–t link model, an extension of the skew–probit model, offering increased flexibility by incorporating both asymmetry and heavy tails, making it suitable for asymmetric and complex data structures. A penalized likelihood-based estimation method is proposed to stabilize parameter estimation, particularly for the asymmetry parameter. Extensive simulation studies demonstrate the model's superior performance in terms of lower bias, root mean squared error (RMSE), and robustness compared to traditional symmetric models like probit and logit. Furthermore, the model is applied to two real-world datasets: one concerning women's labor participation and another related to cardiovascular disease outcomes, both showing superior fitting capabilities compared to more traditional models (with probit and the skew–probit links). These findings highlight the model's applicability to socioeconomic and medical research, characterized by skew and asymmetric data. Moreover, the proposed model could be applied in various domains where data exhibit asymmetry and complex structures.

Keywords: binomial response data; skew–probit link model; model flexibility; penalized likelihood

MSC: 62P12; 62J20; 62J12

1. Introduction

When analyzing binomial response data, models with probit, logit, and cloglog links are commonly considered. Probit and logit links are symmetric, while the cloglog link is asymmetric. Ref. [1] explores these common links. The researchers conduct various simulation studies to investigate whether the choice of the link influences the model's fit or predictive ability. Additionally, they perform analyses on three sets of real-world data. Both simulation studies and real data analysis highlight that an incorrect choice of the link can lead to underfitting or overfitting. They conclude that making a wrong decision can occur if the link function is specified incorrectly. Therefore, one option for a specified link is an asymmetric link that has a symmetric link as a particular case. One of the links that has gained importance in various contexts is the skew–probit link, which incorporates a parameter to regulate the asymmetry of the link function and considers the probit link as a specific case. This link was proposed by [2] in the field of item response theory from a Bayesian perspective. Furthermore, the skew–probit link has been examined in the context of binary response data, both from a Bayesian perspective in [3] and from a frequentist perspective in [4]. The skew–probit link is the inverse of the cumulative distribution function of the skew–normal distribution proposed by [5]. The literature, from the work of [5,6], highlights the difficulties associated with estimating the skewness parameter in these distributions. Therefore, Refs. [7,8] suggest the application of a penalty function.

Recognizing the need for a more flexible and adaptable link function in the analysis of binomial response data, we introduce the skew–t link model in this work. Our proposed model significantly extends the capabilities of existing methods by offering greater flexibility compared to traditional links, including the skew–probit link, which it encompasses as a special case. A key innovation of our approach lies in the use of penalized maximum likelihood estimation, which enhances the stability and accuracy of parameter estimation, particularly in handling the skewness parameter. This combination of flexibility and robust estimation makes our skew–t link model a powerful tool for addressing complex data structures in binomial response models.

The structure of this article is organized systematically as follows. Section 2 presents the proposed skew–t link model for analyzing binomial response data, detailing its formulation and the penalized log-likelihood function. In Section 3, we focus on parameter estimation, including the derivation of the score function and relevant asymptotic results. Section 4 evaluates the performance of the proposed model through two comprehensive simulation studies, each considering different data generation configurations. The application of the model to real-world datasets is presented in Section 5, where we analyze both binomial and binary response data. Finally, Sections 6 and 7 offer a detailed discussion of the findings and conclude the paper.

2. Skew–t Link Model

2.1. Formulation

As a starting point, we establish an essential part of the general notation. Let us assume that $\mathbf{x}_i = (x_{i1}, \ldots, x_{ik})^\top$ is a vector of covariates and $\boldsymbol{\beta} = (\beta_1, \ldots, \beta_k)^\top$ is a vector of regression coefficients, both of dimension $k \times 1$, where $i = 1, \ldots, m$. Additionally, $x_{i1} = 1$ due to the intercept term. In this context, the skew–t link model is specified by

$$\begin{aligned} y_i &\overset{ind.}{\sim} \text{Binomial}(n_i, p_i) \\ p_i &= \Psi_\alpha(\mathbf{x}_i^\top \boldsymbol{\beta}; \nu), \end{aligned} \tag{1}$$

where $\Psi_\alpha(\cdot;\nu)$ is the cumulative distribution function of the skew–t distribution introduced by [9,10] with skewness parameter $-\infty < \alpha < \infty$ and degrees of freedom $\nu > 0$. In the context of the Generalized Linear Models theory, $\Psi_\alpha(\cdot;\nu)$ is the inverse link function [11],

$$\Psi_\alpha^{-1}(p_i;\nu) = \mathbf{x}_i^\top \boldsymbol{\beta}.$$

The model (1) will be represented as $\mathcal{M}_{\alpha,\nu}$.

By definition, the cumulative distribution function for the skew–t distribution is given by

$$\Psi_\alpha(\eta;\nu) = 2\int_{-\infty}^{\eta} \psi_0(t;\nu)\Psi_0\left(\alpha t\sqrt{\frac{\nu+1}{\nu+t^2}};\nu+1\right)\mathrm{d}t, \tag{2}$$

where $\psi_0(\cdot;\nu^*)$ and $\Psi_0(\cdot;\nu^*)$ denote the probability density function and cumulative distribution function of the standard Student's t-distribution with degrees of freedom $\nu^* > 0$, respectively,

$$\psi_0(\eta;\nu) = \frac{\Gamma((\nu+1)/2)}{\sqrt{\nu\pi}\Gamma(\nu/2)}\left(1+\frac{\eta^2}{\nu}\right)^{-\frac{\nu+1}{2}}.$$

$\Psi_\alpha(\cdot;\nu)$ is continuous, smooth, and infinitely differentiable. By the fundamental theorem of calculus, the first derivative of (2) with respect to η is the probability density function of the skew–t distribution,

$$\psi_\alpha(\eta;\nu) = 2\psi_0(\eta;\nu)\Psi_0\left(\alpha\eta\sqrt{\frac{\nu+1}{\nu+\eta^2}};\nu+1\right). \tag{3}$$

The second derivative of (2) with respect to η is

$$\frac{\partial}{\partial\eta}\psi_\alpha(\eta;\nu) = -\frac{\nu+1}{\nu}\eta\left(1+\frac{\eta^2}{\nu}\right)^{-1}\psi_\alpha(\eta;\nu) + \frac{\alpha}{2}\psi_0(\eta;\nu)\psi_0\left(\alpha\eta\sqrt{\frac{\nu+1}{\nu+\eta^2}};\nu+1\right)\left\{\sqrt{\frac{\nu+1}{\nu+\eta^2}} - \frac{\sqrt{\nu+1}}{(\nu+\eta^2)^{3/2}}\eta^2\right\}.$$

Refs. [12,13] derived explicit expressions for the cumulative distribution function when $\nu = 1,2,3,4$. Ref. [12] for $\nu = 1$,

$$\Psi_\alpha(\eta;1) = \frac{1}{\pi}\left[\tan^{-1}(\eta) + \cos^{-1}\left\{\frac{\alpha}{\sqrt{(1+\alpha^2)(1+\eta^2)}}\right\}\right]$$

and Ref. [13] for $\nu = 2,3,4$, for example,

$$\Psi_\alpha(\eta;2) = \frac{1}{2} - \frac{1}{\pi}\tan^{-1}(\alpha) + \frac{\eta}{\sqrt{2+\eta^2}}\left\{\frac{1}{2} + \frac{1}{\pi}\tan^{-1}\left(\frac{\alpha\eta}{\sqrt{2+\eta^2}}\right)\right\}.$$

The model $\mathcal{M}_{\alpha,\nu}$ is connected to several other important models. When $\nu = 1$, it reduces to the new skew–Cauchy link model. As $\nu \longrightarrow \infty$, it converges to the skew–probit link model, represented by $\mathcal{M}_\alpha$. When $\alpha = 0$, the model simplifies to the t-link model, represented by $\mathcal{M}_\nu$. When $\alpha = 0$ and $\nu = 1$, it becomes the Cauchy link model. Finally, as $\alpha = 0$ and $\nu \longrightarrow \infty$, the model converges to the probit link model, represented by $\mathcal{M}_0$. These relationships are illustrated in Figure 1.

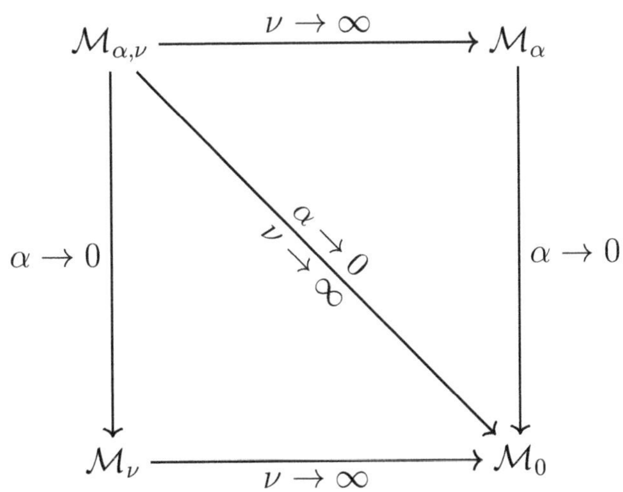

Figure 1. Some of the relationships between models derived from the $\mathcal{M}_{\alpha,\nu}$ model.

Figure 2 displays the probability as a function of η for selected values of the parameters α and ν. This figure is highly informative. When $\alpha = 0$, the probability approaches both zero and one at the same rate. However, when $\alpha > 0$, the probability approaches zero more rapidly than it does one. The inverse behavior is observed when $\alpha < 0$. Additionally, as the degrees of freedom decrease, the tails of the distribution become heavier. These characteristics highlight the advantage of this model compared to those that use symmetric links, such as $\mathcal{M}_0$ and $\mathcal{M}_\nu$, as well as models that employ asymmetric links, such as $\mathcal{M}_\alpha$. Furthermore, this model can adapt to the aforementioned models, making it a flexible link option.

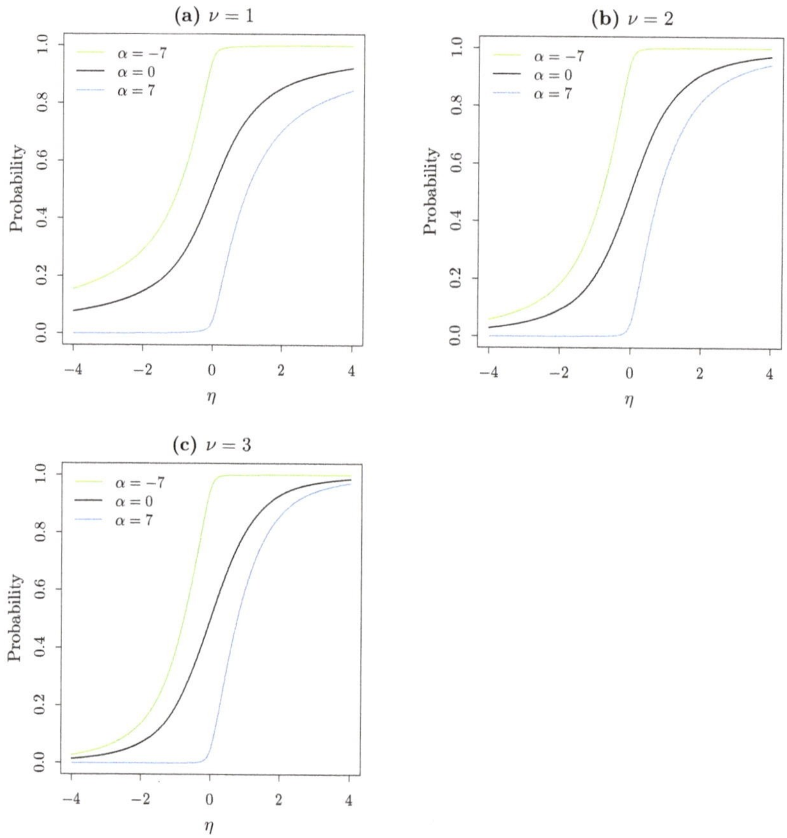

Figure 2. Probability curves of $\mathcal{M}_{\alpha,\nu}$ for some values of α and ν.

2.2. Penalized Log-Likelihood Function

In the Student's t-distribution, estimating the degrees of freedom parameter presents considerable challenges, which also impact the proposed model. According to [14], in a general regression model, two estimation scenarios are considered. In the first, all parameters are estimated simultaneously, while in the second, a subset of parameters is estimated, with the remaining parameters fixed at their true values. In this work, the parameters $\boldsymbol{\beta}$ and α will be estimated, while the parameter ν is fixed at its true value, ν_0.

Consider the complete dataset, $\mathcal{D} = \{(y_i, n_i, \mathbf{x}_i)\}$ and $\eta_i = \mathbf{x}_i^\top \boldsymbol{\beta}$. The log-likelihood function is

$$\ell(\boldsymbol{\theta}) = \sum_{i=1}^{m} \ell_i(\boldsymbol{\theta}), \tag{4}$$

where

$$\ell_i(\boldsymbol{\theta}) \propto y_i \log(p_i) + (n_i - y_i)\log(1 - p_i)$$

with parameter vector $\boldsymbol{\theta} = (\boldsymbol{\beta}^\top, \alpha)^\top$ of dimension $(k+1) \times 1$.

A second challenge arises in the stability of estimating the skewness parameter in the skew–t distribution, a problem that also impacts the proposed model, as it relies on the cumulative distribution function of this distribution. According to [8], available methods to address this issue, both frequentist and Bayesian, are limited to simple scenarios. This study adopts the penalized log-likelihood approach, which necessitates an appropriate penalty function. This function, also known as shrinkage estimation, semi-Bayes, or partial-Bayes, is implemented without requiring a strictly Bayesian justification [15].

Given $\mathcal{D}$, the penalized log-likelihood function is given by

$$\ell_{\mathrm{p}}(\boldsymbol{\theta}) = \ell(\boldsymbol{\theta}) - Q(\alpha), \tag{5}$$

where $Q(\cdot)$ is the penalty function.

Ref. [8] proposes that the penalization function should meet the following properties:

1. $Q(\alpha) \geq 0$
2. $Q(\alpha)\big|_{\alpha=0} = 0$ and
3. $\lim_{\alpha \to \pm\infty}(\alpha) = \infty$.

The penalization function that we can derive from the proposal of [8] is

$$Q(\alpha) = c_1 \log(1 + c_2\alpha^2), \tag{6}$$

where c_1 and c_2 are positive constants. In [3,4], this penalty function was incorporated into the skew–probit link model for binary response data without prior knowledge of its formulation. In [3], from a Bayesian perspective, the values were set as $c_1 = 3/2$ and $c_2 = 1$. Meanwhile, in [4], a frequentist approach was taken, setting $c_1 = 1$ and $c_2 = 4/25$. These values were derived using the kernel of the density of the Student's t distribution, based on the following relationship:

$$\exp\{-Q(\alpha)\} = \left(1 + \frac{\alpha^2}{\sigma^2 \nu}\right)^{-(\nu+1)/2}.$$

Ref. [3] used the parameters $\sigma^2 = 1/2$ and $\nu = 2$, while [4] employed $\sigma^2 = 25/4$ and $\nu = 1$. In the estimation scenario, where ν is assumed to be known, we adopt the approach of [8], selecting the following values:

$$c_1 = \frac{1}{4\nu_2} \quad \text{and} \quad c_2 = \frac{\nu_2}{\nu_1},$$

where

$$\nu_1 = \frac{(\nu+2)(\nu+3)}{3(\nu+1)^2} \quad \text{and} \quad \nu_2 = 0.285 \times \left(1 + \frac{4}{\nu + 0.577}\right).$$

Figure 3 shows the behavior of the penalty functions for both types of links.

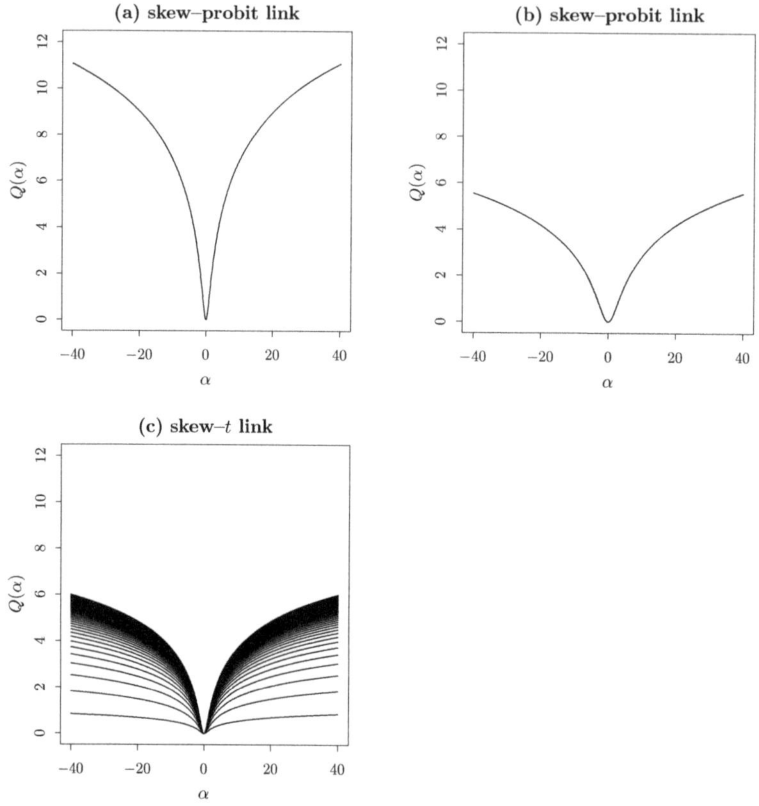

Figure 3. Penalty functions for link models: (**a**) skew–probit by Bazán et al. (2010) [3]; (**b**) skew–probit by Lee and Sinha (2019) [4]; and (**c**) skew–t by Azzalini and Arellano-Valle (2013) [8].

3. Parameter Estimation

3.1. Score Function

The estimation of the model parameters with skew–t link is carried out using the maximum penalized likelihood method. The penalized score function, obtained as the partial derivative of the penalized log-likelihood function with respect to the parameters, provides the estimation equations that must be solved to find the penalized maximum likelihood estimators. The strategy of fitting a model based on the penalized likelihood function has been widely used in various fields. Moreover, the asymptotic properties of these estimators have been extensively studied and documented in the literature for different models; see, for example, [16–18]. A key reference on this method is the book by [19].

Given the function (5) and $\mathcal{D}$, the penalized score function of $\boldsymbol{\theta}$ is given by

$$\mathbf{s}_{\mathrm{P}}(\boldsymbol{\theta}) = \frac{\partial \ell_{\mathrm{P}}(\boldsymbol{\theta})}{\partial \boldsymbol{\theta}} = \begin{bmatrix} \mathbf{s}_{\mathrm{P}}^{\boldsymbol{\beta}}(\boldsymbol{\theta}) \\ s_{\mathrm{P}}^{\alpha}(\boldsymbol{\theta}) \end{bmatrix}, \tag{7}$$

where

$$\mathbf{s}_{\mathrm{p}}^{\beta}(\boldsymbol{\theta}) = \mathbf{X}^{\top}\mathrm{diag}(\mathbf{u}_1)(\mathbf{y} - \boldsymbol{\mu})$$
$$\mathrm{s}_{\mathrm{p}}^{\alpha}(\boldsymbol{\theta}) = \mathbf{u}_2^{\top}(\mathbf{y} - \boldsymbol{\mu}) - \frac{2c_1c_2\alpha}{1 + c_2\alpha^2}.$$

In (7), $\mathbf{u}_1 = (u_{11}, \ldots, u_{1m})^{\top}$ and $\mathbf{u}_2 = (u_{21}, \ldots, u_{2m})^{\top}$, where

$$u_{1i} = \frac{v_{1i}}{p_i(1 - p_i)} \qquad \text{and} \qquad u_{2i} = \frac{v_{2i}}{p_i(1 - p_i)}$$

with

$$v_{1i} = \psi_{\alpha}(\eta_i; \nu) \qquad \text{and} \qquad v_{2i} = 2\int_{-\infty}^{\eta_i} t\sqrt{\frac{\nu + 1}{\nu + t^2}}\psi_0(t; \nu)\psi_0\left(\alpha t\sqrt{\frac{\nu + 1}{\nu + t^2}}; \nu + 1\right)\mathrm{d}t.$$

Also, $\boldsymbol{\mu} = (n_1p_1, \ldots, n_mp_m)^{\top}$, $\mathbf{y} = (y_1, \ldots, y_m)^{\top}$ and $\mathbf{X} = (\mathbf{x}_1, \ldots, \mathbf{x}_m)^{\top}$.

The maximum penalized likelihood estimator $\widehat{\boldsymbol{\theta}}_{\mathrm{p}}$ of $\boldsymbol{\theta}$ is obtained by solving the score equation,

$$\mathbf{s}_{\mathrm{p}}(\widehat{\boldsymbol{\theta}}_{\mathrm{p}}) = \mathbf{0},$$

with $\mathbf{0}$ being the zero vector of dimension $(k + 1) \times 1$.

3.2. Asymptotic Results

In asymptotic theory, maximum penalized likelihood estimators are shown to be consistent and have an approximate multivariate normal distribution in large samples. This approach allows us to construct confidence intervals and perform hypothesis tests on the model parameters, using the expected penalized information matrix and its inverse.

Given the function (5) and $\mathcal{D}$, the expectation of the penalized information matrix is given by

$$\mathcal{I}_{\mathrm{p}}(\boldsymbol{\theta}) = \mathbb{E}[\mathbf{s}_{\mathrm{p}}(\boldsymbol{\theta})\mathbf{s}_{\mathrm{p}}(\boldsymbol{\theta})^{\top}] = \begin{bmatrix} \mathcal{I}_{11} & \mathbf{i}_{12} \\ \mathbf{i}_{12}^{\top} & i_{22} \end{bmatrix}, \tag{8}$$

where

$$\mathcal{I}_{11} = \mathbf{X}^{\top}\mathrm{diag}(\mathbf{u}_1 \circ \mathbf{v}_1)\mathbf{X}$$
$$\mathbf{i}_{12} = \mathbf{X}^{\top}\mathrm{diag}(\mathbf{u}_1)\mathbf{v}_2$$
$$i_{22} = \mathrm{trace}\{\mathrm{diag}(\mathbf{u}_2 \circ \mathbf{v}_2)\} + \frac{2a_1a_2(1 - a_2)\alpha^2}{(1 + a_2\alpha^2)^2},$$

with $\circ$ denoting the Hadamard product. In (8), $\mathbf{v}_1 = (v_{11}, \ldots, v_{1m})^{\top}$and $\mathbf{v}_2 = (v_{21}, \ldots, v_{2m})^{\top}$.

Consequently, the inverse from $\mathcal{I}_{\mathrm{p}}(\boldsymbol{\theta})$ is

$$\boldsymbol{\Omega}_{\mathrm{p}}(\boldsymbol{\theta}) = \begin{bmatrix} \boldsymbol{\Omega}_{11} & \boldsymbol{\omega}_{12} \\ \boldsymbol{\omega}_{12}^{\top} & \omega_{22} \end{bmatrix}, \tag{9}$$

where

$$\boldsymbol{\Omega}_{11} = \mathcal{I}_{11}^{-1}\{\mathbf{I}_k + \mathbf{i}_{12}\omega_{22}\mathbf{i}_{12}^{\top}\mathcal{I}_{11}^{-1}\}$$
$$\boldsymbol{\omega}_{12} = -\mathcal{I}_{11}^{-1}\mathbf{i}_{12}\omega_{22}$$
$$\omega_{22} = \{i_{22} - \mathbf{i}_{12}^{\top}\mathcal{I}_{11}^{-1}\mathbf{i}_{12}\}^{-1},$$

with $\mathbf{I}_k$ being the identity matrix of dimension $k \times k$. The convenient formula for the inverse of a partitioned matrix can be seen, for example, in [20].

Assuming that $\widehat{\boldsymbol{\theta}}_{\mathrm{p}}$ is consistent, we can replace (9) with $\boldsymbol{\Omega}_{\mathrm{p}}(\widehat{\boldsymbol{\theta}}_{\mathrm{p}})$. Consequently,

$$\widehat{\boldsymbol{\theta}}_{\mathrm{p}} \dot{\sim} N_{k+1}(\boldsymbol{\theta}, \boldsymbol{\Omega}_{\mathrm{p}}(\widehat{\boldsymbol{\theta}}_{\mathrm{p}})). \tag{10}$$

The result (10) is essential for constructing confidence intervals for both β_j and α.

In this article, we utilize the open-source software R-4.4.1 [21], specifically the `maxLik` package [22]. This package provides a range of optimization routines that facilitate the implementation of advanced features, such as fixing specific parameter values, which is essential for the proposed model in this study. For the estimation of the parameters of the model $\mathcal{M}_{\alpha,\nu}$, the following procedure is adopted for selecting the initial values. The regression coefficients are initialized based on the estimates from the baseline model $\mathcal{M}_0$, represented as $\widehat{\boldsymbol{\beta}}^{\text{probit}}_{\text{initial}} = (\widehat{\beta}_{01}, \ldots, \widehat{\beta}_{0k})^\top$, where $\widehat{\beta}_{0j}$ corresponds to the estimates obtained under the probit model. Additionally, the asymmetry parameter α is initialized at zero, $\widehat{\alpha}_{\text{initial}} = 0$. These initial values are chosen to ensure a stable foundation for the iterative optimization process.

4. Simulation Study

This section aims to verify the accuracy of the parameter estimates for the $\mathcal{M}_{\alpha,\nu}$ model under the proposed methodology. It also assesses the adaptability of the proposed model to two asymmetric links and describes the process for determining the parameter ν.

4.1. Study 1

This study will address 2 scenarios for generating datasets, creating a total of 500 datasets for each scenario. The construction of the complete datasets follows the outlined procedure: in Step (1), the values for $\boldsymbol{\beta}$ and α are chosen, where $\nu_0 = 1, 2, 3$. For scenario 1, the values are set as $\theta_1 = \beta_1 = 0.5, \theta_2 = \beta_2 = 1, \theta_3 = \beta_3 = 1.5$ and $\theta_4 = \alpha = 0.2$. For scenario 2, the values are set as $\theta_1 = \beta_1 = -0.7, \theta_2 = \beta_2 = 1.3, \theta_3 = \beta_3 = -2.5$ and $\theta_4 = \alpha = 2$. In Step (2), the values for m and n_i are chosen, where $n_i = 50$. For scenario 1, the values are chosen as $m = 20, 40, \ldots, 200$. For scenario 2, the values are chosen as $m = 200, 400, \ldots, 2000$. In Step (3), x_{i2} and x_{i3} are generated using the normal distribution. For scenario 1, the values $x_{i2} \sim N(0, 2)$ and $x_{i3} \sim N(0, 3)$ are generated. For scenario 2, the values $x_{i2} \sim N(-3, 7)$ and $x_{i3} \sim N(3, 7)$ are generated. In Step (4), p_i is structured, $p_i = \Psi_\alpha(\beta_1 + \beta_2 x_{i2} + \beta_3 x_{i3}; \nu_0)$. In Step (5), y_i is generated using the binomial distribution, $y_i \overset{ind.}{\sim} \text{Binomial}(n_i, p_i)$.

Assuming that $\widehat{\theta}^{(j)}$ is the estimator of θ in the j-th dataset crafted, the Monte Carlo mean of these estimates is consequently

$$\overline{\widehat{\theta}} = \frac{1}{500} \sum_{j=1}^{500} \widehat{\theta}^{(j)}. \tag{11}$$

The absolute bias (AB) is defined as

$$\text{AB}(\widehat{\theta}) = |\overline{\widehat{\theta}} - \theta|. \tag{12}$$

The Monte Carlo standard deviation (SD) and the root mean square error (RMSE) are expressed as

$$\text{SD}(\widehat{\theta}) = \sqrt{\frac{1}{499} \sum_{j=1}^{500} (\widehat{\theta}^{(j)} - \overline{\widehat{\theta}})^2} \tag{13}$$

and

$$\text{RMSE}(\widehat{\theta}) = \sqrt{\text{SD}^2(\widehat{\theta}) + \text{AB}^2(\widehat{\theta})}, \tag{14}$$

respectively.

The results of the estimations for scenarios 1 and 2 are detailed in Tables 1 and 2, respectively. Overall, the absolute bias (12) values are close to zero. Additionally, both the SD (13) and RMSE (14) tend to decrease as the simulation size m increases, indicating greater precision in parameter estimation. These results are illustrated in Figures 4 and 5, corresponding to scenarios 1 and 2, respectively. In both figures, a diagonal line highlights the proximity between the SD and RMSE values, confirming that absolute biases are practically negligible.

Table 1. Simulation study results for the first scenario: AB, SD, and RMSE in the parameter estimation of $\mathcal{M}_{\alpha,\nu}$ under three values of ν and five values of m.

Parameter	m	$\nu = 1$			$\nu = 2$			$\nu = 3$		
		AB	SD	RMSE	AB	SD	RMSE	AB	SD	RMSE
β_1	20	0.001	0.304	0.304	0.024	0.330	0.331	0.033	0.376	0.377
	60	0.008	0.165	0.165	0.005	0.190	0.189	0.008	0.214	0.214
	100	0.003	0.121	0.120	0.000	0.140	0.140	0.003	0.166	0.166
	140	0.002	0.112	0.112	0.001	0.130	0.129	0.004	0.154	0.154
	180	0.000	0.092	0.092	0.005	0.105	0.105	0.006	0.125	0.125
β_2	20	0.002	0.148	0.148	0.014	0.128	0.129	0.029	0.123	0.126
	60	0.001	0.074	0.074	0.005	0.064	0.064	0.010	0.063	0.063
	100	0.004	0.056	0.056	0.000	0.047	0.047	0.004	0.046	0.046
	140	0.000	0.044	0.044	0.003	0.037	0.037	0.006	0.036	0.036
	180	0.001	0.043	0.043	0.002	0.036	0.036	0.005	0.035	0.035
β_3	20	0.002	0.173	0.173	0.021	0.149	0.150	0.046	0.147	0.154
	60	0.000	0.091	0.091	0.009	0.079	0.080	0.017	0.080	0.082
	100	0.007	0.071	0.071	0.000	0.059	0.059	0.006	0.060	0.060
	140	0.000	0.060	0.060	0.004	0.050	0.050	0.009	0.050	0.051
	180	0.002	0.054	0.054	0.003	0.046	0.046	0.007	0.045	0.045
α	20	0.018	0.254	0.255	0.042	0.836	0.836	0.123	1.925	1.927
	60	0.010	0.127	0.127	0.016	0.194	0.194	0.029	0.251	0.253
	100	0.004	0.092	0.092	0.007	0.141	0.141	0.008	0.188	0.188
	140	0.004	0.083	0.083	0.004	0.125	0.125	0.005	0.167	0.167
	180	0.002	0.068	0.068	0.001	0.101	0.101	0.002	0.137	0.137

Table 2. Simulation study results for the second scenario: AB, SD, and RMSE in the parameter estimation of $\mathcal{M}_{\alpha,\nu}$ under three values of ν and five values of m.

Parameter	m	$\nu = 1$			$\nu = 2$			$\nu = 3$		
		AB	SD	RMSE	AB	SD	RMSE	AB	SD	RMSE
β_1	200	0.054	0.301	0.306	0.061	0.327	0.332	0.074	0.378	0.384
	600	0.008	0.139	0.139	0.009	0.153	0.153	0.015	0.180	0.180
	1000	0.012	0.113	0.114	0.013	0.124	0.125	0.021	0.148	0.149
	1400	0.001	0.092	0.092	0.003	0.099	0.099	0.005	0.119	0.119
	1800	0.006	0.081	0.081	0.005	0.092	0.092	0.001	0.104	0.104
β_2	200	0.035	0.210	0.213	0.035	0.203	0.206	0.038	0.219	0.222
	600	0.004	0.097	0.097	0.003	0.095	0.095	0.006	0.104	0.104
	1000	0.006	0.080	0.081	0.007	0.078	0.078	0.010	0.087	0.087
	1400	0.002	0.067	0.067	0.002	0.064	0.064	0.003	0.070	0.070
	1800	0.003	0.060	0.060	0.003	0.060	0.060	0.001	0.063	0.063
β_3	200	0.069	0.385	0.391	0.069	0.378	0.384	0.075	0.412	0.419
	600	0.009	0.185	0.185	0.007	0.180	0.180	0.012	0.197	0.197
	1000	0.011	0.154	0.154	0.012	0.150	0.151	0.019	0.166	0.167
	1400	0.002	0.128	0.128	0.004	0.122	0.122	0.005	0.135	0.135
	1800	0.006	0.111	0.111	0.005	0.112	0.113	0.002	0.119	0.119
α	200	0.012	0.181	0.181	0.069	0.311	0.311	0.075	1.095	1.097
	600	0.001	0.088	0.087	0.007	0.149	0.149	0.014	0.218	0.218
	1000	0.002	0.075	0.075	0.012	0.126	0.126	0.003	0.179	0.179
	1400	0.003	0.061	0.061	0.004	0.099	0.099	0.008	0.140	0.140
	1800	0.000	0.052	0.052	0.005	0.092	0.092	0.011	0.126	0.126

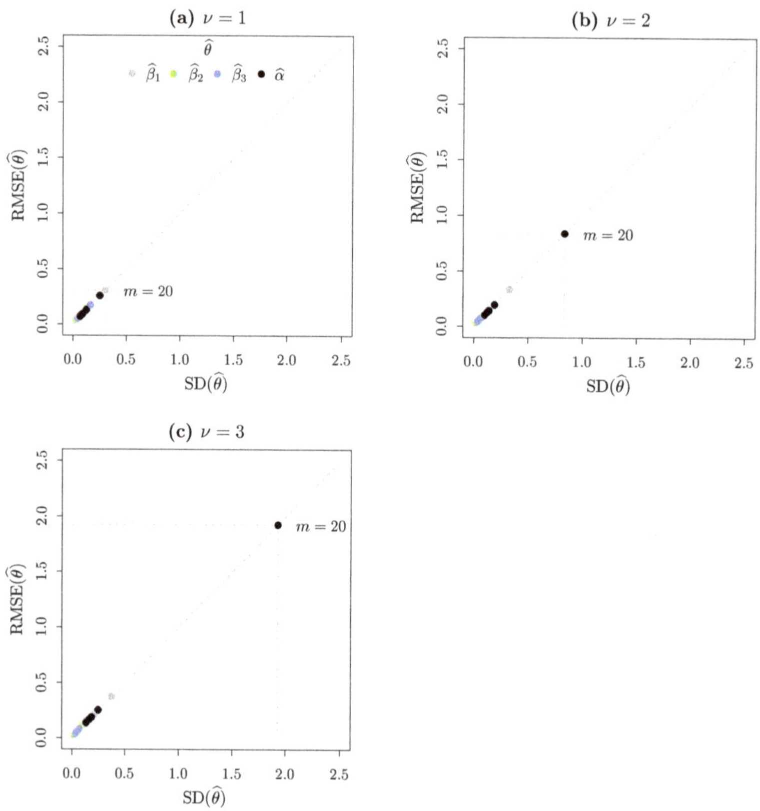

Figure 4. Simulation study results for the first scenario: SD versus RMSE in the parameter estimation of $\mathcal{M}_{\alpha,\nu}$ under three values of ν and ten values of m.

However, it is important to note that in the scenarios with less available information, the variability of the estimators can increase significantly. This effect is observed in Figure 4, where for $m = 20$ and $\nu = 3$, the SD of the skewness parameter estimator reaches a value of 1.925, while the RMSE is 1.927. This behavior explains why the SD and RMSE values for the skewness estimator deviate from the main group of estimates. Additionally, this dispersion may be influenced by the inherent variability in data generation, which emphasizes the need for a more detailed analysis in scenarios with smaller sample sizes.

4.2. Study 2

This subsection presents a second simulation study aimed at evaluating the adaptability of the proposed model in comparison with other asymmetric link models, specifically the cloglog and loglog links. Additionally, the process for setting the parameter ν is detailed. The dataset construction for each link follows the procedure outlined below. In Step (1), the value of $\beta = 1$ is set. In Step (2), the value $m = 70$ is selected. In Step (3), the values $n_i \sim \text{Poisson}(\lambda = 15)$ and $x_{i2} \sim N(0,3)$ are generated. In Step (4), the probability p_i is defined as

$$p_i = \begin{cases} 1 - \exp(-\exp(x_i)), & \text{for the cloglog link (Scenario 1)} \\ \exp(-\exp(-x_i)), & \text{for the loglog link (Scenario 2).} \end{cases}$$

In Step (5), finally, the responses y_i are generated using a binomial distribution, i.e., $y_i \overset{ind.}{\sim} \text{Binomial}(n_i, p_i)$.

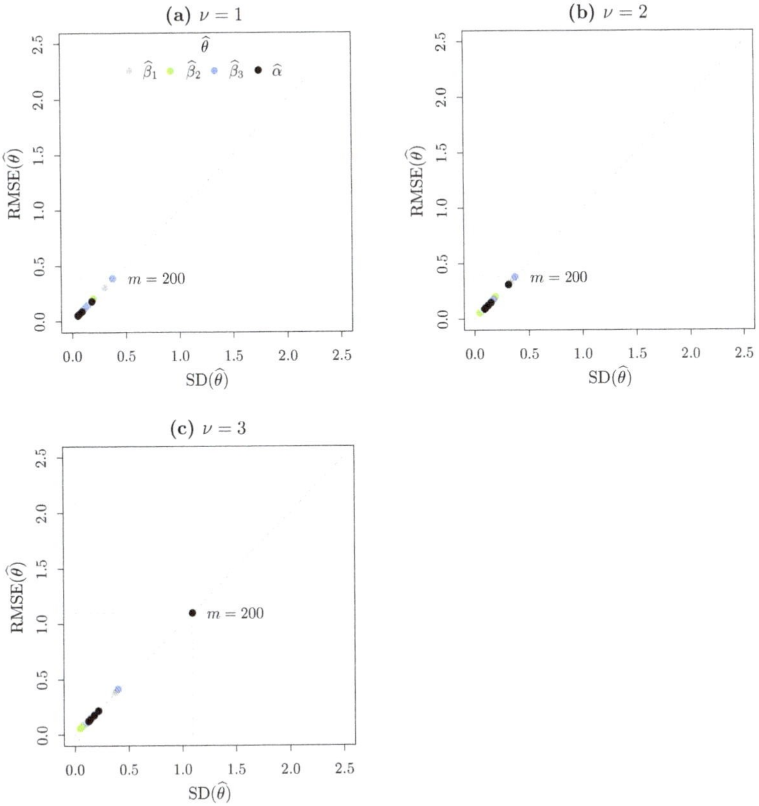

Figure 5. Simulation study results for the second scenario: SD versus RMSE in the parameter estimation of $\mathcal{M}_{\alpha,\nu}$ under three values of ν and ten values of m.

In both scenarios, the cloglog, loglog, and $\mathcal{M}_{\alpha,\nu}$ models are fitted. The determination of the degrees of freedom is performed using the profile likelihood procedure described by [23]. Figure 6 displays the profile likelihood curves as a function of ν. The sequence used for ν is $0.1, 0.2, \ldots, 30$ (with an increment of 0.1). For data generated using the cloglog link, the appropriate degrees of freedom, where the profile-penalized log-likelihood reaches its maximum, is $\nu_0 = 2.8$. For data generated using the loglog link, the appropriate degrees of freedom, corresponding to the maximum of the profile-penalized log-likelihood, is $\nu_0 = 1.9$.

Table 3 focuses on the parameter estimates for the $\mathcal{M}_{\alpha,\nu}$ model in both scenarios. The estimates of β are very close to the true values, and the 95% confidence interval includes the true value. The 95% confidence interval for α does not include zero, which suggests the continued need for a model such as the one proposed, as it is adapting to datasets generated from asymmetric links.

Reinforcing the flexibility of the proposed model, the formula for calculating the distance between two cumulative distribution functions of interest is presented below,

$$\text{D}(x) = \begin{cases} |\Psi_{-0.431}(1.085x; 2.8) - \{1 - \exp(-\exp(x))\}|, & \text{for the cloglog link} \\ |\Psi_{0.523}(1.121x; 1.9) - \exp(-\exp(-x))|, & \text{for the loglog link.} \end{cases}$$

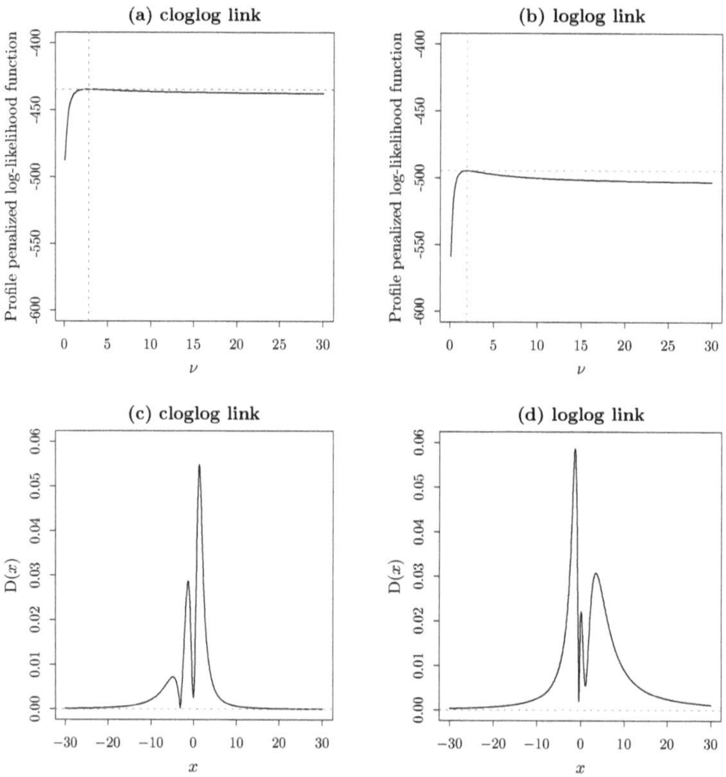

Figure 6. Profile log-likelihood function and distance between the $\mathcal{M}_{\alpha,\nu}$ model and the cloglog and loglog models: (**a**) profile log-likelihood, scenario 1; (**b**) profile log-likelihood, scenario 2; (**c**) distance, scenario 1; (**d**) distance, scenario 2.

Table 3. Summary of parameter estimation for the cloglog, loglog and $\mathcal{M}_{\alpha,\nu}$ models in simulated data.

Scenario	Model	Parameter	Estimation	SD	2.5%	97.5%
1	cloglog	β	0.952	0.056	0.844	1.061
	$\mathcal{M}_{\alpha,\nu}$	β	1.085	0.077	0.932	1.237
		α	−0.431	0.066	−0.559	−0.302
		$\nu_0 = 2.8$				
2	loglog	β	0.951	0.055	0.843	1.059
	$\mathcal{M}_{\alpha,\nu}$	β	1.121	0.080	0.964	1.278
		α	0.523	0.074	0.377	0.668
		$\nu_0 = 1.9$				

Figure 6 illustrates how this distance behaves, with the horizontal axis at zero.

A notable implication of Table 3 and Figure 6 is that the inverse of the skew–t link function approximates the inverse of the cloglog and loglog links,

$$\Psi_{-0.431}(1.085\eta; 2.8) \approx 1 - \exp(-\exp(\eta)) \tag{15}$$

and

$$\Psi_{0.523}(1.121\eta; 1.9) \approx \exp(-\exp(-\eta)), \tag{16}$$

respectively.

5. Applications

In this section, we motivate the proposed link by comparing it with the probit and skew–probit links by fitting them to two real datasets. The first dataset has binomial response data, while the second dataset has binary response data.

5.1. Women's Labor

The National Institute of Statistics (Instituto Nacional de Estadística: INE) of Bolivia conducts the Household Survey (Encuesta de Hogares: EH) semi-annually with the aim of assessing income poverty and collecting essential socioeconomic data to monitor the Sustainable Development Goals. The EH 2021 covers topics such as health, education, employment, non-labor income, and housing, and is publicly available on the INE website at https://www.ine.gob.bo, accessed on 1 January 2024 .

For this illustration, specific data from the EH 2021 were processed. The following variables were considered: the total number of women in a specific age group (n_i), the number of women who worked at least one hour in the previous week (y_i), and the age of the women in years (x_i). Additionally, this process was carried out by differentiating between urban and rural areas, considering women aged 10 to 55, in accordance with current legislation, such as the "Law 321/2013-2014 of the Code of Girls, Boys, and Adolescents" and the "Pension Law 065". The dataset is presented in Table 4, which also includes the proportion of women who worked at least one hour in the previous week (p_i^*).

It is important to note that women participating in labor activities demonstrated a wide diversity of productive and commercial occupations.

Table 5 presents the parameter estimates, standard deviations and 95% confidence intervals for models $\mathcal{M}_0$ (with probit link), $\mathcal{M}_\alpha$ (with skew–probit link) and $\mathcal{M}_{\alpha,\nu}$ (with skew–t link). It also includes model comparison criteria such as the Akaike Information Criterion (AIC), Bayesian Information Criterion (BIC), and Hannan–Quinn Information Criterion (HQIC). The information criterion values unanimously indicate that the model to consider for analysis is $\mathcal{M}_{\alpha,\nu}$.

Figure 7 shows the proportion of women who participated in work activities according to their area of residence, with the lines representing the fitted model. This figure demonstrates that, when comparing models $\mathcal{M}_0$ and $\mathcal{M}_\alpha$ with $\mathcal{M}_{\alpha,\nu}$, the first two do not fit the data in any of the three scenarios. This underscores the need for a model with a flexible link function, which $\mathcal{M}_{\alpha,\nu}$ successfully addresses.

Table 4. Women's labor data.

Urban					Rural				
i	x_i	n_i	y_i	p_i^*	i	x_i	n_i	y_i	p_i^*
1	10	368	1	0.003	1	10	136	9	0.066
2	11	296	5	0.017	2	11	95	14	0.147
3	12	296	4	0.014	3	12	108	15	0.139
4	13	327	12	0.037	4	13	108	18	0.167
5	14	308	12	0.039	5	14	98	33	0.337
6	15	325	16	0.049	6	15	99	27	0.273
7	16	286	27	0.094	7	16	82	25	0.305
8	17	301	34	0.113	8	17	88	29	0.330
9	18	313	58	0.185	9	18	61	20	0.328
10	19	275	61	0.222	10	19	58	19	0.328
11	20	306	94	0.307	11	20	59	22	0.373
12	21	338	101	0.299	12	21	72	29	0.403
13	22	295	104	0.353	13	22	47	17	0.362
14	23	299	116	0.388	14	23	53	22	0.415
15	24	292	119	0.408	15	24	49	20	0.408
16	25	324	144	0.444	16	25	64	32	0.500
17	26	310	151	0.487	17	26	65	33	0.508
18	27	291	145	0.498	18	27	63	38	0.603
19	28	307	156	0.508	19	28	65	38	0.585
20	29	255	130	0.510	20	29	48	26	0.542

Table 4. *Cont.*

Urban					Rural				
i	x_i	n_i	y_i	p_i^*	i	x_i	n_i	y_i	p_i^*
21	30	319	186	0.583	21	30	47	26	0.553
22	31	206	111	0.539	22	31	45	23	0.511
23	32	263	148	0.563	23	32	57	29	0.509
24	33	240	135	0.562	24	33	58	35	0.603
25	34	226	140	0.619	25	34	52	30	0.577
26	35	319	181	0.567	26	35	65	42	0.646
27	36	253	162	0.640	27	36	66	40	0.606
28	37	233	151	0.648	28	37	50	32	0.640
29	38	291	176	0.605	29	38	62	43	0.694
30	39	221	147	0.665	30	39	50	34	0.680
31	40	272	177	0.651	31	40	61	43	0.705
32	41	209	144	0.689	32	41	62	40	0.645
33	42	245	158	0.645	33	42	58	41	0.707
34	43	203	129	0.635	34	43	55	36	0.655
35	44	171	106	0.620	35	44	49	41	0.837
36	45	235	160	0.681	36	45	68	49	0.721
37	46	153	103	0.673	37	46	36	21	0.583
38	47	159	100	0.629	38	47	44	29	0.659
39	48	195	124	0.636	39	48	58	39	0.672
40	49	174	117	0.672	40	49	46	28	0.609
41	50	197	121	0.614	41	50	71	46	0.648
42	51	151	99	0.656	42	51	44	33	0.750
43	52	157	101	0.643	43	52	55	37	0.673
44	53	143	101	0.706	44	53	41	24	0.585
45	54	132	76	0.576	45	54	30	18	0.600
46	55	154	95	0.617	46	55	45	32	0.711

Table 5. Summary of parameter estimation for $\mathcal{M}_0$, $\mathcal{M}_\alpha$ and $\mathcal{M}_{\alpha,\nu}$, along with model selection performance evaluation using AIC, BIC, and HQIC on data related to women's labor.

Area	Model	Parameter	Estimation	SD	2.5%	97.5%	AIC	BIC	HQIC
Urban	$\mathcal{M}_0$	β_1	−1.653	0.035	−1.721	−1.585	13,544.280	13,547.940	13,545.650
		β_2	0.048	0.001	0.046	0.050			
	$\mathcal{M}_\alpha$	β_1	−0.346	0.020	−0.385	−0.306	13,442.100	13,447.590	13,444.160
		β_2	0.031	0.001	0.030	0.032			
		α	4.152	0.401	3.367	4.937			
	$\mathcal{M}_{\alpha,\nu}$	β_1	−2.531	0.123	−2.772	−2.290	12,821.050	12,826.540	12,823.110
		β_2	0.157	0.006	0.145	0.168			
		α	4.111	0.418	3.292	4.931			
		$\nu_0 = 0.40$							
Rural	$\mathcal{M}_0$	β_1	−1.134	0.060	−1.251	−1.017	3595.020	3598.677	3596.390
		β_2	0.036	0.002	0.033	0.040			
	$\mathcal{M}_\alpha$	β_1	−1.134	0.180	−1.487	−0.780	3597.020	3602.506	3599.075
		β_2	0.036	0.002	0.033	0.040			
		α	0.000	0.213	−0.417	0.417			
	$\mathcal{M}_{\alpha,\nu}$	β_1	−1.699	0.222	−2.134	−1.265	3546.702	3552.188	3548.757
		β_2	0.110	0.010	0.092	0.129			
		α	1.003	0.261	0.493	1.514			
		$\nu_0 = 0.40$							
Total	$\mathcal{M}_0$	β_1	−1.528	0.030	−1.587	−1.469	17,201.110	17,204.760	17,202.480
		β_2	0.045	0.001	0.043	0.047			
	$\mathcal{M}_\alpha$	β_1	−0.270	0.018	−0.306	−0.234	17,106.840	17,112.330	17,108.900
		β_2	0.029	0.001	0.028	0.030			
		α	3.784	0.339	3.118	4.449			
	$\mathcal{M}_{\alpha,\nu}$	β_1	−2.341	0.117	−2.571	−2.111	16,545.460	16,550.950	16,547.520
		β_2	0.144	0.005	0.134	0.154			
		α	2.338	0.196	1.953	2.722			
		$\nu_0 = 0.40$							

Table 6 presents the results of the Kolmogorov–Smirnov (K-S) test for assessing the normality of the residuals. Following the fitting of the three models, $\mathcal{M}_0$, $\mathcal{M}_\alpha$ and $\mathcal{M}_{\alpha,\nu}$, we calculated the estimated probabilities and Pearson residuals. The K-S test was then applied to compare the distribution of the residuals with a theoretical normal distribution. In this table, the D value represents the K-S statistic, which measures the maximum difference between the empirical and theoretical distributions. At a significance level of τ, the null hypothesis is rejected if the p-value falls below this threshold, indicating a departure from normality. Conversely, if the p-value exceeds this level, it suggests that the residuals can be considered normally distributed, thereby supporting the model's adequacy. Specifically, with $\tau = 0.05$, the p-values for both the urban area and the total area indicate that the proposed model is adequate. Furthermore, at $\tau = 0.1$, all p-values suggest that the proposed model is appropriate.

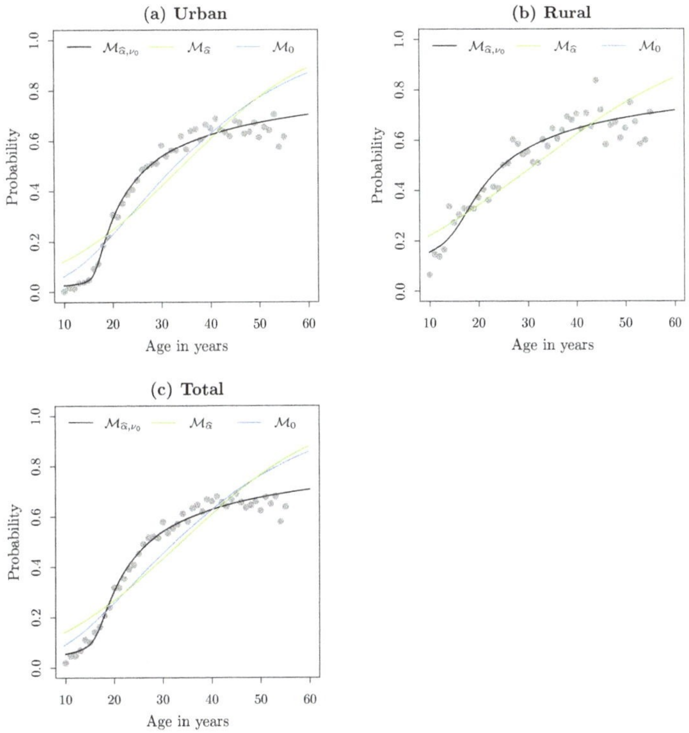

Figure 7. Proportion of women who participated in work activities for at least one hour during the previous week, according to the area of residence in Bolivia. The lines represent the fitted model.

Table 6. Kolmogorov–Smirnov test results for assessing the normality of residuals by area and model on data related to women's labor.

Area	Model	D	p-Value
Urban	$\mathcal{M}_0$	0.394	0.000
	$\mathcal{M}_\alpha$	0.370	0.000
	$\mathcal{M}_{\alpha,\nu}$	0.103	0.672
Rural	$\mathcal{M}_0$	0.180	0.089
	$\mathcal{M}_\alpha$	0.180	0.089
	$\mathcal{M}_{\alpha,\nu}$	0.134	0.351
Total	$\mathcal{M}_0$	0.431	0.000
	$\mathcal{M}_\alpha$	0.364	0.000
	$\mathcal{M}_{\alpha,\nu}$	0.099	0.724

5.2. *Cardiovascular Disease*

One of the leading causes of death in the world is cardiovascular disease (CVD). Ref. [24] proposes a methodology to predict cardiovascular diseases. The study [24] is from the Sleep Heart Health Study (SHHS), a multicenter cohort study implemented by the National Heart, Lung, and Blood Institute to determine the cardiovascular and other consequences of sleep-disordered breathing (the full dataset can be downloaded from https://sleepdata.org, accessed on 1 January 2024). In the original study, the SHHS was designed to determine whether sleep-disordered breathing and obstructive sleep apnea were a risk factor for cardiovascular and cerebrovascular disease [25]. The SHHS dataset is a prospective cohort study that recruited participant data from nine cohort studies. It contains the data of 5804 adults (40+ years), divided into 2 datasets: SHHS1 as a baseline for measuring the health status of the subjects, based on the polysomnography test and medical indices, collected between 1995 and 1998; and SHHS2, which contains the results of the selected cohort follow-up from January 2001 to June 2003, classifying the subjects who did or did not present cardiovascular disease (CVD) or related health problems during that period of time. Given that the dataset includes more than 1200 variables, the main challenge in CVD prediction is to select a subset of variables that might be most useful in explaining CVD. Although many alternatives have been proposed, we use the variables selected by [24] as its use in a machine learning model seems to outperform other options in terms of prediction ability.

The variables considered are the following: y, indicating cardiovascular disease (CVD) events (TRUE = a CVD event occurred, FALSE, otherwise) since Sleep Heart Health Study Visit One (Sleep Heart Health Study Visit One: SHHS1); x_2, indicating age at time of study in years, based on start date of Sleep Heart Health Study Visit One (SHHS1) Polysomnography (PSG) recording; x_3, indicating history of diabetes (Sleep Heart Health Study Visit One (SHHS1)); x_4, indicating Doctor of Medicine (MD)-reported coronary artery bypass graft (CABG) since Sleep Heart Health Study Visit One (SHHS1); x_5, indicating cigarette pack-years since Sleep Heart Health Study Visit One (SHHS1).

The minimum age in years at the time of the study is 39, the maximum age is 90, and the mean age is approximately 65 years. The proportion of patients with a history of diabetes is 0.067. The proportion of patients with coronary artery graft report is 0.035. The mean number of packs of cigarettes consumed per year by patients is approximately 13. The variable y is labeled with one and zero, which represent the presence or not, respectively, of CVD events from SHHS2. Out of a total of 2939 patients (patients belonging to the first and second studies), 749 had almost 1 of the CVD events, which shows an imbalance in the dataset.

The skew–t link model for binary response data is specified by

$$\begin{aligned} y_i &\overset{ind.}{\sim} \text{Bernoulli}(p_i) \\ p_i &= \Psi_\alpha(\mathbf{x}_i^\top \boldsymbol{\beta}; \nu), \end{aligned} \tag{17}$$

where $i = 1, 2, \ldots, 2939$.

Table 7 provides a summary of the parameter estimates and model comparison criteria applied to the dataset. The information criteria values indicate that the most suitable model for the analysis is $\mathcal{M}_{\alpha,\nu}$, which underscores once again the need for a model with a flexible link function, a need that $\mathcal{M}_{\alpha,\nu}$ effectively meets. It is worth noting that the estimated skewness parameter is 2.943. As shown in Figure 2, when $\alpha > 0$, the probability p_i tends to approach zero more rapidly than one, which explains the imbalance observed in the binary response data.

The assessment of residual normality using the K-S test showed that the K-S statistics for models $\mathcal{M}_0$, $\mathcal{M}_\alpha$ and $\mathcal{M}_{\alpha,\nu}$ were $D_{\mathcal{M}_0} = 0.306$, $D_{\mathcal{M}_\alpha} = 0.285$ and $D_{\mathcal{M}_{\alpha,\nu}} = 0.312$, respectively, with p-values less than 2.2×10^{-16}. These results suggest a significant deviation from normality in the residuals of all three models. However, the K-S test is known for its sensitivity to large sample sizes, which may result in detecting minor deviations from normality that do not necessarily affect the overall model fit.

Table 7. Summary of parameter estimation for $\mathcal{M}_0$, $\mathcal{M}_\alpha$ and $\mathcal{M}_{\alpha,\nu}$, along with model selection performance evaluation using AIC, BIC, and HQIC on data related to cardiovascular disease.

Model	Parameter	Estimation	SD	2.5%	97.5%	AIC	BIC	HQIC
$\mathcal{M}_0$	β_1	−3.826	0.203	−4.228	−3.429	2944.676	2974.605	2955.453
	β_2	0.045	0.003	0.039	0.051			
	β_3	0.532	0.097	0.344	0.720			
	β_4	0.831	0.134	0.573	1.092			
	β_5	0.007	0.001	0.004	0.009			
$\mathcal{M}_\alpha$	β_1	−1.156	0.187	−1.522	−0.790	2935.866	2971.781	2948.798
	β_2	0.021	0.002	0.016	0.026			
	β_3	0.303	0.063	0.179	0.426			
	β_4	0.504	0.096	0.315	0.692			
	β_5	0.003	0.001	0.002	0.005			
	α	4.129	1.218	1.742	6.515			
$\mathcal{M}_{\alpha,\nu}$	β_1	−2.095	0.312	−2.706	−1.484	2930.889	2966.803	2943.821
	β_2	0.035	0.004	0.027	0.043			
	β_3	0.590	0.133	0.329	0.851			
	β_4	1.177	0.315	0.560	1.794			
	β_5	0.007	0.001	0.004	0.009			
	α	2.943	0.723	1.527	4.360			
	$\nu_0 = 0.80$							

6. Discussion

The skew–t link model proposed in this paper provides a significant contribution to the field of binomial and binary response data analysis by addressing the limitations of traditional symmetric link functions like probit and logit, as well as the less flexible skew–probit link. This model introduces an additional level of flexibility through the incorporation of both an asymmetry parameter and degrees of freedom, enabling it to handle more complex data patterns. The effectiveness of the skew–t link model is demonstrated in both simulation studies and real-world applications, highlighting its potential as a valuable tool for researchers in various fields.

Another main contribution of the paper is the use of a penalized likelihood-based estimation method to stabilize the estimation process, particularly for the asymmetry parameter. Estimating this parameter can be challenging due to potential divergence, but the penalization strategy mitigates this issue, leading to more robust and reliable parameter estimates. This approach is essential in cases where traditional maximum likelihood estimation methods may fail, making the model more practical for real-world applications.

The comprehensive simulation studies conducted in this paper demonstrate the accuracy and reliability of the skew–t link model. In both scenarios tested, the model consistently exhibited low absolute bias and decreasing Monte Carlo standard deviations and root mean squared errors as the sample size increased. These findings underscore the model's ability to provide consistent and reliable parameter estimates across different data configurations. The second study, which highlights the model's adaptability to asymmetric link functions such as cloglog and loglog, further emphasizes its flexibility in handling a variety of data structures.

Additionally, an alternative approach that could complement the findings of this study is the implementation of a Bayesian perspective. Specifically, one could consider a hierarchical representation where the response y_i follows a binomial distribution given by $y_i|\boldsymbol{\beta}, \alpha, \nu \overset{ind.}{\sim} \text{Binomial}(n_i, p_i)$ with $p_i = \Psi_\alpha(\mathbf{x}_i^\top \boldsymbol{\beta}; \nu)$, where $\boldsymbol{\beta} \sim \pi_1(\boldsymbol{\beta})$, $\alpha \sim \pi_2(\alpha)$ and $\nu \sim \pi_3(\nu)$. Here, $\pi_1(\cdot)$, $\pi_2(\cdot)$ and $\pi_3(\cdot)$ represent suitable prior distributions. Notably, the estimation of the degrees of freedom parameter can be complex; the authors of [26] suggest employing the Jeffreys prior distribution proposed by [27] for the skew–t distribution, which can be expressed as

$$\pi_3(\nu) \propto \sqrt{\frac{\nu}{\nu+3}\left\{\psi_3\left(\frac{\nu}{2}\right) - \psi_3\left(\frac{\nu+1}{2}\right) - \frac{2(\nu+3)}{\nu(\nu+1)^2}\right\}},$$

where $\psi_3(\cdot)$ is the trigamma function. Alternatively, one might consider fixing the degrees of freedom in the estimation scenario presented in this article.

The application of the skew–t link model to two real-world datasets, women's labor and cardiovascular disease data, further validates its practical utility. In both cases, the model outperformed traditional symmetric link functions and the skew–probit link in terms of model fit, as indicated by lower AIC, BIC, and HQIC values. These results indicate that the skew–t link model is particularly well suited for datasets with inherent asymmetry, which is commonly found in socioeconomic and medical research as well as in other fields like environmental science and finance. For instance, in environmental and atmospheric sciences, the skew–t link model can be applied to analyze data related to events such as pollution levels or extreme weather occurrences, where outcome distributions often exhibit non-symmetry due to natural variability. Additionally, in finance and economics, this model can enhance the analysis of binary outcomes such as credit defaults, investment decisions, or market participation, where irregularities in data distributions frequently challenge traditional models. We believe the skew–t model provides a flexible alternative that can more effectively capture the complexities of asymmetric and heavy-tailed data across these diverse domains.

Despite the clear advantages of the skew–t link model, there are several limitations that warrant further exploration. First, while the penalized likelihood estimation method effectively addresses the challenges in estimating the asymmetry parameter, the choice of penalty function could potentially influence the results. Future research could explore alternative penalty functions and assess their impact on model performance. Second, the skew–t link model, as presented in this paper, is limited to binomial and binary response data. Extending this model to more complex data structures, such as multinomial or mixed response models, could significantly broaden its applicability. Additionally, exploring the use of the skew–t link in hierarchical or multilevel models could provide further insights into its potential for analyzing nested data structures, which are common in fields like education and healthcare. Another promising direction for future research lies in the development of computational tools and algorithms that can efficiently estimate the skew–t link model's parameters for larger datasets. Although the penalized likelihood estimation method is effective, its computational cost may increase with larger sample sizes or more complex data configurations. Developing optimized algorithms for parameter estimation could make the skew–t link model more accessible for big data applications.

7. Conclusions

The skew–t link model introduced in this work represents a significant advance in the analysis of binomial and binary response data. Its flexibility, particularly in handling asymmetric distributions and heavy tails, makes it a valuable tool for researchers in a range of fields. The model's ability to outperform traditional symmetric links and the skew–probit link in both simulated and real-world data underscores its potential to address longstanding challenges in statistical modeling. Future research should focus on extending the model to more complex data structures, exploring alternative estimation methods, and optimizing computational tools to improve its applicability in diverse research settings.

Author Contributions: Conceptualization, O.C.-P., G.I.-P. and O.N.; methodology, O.C.-P., O.N. and G.I.-P.; software, O.C.-P.; validation, O.C.-P., O.N. and G.I.-P.; formal analysis, O.C.-P.; investigation, O.C.-P.; data curation, O.N. and O.C.-P.; writing—original draft preparation, O.C.-P.; writing—review and editing, O.N., G.I.-P. and O.C.-P.; visualization, O.C.-P.; supervision, O.N. and G.I.-P.; project administration, O.N.; funding acquisition, O.N. All authors have read and agreed to the published version of the manuscript.

Funding: O.C.-P.'s research was partially supported by the PhD scholarship of the Universidad de Valparaíso (Chile), and O.N. was partially funded by the Chilean national ANID-Fondecyt grant 1241881-E2024.

Data Availability Statement: The original contributions presented in the study are included in the article, further inquiries can be directed to the corresponding authors.

Acknowledgments: The authors thank the editor and the three anonymous reviewers for their valuable comments and suggestions.

Conflicts of Interest: The authors declare no conflicts of interest.

References

1. Chen, M.-H.; Dey, D.K.; Shao, Q.-M. On robustness of choice of links in binomial regression. *Calcutta Stat. Assoc. Bull.* **2022**, *53*, 145–164. [CrossRef]
2. Bazán, J.L.; Bolfarine, H.; Branco, M.D. A skew item response model. *Bayesian Anal.* **2006**, *1*, 861–892. [CrossRef]
3. Bazán, J.L.; Bolfarine, H.; Branco, M.D. A framework for skew-probit links in binary regression. *Commun. Stat.-Theory Methods* **2010**, *4*, 678–697. [CrossRef]
4. Lee, D.; Sinha, S. Identifiability and bias reduction in the skew-probit model for a binary response. *J. Stat. Comput. Simul.* **2019**, *89*, 1621–1648. [CrossRef]
5. Azzalini, A. A class of distributions which includes the normal ones. *Scand. J. Stat.* **1985**, *12*, 171–178.
6. Liseo, B.; Loperfido, N. A note on reference priors for the scalar skew-normal distribution. *J. Stat. Plan. Inference* **2006**, *136*, 373–389. [CrossRef]
7. Sartori, N. Bias prevention of maximum likelihood estimates for scalar skew normal and skew t distributions. *J. Stat. Plan. Inference* **2006**, *136*, 4259–4275. [CrossRef]
8. Azzalini, A.; Arellano-Valle, R.B. Maximum penalized likelihood estimation for skew-normal and skew-t distributions. *J. Stat. Plan. Inference* **2013**, *143*, 419–433. [CrossRef]
9. Branco, M.D.; Dey, D.K. A general class of multivariate skew-elliptical distributions. *J. Multivar. Anal.* **2001**, *79*, 99–113. [CrossRef]
10. Azzalini, A.; Capitanio, A. Distributions generated by perturbation of symmetry with emphasis on a multivariate skew t-distribution. *J. R. Stat. Soc. B Stat. Methodol.* **2003**, *65*, 367–389. [CrossRef]
11. Nelder, J.A.; Wedderburn, R.W.M. Generalized linear models. *J. R. Stat. Soc. Ser. A* **1972**, *135*, 370–384. [CrossRef]
12. Behboodian, J.; Jamalizadeh, A.; Balakrishnan, N. A new class of skew-cauchy distributions. *Stat. Probab. Lett.* **2006**, *76*, 1488–1493. [CrossRef]
13. Jamalizadeh, A.; Khosravi, M.; Balakrishnan, N. Recurrence relations for distributions of a skew-t and a linear combination of order statistics from a bivariate-t. *Comput. Stat. Data Anal.* **2009**, *53*, 847–852. [CrossRef]
14. Taylor, J.M.G.; Siqueira, T.A.; Weiss, R.E. The cost of adding parameters to a model. *J. R. Stat. Soc. B Stat. Methodol.* **1996**, *58*, 593–607. [CrossRef]
15. Cole, S.R.; Chu, H.; Greenland, S. Maximum likelihood, profile likelihood, and penalized likelihood: A primer. *Am. J. Epidemiol.* **2013**, *179*, 252–260. [CrossRef]
16. Ciuperca, G.; Ridolfi, A.; Idier, J. Penalized maximum likelihood estimator for normal mixtures. *Scand. J. Stat.* **2003**, *30*, 45–59. [CrossRef]
17. Otsu, T. Penalized empirical likelihood estimation of semiparametric models. *J. Multivar. Anal.* **2007**, *98*, 1923–1954. [CrossRef]
18. Pötscher, B.M.; Leeb, H. On the distribution of penalized maximum likelihood estimators: The LASSO, SCAD, and thresholding. *J. Multivar. Anal.* **2009**, *100*, 2065–2082. [CrossRef]
19. Eggermont, P.P.; LaRiccia, V.N. *Maximum Penalized Likelihood Estimation: Volume II: Regression*, 1st ed.; Springer: New York, NY, USA, 2009; p. 7.
20. Abadir, K.M.; Magnus, J.R. *Matrix Algebra*, 1st ed.; Cambridge University Press: New York, NY, USA, 2005; p. 106.
21. R Core Team. *R: A Language and Environment for Statistical Computing;* R Foundation for Statistical Computing: Vienna, Austria, 2024.
22. Henningsen, A.; Toomet, O. maxLik: A package for maximum likelihood estimation in R. *Comput. Stat.* **2010**, *26*, 443–458. [CrossRef]
23. Murphy, S.A.; Van Der Vaart, A.W. On profile likelihood. *J. Am. Stat. Assoc.* **2000**, *95*, 449–465. [CrossRef]
24. Rodriguez-Segura, M.; Nicolis, O.; Peralta-Marquez, B.; Carrillo-Azocar, J. Predicting cardiovascular disease by combining optimal feature selection methods with machine learning. In Proceedings of the 2020 39th International Conference of the Chilean Computer Science Society (SCCC), Coquimbo, Chile, 16–20 November 2020; pp. 1–8.
25. Quan, S.F.; Howard, B.V.; Iber, C.; Kiley, J.P.; Nieto, F.J.; O'Connor G.T.; Rapoport, D.M.; Redline, S.; Robbins, J.; Samet, J.M.; et al. The sleep heart health study: Design, rationale, and methods. *Sleep* **1997**, *20*, 1077–1085. [PubMed]
26. Branco, M.D.; Genton, M.G.; Liseo, B. Objective bayesian analysis of skew-t distributions. *Scand. J. Stat.* **2012**, *40*, 63–85. [CrossRef]
27. Fonseca, T.C.O.; Ferreira, M.A.R.; Migon, H.S. Objective bayesian analysis for the Student-t regression model. *Biometrika* **2008**, *95*, 325–333. [CrossRef]

axioms

MDPI

Article

Goodness-of-Fit Test for the Bivariate Negative Binomial Distribution

Francisco Novoa-Muñoz [1,*] and Juan Pablo Aguirre-González [2]

[1] Departamento de Enfermería, Facultad de Ciencias de la Salud y de los Alimentos, Universidad del Bío-Bío, Chillán 3800708, Chile

[2] Departamento de Estadística, Universidad del Bío-Bío, Concepción 4051381, Chile; jpaguirregonzalez@gmail.com

* Correspondence: fnovoa@ubiobio.cl; Tel.: +56-422463088

Abstract: When modeling real-world data, we face the challenge of determining which probability distribution best represents the data. To address this intricate problem, we rely on goodness-of-fit tests. However, when the data come from a bivariate negative binomial distribution, the literature reveals no existing goodness-of-fit test for this distribution. For this reason, in this article, we propose and study a computationally convenient goodness-of-fit test for the bivariate negative binomial distribution. This test is based on a bootstrap approximation and a parallelization strategy. To this end, we use a reparameterization technique based on the probability generating function and a Cramér-von Mises-type statistic. From the simulation studies, we conclude that the results converge to the established nominal levels as the sample size increases, and in all cases considered, the parametric bootstrap method provides an accurate approximation of the null distribution of the statistic we propose. Additionally, we verify the power of the proposed test, as well as its application to five real datasets. To accelerate the massive computational work, we employ the parallelization strategy that, according to Novoa-Muñoz (2024), was the most efficient among the techniques he analyzed.

Keywords: bivariate negative binomial distribution; goodness-of-fit; statistical simulation; simulation techniques; bootstrap distribution estimator; parallel programming

MSC: 62F03; 62F05; 62F12; 62F40

1. Introduction

In today's world, where large volumes of data proliferate, it is common to encounter count data, with the Univariate Negative Binomial Distribution (UNBD) being a useful discrete method for representing such data. This distribution has been used to model insurance policy allocation in actuarial practice (see Shi and Valdez [1]), football betting (see Van Gemert and Van Ophem [2]), and, interestingly, the population dynamics of invasive species (see Krkošek et al. [3]).

By extending the idea of modeling, the Bivariate Negative Binomial Distribution (BNBD) was developed, which is used to describe phenomena involving workplace accidents (see Arbus and Kerrich [4]; Edwards and Gurland [5]), ecological data (see Holgate [6]), migration data related to traffic accidents (see Maher [7]), and bus accident data within London's vehicle fleet (see Kopocińska [8]).

But in a real-life situation, when bivariate count data are available, how can one determine if the BNBD is appropriate for modeling such data? According to González-

Albornoz and Novoa-Muñoz [9], a crucial aspect of data analysis is testing the goodness of fit (gof) of given observations with a probabilistic model. In this regard, and to the best of our knowledge, the only goodness-of-fit tests related to the Negative Binomial distribution that we have found in the literature are those developed by (a) Heller [10], which was applied to a set of microbiological data; (b) Beltrán-Beltrán and O'Reilly [11], who applied it to two datasets (deaths caused by horse kicks and laboratory mice); and (c) Meintanis [12], who applied it to accident data in the Netherlands over the period 1997–2004. However, cases (a) and (b) are tests for univariate data, while case (c) is bivariate but corresponds to a Poisson–Negative Binomial distribution model. More recently, Hudecová et al. [13] and Wang et al. [14] published goodness-of-fit tests for bivariate count time series based on a bivariate Poisson model. Moreover, as far as we know, there is no literature on gof tests for the BNBD. For this reason, the objective of this article is to propose and study a gof test for the BNBD that is consistent against any fixed alternative.

The test we propose employs the probability-generating function (pgf) of the BNBD and its counterpart, the empirical probability-generating function (epgf). The foundation of this proposal lies in the fact that the pgf characterizes the distribution of a random vector and can be consistently estimated by the epgf (see for example Novoa-Muñoz [15]; Novoa-Muñoz and Jiménez-Gamero [16]). This statistical test compares the epgf of the data with an estimator of the pgf of the BNBD.

To decide when to reject the null hypothesis, we need to know the null distribution of the statistic or at least an approximation of it. Since the proposed statistic is of the Cramér-von Mises type, obtaining the null distribution for finite sample sizes is not feasible. The asymptotic alternative we used was to approximate the null distribution using a parametric bootstrap estimator, whose properties can be found in Novoa-Muñoz and Jiménez-Gamero [17].

Since infinite sample sizes do not exist in the real world, we conducted a simulation study to evaluate the performance of the proposed test for finite sample sizes. Due to the computational intensity of the parametric bootstrap method, we used the parallel algorithm parRapply to reduce the simulation runtime. This algorithm proved to be the most efficient among the parallel versions analyzed in Novoa-Muñoz [18].

The present study follows the following sequence: In Section 2, we present the pgf of the DBNB and a reparameterization that makes it computationally more efficient. In Section 3, we develop the test statistic we propose, which, since it does not have a known distribution, we show can be approximated by its null asymptotic distribution. However, as this approximation still depends on the true parameter, in Section 4, we propose a parametric bootstrap estimator. Section 5 is dedicated to presenting the three techniques we used to estimate the parameters of the BNBD. In Section 6, we present and discuss the results of a simulation study and the application of the proposed test to two real datasets. The simulation study was conducted to evaluate the performance of the proposed test and analyze its power.

The notation we use below is detailed in the abbreviations listed at the end of the manuscript.

2. Reparametrization of the Probability Generating Function of the BNBD

From now on, we will consider that $\gamma = (\gamma_0, \gamma_1, \gamma_2) \in \Theta$, where

$$\Theta = \left\{(\gamma_0, \gamma_1, \gamma_2) \in \mathbb{R}^3 : \gamma_0 > \gamma_2,\ \gamma_1 > \gamma_2, \gamma_2 > 0\right\},$$

is the respective parameter space.

On the other hand, according to Kocherlakota and Kocherlakota [19], the genesis of the BNBD depends on the underlying random mechanism. One such mechanism, composition, gives rise to the following probability generating function (pgf):

$$g(t_1, t_2) = (1 - p_1 - p_2 - p_3)^v (1 - p_1 t_1 - p_2 t_2 - p_3 t_1 t_2)^{-v}, \tag{1}$$

where $p_1, p_2, p_3 \in [0,1]$, $v \in \mathbb{N}$ represents the number of trials before the first success or failure.

From (1), Edwards and Gurland [5] and Subrahmaniam [20] derived the probability mass function of the BNBD given below (see Min et al. [21]):

$$P(X_1 = r, X_2 = s) = (1 - p_1 - p_2 - p_3)^v \sum_{i=0}^{min(r,s)} \frac{\Gamma(v + r + s - i)}{\Gamma(v)\ i!\ (r-i)!\ (s-i)!}\, p_1^{r-i}\, p_2^{s-i}\, p_3^i,$$

where Γ is the Gamma function.

For computational purposes and to facilitate the estimation of the distribution parameters, it is highly convenient to incorporate the following reparameterization:

$$p_1 = \frac{\gamma_0 - \gamma_2}{1 + \gamma_0 + \gamma_1 - \gamma_2},\quad p_2 = \frac{\gamma_1 - \gamma_2}{1 + \gamma_0 + \gamma_1 - \gamma_2},\quad p_3 = \frac{\gamma_2}{1 + \gamma_0 + \gamma_1 - \gamma_2}.$$

Thus, the random vector (X_1, X_2) follows a Bivariate Negative Binomial distribution with parameter $\gamma = (\gamma_0, \gamma_1, \gamma_2)$, which we will denote as $(X_1, X_2) \sim BNB(\gamma)$, and its probability mass function (pmf), with which we will work in this article, is given by

$$P_\gamma(X_1 = r, X_2 = s) = \frac{(\gamma_0 - \gamma_2)^r\ (\gamma_1 - \gamma_2)^s\ \Gamma(v + r + s)}{r!\ s!\ \Gamma(v)\ (1 + \gamma_0 + \gamma_1 - \gamma_2)^{v+r+s}}\, S(r,s), \tag{2}$$

where

$$S(r,s) = \sum_{i=0}^{min(r,s)} \frac{\binom{r}{i}\binom{s}{i}}{\binom{v+r+s-1}{i}}\, \tau^i \quad \text{with} \quad \tau = \frac{\gamma_2(1 + \gamma_0 + \gamma_1 - \gamma_2)}{(\gamma_0 - \gamma_2)\ (\gamma_1 - \gamma_2)}.$$

With this reparameterization and considering the parameter γ, the pgf (1) of the BNBD can be written as

$$g(t;\gamma) := E\left(t_1^{X_1} t_2^{X_2}\right) = (1 + (1 - t_1)\gamma_0 + (1 - t_2)\gamma_1 - (t_1 - 1)(t_2 - 1)\gamma_2)^{-v},$$

where $t = (t_1, t_2) \in \mathbb{R}^2$ and $\gamma \in \Theta$.

3. Cramér-Von Mises-Type Statistic and Its Asymptotic Null Distribution

In this section, we introduce the test statistic, which is of the Cramér-von Mises type. The essence of the Cramér-von Mises statistic lies in measuring the distance between two continuous distribution functions. In particular, we use it to measure the distance between the pgf, $g(t;\gamma)$, and its empirical counterpart, the epgf $g_n(t)$, which is defined below. For a detailed explanation of the Cramér-von Mises distance, see Baringhaus and Henze [22].

In order to test the hypothesis

$$H_0 : (X_1, X_2) \sim BNB(\gamma), \text{ for some } \gamma \in \Theta,$$

against the alternative

$$H_1 : (X_1, X_2) \nsim BNB(\gamma),\ \forall \gamma \in \Theta,$$

let $\boldsymbol{X}_1 = (X_{11}, X_{12}), \ldots, \boldsymbol{X}_n = (X_{n1}, X_{n2})$ be independent and identically distributed (iid) random vectors defined on a probability space $(\Omega, \mathcal{A}, P)$ and taking values in $\mathbb{N}_0^2$. Moreover, let

$$g_n(t) = \frac{1}{n}\sum_{i=1}^{n} t_1^{X_{i1}} t_2^{X_{i2}},$$

be the epgf of $\boldsymbol{X}_1, \ldots, \boldsymbol{X}_n$ for some appropriate $W \subseteq \mathbb{R}^2$.

To develop our statistical test, the following result is fundamental, and its proof, for the d-dimensional case, can be reviewed in Novoa-Muñoz and Jiménez-Gamero [17]:

Proposition 1. *Let $\boldsymbol{X}_1, \ldots, \boldsymbol{X}_n$ be iid from a random vector $\boldsymbol{X} = (X_1, X_2) \in \mathbb{N}_0^2$. Let $g(t) = E\left(t_1^{X_1} t_2^{X_2}\right)$ be the pgf of $\boldsymbol{X}$, which is defined on $W \subseteq \mathbb{R}^2$. Let $0 \le b_j \le c_j < \infty$, $j = 1, 2$ such that $R = [b_1, c_1] \times [b_2, c_2] \subseteq W$; then,*

$$\sup_{t \in R} |g_n(t) - g(t)| \xrightarrow{a.s.} 0.$$

According to Proposition 1, the empirical probability-generating function (epgf) consistently estimates the pgf. Moreover, if $\hat{\gamma}_n$ is a consistent estimator of γ and H_0 is true, then the pgf is consistently estimated by $g(t; \hat{\gamma}_n)$, since g is a continuous function. On the other hand, because the distribution of $\boldsymbol{X}$ is determined solely by its pgf, $g(t), t \in [0,1]^2$, it is reasonable to think that H_0 should reject the null hypothesis for large values of $B_{n,w}(\hat{\gamma}_n)$, which are defined by

$$B_{n,w}(\hat{\gamma}_n) = \int_{[0,1]^2} B_n^2(t; \hat{\gamma}_n) w(t) dt, \tag{3}$$

where

$$B_n(t; \gamma) = \sqrt{n}\{g_n(t) - g(t; \gamma)\},$$

$\hat{\gamma}_n = \hat{\gamma}_n(\boldsymbol{X}_1, \boldsymbol{X}_2, \ldots, \boldsymbol{X}_n)$ is a consistent estimator of γ. Additionally, $w(t)$ is a measurable and non-negative weight function to which we will impose the condition of being finite to ensure that the double integral in (3) is finite for each fixed n. That is,

$$0 \le \int_{[0,1]^2} w(t) dt < \infty. \tag{4}$$

The next step is to determine what constitutes large samples of $B_{n,w}(\hat{\gamma}_n)$. To do this, the first alternative is to understand its null distribution. However, since $B_{n,w}(\hat{\gamma}_n)$ is a Cramér-von Mises-type statistic, it does not have a known distribution. Therefore, we will estimate it through its asymptotic null distribution. To achieve this, we will assume that the estimator $\hat{\gamma}_n$ satisfies the following regularity condition:

Assumption 1. *Under H_0, if $\gamma = (\gamma_0, \gamma_1, \gamma_2) \in \Theta$ denotes the true parameter value, then*

$$\sqrt{n}(\hat{\gamma}_n - \gamma) = \frac{1}{\sqrt{n}}\sum_{i=1}^{n} \boldsymbol{\ell}(\boldsymbol{X}_i; \gamma) + \mathbf{o}_P(1),$$

where $\boldsymbol{\ell} : \mathbb{N}_0^2 \times \Theta \longrightarrow \mathbb{R}^3$ is such that $E_\gamma\{\boldsymbol{\ell}(\boldsymbol{X}_1; \gamma)\} = \mathbf{0}$ and $J(\gamma) = E_\gamma\left\{\boldsymbol{\ell}(\boldsymbol{X}_1; \gamma)^\top \boldsymbol{\ell}(\boldsymbol{X}_1; \gamma)\right\} < \infty$. Here, $\mathbf{o}_P(1)$ is a vector consisting of three $o_P(1)$ elements.

Assumption 1 is fulfilled by most commonly used estimators; see [19,23].

The regularity conditions for a parameter estimator have important practical implications, as they ensure the validity and good behavior of the estimators obtained. These conditions allow for the derivation of asymptotic properties such as consistency, asymptotic normality, and efficiency. Some key practical implications are the following:

- Ensuring the consistency of the estimator: This guarantees that the estimator converges to the true value of the parameter as the sample size increases. This is crucial for ensuring that the model's results are representative of the underlying phenomenon.
- Asymptotic normality: This allows the distribution of the estimator to approximate a normal distribution as the sample size grows. This facilitates inference, such as hypothesis testing and confidence interval construction.
- Efficiency of the estimator: This can enable the estimator to reach the Cramér–Rao bound, meaning it has the lowest possible variance among unbiased estimators.
- Mathematical interpretability and proper modeling: They ensure that the probability or likelihood functions have appropriate properties, such as being differentiable, non-degenerate, and well-defined. This enables reliable analytical derivations and numerical computations.
- Robustness to minor violations: Although some regularity conditions may be difficult to verify in practice, this provides a solid theoretical framework that allows models to adapt to small violations or approximations.

In summary, regularity conditions ensure that estimators are reliable, accurate, and suitable for making valid inferences, which is essential in practical statistical applications, such as scientific research, economics, biology, and other fields.

The next result gives the asymptotic null distribution of $B_{n,w}(\hat{\gamma}_n)$.

Theorem 1. *Let $\mathbf{X}_1, \ldots, \mathbf{X}_n$ be iid from $\mathbf{X} = (X_1, X_2) \sim BNB(\gamma)$. Suppose that Assumption 1 holds. Then,*

$$B_{n,w}(\hat{\gamma}_n) = ||V_n||^2_{\mathcal{H}} + o_p(1),$$

where $V_n(t) = \frac{1}{\sqrt{n}} \sum_{i=1}^n B^0(\mathbf{X}_i; t; \gamma)$, with

$$B^0(\mathbf{X}_i; t; \gamma) = t_1^{X_{i1}} t_2^{X_{i2}} - g(t;\gamma) - v\{g(t;\gamma)\}^{\frac{v+1}{v}} (t_1 - 1, t_2 - 1, (t_1 - 1)(t_2 - 1)) \boldsymbol{\ell}(\mathbf{X}_i; \gamma)^\top,$$

$i = 1, \ldots, n$. Moreover,

$$B_{n,w}(\hat{\gamma}_n) \xrightarrow{L} \sum_{j \geq 1} \lambda_j \chi^2_{1j}, \tag{5}$$

where $\chi^2_{11}, \chi^2_{12}, \ldots$ are independent χ^2 variates with one degree of freedom, and the set $\{\lambda_j\}$ is the non-null eigenvalues of the operator $C(\gamma)$ defined on the function space $\{\xi : \mathbb{N}_0^2 \to \mathbb{R}$, such that $E_\gamma\{\xi^2(\mathbf{X})\} < \infty, \forall \gamma \in \Theta\}$ as follows:

$$C(\gamma)\xi(\mathbf{x}) = E_\gamma\{h(\mathbf{x}, \mathbf{Y}; \gamma)\xi(\mathbf{Y})\},$$

where

$$h(\mathbf{x}, \mathbf{y}; \gamma) = \int_{[0,1]^2} B^0(\mathbf{x}; t; \gamma) B^0(\mathbf{y}; t; \gamma) w(t) dt. \tag{6}$$

Proof. By definition, $B_{n,w}(\hat{\gamma}_n) = \|B_n(t; \hat{\gamma}_n)\|^2_{\mathcal{H}}$. Note that

$$B_n(t; \hat{\gamma}_n) = \frac{1}{\sqrt{n}} \sum_{i=1}^n B(\mathbf{X}_i; t; \hat{\gamma}_n), \text{ with } B(\mathbf{X}_i; t; \gamma) = t_1^{X_{i1}} t_2^{X_{i2}} - g(t;\gamma). \tag{7}$$

By Taylor expansion of $B(\mathbf{X}_i; t; \hat{\gamma}_n)$ around γ,

$$B_n(t;\hat{\gamma}_n) = \frac{1}{\sqrt{n}}\sum_{i=1}^{n} B(\mathbf{X}_i;t;\gamma) + \frac{1}{n}\sum_{i=1}^{n} B^{(1)}(\mathbf{X}_i;t;\gamma)\,\sqrt{n}(\hat{\gamma}_n-\gamma)^\top + \frac{1}{2}\sqrt{n}(\hat{\gamma}_n-\gamma)\,\frac{1}{n}\sum_{i=1}^{n} B^{(2)}(\mathbf{X}_i;t;\gamma)\,\sqrt{n}(\hat{\gamma}_n-\gamma)^\top + r_n, \quad (8)$$

where

$$r_n = \frac{1}{3!}\frac{1}{\sqrt{n}}\sum_{i=1}^{n}\sum_{k_1+k_2+k_3=3} \left.\frac{\partial^3 B(\mathbf{X}_i;t;\gamma)}{\partial\gamma_0^{k_1}\,\partial\gamma_1^{k_2}\,\partial\gamma_2^{k_3}}\right|_{\gamma=\tilde{\gamma}} (\hat{\gamma}_{0n}-\gamma_0)(\hat{\gamma}_{1n}-\gamma_1)(\hat{\gamma}_{2n}-\gamma_2),$$

and $\tilde{\gamma} = \alpha\hat{\gamma}_n + (1-\alpha)\gamma$, for some $0 < \alpha < 1$, $B^{(1)}(x;t;\tau)$, is the vector of the first derivatives, and $B^{(2)}(x;t;\tau)$ is the matrix of the second derivatives of $B(x;t;\tau)$ with respect to $\tau = (\tau_0, \tau_1, \tau_2)$. That is,

$$B^{(1)}(x;t;\tau) = \left(B_1^{(1)}(x;t;\tau), B_2^{(1)}(x;t;\tau), B_3^{(1)}(x;t;\tau)\right),\; B_j^{(1)}(x;t;\tau) = \frac{\partial B(x;t;\tau)}{\partial\tau_{j-1}},\; j = 1,2,3.$$

As the first derivatives are

$$B_1^{(1)}(x;t;\tau) = v(1-t_1)q,\;\; B_2^{(1)}(x;t;\tau) = v(1-t_2)q,\;\; B_3^{(1)}(x;t;\tau) = -v(t_1-1)(t_2-1)q, \quad (9)$$

where $q = \{g(t;\tau)\}^{\frac{v+1}{v}}$, then $\left|B_j^{(1)}(\mathbf{X}_1;t;\tau)\right| \le v < \infty$ for $j = 1,2,3$ $\forall t \in [0,1]^2$.

Thus, considering (4), it results that

$$E_\gamma\left\{\left\|B_j^{(1)}(\mathbf{X}_1;t;\gamma)\right\|_{\mathcal{H}}^2\right\} < \infty,\;\; j = 1,2,3. \quad (10)$$

Since, for $j = 1,2,3$, we have that

$$E_\gamma\left[\left\{\frac{1}{n}\sum_{i=1}^{n} B_j^{(1)}(\mathbf{X}_i;t;\gamma)\right\}^2\right] = \frac{1}{n}E_\gamma\left[\left\{B_j^{(1)}(\mathbf{X}_1;t;\gamma)\right\}^2\right] + \frac{n-1}{n}\left[E_\gamma\left\{B_j^{(1)}(\mathbf{X}_1;t;\gamma)\right\}\right]^2,$$

then

$$\begin{aligned} E_\gamma&\left[\left\{\frac{1}{n}\sum_{i=1}^{n} B_j^{(1)}(\mathbf{X}_i;t;\gamma) - E_\gamma\left\{B_j^{(1)}(\mathbf{X}_1;t;\gamma)\right\}\right\}^2\right] \\ &= \frac{1}{n}E_\gamma\left[\left\{B_j^{(1)}(\mathbf{X}_1;t;\gamma)\right\}^2\right] - \frac{1}{n}\left[E_\gamma\left\{B_j^{(1)}(\mathbf{X}_1;t;\gamma)\right\}\right]^2 \\ &\le \frac{1}{n}E_\gamma\left[\left\{B_j^{(1)}(\mathbf{X}_1;t;\gamma)\right\}^2\right]. \end{aligned}$$

Using the Markov inequality and (10) for $j = 1,2,3$, we obtain

$$P_\gamma\left[\left\|\frac{1}{n}\sum_{i=1}^{n} B_j^{(1)}(\mathbf{X}_i;t;\gamma) - E_\gamma\left\{B_j^{(1)}(\mathbf{X}_1;t;\gamma)\right\}\right\|_{\mathcal{H}} > \varepsilon\right] \le \frac{1}{n\,\varepsilon^2}E_\gamma\left[\left\|B_j^{(1)}(\mathbf{X}_1;t;\gamma)\right\|_{\mathcal{H}}^2\right] \to 0.$$

Thus, in the space $\mathcal{H}$, we obtain that

$$\frac{1}{n}\sum_{i=1}^{n} B^{(1)}(\mathbf{X}_i;t;\gamma) \xrightarrow{P} E_\gamma\left\{B^{(1)}(\mathbf{X}_1;t;\gamma)\right\} = -v\{g(t;\gamma)\}^{\frac{v+1}{v}}(t_1-1, t_2-1, (t_1-1)(t_2-1)).$$

For the second derivatives, it follows from (9) that

$$B^{(2)}(x;t;\tau) = -v(v+1)\{g(t;\tau)\}^{\frac{v+2}{v}} A_t,$$

where $A_t = \begin{pmatrix} (t_1-1)^2 & (t_1-1)(t_2-1) & (t_1-1)^2(t_2-1) \\ (t_1-1)(t_2-1) & (t_2-1)^2 & (t_1-1)(t_2-1)^2 \\ (t_1-1)^2(t_2-1) & (t_1-1)(t_2-1)^2 & \{(t_1-1)(t_2-1)\}^2 \end{pmatrix}$.

Therefore, $\left|B^{(2)}_{jk}(\mathbf{X}_1;t;\tau)\right| \le v(v+1) < \infty$ for $j,k \in \{1,2,3\}$ $\forall t \in [0,1]^2$.
Thus, considering (4), it results that

$$E_\gamma\left\{\left\|B^{(2)}_{jk}(\mathbf{X}_1;t;\gamma)\right\|^2_{\mathcal{H}}\right\} < \infty, \ \ j,k \in \{1,2,3\}.$$

Following similar steps as those for the vector $B^{(1)}(\mathbf{X}_i;t;\gamma)$ for the matrix of second derivatives, we obtain that in the space $\mathcal{H}$ it results in

$$\frac{1}{n}\sum_{i=1}^{n} B^{(2)}(\mathbf{X}_i;t;\gamma) \xrightarrow{P} E_\gamma\left\{B^{(2)}(\mathbf{X}_1;t;\gamma)\right\} = -v(v+1)\{g(t;\gamma)\}^{\frac{v+2}{v}} A_t.$$

Additionally, using Assumption 1, we obtain

$$\frac{1}{2}\sqrt{n}(\hat{\gamma}_n-\gamma)\,\frac{1}{n}\sum_{i=1}^{n} B^{(2)}(\mathbf{X}_i;t;\gamma)\,\sqrt{n}(\hat{\gamma}_n-\gamma)^\top =$$

$$\frac{1}{2}E_\gamma\{\boldsymbol{\ell}(\mathbf{X}_1;\gamma)\}\,E_\gamma\left\{B^{(2)}(\mathbf{X}_1;t;\gamma)\right\}\frac{1}{\sqrt{n}}\sum_{k=1}^{n}\boldsymbol{\ell}(\mathbf{X}_k;\gamma)^\top$$
$$+\,E_\gamma\{\boldsymbol{\ell}(\mathbf{X}_1;\gamma)\}\,E_\gamma\left\{B^{(2)}(\mathbf{X}_1;t;\gamma)\right\}\mathbf{o}_p(1)^\top + o_p(1)$$

On the other hand, using similar arguments to the previous ones, we obtain $\|r_n\|_{\mathcal{H}} = o_p(1)$; then, using Assumption 1, (8) can be written as

$$B_n(t;\hat{\gamma}_n) = B_n(t;\gamma) + b_n,$$

where $\|b_n\|_{\mathcal{H}} = o_p(1)$, and

$$B_n(t;\gamma) = \frac{1}{\sqrt{n}}\sum_{i=1}^{n}\left[B(\mathbf{X}_i;t;\gamma) + E_\gamma\left\{B^{(1)}(\mathbf{X}_1;t;\gamma)\right\}\boldsymbol{\ell}(\mathbf{X}_i;\gamma)^\top\right].$$

On the other hand, observe that

$$\|B_n(\gamma)\|^2_{\mathcal{H}} = \frac{1}{n}\sum_{i=1}^{n}\sum_{j=1}^{n} h(\mathbf{X}_i,\mathbf{X}_j;\gamma),$$

where $h(\boldsymbol{x},\boldsymbol{y};\gamma)$ is defined in (6) and satisfies $h(\boldsymbol{x},\boldsymbol{y};\gamma) = h(\boldsymbol{y},\boldsymbol{x};\gamma)$, $E_\gamma\{h^2(\mathbf{X}_1,\mathbf{X}_2;\gamma)\} < \infty$, $E_\gamma\{|h(\mathbf{X}_1,\mathbf{X}_1;\gamma)|\} < \infty$ and $E_\gamma\{h(\mathbf{X}_1,\mathbf{X}_2;\gamma)\} = 0$. Thus, from Theorem 6.4.1.B in Serfling [24],

$$\|B_n(\gamma)\|^2_{\mathcal{H}} \xrightarrow{L} \sum_{j\ge 1}\lambda_j \chi^2_{1j}$$

where $\chi^2_{11}, \chi^2_{12}, \ldots$ and the set $\{\lambda_j\}$ is as defined in the statement of the Theorem. In particular, $\|B_n(\gamma)\|^2_{\mathcal{H}} = O_P(1)$, which implies (5). □

As seen in Theorem 1, the null asymptotic distribution of $B_{n,w}(\hat{\gamma}_n)$ still depends on the true value of the parameter γ, which, being unknown, does not provide a useful solution. This issue is resolved by replacing γ with $\hat{\gamma}$.

However, a greater challenge lies in determining the set $\{\lambda_j\}_{j\geq 1}$, since calculating the eigenvalues of an operator is not straightforward. Moreover, it is also necessary to obtain the expression for $h(x, y; \gamma)$, which is difficult to derive, because it depends on the function $\boldsymbol{\ell}$, which generally does not have a simple expression.

Thus, in the following section, we employ the parametric bootstrap method to approximate the null distribution of the test statistic.

4. Bootstrap Approximation of the Null Distribution

The parametric bootstrap method provides an alternative way to estimate the null distribution of the proposed statistic. For this, let $\boldsymbol{X}_1, \ldots, \boldsymbol{X}_n$ be iid random vectors taking values in $\mathbb{N}_0^2$, and suppose that $\hat{\gamma}_n = \hat{\gamma}_n(\boldsymbol{X}_1, \ldots, \boldsymbol{X}_n) \in \Theta$.

Furthermore, to use the bootstrap method, we must consider that $\boldsymbol{X}_1^*, \ldots, \boldsymbol{X}_n^*$ are iid random vectors from a population distributed according to the $BNB(\hat{\gamma}_n)$ law given that $\boldsymbol{X}_1, \ldots, \boldsymbol{X}_n$. Also, let $B_{n,w}^*(\hat{\gamma}_n^*)$ be the bootstrap version of $B_{n,w}(\hat{\gamma}_n)$, which is obtained by replacing $\boldsymbol{X}_1, \ldots, \boldsymbol{X}_n$ and $\hat{\gamma}_n = \hat{\gamma}_n(\boldsymbol{X}_1, \ldots, \boldsymbol{X}_n)$ with $\boldsymbol{X}_1^*, \ldots, \boldsymbol{X}_n^*$ and $\hat{\gamma}_n^* = \hat{\gamma}_n(\boldsymbol{X}_1^*, \ldots, \boldsymbol{X}_n^*)$, respectively, in the expression for $B_{n,w}(\hat{\gamma}_n)$.

Theorem 2, presented later, demonstrates that the parametric bootstrap method consistently approximates the null distribution of $B_{n,w}(\hat{\gamma}_n)$. To achieve this, we must assume the following hypotheses, which are satisfied by commonly used estimators, as mentioned after Assumption 1.

Assumption 2. *Assumption 1 holds and the functions $\boldsymbol{\ell}$ and J satisfy*

(1) $\sup_{\varrho\in\Theta_0} E_\varrho\left[\|\boldsymbol{\ell}(\boldsymbol{X};\varrho)\|^2 I\{\|\boldsymbol{\ell}(\boldsymbol{X};\varrho)\| > \tau\}\right] \longrightarrow 0$ *as* $\tau \to \infty$, *where* $\Theta_0 \subseteq \Theta$ *is an open neighborhood of* γ.

(2) $\boldsymbol{\ell}(\boldsymbol{X};\varrho)$ *and* $J(\varrho)$ *are continuous as functions of* ϱ *at* $\varrho = \gamma$, *and* $J(\varrho)$ *is finite* $\forall \varrho \in \Theta_0$.

Theorem 2. *Let* $\boldsymbol{X}_1, \ldots, \boldsymbol{X}_n$ *be iid from a random vector* $\boldsymbol{X} = (X_1, X_2) \in \mathbb{N}_0^2$. *Suppose that Assumption 2 holds and that* $\hat{\gamma}_n = \gamma + o(1)$ *for some* $\gamma \in \Theta$. *Then,*

$$\sup_{x\in\mathbb{R}}\left|P_*\{B_{n,w}^*(\hat{\gamma}_n^*) \leq x\} - P_\gamma\{B_{n,w}(\hat{\gamma}_n) \leq x\}\right| \xrightarrow{a.s.} 0.$$

Proof. By definition, $B_{n,w}^*(\hat{\gamma}_n^*) = \|B_n^*(t;\hat{\gamma}_n^*)\|_{\mathcal{H}}^2$, with

$$B_n^*(t;\hat{\gamma}_n^*) = \frac{1}{\sqrt{n}}\sum_{i=1}^n B(\boldsymbol{X}_i^*;t;\hat{\gamma}_n^*)$$

and $B(\boldsymbol{X};t;\gamma)$ defined in (7).

Following similar steps to those given in the proof of Theorem 1, it can be seen that $B_{n,w}^*(\hat{\gamma}_n^*) = \|V_n^*\|_{\mathcal{H}}^2 + o_{P_*}(1)$, where $V_n^*(t)$ is defined as $V_n(t)$, with $\boldsymbol{X}_i$ and γ replaced by $\boldsymbol{X}_i^*$ and $\hat{\gamma}_n$, respectively.

Now, the result follows by applying Theorem 1.1 in Kundu et al. [25] to V_n^* and the continuous mapping theorem. □

From Theorem 2, the test function

$$\Psi^* = \begin{cases} 1, & \text{if } B_{n,w}^*(\hat{\gamma}_n^*) \geq b_{n,w,\alpha}^*, \\ 0, & \text{otherwise,} \end{cases}$$

or, equivalently, the test that rejects H_0 when $p^* = P_*\{B_{n,w}^*(\hat{\gamma}_n^*) \geq B_{obs}\} \leq \alpha$, is asymptotically correct in the sense that, when H_0 is true, $\lim P_\gamma(\Psi^* = 1) = \alpha$, where $b_{n,w,\alpha}^* = \inf\{x : P_*(B_{n,w}^*(\hat{\gamma}_n^*) \geq x) \leq \alpha\}$ is the α upper percentile of the bootstrap distribution of $B_{n,w}(\hat{\gamma}_n)$, and B_{obs} is the observed value of the test statistic.

5. Parameter Estimation

In this research, three techniques were analyzed to estimate the parameters established in parameterization (2), namely, the (a) method of moments, (b) zero–zero cell frequency, and (c) maximum likelihood. In what follows, we will use different notation to denote the estimator of γ depending on the method employed: $\tilde{\gamma}$ for the method of moments, $\tilde{\tilde{\gamma}}$ for the zero–zero cell frequency method, and $\tilde{\tilde{\tilde{\gamma}}}$ for the maximum likelihood. For this, let us consider $(X_1, X_2) \sim BNB(\gamma)$.

5.1. Method of Moments

The usual procedure for obtaining the moment estimators is to equate the sample moments to the population moments and solve the resulting equations. According to [26], we shall use the two first marginal moments and the first mixed central moment $m_{1,1}$.

The moments of the distribution in (2) are

$$
\begin{aligned}
&\mu'_{1,0} = v\,\gamma_0, \quad \mu'_{0,1} = v\,\gamma_1, \quad \mu_{1,1} = v\,(\gamma_2 + \gamma_0\,\gamma_1), \quad \mu_{2,0} = v\,\gamma_0\,(1+\gamma_0),\\
&\mu_{0,2} = v\,\gamma_1\,(1+\gamma_1), \quad \mu_{2,1} = v(2\gamma_0+1)(\gamma_2+\gamma_0\gamma_1), \quad \mu_{1,2} = v(2\gamma_0+1)(\gamma_1+\gamma_0\gamma_1),\\
&\mu_{2,2} = v\left\{2(v+1)\gamma_2^2 + 2\,(v+2)\,\gamma_0\,\gamma_1\,\gamma_2 + 3\,(v+2)\,\gamma_0^2\,\gamma_1^2 + \gamma_2(2\gamma_0+2\gamma_1+1)\right.\\
&\qquad\qquad \left. +\ (v+1)\gamma_0\,\gamma_1\,(1+\gamma_0+\gamma_1) + \gamma_0\,\gamma_1\,(\gamma_0+\gamma_1)\right\}.
\end{aligned}
$$

5.1.1. Estimators of $\tilde{\gamma}$

Using the sample marginal first moments $\bar{X}_1$ and $\bar{X}_2$, as well as the mixed moment $m_{1,1}$, we have the moment estimators

$$
\tilde{\gamma}_0 = \frac{\bar{X}_1}{v}, \quad \tilde{\gamma}_1 = \frac{\bar{X}_2}{v}, \quad \tilde{\gamma}_2 = \frac{m_{1,1}}{v} - \frac{\bar{X}_1\,\bar{X}_2}{v^2}.
$$

5.1.2. Asymptotic Variance Matrix of $\tilde{\gamma}$

The asymptotic variance–covariance matrix of the estimators obtained through the method of moments, Σ_{MM}, is given by

$$
\Sigma_{MM} = \frac{1}{n\,v}\begin{pmatrix} \gamma_0(1+\gamma_0) & \gamma_2+\gamma_0\gamma_1 & (2\gamma_0+1)(\gamma_2+\gamma_0\gamma_1)\\ \gamma_2+\gamma_0\gamma_1 & \gamma_1(1+\gamma_1) & (2\gamma_0+1)(\gamma_1+\gamma_0\gamma_1)\\ (2\gamma_0+1)(\gamma_2+\gamma_0\gamma_1) & (2\gamma_0+1)(\gamma_1+\gamma_0\gamma_1) & \varsigma \end{pmatrix},
$$

where $\varsigma = (v+2)\gamma_2^2 + \gamma_0\gamma_1\{4\gamma_2 + 2(v+3)\gamma_0\gamma_1 + (v+2)(\gamma_0+\gamma_1) + v + 1\}$.

5.1.3. Asymptotic Distribution of $\tilde{\gamma}$

Since $\tilde{\gamma}$ is a function of sample moments, applying Theorem 11.2.14 (Delta Method) given in Lehmann and Romano [27], it follows that

$$
\sqrt{n}(\tilde{\gamma} - \gamma) \xrightarrow{L} N_3(\mathbf{0}, \Sigma_{MM}).
$$

5.1.4. Asymptotic Properties of $\tilde{\gamma}$

According to the results of Section 5.1.3, $\tilde{\gamma}$ is a consistent and asymptotically normal estimator.

5.2. Zero–Zero Cell Frequency

5.2.1. Estimators of $\tilde{\tilde{\gamma}}$

From (2),

$$
P_\gamma(0,0) = (1+\gamma_0+\gamma_1-\gamma_2)^{-v}.
$$

A combination of $\bar{X}_1$, $\bar{X}_2$ and the observed zero–zero cell relative frequency $\frac{n_{00}}{n}$ can be used to estimate the parameters γ_0, γ_1 and γ_2:

$$\tilde{\tilde{\gamma}}_0 = \frac{\bar{X}_1}{v}, \quad \tilde{\tilde{\gamma}}_1 = \frac{\bar{X}_2}{v}, \quad \tilde{\tilde{\gamma}}_2 = 1 + \frac{\bar{X}_1}{v} + \frac{\bar{X}_2}{v} - \left\{\frac{n_{00}}{n}\right\}^{-\frac{1}{v}}.$$

5.2.2. Asymptotic Variance Matrix of $\tilde{\tilde{\gamma}}$

The asymptotic variance–covariance matrix of the estimators obtained through the zero–zero cell frequency method, Σ_{ZZ}, is given by

$$\Sigma_{ZZ} = \frac{1}{v\,n}\begin{pmatrix} \gamma_0(1+\gamma_0) & \gamma_2+\gamma_0\gamma_1 & \gamma_2(1+\gamma_0) \\ \gamma_2+\gamma_0\gamma_1 & \gamma_1(1+\gamma_1) & \gamma_2(1+\gamma_1) \\ \gamma_2(1+\gamma_0) & \gamma_2(1+\gamma_1) & (1+\gamma_0+\gamma_1)(2\gamma_2-\gamma_0-\gamma_1)+\zeta \end{pmatrix},$$

where $\zeta = \frac{1}{v}\left(\frac{1}{P_\gamma(0,0)} - 1\right)(1+\gamma_0+\gamma_1-\gamma_2)^2$.

5.2.3. Asymptotic Distribution of $\tilde{\tilde{\gamma}}$

Since $\tilde{\tilde{\gamma}}$ is a function of sample moments, applying Theorem 11.2.14 (Delta Method) given in Lehmann and Romano [27], it follows that

$$\sqrt{n}(\tilde{\tilde{\gamma}} - \gamma) \xrightarrow{L} N_3(\mathbf{0}, \Sigma_{ZZ}).$$

5.2.4. Asymptotic Properties of $\tilde{\tilde{\gamma}}$

According to the results of Section 5.2.3 $\tilde{\tilde{\gamma}}$ is a consistent and asymptotically normal estimator.

5.3. Maximum Likelihood Estimators

5.3.1. Estimators of $\tilde{\tilde{\tilde{\gamma}}}$

Differentiating the pmf given in (2) with respect to γ_0, γ_1, and γ_2 successively, we have

$$\frac{1}{P_\gamma(r,s)}\frac{\partial P_\gamma(r,s)}{\partial \gamma_0} = \frac{r}{\gamma_0-\gamma_2} - \frac{v+r+s}{1+\gamma_0+\gamma_1-\gamma_2} - \frac{(1+\gamma_1)R(r,s)}{(\gamma_0-\gamma_2)(1+\gamma_0+\gamma_1-\gamma_2)}, \tag{11}$$

where $R(r,s) = \frac{S'(r,s)}{S(r,s)}$, and

$$S'(r,s) = \sum_{i=0}^{min(r,s)} \frac{\binom{r}{i}\binom{s}{i}}{\binom{v+r+s-1}{i}}\, i\,\tau^i.$$

A similar procedure yields

$$\frac{1}{P_\gamma(r,s)}\frac{\partial P_\gamma(r,s)}{\partial \gamma_1} = \frac{s}{\gamma_1-\gamma_2} - \frac{v+r+s}{1+\gamma_0+\gamma_1-\gamma_2} - \frac{(1+\gamma_0)R(r,s)}{(\gamma_1-\gamma_2)(1+\gamma_0+\gamma_1-\gamma_2)}, \tag{12}$$

and

$$\begin{aligned}\frac{1}{P_\gamma(r,s)}\frac{\partial P_\gamma(r,s)}{\partial \gamma_2} = &-\frac{r}{\gamma_0-\gamma_2} - \frac{s}{\gamma_1-\gamma_2} - \frac{v+r+s}{1+\gamma_0+\gamma_1-\gamma_2} \\ &+\left(\frac{1}{\gamma_2} + \frac{1}{\gamma_0-\gamma_2} + \frac{1}{\gamma_1-\gamma_2} - \frac{1}{1+\gamma_0+\gamma_1-\gamma_2}\right)R(r,s).\end{aligned} \tag{13}$$

The estimating equations are

$$\sum_{r,s} \frac{1}{P_\gamma(r,s)} \frac{\partial P_\gamma(r,s)}{\partial \gamma_0} = 0, \quad \sum_{r,s} \frac{1}{P_\gamma(r,s)} \frac{\partial P_\gamma(r,s)}{\partial \gamma_1} = 0, \quad \sum_{r,s} \frac{1}{P_\gamma(r,s)} \frac{\partial P_\gamma(r,s)}{\partial \gamma_1} = 0,$$

which yield the maximum likelihood estimators $\tilde{\tilde{\tilde{\gamma}}}$ as

$$\frac{\bar{X}_1}{\tilde{\tilde{\tilde{\gamma}}}_0 - \tilde{\tilde{\tilde{\gamma}}}_2} - \frac{v + \bar{X}_1 + \bar{X}_2}{\xi} - \frac{\left(1 + \tilde{\tilde{\tilde{\gamma}}}_1\right)\bar{R}}{\xi\left(\tilde{\tilde{\tilde{\gamma}}}_0 - \tilde{\tilde{\tilde{\gamma}}}_2\right)} = 0,$$

$$-\frac{v + \bar{X}_1 + \bar{X}_2}{\xi} + \frac{\bar{X}_2}{\tilde{\tilde{\tilde{\gamma}}}_1 - \tilde{\tilde{\tilde{\gamma}}}_2} - \frac{\left(1 + \tilde{\tilde{\tilde{\gamma}}}_0\right)\bar{R}}{\xi\left(\tilde{\tilde{\tilde{\gamma}}}_1 - \tilde{\tilde{\tilde{\gamma}}}_2\right)} = 0,$$

$$-\frac{\bar{X}_1}{\tilde{\tilde{\tilde{\gamma}}}_0 - \tilde{\tilde{\tilde{\gamma}}}_2} - \frac{\bar{X}_2}{\tilde{\tilde{\tilde{\gamma}}}_1 - \tilde{\tilde{\tilde{\gamma}}}_2} + \frac{v + \bar{X}_1 + \bar{X}_2}{\xi} + \left\{\frac{1}{\tilde{\tilde{\tilde{\gamma}}}_2} + \frac{1}{\tilde{\tilde{\tilde{\gamma}}}_0 - \tilde{\tilde{\tilde{\gamma}}}_2} + \frac{1}{\tilde{\tilde{\tilde{\gamma}}}_1 - \tilde{\tilde{\tilde{\gamma}}}_2} - \frac{1}{\xi}\right\}\bar{R} = 0,$$

where $\xi = 1 + \tilde{\tilde{\tilde{\gamma}}}_0 + \tilde{\tilde{\tilde{\gamma}}}_1 - \tilde{\tilde{\tilde{\gamma}}}_2$.

Here, $\bar{R}$ is the sample mean of $R(x,y)$. Solving these equations leads to

$$\tilde{\tilde{\tilde{\gamma}}}_0 = \frac{\bar{X}_1}{v}, \quad \tilde{\tilde{\tilde{\gamma}}}_1 = \frac{\bar{X}_2}{v},$$

while $\tilde{\tilde{\tilde{\gamma}}}_2$ is the solution to the equation

$$v\,\tilde{\tilde{\tilde{\gamma}}}_2 = \bar{R}.$$

This equation for $\tilde{\tilde{\tilde{\gamma}}}_2$ can be solved iteratively using either the moment or zero–zero cell frequency estimate as an initial value.

5.3.2. Asymptotic Variance Matrix of $\tilde{\tilde{\tilde{\gamma}}}$

By definition, The third-order information matrix, F_3, is given by (for large n)

$$F_3 = n\left(\sum_{r,s} \frac{1}{P_\gamma(r,s)} \frac{\partial P_\gamma(r,s)}{\partial \gamma_i} \frac{\partial P_\gamma(r,s)}{\partial \gamma_j}\right), \quad \text{with } i,j \in \{0,1,2\}.$$

Returning to Equations (11)–(13) and recalling that the asymptotic variance–covariance matrix of the estimators obtained by the maximum likelihood method, Σ_{ML}, is the inverse of the information matrix, then

$$\Sigma_{ML} = \frac{1}{n}\left(\sum_{r,s} Q_i(r,s) Q_j(r,s) P_\gamma(r,s)\right)^{-1}, \quad i,j \in \{0,1,2\},$$

where

$$Q_i(r,s) = \frac{1}{P_\gamma(r,s)} \frac{\partial P_\gamma(r,s)}{\partial \gamma_i}, \quad i = 0,1,2.$$

5.3.3. Asymptotic Distribution of $\tilde{\tilde{\tilde{\gamma}}}$

Since $\tilde{\tilde{\tilde{\gamma}}}$ is a function of sample moments, applying Theorem 11.2.14 (Delta Method) given in Lehmann and Romano [27], it follows that

$$\sqrt{n}\left(\tilde{\tilde{\tilde{\gamma}}} - \gamma\right) \xrightarrow{L} N_3(\mathbf{0}, \Sigma_{ML}).$$

5.3.4. Asymptotic Properties of $\tilde{\tilde{\tilde{\gamma}}}$

According to the results of Section 5.3.3, $\tilde{\tilde{\tilde{\gamma}}}$ is a consistent and asymptotically normal estimator.

6. Numerical Results and Discussion

The properties of the statistic $B_{n,w}(\hat{\gamma}_n)$ are asymptotic (see, for example, [17]). However, we need to apply the test statistic in the real world, i.e., for finite sample sizes. This section is dedicated to investigating the behavior of the bootstrap approximation of the proposed statistic in a finite scenario. To this end, we conducted a simulation study and present the results obtained.

It is important to note that, as we did not find another consistent test statistic for the BNBD, the numerical study presented has no point of comparison. This is the reason why the study was carried out using three estimation techniques.

Given the massive volume of calculations performed, we minimized computation time by using the parallelization algorithm called parRapply, which has been suggested in [18]. All computational work was done through codes written in the R programming language [28].

It is important to point out that parRapply is a function from the parallel package, which is available in [18]. parRapply is a computational technique based on task simultaneity, allowing for faster computation times by partitioning the work to be executed across the different cores available on a computer. Its main goal is to reduce the execution time of a program. For more detailed information about parRapply, you can refer to the documentation available in [18].

To calculate $B_{n,w}(\hat{\gamma}_n)$, we used the weight function

$$w(t;a_1,a_2) = t_1^{a_1} t_2^{a_2}, \tag{14}$$

with $a_1 > -1$ and $a_2 > -1$, resulting in the following explicit form of the test statistic:

$$B_{n,w}(\hat{\gamma}_n) = \frac{1}{n}\sum_{i=1}^{n}\sum_{j=1}^{n}\left(\frac{1}{X_{i1}+X_{j1}+a_1+1}\right)\left(\frac{1}{X_{i2}+X_{j2}+a_2+1}\right)$$
$$+q^{v}\sum_{k=0}^{\infty}\sum_{l=0}^{k}\sum_{m=0}^{k-l}\frac{(\hat{\gamma}_0-\hat{\gamma}_1)^{k-l-m}(\hat{\gamma}_1-\hat{\gamma}_2)^{l}\hat{\gamma}_2^{m}}{l!\,m!(k-m-l)!\,q^{k}}\left(\frac{nq^{v}(2v+k-1)!}{(2v-1)!\,A_{kl}\,C_{lm}}-\frac{2(v+k-1)!}{(v-1)!}\sum_{i=1}^{n}\frac{1}{D_{iklm}}\right),$$

where $q = 1+\hat{\gamma}_0+\hat{\gamma}_1-\hat{\gamma}_2$, $A_{kl} = a_1+k-l+1$, $C_{lm} = a_2+l+m+1$, and $D_{iklm} = (X_{i1}+A_{kl})(X_{i2}+C_{lm})$.

Remark 1. *For practical purposes, truncating the infinite series to the first 20 terms yielded sufficiently accurate values for the test statistic and good performance of the corresponding subroutine.*

6.1. Simulated Data for Type I Error

In practice, the exact bootstrap estimator of the null distribution of $B_{n,w}(\hat{\gamma}_n)$ cannot be calculated. As usual, we approximate it by simulation as follows:

1. Estimate γ through $\hat{\gamma}$ and compute the observed value of the test statistic B_{obs}.
2. For some large integer K, repeat for every $k \in \{1,\ldots,K\}$:
   (a) Generate $\boldsymbol{X}^{*k} = (\boldsymbol{X}_1^{*k},\ldots,\boldsymbol{X}_n^{*k})$, where $\boldsymbol{X}_1^{*k},\ldots,\boldsymbol{X}_n^{*k}$ are iid from a $BNB(\hat{\gamma})$
   (b) Calculate the test statistic evaluated at $\boldsymbol{X}^{*k}$, obtaining $B_n^{*k}(\hat{\gamma}^{*k})$.
3. Approximate the p-value by $\hat{p} = \frac{1}{K}\sum_{k=1}^{K} I\{B_n^{*k}(\hat{\gamma}^{*k}) > B_{obs}\}$.

It is important to note that in Appendix A, we present the computational implementation of the parametric bootstrap algorithm written in R code.

To study the goodness of the bootstrap approximation of $B_{n,w}(\hat{\gamma}_n)$ for finite sample sizes, we generated samples of size $n = 30(20)70$ from $BNB(\gamma_0, \gamma_1, \gamma_2)$, with $\gamma_0 = \gamma_1$, where $\gamma_0, \gamma_1 \in \{0.29, 0.30, 0.31, 0.32\}$ and the parameter γ_2 were chosen such that the correlation coefficient, $\rho = \frac{\gamma_0\gamma_1+\gamma_2}{\sqrt{\gamma_0\gamma_1(1+\gamma_0)(1+\gamma_1)}}$, equaled to 0.25, 0.50, and 0.75 in order to evaluate the quality of the approximations for data with low, moderate, and high correlations, respectively.

To estimate the parameter γ, we employed the three techniques described in Section 5. Then, we approximated the bootstrap p-values, p^*, for the proposed test. For this purpose, we used the weighting function given in (14) for $(a_1, a_2) \in \{(0,0), (1,0), (0,1)\}$ and generated $K = 500$ bootstrap samples.

The above procedure was repeated 1000 times, and we calculated the fraction of the estimated p-values that were less than or equal to 0.05 and 0.10. These fractions correspond to the estimated probabilities of Type I error for $\alpha = 0.05, 0.10$, respectively.

Next, we repeat the previous experiment for $\gamma_0 \neq \gamma_1$, where $\gamma_0, \gamma_1 \in \{0.29, 0.30, 0.31, 0.32\}$ and γ_2 were chosen such that the correlation coefficient, $\rho = \frac{\gamma_0\gamma_1+\gamma_2}{\sqrt{\gamma_0\gamma_1(1+\gamma_0)(1+\gamma_1)}}$, was approximately equal to 0.25, 0.50, and 0.75.

In both scenarios, $\gamma_0 = \gamma_1$ and $\gamma_0 \neq \gamma_1$, we experimented with different numbers of trials before the first event occurred, v. We obtained similar results for the different simulated cases; here, we only report the results for $v = 5$.

Tables 1–6 summarize the obtained results. We denote the test statistic by $B_{n,a}(\hat{\gamma})$ when the weight function w takes the form given by (14) for some $a = (a_1, a_2)$. Additionally, note that we used the notation detailed in Section 5 to represent the technique employed to estimate the parameter γ.

Table 1. Simulation results for the probability of type I error for $\rho = 0.25$ and $E(X_1) = E(X_2)$.

	$n = 30$		$n = 50$		$n = 70$	
	$\alpha = 0.05$	$\alpha = 0.10$	$\alpha = 0.05$	$\alpha = 0.10$	$\alpha = 0.05$	$\alpha = 0.10$
$\gamma = (0.29, 0.29, 0.009425)$						
$B_{n,(0,0)}(\tilde{\gamma})$	0.033	0.080	0.036	0.087	0.061	0.110
$B_{n,(1,0)}(\tilde{\gamma})$	0.034	0.081	0.035	0.088	0.060	0.109
$B_{n,(0,1)}(\tilde{\gamma})$	0.032	0.080	0.036	0.087	0.058	0.111
$B_{n,(0,0)}(\tilde{\tilde{\gamma}})$	0.038	0.083	0.042	0.089	0.056	0.107
$B_{n,(1,0)}(\tilde{\tilde{\gamma}})$	0.039	0.083	0.043	0.090	0.057	0.108
$B_{n,(0,1)}(\tilde{\tilde{\gamma}})$	0.040	0.082	0.044	0.090	0.057	0.109
$B_{n,(0,0)}(\tilde{\tilde{\tilde{\gamma}}})$	0.042	0.088	0.045	0.095	0.051	0.102
$B_{n,(1,0)}(\tilde{\tilde{\tilde{\gamma}}})$	0.041	0.090	0.047	0.097	0.050	0.101
$B_{n,(0,1)}(\tilde{\tilde{\tilde{\gamma}}})$	0.042	0.087	0.046	0.097	0.051	0.102
$\gamma = (0.30, 0.30, 0.007500)$						
$B_{n,(0,0)}(\tilde{\gamma})$	0.030	0.084	0.035	0.085	0.061	0.112
$B_{n,(1,0)}(\tilde{\gamma})$	0.034	0.083	0.035	0.087	0.062	0.113
$B_{n,(0,1)}(\tilde{\gamma})$	0.033	0.080	0.038	0.089	0.059	0.112
$B_{n,(0,0)}(\tilde{\tilde{\gamma}})$	0.037	0.086	0.042	0.091	0.056	0.107
$B_{n,(1,0)}(\tilde{\tilde{\gamma}})$	0.038	0.085	0.041	0.093	0.057	0.106
$B_{n,(0,1)}(\tilde{\tilde{\gamma}})$	0.037	0.085	0.044	0.093	0.055	0.105
$B_{n,(0,0)}(\tilde{\tilde{\tilde{\gamma}}})$	0.041	0.090	0.047	0.095	0.052	0.102
$B_{n,(1,0)}(\tilde{\tilde{\tilde{\gamma}}})$	0.040	0.087	0.048	0.094	0.051	0.102
$B_{n,(0,1)}(\tilde{\tilde{\tilde{\gamma}}})$	0.040	0.092	0.049	0.095	0.050	0.101

Table 1. *Cont.*

	$n = 30$		$n = 50$		$n = 70$	
	$\alpha = \mathbf{0.05}$	$\alpha = \mathbf{0.10}$	$\alpha = \mathbf{0.05}$	$\alpha = \mathbf{0.10}$	$\alpha = \mathbf{0.05}$	$\alpha = \mathbf{0.10}$
$\gamma = (0.32, 0.32, 0.003200)$						
$B_{n,(0,0)}(\tilde{\gamma})$	0.030	0.083	0.037	0.086	0.060	0.108
$B_{n,(1,0)}(\tilde{\gamma})$	0.031	0.082	0.035	0.089	0.061	0.109
$B_{n,(0,1)}(\tilde{\gamma})$	0.032	0.081	0.036	0.087	0.060	0.107
$B_{n,(0,0)}(\tilde{\tilde{\gamma}})$	0.039	0.087	0.041	0.091	0.058	0.107
$B_{n,(1,0)}(\tilde{\tilde{\gamma}})$	0.037	0.087	0.043	0.093	0.057	0.105
$B_{n,(0,1)}(\tilde{\tilde{\gamma}})$	0.036	0.086	0.043	0.093	0.055	0.104
$B_{n,(0,0)}(\tilde{\tilde{\tilde{\gamma}}})$	0.040	0.089	0.045	0.096	0.053	0.102
$B_{n,(1,0)}(\tilde{\tilde{\tilde{\gamma}}})$	0.042	0.091	0.046	0.095	0.053	0.103
$B_{n,(0,1)}(\tilde{\tilde{\tilde{\gamma}}})$	0.042	0.093	0.045	0.096	0.052	0.101

Table 2. Simulation results for the probability of type I error for $\rho \approx 0.25$ and $E(X_1) \neq E(X_2)$.

	$n = 30$		$n = 50$		$n = 70$	
	$\alpha = \mathbf{0.05}$	$\alpha = \mathbf{0.10}$	$\alpha = \mathbf{0.05}$	$\alpha = \mathbf{0.10}$	$\alpha = \mathbf{0.05}$	$\alpha = \mathbf{0.10}$
$\gamma = (0.29, 0.30, 0.008492)$						
$B_{n,(0,0)}(\tilde{\gamma})$	0.031	0.079	0.039	0.085	0.058	0.113
$B_{n,(1,0)}(\tilde{\gamma})$	0.034	0.081	0.039	0.087	0.056	0.111
$B_{n,(0,1)}(\tilde{\gamma})$	0.033	0.075	0.035	0.084	0.057	0.114
$B_{n,(0,0)}(\tilde{\tilde{\gamma}})$	0.039	0.086	0.042	0.089	0.056	0.110
$B_{n,(1,0)}(\tilde{\tilde{\gamma}})$	0.037	0.085	0.041	0.089	0.056	0.109
$B_{n,(0,1)}(\tilde{\tilde{\gamma}})$	0.039	0.085	0.042	0.088	0.055	0.110
$B_{n,(0,0)}(\tilde{\tilde{\tilde{\gamma}}})$	0.041	0.092	0.046	0.096	0.053	0.101
$B_{n,(1,0)}(\tilde{\tilde{\tilde{\gamma}}})$	0.043	0.093	0.045	0.095	0.052	0.103
$B_{n,(0,1)}(\tilde{\tilde{\tilde{\gamma}}})$	0.040	0.090	0.044	0.096	0.052	0.100
$\gamma = (0.29, 0.31, 0.007543)$						
$B_{n,(0,0)}(\tilde{\gamma})$	0.032	0.079	0.035	0.083	0.059	0.115
$B_{n,(1,0)}(\tilde{\gamma})$	0.033	0.083	0.035	0.085	0.058	0.112
$B_{n,(0,1)}(\tilde{\gamma})$	0.031	0.077	0.033	0.081	0.059	0.116
$B_{n,(0,0)}(\tilde{\tilde{\gamma}})$	0.037	0.081	0.040	0.087	0.057	0.110
$B_{n,(1,0)}(\tilde{\tilde{\gamma}})$	0.036	0.087	0.043	0.089	0.055	0.109
$B_{n,(0,1)}(\tilde{\tilde{\gamma}})$	0.038	0.085	0.044	0.090	0.056	0.108
$B_{n,(0,0)}(\tilde{\tilde{\tilde{\gamma}}})$	0.041	0.093	0.044	0.095	0.053	0.103
$B_{n,(1,0)}(\tilde{\tilde{\tilde{\gamma}}})$	0.042	0.090	0.045	0.094	0.053	0.102
$B_{n,(0,1)}(\tilde{\tilde{\tilde{\gamma}}})$	0.041	0.089	0.046	0.092	0.050	0.100
$\gamma = (0.30, 0.31, 0.006492)$						
$B_{n,(0,0)}(\tilde{\gamma})$	0.031	0.081	0.037	0.084	0.060	0.112
$B_{n,(1,0)}(\tilde{\gamma})$	0.033	0.078	0.038	0.084	0.059	0.112
$B_{n,(0,1)}(\tilde{\gamma})$	0.033	0.076	0.037	0.086	0.060	0.110
$B_{n,(0,0)}(\tilde{\tilde{\gamma}})$	0.035	0.081	0.041	0.086	0.055	0.109
$B_{n,(1,0)}(\tilde{\tilde{\gamma}})$	0.038	0.083	0.043	0.087	0.055	0.107
$B_{n,(0,1)}(\tilde{\tilde{\gamma}})$	0.035	0.082	0.041	0.084	0.056	0.111
$B_{n,(0,0)}(\tilde{\tilde{\tilde{\gamma}}})$	0.042	0.086	0.044	0.092	0.054	0.102
$B_{n,(1,0)}(\tilde{\tilde{\tilde{\gamma}}})$	0.040	0.085	0.045	0.095	0.051	0.101
$B_{n,(0,1)}(\tilde{\tilde{\tilde{\gamma}}})$	0.043	0.085	0.045	0.095	0.052	0.101

Table 3. Simulation results for the probability of type I error for $\rho = 0.50$ and $E(X_1) = E(X_2)$.

	$n = 30$		$n = 50$		$n = 70$	
	$\alpha = 0.05$	$\alpha = 0.10$	$\alpha = 0.05$	$\alpha = 0.10$	$\alpha = 0.05$	$\alpha = 0.10$
$\gamma = (0.29, 0.29, 0.102950)$						
$B_{n,(0,0)}(\tilde{\gamma})$	0.033	0.075	0.035	0.083	0.060	0.115
$B_{n,(1,0)}(\tilde{\gamma})$	0.031	0.083	0.037	0.084	0.059	0.112
$B_{n,(0,1)}(\tilde{\gamma})$	0.033	0.082	0.038	0.086	0.058	0.113
$B_{n,(0,0)}(\tilde{\tilde{\gamma}})$	0.038	0.082	0.043	0.084	0.055	0.112
$B_{n,(1,0)}(\tilde{\tilde{\gamma}})$	0.039	0.083	0.044	0.087	0.055	0.111
$B_{n,(0,1)}(\tilde{\tilde{\gamma}})$	0.039	0.085	0.042	0.089	0.055	0.111
$B_{n,(0,0)}(\tilde{\tilde{\tilde{\gamma}}})$	0.043	0.088	0.045	0.095	0.052	0.104
$B_{n,(1,0)}(\tilde{\tilde{\tilde{\gamma}}})$	0.040	0.090	0.047	0.096	0.051	0.102
$B_{n,(0,1)}(\tilde{\tilde{\tilde{\gamma}}})$	0.043	0.093	0.045	0.097	0.052	0.100
$\gamma = (0.30, 0.30, 0.105000)$						
$B_{n,(0,0)}(\tilde{\gamma})$	0.034	0.074	0.038	0.084	0.059	0.114
$B_{n,(1,0)}(\tilde{\gamma})$	0.033	0.075	0.037	0.085	0.060	0.112
$B_{n,(0,1)}(\tilde{\gamma})$	0.034	0.076	0.041	0.084	0.058	0.114
$B_{n,(0,0)}(\tilde{\tilde{\gamma}})$	0.038	0.083	0.044	0.086	0.054	0.109
$B_{n,(1,0)}(\tilde{\tilde{\gamma}})$	0.039	0.085	0.042	0.087	0.056	0.111
$B_{n,(0,1)}(\tilde{\tilde{\gamma}})$	0.038	0.082	0.042	0.086	0.055	0.110
$B_{n,(0,0)}(\tilde{\tilde{\tilde{\gamma}}})$	0.041	0.089	0.046	0.095	0.053	0.103
$B_{n,(1,0)}(\tilde{\tilde{\tilde{\gamma}}})$	0.043	0.091	0.044	0.095	0.053	0.103
$B_{n,(0,1)}(\tilde{\tilde{\tilde{\gamma}}})$	0.041	0.093	0.045	0.096	0.050	0.102
$\gamma = (0.32, 0.32, 0.108800)$						
$B_{n,(0,0)}(\tilde{\gamma})$	0.032	0.080	0.039	0.084	0.060	0.113
$B_{n,(1,0)}(\tilde{\gamma})$	0.035	0.076	0.036	0.083	0.061	0.114
$B_{n,(0,1)}(\tilde{\gamma})$	0.030	0.078	0.038	0.084	0.060	0.113
$B_{n,(0,0)}(\tilde{\tilde{\gamma}})$	0.037	0.081	0.042	0.087	0.057	0.109
$B_{n,(1,0)}(\tilde{\tilde{\gamma}})$	0.039	0.084	0.042	0.086	0.056	0.109
$B_{n,(0,1)}(\tilde{\tilde{\gamma}})$	0.037	0.082	0.041	0.085	0.057	0.108
$B_{n,(0,0)}(\tilde{\tilde{\tilde{\gamma}}})$	0.041	0.087	0.044	0.095	0.051	0.100
$B_{n,(1,0)}(\tilde{\tilde{\tilde{\gamma}}})$	0.042	0.091	0.045	0.094	0.053	0.104
$B_{n,(0,0)}(\tilde{\tilde{\tilde{\gamma}}})$	0.040	0.093	0.046	0.095	0.051	0.103

Table 4. Simulation results for the probability of type I error for $\rho \approx 0.50$ and $E(X_1) \neq E(X_2)$.

	$n = 30$		$n = 50$		$n = 70$	
	$\alpha = 0.05$	$\alpha = 0.10$	$\alpha = 0.05$	$\alpha = 0.10$	$\alpha = 0.05$	$\alpha = 0.10$
$\gamma = (0.29, 0.31, 0.104990)$						
$B_{n,(0,0)}(\tilde{\gamma})$	0.032	0.078	0.038	0.083	0.060	0.114
$B_{n,(1,0)}(\tilde{\gamma})$	0.032	0.076	0.037	0.084	0.060	0.113
$B_{n,(0,1)}(\tilde{\gamma})$	0.034	0.081	0.037	0.083	0.059	0.113
$B_{n,(0,0)}(\tilde{\tilde{\gamma}})$	0.038	0.080	0.041	0.084	0.057	0.111
$B_{n,(1,0)}(\tilde{\tilde{\gamma}})$	0.039	0.081	0.043	0.085	0.055	0.110
$B_{n,(0,1)}(\tilde{\tilde{\gamma}})$	0.038	0.082	0.042	0.087	0.056	0.109
$B_{n,(0,0)}(\tilde{\tilde{\tilde{\gamma}}})$	0.041	0.086	0.046	0.096	0.053	0.102
$B_{n,(1,0)}(\tilde{\tilde{\tilde{\gamma}}})$	0.043	0.090	0.044	0.095	0.053	0103
$B_{n,(0,1)}(\tilde{\tilde{\tilde{\gamma}}})$	0.043	0.091	0.047	0.094	0.051	0.103
$\gamma = (0.30, 0.31, 0.105984)$						
$B_{n,(0,0)}(\tilde{\gamma})$	0.031	0.072	0.037	0.083	0.059	0.115
$B_{n,(1,0)}(\tilde{\gamma})$	0.033	0.079	0.035	0.083	0.060	0.115
$B_{n,(0,1)}(\tilde{\gamma})$	0.033	0.074	0.038	0.085	0.058	0.114
$B_{n,(0,0)}(\tilde{\tilde{\gamma}})$	0.037	0.080	0.042	0.084	0.056	0.109

Table 4. *Cont.*

	$n = 30$		$n = 50$		$n = 70$	
	$\alpha = 0.05$	$\alpha = 0.10$	$\alpha = 0.05$	$\alpha = 0.10$	$\alpha = 0.05$	$\alpha = 0.10$
$B_{n,(1,0)}(\tilde{\tilde{\gamma}})$	0.037	0.081	0.043	0.085	0.055	0.111
$B_{n,(0,1)}(\tilde{\tilde{\gamma}})$	0.039	0.082	0.041	0.087	0.056	0.109
$B_{n,(0,0)}(\tilde{\tilde{\tilde{\gamma}}})$	0.043	0.087	0.045	0.094	0.052	0.103
$B_{n,(1,0)}(\tilde{\tilde{\tilde{\gamma}}})$	0.040	0.090	0.044	0.093	0.053	0.103
$B_{n,(0,1)}(\tilde{\tilde{\tilde{\gamma}}})$	0.040	0.087	0.047	0.095	0.051	0.101
$\gamma = (0.30, 0.32, 0.106939)$						
$B_{n,(0,0)}(\tilde{\gamma})$	0.031	0.079	0.034	0.081	0.061	0.115
$B_{n,(1,0)}(\tilde{\gamma})$	0.032	0.076	0.035	0.083	0.060	0.112
$B_{n,(0,1)}(\tilde{\gamma})$	0.032	0.077	0.035	0.082	0.061	0.114
$B_{n,(0,0)}(\tilde{\tilde{\gamma}})$	0.039	0.082	0.042	0.087	0.054	0.111
$B_{n,(1,0)}(\tilde{\tilde{\gamma}})$	0.038	0.082	0.041	0.088	0.053	0.106
$B_{n,(0,1)}(\tilde{\tilde{\gamma}})$	0.038	0.081	0.043	0.088	0.054	0.107
$B_{n,(0,0)}(\tilde{\tilde{\tilde{\gamma}}})$	0.042	0.088	0.046	0.095	0.051	0.104
$B_{n,(1,0)}(\tilde{\tilde{\tilde{\gamma}}})$	0.041	0.086	0.044	0.096	0.050	0.102
$B_{n,(0,1)}(\tilde{\tilde{\tilde{\gamma}}})$	0.041	0.088	0.044	0.095	0.053	0.103

Table 5. Simulation results for the probability of type I error for $\rho = 0.75$ and $E(X_1) = E(X_2)$.

	$n = 30$		$n = 50$		$n = 70$	
	$\alpha = 0.05$	$\alpha = 0.10$	$\alpha = 0.05$	$\alpha = 0.10$	$\alpha = 0.05$	$\alpha = 0.10$
$\gamma = (0.29, 0.29, 0.196475)$						
$B_{n,(0,0)}(\tilde{\gamma})$	0.034	0.085	0.038	0.089	0.059	0.110
$B_{n,(1,0)}(\tilde{\gamma})$	0.033	0.084	0.036	0.088	0.060	0.111
$B_{n,(0,1)}(\tilde{\gamma})$	0.032	0.084	0.037	0.087	0.058	0.111
$B_{n,(0,0)}(\tilde{\tilde{\gamma}})$	0.037	0.085	0.042	0.089	0.057	0.107
$B_{n,(1,0)}(\tilde{\tilde{\gamma}})$	0.038	0.086	0.045	0.090	0.054	0.104
$B_{n,(0,1)}(\tilde{\tilde{\gamma}})$	0.037	0.084	0.043	0.089	0.056	0.109
$B_{n,(0,0)}(\tilde{\tilde{\tilde{\gamma}}})$	0.044	0.088	0.047	0.095	0.051	0.104
$B_{n,(1,0)}(\tilde{\tilde{\tilde{\gamma}}})$	0.041	0.090	0.044	0.096	0.052	0.102
$B_{n,(0,1)}(\tilde{\tilde{\tilde{\gamma}}})$	0.042	0.093	0.045	0.097	0.052	0.100
$\gamma = (0.30, 0.30, 0.202500)$						
$B_{n,(0,0)}(\tilde{\gamma})$	0.035	0.076	0.039	0.086	0.058	0.110
$B_{n,(1,0)}(\tilde{\gamma})$	0.034	0.075	0.039	0.085	0.059	0.111
$B_{n,(0,1)}(\tilde{\gamma})$	0.034	0.075	0.040	0.084	0.057	0.112
$B_{n,(0,0)}(\tilde{\tilde{\gamma}})$	0.036	0.083	0.043	0.087	0.054	0.108
$B_{n,(1,0)}(\tilde{\tilde{\gamma}})$	0.038	0.085	0.044	0.088	0.055	0.109
$B_{n,(0,1)}(\tilde{\tilde{\gamma}})$	0.039	0.086	0.044	0.089	0.055	0.107
$B_{n,(0,0)}(\tilde{\tilde{\tilde{\gamma}}})$	0.043	0.090	0.046	0.095	0.052	0.101
$B_{n,(1,0)}(\tilde{\tilde{\tilde{\gamma}}})$	0.043	0.091	0.046	0.095	0.052	0.102
$B_{n,(0,1)}(\tilde{\tilde{\tilde{\gamma}}})$	0.042	0.092	0.045	0.096	0.051	0.101
$\gamma = (0.31, 0.31, 0.208475)$						
$B_{n,(0,0)}(\tilde{\gamma})$	0.033	0.078	0.039	0.085	0.059	0.112
$B_{n,(1,0)}(\tilde{\gamma})$	0.035	0.079	0.039	0.086	0.060	0.113
$B_{n,(0,1)}(\tilde{\gamma})$	0.033	0.078	0.038	0.084	0.050	0.112
$B_{n,(0,0)}(\tilde{\tilde{\gamma}})$	0.038	0.084	0.043	0.088	0.054	0.107
$B_{n,(1,0)}(\tilde{\tilde{\gamma}})$	0.040	0.085	0.045	0.089	0.053	0.108
$B_{n,(0,1)}(\tilde{\tilde{\gamma}})$	0.040	0.086	0.046	0.090	0.052	0.106
$B_{n,(0,0)}(\tilde{\tilde{\tilde{\gamma}}})$	0.042	0.089	0.046	0.095	0.051	0.100
$B_{n,(1,0)}(\tilde{\tilde{\tilde{\gamma}}})$	0.042	0.091	0.046	0.094	0.052	0.101
$B_{n,(0,0)}(\tilde{\tilde{\tilde{\gamma}}})$	0.041	0.092	0.044	0.096	0.050	0.100

Table 6. Simulation results for the probability of type I error for $\rho \approx 0.75$ and $E(X_1) \neq E(X_2)$.

	$n = 30$		$n = 50$		$n = 70$	
	$\alpha = 0.05$	$\alpha = 0.10$	$\alpha = 0.05$	$\alpha = 0.10$	$\alpha = 0.05$	$\alpha = 0.10$
$\gamma = (0.29, 0.30, 0.199475)$						
$B_{n,(0,0)}(\tilde{\gamma})$	0.031	0.084	0.037	0.089	0.060	0.109
$B_{n,(1,0)}(\tilde{\gamma})$	0.030	0.083	0.036	0.088	0.061	0.108
$B_{n,(0,1)}(\tilde{\gamma})$	0.030	0.084	0.036	0.089	0.059	0.109
$B_{n,(0,0)}(\tilde{\tilde{\gamma}})$	0.036	0.084	0.044	0.089	0.057	0.106
$B_{n,(1,0)}(\tilde{\tilde{\gamma}})$	0.037	0.086	0.045	0.091	0.056	0.105
$B_{n,(0,1)}(\tilde{\tilde{\gamma}})$	0.037	0.085	0.045	0.089	0.055	0.107
$B_{n,(0,0)}(\tilde{\tilde{\tilde{\gamma}}})$	0.043	0.089	0.047	0.094	0.052	0.104
$B_{n,(1,0)}(\tilde{\tilde{\tilde{\gamma}}})$	0.042	0.090	0.045	0.096	0.053	0.102
$B_{n,(0,1)}(\tilde{\tilde{\tilde{\gamma}}})$	0.042	0.092	0.045	0.096	0.053	0.101
$\gamma = (0.30, 0.31, 0.205476)$						
$B_{n,(0,0)}(\tilde{\gamma})$	0.034	0.076	0.039	0.085	0.058	0.111
$B_{n,(1,0)}(\tilde{\gamma})$	0.034	0.075	0.038	0.086	0.057	0.110
$B_{n,(0,1)}(\tilde{\gamma})$	0.035	0.075	0.039	0.086	0.058	0.111
$B_{n,(0,0)}(\tilde{\tilde{\gamma}})$	0.037	0.084	0.043	0.087	0.054	0.109
$B_{n,(1,0)}(\tilde{\tilde{\gamma}})$	0.039	0.086	0.044	0.089	0.055	0.108
$B_{n,(0,1)}(\tilde{\tilde{\gamma}})$	0.039	0.086	0.044	0.089	0.054	0.108
$B_{n,(0,0)}(\tilde{\tilde{\tilde{\gamma}}})$	0.044	0.091	0.046	0.096	0.052	0.101
$B_{n,(1,0)}(\tilde{\tilde{\tilde{\gamma}}})$	0.043	0.091	0.045	0.095	0.053	0.102
$B_{n,(0,1)}(\tilde{\tilde{\tilde{\gamma}}})$	0.044	0.092	0.045	0.096	0.052	0.101
$\gamma = (0.30, 0.32, 0.208408)$						
$B_{n,(0,0)}(\tilde{\gamma})$	0.035	0.079	0.039	0.085	0.058	0.112
$B_{n,(1,0)}(\tilde{\gamma})$	0.035	0.080	0.039	0.087	0.059	0.110
$B_{n,(0,1)}(\tilde{\gamma})$	0.034	0.079	0.039	0.085	0.056	0.112
$B_{n,(0,0)}(\tilde{\tilde{\gamma}})$	0.037	0.084	0.044	0.088	0.054	0.106
$B_{n,(1,0)}(\tilde{\tilde{\gamma}})$	0.037	0.084	0.044	0.088	0.054	0.109
$B_{n,(0,1)}(\tilde{\tilde{\gamma}})$	0.038	0.085	0.045	0.089	0.053	0.107
$B_{n,(0,0)}(\tilde{\tilde{\tilde{\gamma}}})$	0.042	0.090	0.046	0.094	0.051	0.100
$B_{n,(1,0)}(\tilde{\tilde{\tilde{\gamma}}})$	0.042	0.091	0.046	0.094	0.052	0.101
$B_{n,(0,0)}(\tilde{\tilde{\tilde{\gamma}}})$	0.043	0.092	0.047	0.096	0.050	0.101

In turn, as documented in the literature, the tables show that the maximum likelihood method provided better results than the other two estimation methods analyzed, followed by the method of moments. Furthermore, it is observed that the results converged to the established nominal level as the sample size increased.

These two conclusions can be clearly visualized in the graphs presented in Appendix A. On the one hand, it can be observed that as the sample size increased, the results approached the established nominal level: in the left area of each graph, the convergence toward $\alpha = 0.05$ is evident, while in the right area, the convergence toward $\alpha = 0.10$ is observable. Furthermore, it can be detected that using the maximum likelihood method yielded results closer to the established nominal levels ($\alpha = 0.05$ on the left side and $\alpha = 0.10$ on the right side) compared to the other two methods, with the method of moments following in accuracy.

Observing the values presented in the tables, we conclude that the parametric bootstrap method provides an accurate approximation to the null distribution of $B_{n,w}(\hat{\gamma}_n)$ in all the cases considered. This is also evident in the graphs in Appendix B.

6.2. Power of the Proposed Test Statistic

To analyze the power, we repeated the previous experiment for samples of size $n = 50$ across four alternatives (see, for example, Kocherlakota and Kocherlakota [19] for a description of these distributions):

- Bivariate Binomial distribution $BB(m; p_1, p_2, p_3)$, where $p_1 + p_2 - p_3 \leq 1$, $p_1 \geq p_3$, $p_2 \geq p_3$, and $p_3 > 0$;
- Bivariate Hermite distribution $BH(\mu, \sigma^2; \lambda_1, \lambda_2, \lambda_3)$, where $\mu > \sigma^2(\lambda_1 + \lambda_2 + \lambda_3)$;
- Bivariate Neyman type A distribution $BNTA(\lambda; \lambda_1, \lambda_2, \lambda_3)$, where $0 < \lambda_1 + \lambda_2 + \lambda_3 \leq 1$;
- Bivariate Poisson distribution $BP(\lambda_1, \lambda_2, \lambda_3)$, where $\lambda_1 > \lambda_3$, and $\lambda_2 > \lambda_3 > 0$.

The bivariate Binomial distribution and the bivariate Neyman type A distribution have been used as alternatives in other related articles (see, for example, Loukas and Kemp [29] and Rayner and Best [30]). The other alternative distributions employed are analogous to those used by Gürtler and Henze [31] in the univariate case.

To generate random samples from the bivariate distributions used as alternatives, we implemented computational algorithms following the simulation procedures provided in Kocherlakota and Kocherlakota [19].

Table 7 displays the alternatives considered and the estimated power for nominal significance level $\alpha = 0.05$. Additionally, to estimate the parameter γ, we only used the maximum likelihood method, as it yielded better results in the type I error study. Analyzing this table, we can conclude that all the considered tests, denoted by $B_{(a_1,a_2)}$, were able to detect the alternatives studied and with good power results, especially when $B_{(0,0)}$ was used.

Table 7. Simulation results for the power. The values are in the form of percentages rounded to the nearest integer.

Alternative	$B_{(0,0)}$	$B_{(1,0)}$	$B_{(0,1)}$
$BB(1; 0.41, 0.02, 0.01)$	95	91	88
$BB(1; 0.55, 0.03, 0.02)$	97	92	89
$BB(2; 0.42, 0.02, 0.01)$	98	94	90
$BB(2; 0.51, 0.01, 0.01)$	94	89	88
$BB(2; 0.71, 0.04, 0.03)$	92	86	85
$BH(0.99; 1, 0.66, 0.10, 0.10)$	96	87	92
$BH(1.00; 1, 0.30, 0.30, 0.25)$	95	86	90
$BH(1.00; 1, 0.31, 0.33, 0.24)$	92	86	86
$BH(1.30; 1, 0.61, 0.03, 0.02)$	93	84	85
$BH(1.40; 1, 1.00, 0.26, 0.12)$	95	86	88
$BNTA(0.15; 0.35, 0.33, 0.32)$	94	87	93
$BNTA(0.42; 0.32, 0.35, 0.33)$	92	89	91
$BNTA(0.50; 0.31, 0.34, 0.35)$	93	89	92
$BNTA(0.70; 0.35, 0.30, 0.33)$	91	88	92
$BNTA(0.75; 0.32, 0.34, 0.34)$	94	89	93
$BP(1.00, 1.00, 0.25)$	97	87	90
$BP(1.00, 1.00, 0.50)$	94	83	92
$BP(1.00, 1.00, 0.75)$	96	82	90
$BP(1.50, 1.00, 0.31)$	95	86	89
$BP(1.50, 1.00, 0.92)$	96	86	91

All calculations performed in this research were programmed using the open-source software R [28]. To leverage the potential of parallel programming (see Novoa-Muñoz [18]), the codes were executed utilizing the supercomputing infrastructure of the NLHPC (ECM–02)[2] belonging to the Mathematical Modeling Center of the University of Chile [32].

This infrastructure includes, among other resources, 132 HP computing nodes (128 HP SL230 nodes and 4 HP SL250 nodes), each equipped with two 10-core Intel Xeon Ivy Bridge E5-2660V2 processors.The manufacturer of the NLHPC supercomputer was Atos, located in the city of Bezons, France.

6.3. Real Data Set

The test statistic was applied to two real datasets:

First Case: Biometric Data. This case was analyzed by Dunn [33] to illustrate and represent a real case of the BNBD. The sample was obtained from Arbous and Kerrich [4] in a study on the treatment and analysis of the propensity for workplace accidents in the railway sector among a group of experienced workers. The study involved 122 workers, with the first variable representing a six-year period (1937–1942) and the second variable representing a five-year period (1943–1947). The results correspond to the number of workers who had accidents in the two non-overlapping time periods.

Second Case: Agronomic–Botanical Data. This dataset is based on the number of plants of the species Lacistema aggregatum and Protium guianense in each of 100 contiguous quadrants. The data were first presented by Holgate [6] and later analyzed by various researchers up to 1995, including Gillings [34], Crockett [35], Loukas and Kemp [29], Kocherlakota and Kocherlakota [19], and Rayner and Best [30]. They were also studied by Novoa-Muñoz and Jiménez-Gamero [17]. Researchers Crockett [35], Loukas and Kemp [29], Rayner and Best [30], and Novoa-Muñoz and Jiménez-Gamero [17] examined the data to determine whether they corresponded to a bivariate Poisson model and concluded that the bivariate Poisson distribution did not correctly model the mentioned data.

The following three cases are part of the kaggle.com [36] repository, where companies from around the world can upload their databases for a community of data scientists to generate predictive models. It is a challenge of skills and competencies among developers who seek to identify patterns and trends in the data. These cases correspond to current data recorded in recent times.

kaggle.com [36] also offers modeling and evaluation tools to develop and compare models. It is an online community for learning, sharing, and competing in data science.

It is important to note that, based on the information available to date, we have no evidence that any of these three datasets have previously been analyzed to determine whether they follow a probability distribution.

Third Case: Black Friday Sales Data. This is a public dataset containing information about purchases made during Black Friday. It includes buyer variables such as age, gender, purchase amount, category, and quantity of products purchased. The dataset contains over 550,000 rows and 12 columns. Two columns containing the quantity of products purchased were randomly selected. The dataset can be used to identify patterns and trends in Black Friday purchases.

Fourth Case: Jamboree Education Data. This dataset contains information on students' academic performance in admission exams. It includes variables such as scores in different sections of the exam, the student's age, and gender. The objective is to predict students' academic performance. This dataset is useful for analyzing and improving educational outcomes.

Fifth Case: Insurance Data. This database contains information about insurance customers. It includes variables such as age, gender, marital status, and income level. It also contains information about insurance policies, such as premium amount and insurance type. The dataset aims to predict the likelihood of a customer renewing their insurance policy. It is useful for analyzing and improving customer retention in the insurance industry.

Table 8 shows the p-values for testing the goodness of fit to a BNBD for the five real datasets using the statistical test we have proposed. For this, we used $(a_1, a_2) \in \{(0,0), (1,0), (0,1)\}$. Additionally, for the five real cases, we applied a nominal significance level of $\alpha = 0.05$ and considered $v = 5$, which was employing the same number of trials before the first event occurred.

Table 8. p-values for the real datasets rounded to three decimal places.

Test Statistics	Biometric	Agronomic	Sales	Education	Insurance
$B_{n(0,0)}$	0.434	0.277	0.003	0.892	0.493
$B_{n(1,0)}$	0.443	0.327	0.037	0.836	0.665
$B_{n(0,1)}$	0.440	0.303	0.023	0.878	0.258

The results displayed in this table allow us to conclude the following: For the Black Friday Sales data, the null hypothesis is rejected, meaning that Black Friday sales are not well modeled by a DBNB. On the other hand, for the other four datasets, it is not possible to reject the null hypothesis. Therefore, we conclude that the biometric, agronomic, education, and insurance data can be well modeled by a DBNB.

6.4. Comparisons with Other Goodness-of-Fit Tests

The only goodness-of-fit tests we have found in the statistical literature for bivariate count data are for the bivariate Poisson distribution and the bivariate Hermite distribution. The similarity is that these tests can be defined as follows:

- Consistent: As the sample size increases, the probability of correctly rejecting a false null hypothesis approaches 1. In other words, a consistent test has the ability to detect any deviation from the null hypothesis when sufficient information is available (i.e., with a sufficiently large sample size).
- Based on the probability generating function.
- Of the Cramér-von Mises type.
- With null asymptotic distribution approximated by the parametric bootstrap method.
- Specific tests for bivariate count data.

However, their implementation complexity may be a disadvantage compared to more generic tests like Kolmogorov–Smirnov, Anderson–Darling, or chi-squared.

Author Contributions: Conceptualization, F.N.-M.; methodology, F.N.-M.; software, F.N.-M. and J.P.A.-G.; validation, F.N.-M. and J.P.A.-G.; formal analysis, F.N.-M.; investigation, F.N.-M. and J.P.A.-G.; resources, F.N.-M.; data curation, J.P.A.-G.; writing—original draft preparation, F.N.-M. and J.P.A.-G.; writing—review and editing, F.N.-M.; visualization, F.N.-M. and J.P.A.-G. All authors have read and agreed to the published version of the manuscript.

Funding: This publication was supported by Universidad del Bío-Bío, DICREA [2220529 IF/R].

Data Availability Statement: The original contributions presented in the study are included in the article, further inquiries can be directed to the corresponding author.

Acknowledgments: The corresponding author expresses gratitude to the research project DIUBB 2220529 IF/R, the "Vicerrectoría de Investigación y Postgrado" and the "Departamento de Enfermería" entities of the Universidad del Bío-Bío, Chile. He also thanks the anonymous reviewers and the editor of this journal for their valuable time and their careful comments and suggestions with which the quality of this paper has been improved.

Conflicts of Interest: The authors declare no conflicts of interest.

Abbreviations

The following abbreviations are used in this manuscript:

All vectors are row vectors, and $x^\top$ is the transposed of the row vector x; for any vector, x, x_k denotes its kth coordinate, and $\|x\|$ denotes its Euclidean norm; $\mathbb{N}_0 = \{0, 1, 2, 3, ...\}$; $\mu'_{r,s} = E(X^r\ Y^s)$ denotes the joint moments of the random variables X and Y; $\mu_{r,s} = E[(X - \mu_X)^r\ (Y - \mu_Y)^s]$ denotes the (r, s)th central moment, where μ_Z is the expected value of Z; $I\{A\}$ denotes the indicator function of the set A; P_γ denotes the probability law of the BNBD with parameter γ; E_γ denotes expectation with respect to the probability function P_γ; P_* and E_* denote the conditional probability law and expectation given the data $(X_1, Y_1), \ldots, (X_n, Y_n)$, respectively; all limits in this work are taken as $n \to \infty$; $\xrightarrow{L}$ denotes convergence in distribution; $\xrightarrow{P}$ denotes convergence in probability; $\xrightarrow{a.s.}$ denotes almost sure convergence; let $\{C_n\}$ be a sequence of random variables or random elements, and let $\epsilon \in \mathbb{R}$; then, $C_n = O_P(n^{-\epsilon})$ means that $n^\epsilon C_n$ is bounded in probability, $C_n = o_P(n^{-\epsilon})$ means that $n^\epsilon C_n \xrightarrow{P} 0$, and $C_n = o(n^{-\epsilon})$ means that $n^\epsilon C_n \xrightarrow{a.s.} 0$; $\mathcal{H} = L^2([0, 1]^2, w)$ denotes the separable Hilbert space of the measurable functions $\varphi, w : [0, 1]^2 \to \mathbb{R}$ such that $||\varphi||^2_{\mathcal{H}} = \int_{[0,1]^2} \varphi^2(t)\, w(t) dt < \infty$.

Appendix A

This section presents the R code for the parametric bootstrap implementation used.

```
# The libraries to be used are loaded
library(methods)
library(Runuran)

# generates bivariate negative binomial samples
gbnbs = function(gamma0,gamma1,gamma2,N,v){
 if (gamma0 > gamma2 && gamma1 > gamma2 && gamma2 >= 0){
  q = 1 + gamma0 + gamma1 - gamma2
  p1 = (gamma0 - gamma2)/q
  p2 = (gamma1 - gamma2)/q
  p3 = gamma2/q
  tau = gamma2 * q/((gamma0 - gamma2)*(gamma1 - gamma2))
  x1 = numeric(N)
  x2 = rep(N,0)
  x = rep(N,0)
  y = numeric(N)
  pmf1 = function(a){
   p = abs(1 - (p2 + p3)/(1 - p1))
   return(choose(v + a - 1,v - 1) * p^v * (1 - p)^a)
  }
  dy = unuran.discr.new(pmf = pmf1, lb = 0, ub = 10, mode = 0, sum = 1)
  gen = unuran.new(distr = dy, method = "dari; squeeze = on")
  y = ur(gen,N)
  pmf2 = function(t){
   P = abs(p3/(p2 + p3))
   return(choose(v,t) * P^t * (1 - P)^(v - t))
  }
  dxg = unuran.discr.new(pmf = pmf2, lb = 0, ub = 2, mode = 0, sum = 1)
  gen = unuran.new(distr = dxg, method = "dari; squeeze = on")
  x1 = ur(gen,N)
  for(j in 1:N){
   pmf3 <- function(b){
    px2<- abs(1 - p1)
    return(choose(v + y[j] + b - 1,v + y[j] - 1) * px2^(v + y[j]) * (1 - px2)^b)
   }
   dx2 = unuran.discr.new(pmf = pmf3, lb = 0, ub = 10, mode = 0, sum = 1)
```

```
    gen = unuran.new(distr = dx2, method = "dari; squeeze = on")
    x2[j] = ur(gen,1)
    x[j] = x1[j] + x2[j]
   }
   return(list(x = x,y = y))
 }
}

# Assignment of the fixed values to be used
v = 5   # Number of trials before the first success or failure
n = 70  # Sample size
K = 500 # Bootstrap iterations

#The initial population data is loaded
load("data_BNBD.rda")
data_x = data_BNBD$x
data_y = data_BNBD$y
freq_ini = table(data_x,data_y)

# Step 1 of the parametric Bootstrap algorithm

#The parameters of the initial population are estimated
gamma_0 = mean(data_x)/v
gamma_1 = mean(data_y)/v

#The third parameter is estimated using the three estimation methods
#MZ is the implementation of Zero-Zero frequency method algorithm
#MM is the implementation of the Method of Moments algorithm
#ML is the implementation of the Maximum Likelihood method algorithm
gammaZZ_2 = MZ(g_0 = gamma_0,g_1 = gamma_1,table = freq_ini,n = n,v = v)
gammaMM_2 = MM(g_0 = gamma_0,g_1 = gamma_1,table = freq_ini,n = n,v = v)
gammaML_2 = ML(g_0 = gamma_0,g_1 = gamma_1,table = freq_ini,n = n,v = v)

#The observed value is obtained for each parameter estimation method
#B_est is the implementation of the test statistic.
B_obs_ZZ = B_est(gamma_0,gamma_1,gammaZZ_2,data_x,data_y,n,v)
B_obs_MM = B_est(gamma_0,gamma_1,gammaMM_2,data_x,data_y,n,v)
B_obs_ML = B_est(gamma_0,gamma_1,gammaML_2,data_x,data_y,n,v)

# Implementation of the parametric Bootstrap method
B_bootZZ = B_bootMM = B_bootML = rep(0,K)
for(k in 1:K){
 # Step 2(a) of the parametric Bootstrap algorithm
 sampleB_ZZ = gbnbs(gamma_0, gamma_1, gammaZZ_2, n, v)
 sampleB_MM = gbnbs(gamma_0, gamma_1, gammaMM_2, n, v)
 sampleB_ML = gbnbs(gamma_0, gamma_1, gammaML_2, n, v)
 dataB_ZZ = data.frame(x = sampleB_ZZ$x, y = sampleB_ZZ$y)
 dataB_MM = data.frame(x = sampleB_MM$x, y = sampleB_MM$y)
 dataB_ML = data.frame(x = sampleB_ML$x, y = sampleB_ML$y)
 freqB_ZZ = table(dataB_ZZ$x,dataB_ZZ$y)
 freqB_MM = table(dataB_MM$x,dataB_MM$y)
 freqB_ML = table(dataB_ML$x,dataB_ML$y)

 # The Bootstrap parameters are estimated: gammaB
 gammaB_ZZ_0 = mean(dataB_ZZ$x)/v
```

```
    gammaB_ZZ_1 = mean(dataB_ZZ$y)/v
    gammaB_MM_0 = mean(dataB_MM$x)/v
    gammaB_MM_1 = mean(dataB_MM$y)/v
    gammaB_ML_0 = mean(dataB_ML$x)/v
    gammaB_ML_1 = mean(dataB_ML$y)/v

    # The third parameter is estimated using the three estimation methods
   gammaB_ZZ_2 = MZ(g_0 = gammaB_ZZ_0,g_1 = gammaB_ZZ_1,table = freqB_ZZ,n = n,v = v)
   gammaB_MM_2 = MM(g_0 = gammaB_MM_0,g_1 = gammaB_MM_1,table = freqB_MM,n = n,v = v)
   gammaB_ML_2 = ML(g_0 = gammaB_ML_0,g_1 = gammaB_ML_1,table = freqB_ML,n = n,v = v)

    # Step 2(b) of the parametric Bootstrap algorithm
    B_boot_ZZ[k] = B_est(gammaB_ZZ_0,gammaB_ZZ_1,gammaB_ZZ_2,dataB_ZZ$x,dataB_ZZ$y,n,v)
    B_boot_MM[k] = B_est(gammaB_MM_0,gammaB_MM_1,gammaB_MM_2,dataB_MM$x,dataB_MM$y,n,v)
    B_boot_ML[k] = B_est(gammaB_ML_0,gammaB_ML_1,gammaB_ML_2,dataB_ML$x,dataB_ML$y,n,v)
   }
   # Step 3 of the parametric Bootstrap algorithm
   # An approximation of the p-value is accumulated
   vpZZ_B = sum(rep(1,K)[B_boot_ZZ > B_obs_ZZ])/K
   vpMM_B = sum(rep(1,K)[B_boot_MM > B_obs_MM])/K
   vpML_B = sum(rep(1,K)[B_boot_ML > B_obs_ML])/K
```

Appendix B

This section displays the graphs that complement the numerical tables presented in Section 6.1.

Note that in Figures A1–A18, presented below, the areas with a pink background highlight the convergence of the method at the nominal level $\alpha = 0.05$ represented by the blue dashed line. On the other hand, the areas with an orange background emphasize the convergence of the method at the nominal level $\alpha = 0.10$ described by the blue dashed line.

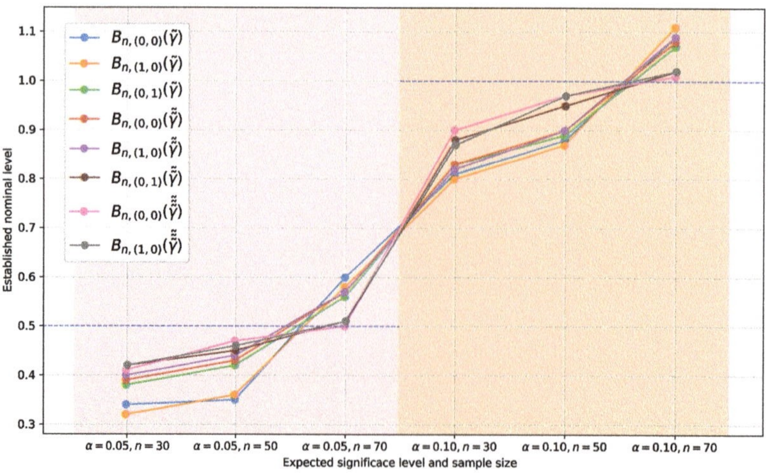

Figure A1. Simulation results for the probability of type I error for $\gamma = (0.29, 0.29, 0.009425)$.

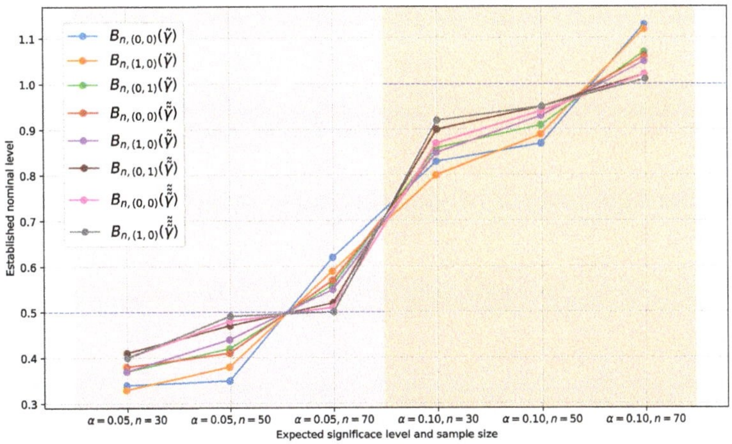

Figure A2. Simulation results for the probability of type I error for $\gamma = (0.30, 0.30, 0.007500)$.

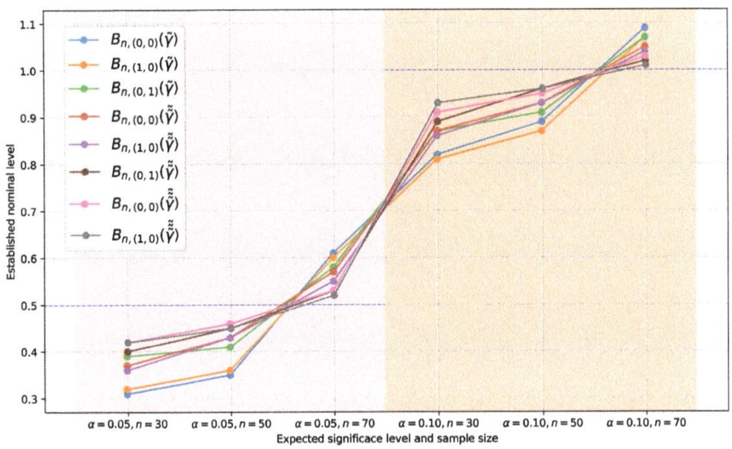

Figure A3. Simulation results for the probability of type I error for $\gamma = (0.32, 0.32, 0.003200)$.

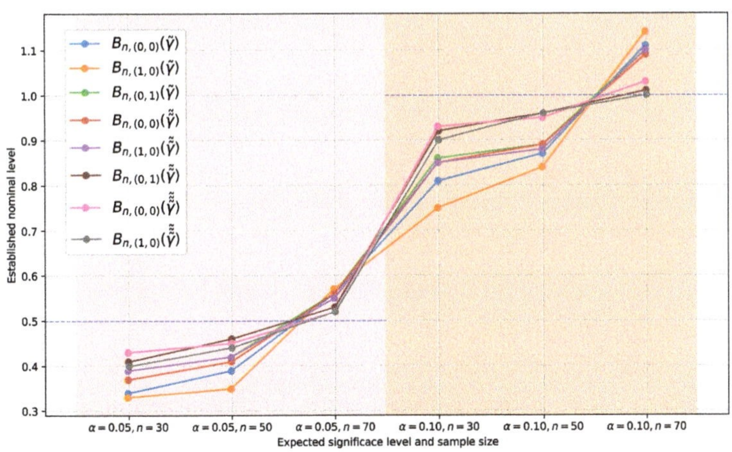

Figure A4. Simulation results for the probability of type I error for $\gamma = (0.29, 0.30, 0.008492)$.

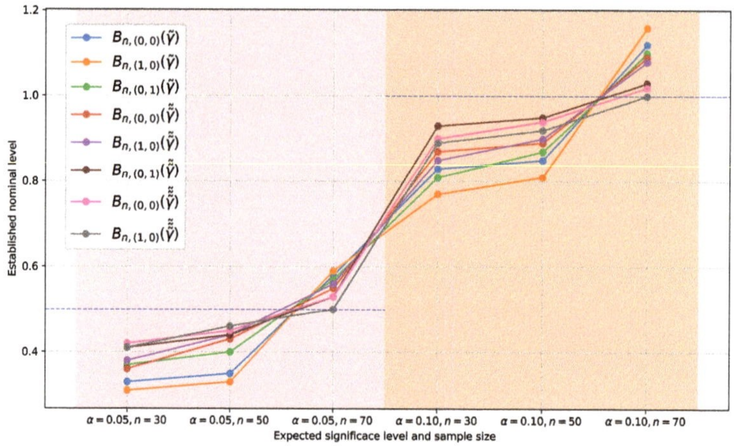

Figure A5. Simulation results for the probability of type I error for $\gamma = (0.29, 0.31, 0.007543)$.

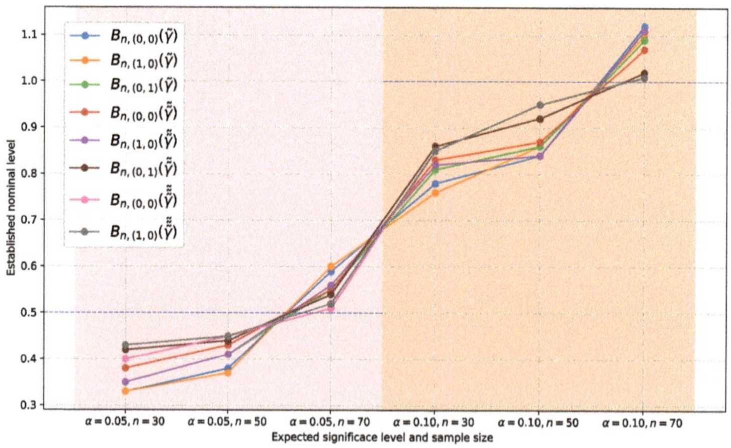

Figure A6. Simulation results for the probability of type I error for $\gamma = (0.30, 0.31, 0.006492)$.

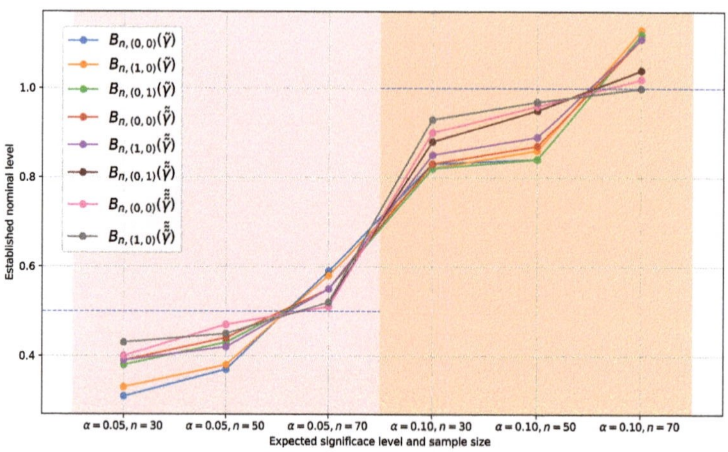

Figure A7. Simulation results for the probability of type I error for $\gamma = (0.29, 0.29, 0.102950)$.

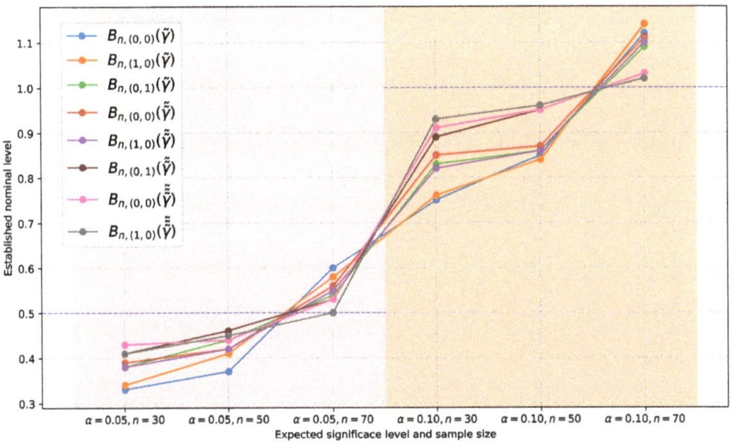

Figure A8. Simulation results for the probability of type I error for $\gamma = (0.30, 0.30, 0.105000)$.

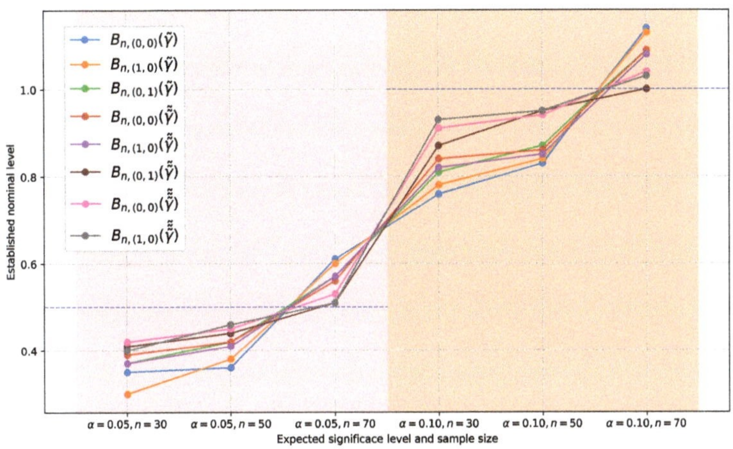

Figure A9. Simulation results for the probability of type I error for $\gamma = (0.32, 0.32, 0.108800)$.

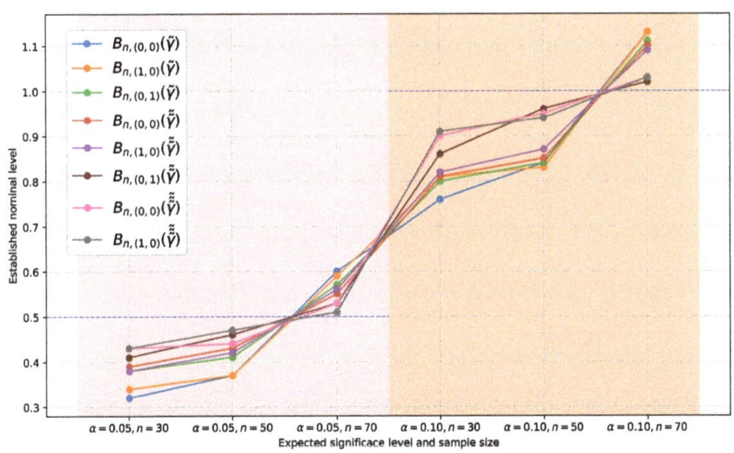

Figure A10. Simulation results for the probability of type I error for $\gamma = (0.29, 0.31, 0.104990)$.

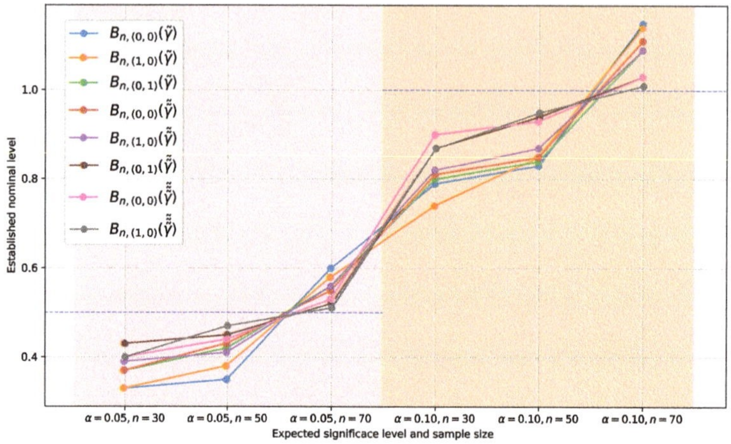

Figure A11. Simulation results for the probability of type I error for $\gamma = (0.30, 0.31, 0.105984)$.

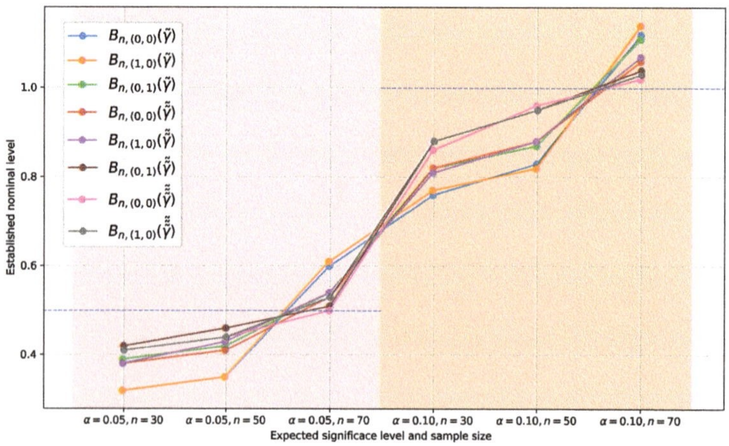

Figure A12. Simulation results for the probability of type I error for $\gamma = (0.30, 0.32, 0.106939)$.

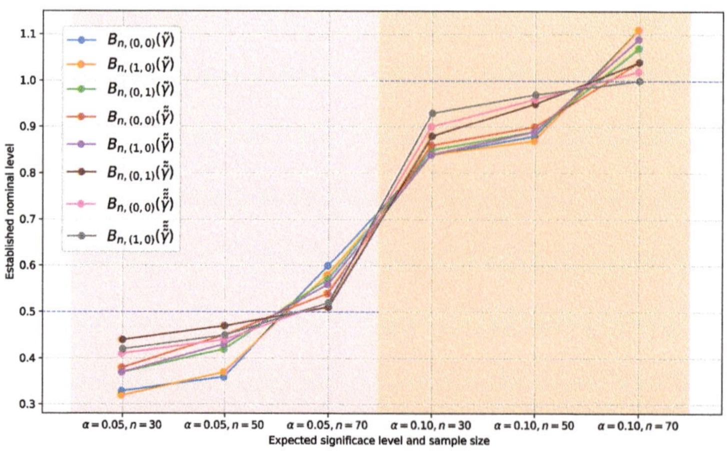

Figure A13. Simulation results for the probability of type I error for $\gamma = (0.29, 0.29, 0.196475)$.

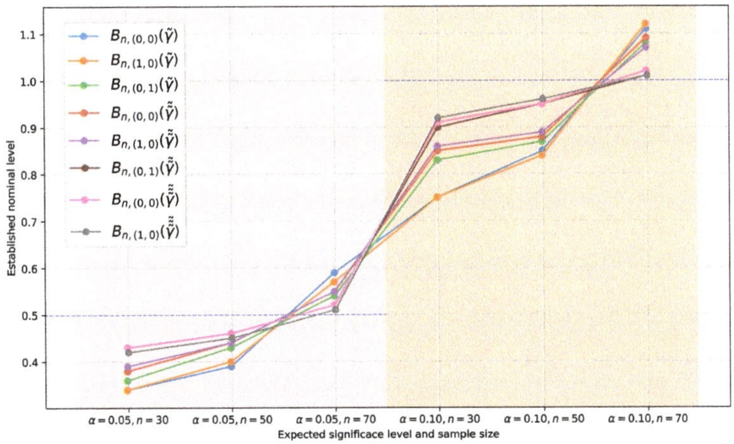

Figure A14. Simulation results for the probability of type I error for $\gamma = (0.30, 0.30, 0.202500)$.

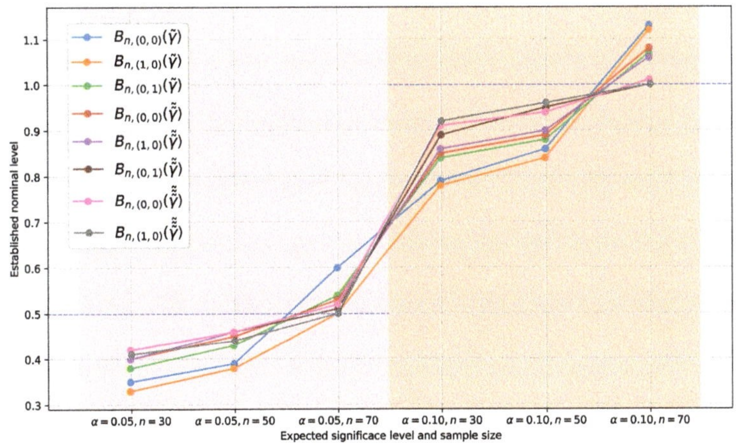

Figure A15. Simulation results for the probability of type I error for $\gamma = (0.31, 0.31, 0.208475)$.

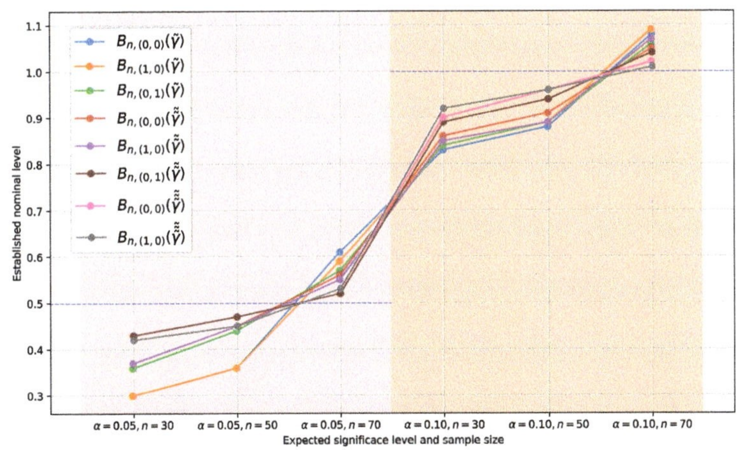

Figure A16. Simulation results for the probability of type I error for $\gamma = (0.29, 0.30, 0.199475)$.

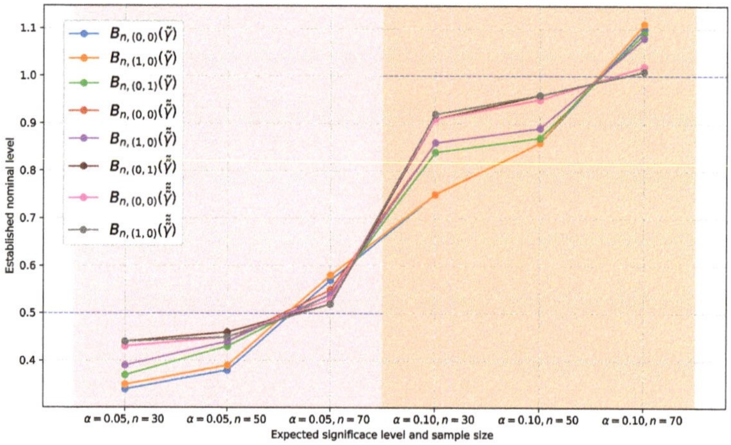

Figure A17. Simulation results for the probability of type I error for $\gamma = (0.30, 0.31, 0.205476)$.

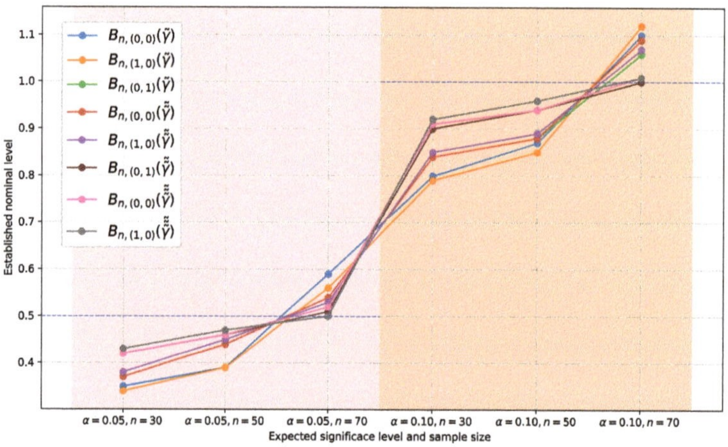

Figure A18. Simulation results for the probability of type I error for $\gamma = (0.30, 0.32, 0.208408)$.

References

1. Shi, P.; Valdez, E. Multivariate Negative Binomial Models for Insurance Claim Counts. *Insur. Math. Econ.* **2014**, *55*, 18–29. [CrossRef]
2. Van Gemert, D.; Van Ophem, J.C.M. Modelling the Scores of Premier League Football Matches. In *Economics, Management and Optimization in Sports*; Springer: Berlin/Heidelberg, Germany, 2004.
3. Krkošek, M.; Connors, B.M.; Lewis, M.A.; Poulin, R. Allee effects may slow the spread of parasites in a coastal marine ecosystem. *Am. Nat.* **2012**, *179*, 401–412. [CrossRef] [PubMed]
4. Arbous, A.G.; Kerrich, J.E. Accident Statistics and the Concept of Accident-Proneness. *Biometrics* **1951**, *7*, 340–432. [CrossRef]
5. Edwards, C.B.; Gurland. J. A Class of Distributions Applicable to Accidents. *J. Am. Stat. Assoc.* **1961**, *56*, 503–517. [CrossRef]
6. Holgate, P. Bivariate generalizations of Neyman's Type A distribution. *Biometrika* **1966**, *53*, 241–245. [CrossRef]
7. Maher, M.J. A bivariate negative binomial model to explain traffic accident migration. *Accid. Anal. Prev.* **1990**, *22*, 487–498. . [CrossRef]
8. Kopocińska, I. Bivariate negative binomial distribution of the Marshall-Olkin type. *Appl. Math.* **1999**, *25*, 457–461. [CrossRef]
9. González-Albornoz, P.; Novoa-Muñoz, F. Goodness-of-Fit Test for the Bivariate Hermite Distribution. *Axioms* **2023**, *12*, 7. [CrossRef]
10. Heller, B. A Goodness-of-Fit test for the Negative Binomial Distribution applicable to Large Sets of Small Samples. *Dev. Water Sci.* **1986**, *27*, 215–220. [CrossRef]

11. Beltrán-Beltrán, J.I.; O'Reilly, F.J. On goodness of fit tests for the Poisson, negative binomial and binomial distributions. *Stat. Pap.* **2019**, *60*, 1–18. [CrossRef]
12. Meintanis, S.G. A new goodness-of-fit test for certain bivariate distributions applicable to traffic accidents. *Stat. Methodol.* **2007**, *4*, 22–34. [CrossRef]
13. Hudecová, Š.; Hušková, M.; Meintanis, S.G. Goodness-of-Fit Tests for Bivariate Time Series of Counts. *Econometrics* **2021**, *9*, 10. [CrossRef]
14. Wang, H.; Weiß, C.H.; Zhang, M. Goodness-of-fit testing in bivariate count time series based on a bivariate dispersion index. *AStA Adv. Stat. Anal.* **2024**. [CrossRef]
15. Novoa-Muñoz, F. Goodness-of-fit tests for the bivariate Poisson distribution. *Commun. Stat. Simul. Comput.* **2019**, *50*, 1998–2014. [CrossRef]
16. Novoa-Muñoz, F.; Jiménez-Gamero, M.D. A goodness-of-fit test for the multivariate Poisson distribution. *SORT* **2016**, *40*, 113–138.
17. Novoa-Muñoz, F.; Jiménez-Gamero, M.D. Testing for the bivariate Poisson distribution. *Metrika* **2014**, *77*, 771–793. [CrossRef]
18. Novoa-Muñoz, F. Implementation of a Parallel Algorithm to Simulate the Type I Error Probability. *Mathematics* **2024**, *12*, 1686. [CrossRef]
19. Kocherlakota, S.; Kocherlakota, K. *Bivariate Discrete Distributions*; John Wiley & Sons: Hoboken, NJ, USA, 1992.
20. Subrahmaniam, K. A test for "intrinsic correlation" in the Theory of Accident Proneness. *J. R. Stat. Soc. Ser. B Methodol.* **1966**, *28*, 180–189. Available online: http://www.jstor.org/stable/2984284 (accessed on 12 February 2023). [CrossRef]
21. Min, C.; Ong, S.; Srivastava, H.M. A class of bivariate negative binomial distributions with different index parameters in the marginals. *Appl. Math. Comput.* **2010**, *217*, 3069–3087. [CrossRef]
22. Baringhaus, L.; Henze, N. Cramér-von Mises distance: Probabilistic interpretation, confidence intervals, and neighborhood-of-model validation. *J. Nonparametr. Stat.* **2017**, *29*, 167–188. [CrossRef]
23. Papageorgiou, H.; Loukas, S. Conditional even point estimation for bivariate discrete distributions. *Commun. Stat. Theory Methods* **1988**, *17*, 3403–3412. [CrossRef]
24. Serfling, R.J. *Approximation Theorems of Mathematical Statistics*; Wiley: New York, NY, USA, 1980.
25. Kundu, S.; Majumdar, S.; Mukherjee, K. Central limits theorems revisited. *Stat. Prob. Lett.* **2000**, *47*, 265–275. [CrossRef]
26. Subrahmaniam, K.; Subrahmaniam, K. On the Estimation of the Parameters in the Bivariate Negative Binomial Distribution. *J. R. Stat. Soc. Ser. B Methodol.* **1973**, *35*, 131–146. [CrossRef]
27. Lehmann, E.L.; Romano, J.P. *Testing Statistical Hypotheses*; Springer: New York, NY, USA, 2005.
28. R Core Team. *R: A Language and Environment for Statistical Computing*; R Foundation for Statistical Computing, Vienna, Austria, 2021. Available online: https://www.R-project.org/ (accessed on 10 January 2021).
29. Loukas, S.; Kemp, C.D. The Index of Dispersion Test for the Bivariate Poisson Distribution. *Biometrics* **1986**, *47*, 941–948. [CrossRef]
30. Rayner, J.C.W.; Best, D.J. Smooth Tests for the Bivariate Poisson Distribution. *Aust. N. Z. J. Stat.* **1995**, *47*, 233–245. [CrossRef]
31. Gürtler, N.; Henze, N. Recent and classical goodness-of-fit tests for the Poisson distribution. *J. Stat. Planningand Inference* **2000**, *90*, 207–225. [CrossRef]
32. Available online: https://www.nlhpc.cl (accessed on 15 January 2021).
33. Dunn, J.E. Characterization of the Bivariate Negative Binomial Distribution. *J. Ark. Acad. Sci.* **1967**, *21*, 77–86.
34. Gillings, D.B. Some further results for bivariate generalizations of the Neyman type A distribution. *Biometrics* **1974**, *30*, 619–628. [CrossRef]
35. Crockett, N.G. A quick test of fit of a bivariate distribution. In *Interactive Statistics*; McNeil, D., Ed.; Elsevier: Amsterdam, The Netherlands, 1979; pp. 185–191.
36. Available online: https://www.kaggle.com/ (accessed on 14 December 2024).

axioms

MDPI

Article

Optimal Minimax Rate of Smoothing Parameter in Distributed Nonparametric Specification Test

Peili Liu [1,†], Yanyan Zhao [1,*,†], Libai Xu [2] and Tao Wang [3]

1 Department of Biostatistics, School of Public Health, Shandong University, Jinan 250021, China; liupeili@mail.sdu.edu.cn
2 School of Mathematical Sciences, Soochow University, Suzhou 215006, China; lbxu@suda.edu.cn
3 School of Mathematics and Statistics, Huaiyin Normal University, Huai'an 223300, China; 8201711075@hytc.edu.cn
* Correspondence: yanyan.zhao@sdu.edu.cn
† These authors contributed equally to this work.

Abstract: A model specification test is a statistical procedure used to assess whether a given statistical model accurately represents the underlying data-generating process. The smoothing-based nonparametric specification test is widely used due to its efficiency against "singular" local alternatives. However, large modern datasets create various computational problems when implementing the nonparametric specification test. The divide-and-conquer algorithm is highly effective for handling large datasets, as it can break down a large dataset into more manageable datasets. By applying divide-and-conquer, the nonparametric specification test can handle the computational problems induced by the massive size of the modern datasets, leading to improved scalability and efficiency and reduced processing time. However, the selection of smoothing parameters for optimal power of the distributed algorithm is an important problem. The rate of the smoothing parameter that ensures rate optimality of the test in the context of testing the specification of a nonlinear parametric regression function is studied in the literature. In this paper, we verified the uniqueness of the rate of the smoothing parameter that ensures the rate optimality of divide-and-conquer-based tests. By employing a penalty method to select the smoothing parameter, we obtain a test with an asymptotic normal null distribution and adaptiveness properties. The performance of this test is further illustrated through numerical simulations.

Keywords: divide-and-conquer; optimal minimax rate; model specification test; bandwidth

MSC: 62-08; 62G10

1. Introduction

Big datasets characterized by large sample sizes N and/or high dimension p are increasingly accessible. In this paper, we focus on datasets with massive sample size N and low dimension p. However, directly making inferences from such large datasets is computationally infeasible due to limitations in processor memory, which makes selecting an appropriate model for big data particularly challenging. The divide-and-conquer approach is intuitive and has been widely employed across various fields to tackle diverse problems. Zaremba et al. [1] utilized this strategy to address two-sample test problems. In situations involving large sample sizes or high-dimensional predictors, Chen and Xie [2] applied the divide-and-conquer methodology for variable selection in generalized linear models. Battey et al. [3] integrated the divide-and-conquer algorithm with high-dimensional hypothesis testing and estimation. Additionally, as noted in [4], samples in big datasets are often aggregated from multiple sources. Therefore, feasible and robust specification testing methods, essential for addressing model misspecification, are critical for handling massive datasets.

Suppose we have a sequence of independent observations $\{(y_i, \mathbf{x}_i)\}_{i=1}^N$ drawn from a population $(Y, \mathbf{X}) \in \mathbb{R} \times [0,1]^p$, where the unknown regression function $E(Y \mid \mathbf{X} = \mathbf{x}) = m(\mathbf{x})$ is assumed to be smooth. In this context, a specification test is necessary to assess the functional form of the regression and justify the use of a parametric model. Given a parametric family of known real functions $g(\mathbf{x}; \boldsymbol{\theta})$, the null and alternative hypotheses can be described as follows:

$$H_0 : m(\mathbf{x}) = g(\mathbf{x}, \boldsymbol{\theta}_0) \quad \text{for some } \boldsymbol{\theta}_0 \in \Theta, \tag{1}$$

$$H_1 : m(\mathbf{x}) \neq g(\mathbf{x}, \boldsymbol{\theta}_0) \quad \text{for all } \boldsymbol{\theta}_0 \in \Theta, \tag{2}$$

where $\Theta \subset \mathbb{R}^q$ denotes the parameter space. This hypothesis testing problem has been widely studied in the literature. One category of approach is to measure the distance between the estimator under the null and the nonparametric estimator under alternative models (see Hardle and Mammen [5], Neumeyer and Van Keilegom [6], González-Manteiga and Crujeiras [7] and the references therein). Another competing approach relies on the empirical process of the residuals from the parametric model [8,9]. An important criterion for evaluating the behavior of these tests is their power performance under local alternatives (see, e.g., [10]). Additionally, Ingster [11,12] proposed an alternative approach to investigating the asymptotic power properties of tests via the minimax approach. Guerre and Lavergne [13] further provided the optimal minimax rate for the smoothing parameter that ensures the rate optimality of the test in the context of testing the specification of a nonlinear parametric regression function. Conditional on a subset of covariates in regression modeling, Cai et al. [14] proposed a significance test for the partial mean independence problem based on machine learning methods and data splitting. Tan and Zhu [15] proposed a residual-marked empirical process that adapts to the underlying model, forming the basis of a goodness-of-fit test for parametric single-index models with a diverging number of predictors. However, existing methods that work well for moderate-sized datasets are not feasible for massive datasets due to computational limitations. Han et al. [16] developed an optimal sampling strategy to select a small subset from a large pool of data to reduce the computation budget for model checking big data. When dealing with test statistics that are quadratic forms [5,17], the computational complexity of the quadratic form test statistic is $O(N^2)$, which presents a significant computational burden for large-scale data.

To address this issue, a divide-and-conquer-based test statistic was proposed in [18,19]. Zhao et al. [18] incorporated a divide-and-conquer strategy into [17] a nonparametric test statistic along with a data-driven bandwidth selection procedure. However, this integrated approach can easily inflate the type I error rate. To mitigate issues associated with choosing smoothing parameters and preserving the type-I error rate, Ref. Zhao et al. [19] proposed randomly splitting the observations into two subsets. In the first subset, an "optimal" smoothing parameter is selected based on a straightforward criterion. Subsequently, a lack-of-fit test grounded in asymptotic theory is conducted using the second subset. This data-splitting strategy effectively controls the type-I error rate. However, the sample splitting will reduce the power, as only a subset of the sample is used to construct the test statistics. Furthermore, the uniqueness of the rate of the smoothing parameter, which ensures the rate optimality of the divide-and-conquer-based test statistic, is not addressed in [18,19]. In this paper, we establish and verify the uniqueness of the rate for the smoothing parameter that guarantees the rate optimality of the divide-and-conquer-based test statistic.

Moreover, it is well known that the optimal smoothing parameters for testing differ from those that are optimal for estimation [11,12,20]. As a result, there has been growing interest in adaptive testing methods. One approach is to consider a set of suitable values for the bandwidth and proceed from there, as discussed in [21,22]. In this paper, we integrate the smoothing parameter selection method in [22] with the divide-and-conquer-based test statistic proposed in [18]. This combination leads to a computationally feasible and adaptive test statistic which retains its asymptotic normality under the null hypothesis.

The paper is organized as follows: Section 2 describes the test statistics and their corresponding asymptotic behavior under the null hypothesis. In Section 3, we demonstrate the unique rate of the smoothing parameter that ensures rate optimality in the DZH test. Section 4 presents simulation studies for illustration. The proofs of the theorems are provided in Section 5.

2. The Divide-and-Conquer-Based Test Statistics

The distributed test statistic proposed in Zhao et al. [18] is based on the test statistic in Zheng [17], where the kernel method is used to estimate the conditional moment $E\{\zeta_i E(\zeta_i \mid \mathbf{X}_i) f(\mathbf{X}_i)\}$, $\zeta_i = y_i - g(\mathbf{x}_i; \boldsymbol{\theta}_0)$, and $f(\cdot)$ is the density function of $\mathbf{x}_i$. The kernel-based sample estimator of the quantity is

$$Q_N(h_N) = \frac{1}{N(N-1)} \sum_{i=1}^{N} \sum_{j \neq i}^{N} \mathcal{K}_{h_N}(\mathbf{x}_i - \mathbf{x}_j) e_i e_j,$$

where $\mathcal{K}_{h_N}(\cdot) = \mathcal{K}(\cdot / h_N)/h_N^p$ denotes a p-dimensional kernel function, h_N is the bandwidth depending on N, $e_i = y_i - g(\mathbf{x}_i, \hat{\boldsymbol{\theta}}_N)$, and $\hat{\boldsymbol{\theta}}_N$ is an estimate of $\boldsymbol{\theta}_0$ under the null hypothesis.

When handling exceptionally large datasets where the sample size N becomes unmanageable, the test statistics combined with the divide-and-conquer procedure is proposed in Zhao et al. [18]. Initially, the dataset is partitioned into K equally sized subsets, each containing n observations. The test statistic based on the observations in the kth subset is

$$V_k(h_n) = \frac{1}{n(n-1)} \sum_{i=1}^{n} \sum_{j \neq i}^{n} \mathcal{K}_{h_n}\left(\mathbf{x}_{ik} - \mathbf{x}_{jk}\right) e_{ik} e_{jk},$$

where e_{ik}'s are the fitted residuals with $\{(\mathbf{x}_{ik}, y_{ik})\}_{i=1}^{n}$. As $nh_n^{p/2} V_k(h_n)$ is asymptotically normal with mean zero and δ^2 under mild conditions [17], where

$$\delta^2 = 2 \int \mathcal{K}^2(\mathbf{u}) d\mathbf{u} \int \{\sigma^2(\mathbf{x})\}^2 f^2(\mathbf{x}) d\mathbf{x},\ \sigma^2(\mathbf{x}) = E(\varepsilon_i^2 \mid \mathbf{x}),\ \varepsilon_i = y_i - m(\mathbf{x}_i)$$

Then, Zhao et al. [18] combined the test statistic by taking an average,

$$T_N(h_n) = \frac{1}{K} \sum_{k=1}^{K} \frac{V_k(h_n)}{\widehat{\delta}(h_n)}, \tag{3}$$

where $\widehat{\delta}^2(h_n)$ is an estimate of δ^2. A natural estimator is $\widehat{\delta}^2(h_n) = K^{-1} \sum_{k=1}^{K} \widehat{\delta}_k^2(h_n)$, where

$$\widehat{\delta}_k^2(h_n) = \frac{2}{n(n-1)} \sum_{i=1}^{n} \sum_{j \neq i}^{n} h_n^p \mathcal{K}_{h_n}^2\left(\mathbf{x}_{ik} - \mathbf{x}_{jk}\right) e_{ik}^2 e_{jk}^2$$

is a consistent estimate of δ^2 based on the kth subset. The test based on statistic $T_N(h_n)$ is denoted as the DZH test in [18]. $T_N(h_n)$ is asymptotic normal under the null hypothesis provided some mild conditions [18]. In this paper, we study the asymptotic behavior of $T_N(h_n)$ by relaxing $nh_n^p/\ln n \to \infty$ to $nh_n^p \to \infty$.

Assumption 1. *The density function $f(\mathbf{x})$ of $\mathbf{x}$ and its first-order derivatives are uniformly bounded, $0 \le \underline{f} \le f(\mathbf{x}) \le \bar{f} < \infty, \forall \mathbf{x} \in [0,1]^p$.*

Assumption 2. *Suppose that $E(\varepsilon_i|\mathbf{X}_i) = 0$ and $\sigma^2(\mathbf{x}_i) \le \bar{\sigma}^2$, $E(\varepsilon_i^4|\mathbf{X}_i) = \sigma^4(\mathbf{x}_i) \le C$ uniformly in i. We also assume that $\sigma^2(\mathbf{x}_i)$ is differentiable and that its first-order derivatives are uniformly bounded for all i.*

Assumption 3. *For any $m(\cdot)$, not necessarily in H_0, let*

$$\boldsymbol{\theta}^* = \arg\min_{\boldsymbol{\theta}\in\Theta} E\{m(\mathbf{X}) - g(\mathbf{X};\boldsymbol{\theta})\}^2.$$

Under H_0, $\boldsymbol{\theta}^* = \boldsymbol{\theta}_0$. For any $m(\cdot)$, $\boldsymbol{\theta}^*$ is unique. $\hat{\boldsymbol{\theta}}_n$ is the estimator of $\boldsymbol{\theta}^*$ such that $\sqrt{nK}(\hat{\boldsymbol{\theta}}_n - \boldsymbol{\theta}^*) = O_p(1)$ uniformly with respect to $m(\cdot)$ with $E\{m^4(\mathbf{X})\} \le C < \infty$, i.e.,

$$\forall \eta > 0, \exists \epsilon > 0 : \limsup_{n,K\to\infty} \sup_{E\{m^4(X)\}\le C} P\left(\sqrt{nK}\|\hat{\boldsymbol{\theta}}_n - \boldsymbol{\theta}^*\| > \epsilon\right) \le \eta.$$

Assumption 4. *$g(\cdot,\cdot)$ is uniformly bounded in $\mathbf{x}$ and $\boldsymbol{\theta}$, is twice continuously differentiable with respect to $\boldsymbol{\theta}$, with first- and second-order derivatives $g_\theta(\cdot,\cdot)$ and $g_{\theta\theta}(\cdot,\cdot)$ uniformly bounded in $\mathbf{x}$ and $\boldsymbol{\theta} \in \Theta$ with upper bound $\bar{g}_\theta$ and $\bar{g}_{\theta\theta}$, respectively.*

Assumption 5. *$\mathcal{K}(u)$ is a nonnegative, bounded, continuous, and symmetric function such that $\int \mathcal{K}(u)du = 1$.*

Assumption 6. *Suppose $\mathcal{K}(u)$'s Fourier transform $\widehat{\mathcal{K}}(u) = \int \exp(-it'u)\mathcal{K}(t)dt$ is strictly positive on its nonempty support.*

Theorem 1 (Null hypothesis). *Suppose Assumptions 1–5 hold; if $nh_n^p \to \infty$, $h_n \to 0$ and $K \to \infty$, then we have $nh_n^{p/2}K^{1/2}T_N(h_n) \xrightarrow{d} N(0,1)$.*

This result suggests that we can reject H_0 at an α level of significance if the normalized $nh_n^{p/2}K^{1/2}T_N(h_n)$ is larger than z_α, where z_α is the upper αth quantile of the standard normal distribution. Given that our focus is to demonstrate the null asymptotic results under the specific bandwidth h_n in Theorem 1, the condition can be relaxed to $nh_n^p \to \infty$. The proof of this theorem closely resembles that of Theorem 1 in Zhao et al. [18], with the exception that we relax the condition from $nh_n^p/\ln n \to \infty$ to $nh_n^p \to \infty$. Therefore, we omit the detailed proof here. However, how to choose an appropriate K via balancing the computation budget and statistical efficiency in practical applications is still an open question.

To develop an adaptive test, we integrate the smoothing parameter selection procedure proposed by Guerre and Lavergne [22] and $T_N(h_n)$. This procedure advocates for a larger smoothing parameter under the null hypothesis and selects h based on this criterion.

$$h_n^* = \underset{h\in\mathcal{H}_n}{\text{argmax}}\{K^{-1}\sum_{k=1}^{K} V_k(h) - \gamma_n \hat{v}_{h,h_0}\}.$$

where $\mathcal{H}_n$ is the given candidate set of h_n and $\hat{v}_{h,h_0}$ is an estimator of the asymptotic null standard deviation of $K^{-1}\sum_{k=1}^{K}(V_k(h) - V_k(h_0))$. The asymptotic null standard deviation of $K^{-1}\sum_{k=1}^{K}(V_k(h) - V_k(h_0))$ is

$$v_{h,h_0} = \sqrt{\frac{2}{Kn(n-1)}\int\left[\mathcal{K}_h(x_1 - x_2) - \mathcal{K}_{h_0}(x_1 - x_2)\right]^2\sigma^2(x_1)\sigma^2(x_2)f(x_1)f(x_2)dx_1dx_2},$$

where an intuitive estimator is

$$\hat{v}_{h,h_0} = \sqrt{\frac{2}{K^2n^2(n-1)^2}\sum_{k=1}^{K}\sum_{i=1}^{n}\sum_{i\neq j}\left[\mathcal{K}_h(x_{ik} - x_{jk}) - \mathcal{K}_{h_0}(x_{ik} - x_{jk})\right]^2 e_{ik}^2e_{jk}^2}.$$

Let h_0 represent the largest element in $\mathcal{H}_n$. The corresponding test statistic based on the selected h_n^* is given by

$$T_N^*(h_n^*) = \frac{1}{K}\sum_{k=1}^{K}\frac{V_k(h_n^*)}{\hat{\delta}(h_0)}$$

Under the null hypothesis, as $\gamma_n \to \infty$, the test statistic $T_N^*(h_n^*)$ tends to favor $T_N(h_0)$. Given that $T_N(h_0)$ is asymptotically normal under Assumptions 1–5, and considering that $nh_0^p \to \infty$, $h_0 \to 0$ and $K \to \infty$, $T_N^*(h_n^*)$ also achieves asymptotic normality under the additional condition that $\gamma_n \to \infty$. Moreover, this statistic exhibits an adaptive property, enhancing its suitability across a broader range of alternative hypotheses.

3. The Unique Rate of the Smoothing Parameter Ensuring Rate-Optimality in the DZH Test

Our previous study in Zhao et al. [18] demonstrated that the optimal power of the test is significantly dependent on the set of bandwidth candidates, $\mathcal{H}_n$. This set should encompass the optimal rate of bandwidth, $\tilde{h}_n \asymp N^{-2/(4s+p)}$ to achieve desired performance. However, the uniqueness of this bandwidth rate was not established. In this section, we will demonstrate the uniqueness of the rate $O(N^{-2/(4s+p)})$, which is critical for ensuring the rate-optimality of the DZH test. Let the Hölder class $C_p(L,s)$ be the set of maps $\ell_N(\cdot)$ from $[0,1]^p$ to $\mathbb{R}$ with

$$C_p(L,s) = \{\ell_N(\cdot) : |\ell_N(\mathbf{x}) - \ell_N(\mathbf{y})| \leq L\|\mathbf{x} - \mathbf{y}\|^s \text{ for all } \mathbf{x},\mathbf{y} \text{ in } [0,1]^p\},\ s \in (0,1],$$
$$C_p(L,s) = \{\ell_N(\cdot) : \text{the } \lfloor s\rfloor\text{th partial derivatives of } \ell_N(\cdot) \text{ are in } C_p(L, s - \lfloor s\rfloor)\},\ s > 1,$$

where $\lfloor s\rfloor$ is the lower integer part of s. Consider the following alternative hypothesis:

$$H_1(\kappa_N\rho_N) = \{m_N(\mathbf{x}) : E\ell_N^2(\mathbf{X},\boldsymbol{\theta}^*) \geq \kappa_N^2\rho_N^2, \ell_N(\cdot) \in C_p(L,s) \text{ for fixed } s > p/4\},$$

where $\ell_N(\cdot) = m_N(\cdot) - g(\cdot;\boldsymbol{\theta}^*)$ and $\rho_N = N^{-2s/(4s+p)}$. ρ_N is the optimal minimax rate for nonparametric specification testing in regression models of known $s > p/4$ for the Hölder class given above (see Guerre and Lavergne [13]).

Theorem 2. *Suppose Assumptions 1–6 hold, $\tilde{h}_n \asymp N^{-2/(4s+p)}$ is the only bandwidth rate such that $I\{nh_n^{p/2}K^{1/2}T_N(h_n) \geq z_\alpha\}$ can consistent uniformly against $\{m_N(\cdot)\}_{N\geq 1} \in H_1(\kappa_N\rho_N)$ for any $\kappa_N \to \infty$.*

4. Simulation Studies

In this section, we present simulation studies to examine the behaviors of the size and power of the tests based on test statistics $T_N(h_n)$ and $T^*(h_n^*)$, denoted as DZH and MD, respectively. We choose $p = 2, N = 2000, 4000, 8000, K = 10, 20, 40$. To demonstrate the adaptiveness of the MD test compared to the DZH test and to maintain the type I error rate for both tests, we select $\mathcal{H}_n = \{h_1 = 0.28, h_2 = 0.14, h_3 = 0.07\}$. For the MD test, we adopt a penalty sequence $\gamma_n = c\sqrt{2\ln(|\mathcal{H}_n|)}$, where $c = 2$, as recommended in Guerre and Lavergne [22], and $|\mathcal{H}_n|$ represents the cardinality of $\mathcal{H}_n$. Two models are used to generate response variable Y.

- M1: $Y = 1 + X_1 + X_2 + \varepsilon$
- M2: $Y = 1 + X_1 + X_2 + \sin(bX_1) + \varepsilon,\ b \in \{0.8, 1, 10\}$

We define the variables X_1 and X_2 where $X_1 = Z_1$ represents a simple assignment, and $X_2 = Z_1 + Z_2/\sqrt{2}$ combines the influences of two independent factors under transformation to maintain variance consistency. To rigorously test the robustness of our proposed statistical method against different models, Z_1 and Z_2 are independently drawn from either the standard normal distribution, which provides a baseline due to its well-known properties, or from the Student's t-distribution with 5 degrees of freedom, known for its heavier tails and greater kurtosis. This choice enables an examination of the test's sensitivity deviating from normality. Furthermore, to assess the impact of error distributions on test performance, we explore three different distributions for the error term ε. These include the standard normal distribution, standardized exponential distribution, and Student's t-distribution with 5 degrees of freedom. Standard normal distribution assumes ideal conditions. The standardized exponential distribution introduces asymmetry and is skewed. Student's t-distribution with 5 degrees of freedom tests the resilience of the method against errors with heavier tails. This comprehensive approach allows us to determine the test's effectiveness and reliability across various scenarios reflective of real-world data complexities. The kernel function $\mathcal{K}$ used is the bivariate standard normal density function. M1 is used to assess the size of the tests. To investigate the power of the test against a high(low)-frequency alternatives, M2 is considered. In model M2, small(large) values of b represent low(high)-frequency alternatives. b is selected to be $\{0.8, 1, 10\}$.

The empirical sizes are reported in Tables 1–4 for different error distributions, demonstrating that both methods effectively maintain the Type-I error rate. We describe the variation trends of the power along sample size N and K in Tables 5 and 6 and Figures 1–4. DZH tests under three distinct bandwidths are included in the power comparison tables. The results indicate that power loss increases with larger K, a consequence of the information loss inherent in the divide-and-conquer procedure. For low-frequency alternatives (when $b = 0.8, 1$), the power of the DZH test improves as h increases. However, for the high-frequency setting $b = 10$, DZH test exhibits an opposite trend with changes in h. The MD test performs comparably to the best scenarios of the DZH test for both low- and high-frequency alternatives, demonstrating its adaptive capability. This adaptiveness makes it suitable for a broader range of alternative hypotheses, accommodating both low- and high-frequency variations. The comparison between Figures 1 and 4 demonstrates that the proposed test exhibits higher power when the variables Z_1 and Z_2 are generated from the Student's t(5) distribution rather than the normal distribution. This underscores the robustness of our method against the heavy-tailed distribution of variables. The power performance of all the tests under the exponential distribution is comparable to that under the normal distribution. However, there is a noticeable decrease in power when the underlying model is the Student's t distribution compared to the other two scenarios. All analyses were conducted using R version 4.3.2.

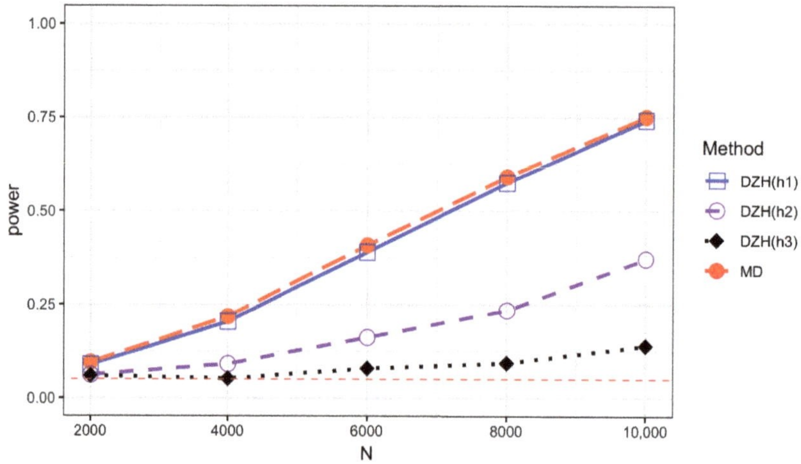

Figure 1. Power comparison of the MD test and DZH test based on different bandwidths under model M2 with $b = 0.8$ and $K = 40$. Error term ε is generated from standard normal distribution.

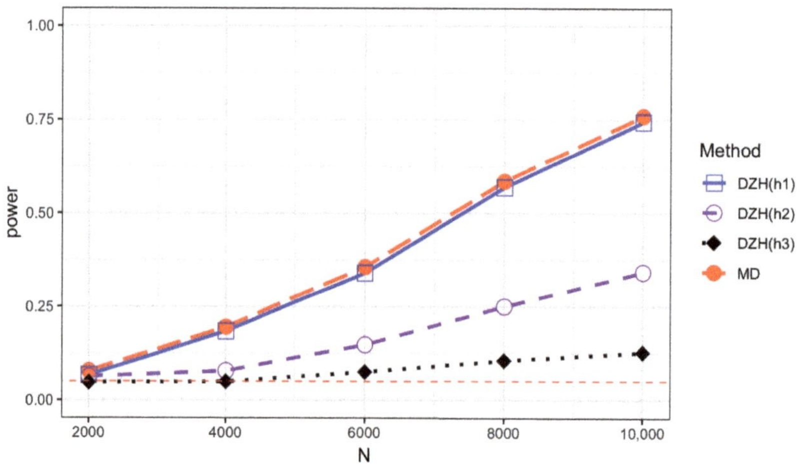

Figure 2. Power comparison of the MD test and DZH test based on different bandwidths under model M2 with $b = 0.8$ and $K = 40$. Error term ε is generated from standardized exponential distribution.

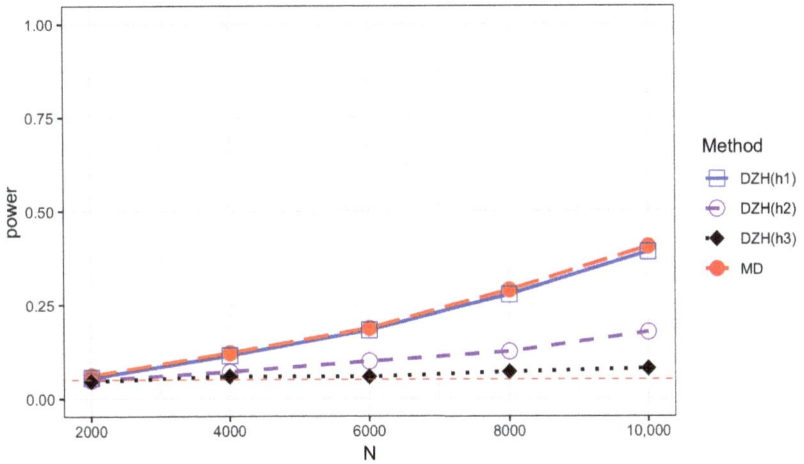

Figure 3. Power comparison of the MD test and DZH test based on different bandwidths under model M2 with $b = 0.8$ and $K = 40$. Error term ε is generated from Student's t distribution with 5 degrees of freedom.

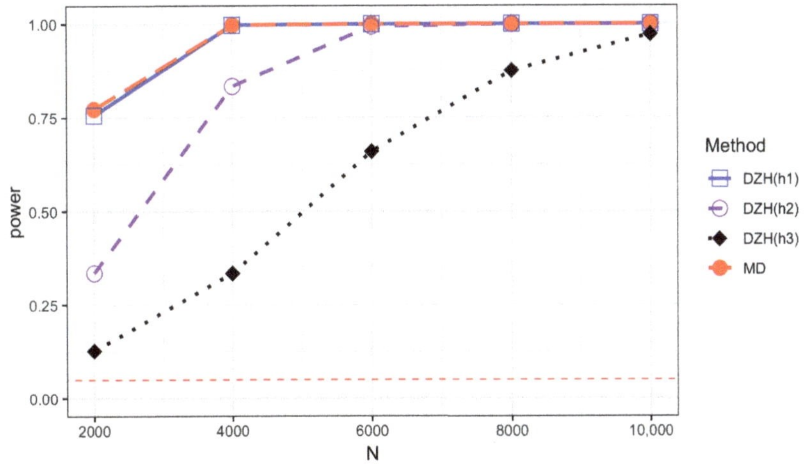

Figure 4. Power comparison of the MD test and DZH test based on different bandwidths under model M2 with $b = 0.8$ and $K = 40$. Error term ε is generated from standard normal distribution. Z_1 and Z_1 are generated from Student's t distribution with 5 degrees of freedom.

Table 1. Empirical sizes for different values of N with $\alpha = 1\%, 5\%, 10\%$ when the error term is normal distribution.

		MD			DZH								
					h_1			h_2			h_3		
N	$\alpha \backslash K$	10	20	40	10	20	40	10	20	40	10	20	40
	1%	1.3	1.3	1.1	0.8	1.0	1.0	0.7	0.7	0.6	0.6	0.9	0.8
2000	5%	5.1	5.8	5.3	4.4	5.3	4.8	5.3	4.3	4.4	4.6	5.8	5.5
	10%	11.1	10.1	11.3	9.9	9.7	10.0	10.3	10.0	10.7	11.6	12.1	11.6
	1%	1.3	1.2	1.1	1.0	1.0	0.9	1.0	0.8	0.7	0.9	0.5	0.6
4000	5%	5.4	5.7	4.8	4.7	5.1	4.2	4.9	4.6	4.6	5.6	4.9	4.3
	10%	9.7	10.4	9.8	9.2	9.9	8.9	9.2	8.8	9.8	10.1	9.2	8.8
	1%	0.5	1.0	0.5	0.4	0.7	0.4	0.4	0.8	0.5	1.0	1.0	0.6
8000	5%	5.2	5.1	4.1	4.2	4.5	3.4	5.0	4.9	4.3	5.2	5.5	4.3
	10%	10.8	10.7	10.2	10.1	9.5	9.3	9.9	9.4	9.3	10.9	10.4	8.7

Table 2. Empirical sizes for different values of N with $\alpha = 1\%, 5\%, 10\%$ when the error term is exponential distribution.

		MD			DZH								
					h_1			h_2			h_3		
N	$\alpha \backslash K$	10	20	40	10	20	40	10	20	40	10	20	40
	1%	1.7	2.2	1.6	1.5	1.9	1.5	0.7	0.8	1.5	1.1	0.7	1.1
2000	5%	5.7	5.5	5.5	5.2	5.1	5.0	5.8	4.9	4.9	6.2	5.1	5.1
	10%	10.6	10.8	9.9	10.0	9.9	9.6	12.1	10.5	9.7	11.5	11.0	9.8
	1%	1.3	0.8	0.7	1.2	0.5	0.7	1.0	0.5	1.2	1.2	0.6	0.6
4000	5%	5.8	5.2	4.8	4.9	4.6	4.3	5.1	4.9	4.6	4.8	4.9	3.8
	10%	11.3	9.7	10.4	10.3	9.0	9.8	8.9	9.4	9.3	8.9	9.8	8.6
	1%	1.0	1.1	1.0	0.9	1.0	0.8	1.4	1.2	0.5	1.1	1.3	0.6
8000	5%	4.9	5.5	3.4	4.3	4.5	2.9	4.5	4.6	2.9	4.7	5.4	4.1
	10%	10.1	10.3	8.1	9.3	9.5	7.4	8.3	9.4	8.3	9.0	9.3	9.8

Table 3. Empirical sizes for different values of N with $\alpha = 1\%, 5\%, 10\%$ when the error term is Student's t distribution.

		MD			DZH								
					h_1			h_2			h_3		
N	$\alpha \backslash K$	10	20	40	10	20	40	10	20	40	10	20	40
	1%	1.1	0.7	1.1	1.1	0.6	0.7	0.6	0.6	0.4	0.7	0.6	0.6
2000	5%	4.8	4.7	4.7	4.3	4.2	4.4	4.0	4.0	4.9	4.3	3.8	4.8
	10%	9.9	9.8	10.4	9.2	9.1	9.2	8.0	8.6	10.1	10.4	8.8	9.0
	1%	1.2	1.6	1.5	1.1	1.1	1.2	1.0	1.3	1.1	0.8	1.1	0.6
4000	5%	5.3	5.6	5.8	4.9	5.1	5.2	5.0	5.5	5.5	5.2	5.4	5.2
	10%	10.0	10.4	10.5	9.0	9.5	9.5	10.2	10.4	9.1	11.6	9.3	9.0
	1%	1.2	1.0	1.5	1.0	0.9	1.2	0.5	0.5	1.3	0.6	0.9	1.1
8000	5%	5.2	3.7	5.2	4.5	3.2	4.5	3.4	3.4	4.8	4.7	4.4	5.0
	10%	9.1	8.8	9.9	8.3	7.9	9.1	8.5	8.6	10.1	9.9	10.1	11.4

Table 4. Empirical sizes for different values of N with $\alpha = 1\%, 5\%, 10\%$ when the Z_1 and Z_2 are generated from Student's t(5) distribution.

		MD			**DZH**								
					h_1			h_2			h_3		
N	$\alpha \setminus K$	**10**	**20**	**40**	**10**	**20**	**40**	**10**	**20**	**40**	**10**	**20**	**40**
	1%	1.2	1.3	1.7	0.9	1.1	1.6	1.5	0.8	1.1	1.0	1.1	1.1
2000	5%	6.0	6.6	6.0	5.6	6.1	5.3	5.0	5.8	5.9	5.3	5.9	5.7
	10%	10.9	10.8	11.5	10.0	10.3	10.5	10.2	10.4	10.2	10.9	10.9	11.0
	1%	0.9	0.5	1.1	0.7	0.5	0.8	0.9	1.0	1.4	1.2	1.3	1.1
4000	5%	5.7	4.9	4.9	4.9	4.3	4.6	4.8	4.2	4.5	5.4	5.4	5.3
	10%	11.3	10.4	9.9	9.6	9.8	8.6	10.1	9.2	9.6	10.8	9.8	10.1
	1%	0.9	1.8	0.5	0.8	1.2	0.3	0.7	1.1	1.1	0.8	1.0	0.6
8000	5%	4.6	5.6	4.6	4.0	4.7	4.3	3.9	5.9	4.3	4.3	4.2	5.5
	10%	9.8	11.7	9.4	9.1	11.1	8.8	9.1	10.8	8.7	8.8	9.4	10.5

Table 5. Empirical power of MD and DZH with $\alpha = 5\%$ when the error term is normal distribution.

		MD			**DZH**								
					h_1			h_2			h_3		
N	b $\setminus K$	**10**	**20**	**40**	**10**	**20**	**40**	**10**	**20**	**40**	**10**	**20**	**40**
2000	1	83.4	60.9	36.8	81.9	59	35.5	45.1	25.9	14.5	17.3	10.9	7.4
	10	100	100	100	18.2	12.4	8.4	100	100	100	100	100	100
4000	1	100	99	88.9	100	98.9	88.3	94.3	74.4	46.5	48.5	27	15.7
	10	100	100	100	62.8	36.6	20	100	100	100	100	100	100
8000	1	100	100	100	100	100	100	100	99.9	94.9	96.3	75.9	48.4
	10	100	100	100	100	93.5	67.1	100	100	100	100	100	100

Table 6. Empirical power of MD and DZH with $\alpha = 5\%$ when the error term is exponential distribution.

		MD			**DZH**								
					h_1			h_2			h_3		
N	b $\setminus K$	**10**	**20**	**40**	**10**	**20**	**40**	**10**	**20**	**40**	**10**	**20**	**40**
2000	1	82.7	61.2	38.2	82.4	59.9	36.7	44.4	26.5	16.1	15.8	9.6	5.6
	10	100	100	100	19.1	11.8	7.5	100	100	99.9	100	100	100
4000	1	99.8	98.5	89.7	99.8	98.4	88.9	94.9	72	44.1	46.9	25.2	13.3
	10	100	100	100	66.3	34.2	19.1	100	100	100	100	100	100
8000	1	100	100	100	100	100	100	100	99.7	96.1	97	78.8	50.6
	10	100	100	100	99.8	94.1	66.4	100	100	100	100	100	100

5. Proofs

Some Lemmas

In this section, we restate three Lemmas in Zhao et al. [18], omitting detailed proofs for brevity. Lemma 2 is restated under assumption $nh_n^p \to \infty$. We assume $q = 1$ without loss of generality. Denote

$$e_{ik} = y_{ik} - g(\mathbf{x}_{ik}; \hat{\theta}_n),\ \varepsilon_{ik} = y_{ik} - m(\mathbf{x}_{ik}),\ u_{ik} = g(\mathbf{x}_{ik}; \hat{\theta}_n) - g(\mathbf{x}_{ik}; \theta^*),\ \ell_{ik} = m(\mathbf{x}_{ik}) - g(\mathbf{x}_{ik}; \theta^*)$$

We introduce the following matrix notations:

$$\mathbf{e}_k = (e_{ik}, 1 \le i \le n)',\ \boldsymbol{\varepsilon}_k = (\varepsilon_{ik}, 1 \le i \le n)',\ \mathbf{u}_k = (u_{ik}, 1 \le i \le n)',\ \boldsymbol{\ell}_k = (\ell_{ik}, 1 \le i \le n)'$$

$$W_k(h_n) = \left[w_{ik,jk} \right]_{1 \le i,j \le n}$$

$$w_{ik,jk} = \begin{cases} \frac{1}{n(n-1)} \mathcal{K}_{h_n}\left(\mathbf{x}_{ik} - \mathbf{x}_{jk}\right), & i \neq j; \\ 0, & i = j \end{cases}$$

Under H_1, $\ell_{ik} \neq 0$,

$$\begin{aligned} V_k &= (\boldsymbol{\ell}_k + \boldsymbol{\varepsilon}_k)' W_k(h_n)(\boldsymbol{\ell}_k + \boldsymbol{\varepsilon}_k) - 2\boldsymbol{\ell}_k' W_k(h_n)\mathbf{u}_k - 2\boldsymbol{\varepsilon}_k' W_k(h_n)\mathbf{u}_k + \mathbf{u}_k' W_k(h_n)\mathbf{u}_k \\ &= V_{1k} - 2V_{2k} - 2V_{3k} + V_{4k} \end{aligned}$$

Under H_0, $\ell_{ik} = 0$, then $V_k = V_{1k} - 2V_{3k} + V_{4k}$, where $V_{1k} = \boldsymbol{\varepsilon}_k' W_k(h_n)\boldsymbol{\varepsilon}_k$. Following Zhao et al. [18], we decompose $nh_n^{p/2}K^{1/2}T_N$ in the following way:

$$\begin{aligned} nh_n^{p/2}K^{1/2}T_N &= nh_n^{p/2}\widehat{\delta}^{-1}K^{-1/2}\sum_{k=1}^{K} V_k \\ &= nh_n^{p/2}\widehat{\delta}^{-1}K^{-1/2}\sum_{k=1}^{K} V_{1k} - 2nh_n^{p/2}\widehat{\delta}^{-1}K^{-1/2}\sum_{k=1}^{K} V_{2k} \\ &\quad - 2nh_n^{p/2}\widehat{\delta}^{-1}K^{-1/2}\sum_{k=1}^{K} V_{3k} + nh_n^{p/2}\widehat{\delta}^{-1}K^{-1/2}\sum_{k=1}^{K} V_{4k} \\ &= \bar{V}_1 - 2\bar{V}_2 - 2\bar{V}_3 + \bar{V}_4 \end{aligned}$$

Lemma 1. *Given Assumptions 1–5, under the null hypothesis, δ^2 can be consistently estimated by $\widehat{\delta}^2(h_n)$, as $nh_n^p \to \infty$, $h_n \to 0$, $K \to \infty$.*

Lemma 2. *Given Assumptions 1–5,*
1. $\bar{V}_2 = O_p(\sqrt{n}h_n^{p/2}\sqrt{E(\ell_N^2(\mathbf{x}))})$ uniformly for $m(\cdot)$ under H_1, as $h_n \to 0$, $nh_n^p \to \infty$, $K \to \infty$.
2. $\bar{V}_3 = O_p(h_n^{p/2}/\sqrt{K}) = o_p(1)$, uniformly for $m(\cdot)$ under H_1 and H_0, as $h_n \to 0$, $nh_n^p \to \infty$, $K \to \infty$.
3. $\bar{V}_4 = O_p(h_n^{p/2}/\sqrt{K}) = o_p(1)$, uniformly for $m(\cdot)$ under H_1 and H_0, as $h_n \to 0$, $nh_n^p \to \infty$, $K \to \infty$.

Lemma 3. *Denote $\tilde{V}_1 = nh_n^{p/2}K^{-1/2}\sum_{k=1}^{K} V_{1k}$. Under Assumptions 1–6, for any $m_N(\cdot) \in H_1(\kappa_N\rho_N)$ and n large enough, where $\rho_N = N^{-\frac{2s}{4s+p}}$, we have*

$$E(\tilde{V}_1) \leq C_1K^{1/2}nh_n^{p/2}E\ell_N^2(\mathbf{X}),\ Var(\tilde{V}_1) \leq C_2nh_n^pE\ell_N^2(\mathbf{x}) + C_3$$

When

$$\kappa_N\rho_N \geq \left(\left(\Lambda_n + \sqrt{r(P_{h_n})}\right)\Big/\left(\Lambda_n - \frac{1}{\sqrt{nh_n^p}}\right)\right)C_0Lh_n^s,\ \Lambda_n = \frac{\sqrt{E(\boldsymbol{\pi}_k'P_{h_n}\boldsymbol{\pi}_k)}}{\sqrt{E(\boldsymbol{\pi}_k'\boldsymbol{\pi}_k)}}$$

we have

$$E(\tilde{V}_1) \geq C_1K^{1/2}nh_n^{p/2}\left(\left(\Lambda_n - \frac{1}{\sqrt{nh_n^p}}\right)\sqrt{E\ell_N^2(\mathbf{x})} - (\Lambda_n + \sqrt{r(P_{h_n})})C_0Lh_n^s\right)^2$$

Proof of Theorem 2. We first construct a alternative $m_N(\cdot)$ based on $\tilde{h}_n$.

$$m_N(\cdot) = g(\cdot;\boldsymbol{\theta}^*) + \ell_N(\cdot)$$

Using the method in Guerre and Lavergne [13] to construct the alternatives $\ell_N(\cdot)$, define

$$I_{\mathbf{t}} = \prod_{i=1}^{p} [t_i \tilde{h}_n, (t_i + 1)\tilde{h}_n)$$

for $\mathbf{t} \in \mathrm{Y}_n$.

$$\mathrm{Y}_n = \{\mathbf{t} : \mathbf{t} = (t_1, \cdots, t_p)' \in \mathbb{N}^p, 0 \le t_i \le \gamma_n - 1\}$$

Then, $I_{\mathbf{t}} \subset [0,1]^p$, without loss of generality, we assume that $\gamma_n = 1/\tilde{h}_n$ is an integer. Let

$$\varphi_{\mathbf{t}}(\mathbf{x}) = \varphi\left(\frac{\mathbf{x} - \mathbf{t}\tilde{h}_n}{\tilde{h}_n}\right), \ \mathbf{t} \in \mathrm{Y}_n$$

where $\varphi_{\mathbf{t}}(\cdot)'s$ are orthogonal with disjoint supports $I_{\mathbf{t}}$, and $\varphi(\cdot)$ is bounded and nonnegative. Let $\{B_{\mathbf{t}}, \mathbf{t} \in \mathrm{Y}_n\}$ be any sequence with $|B_{\mathbf{t}}| = 1$, $\forall \mathbf{t}$,

$$\ell_N(\mathbf{x}) = \kappa_N \rho_N \sum_{\mathbf{t} \in \mathrm{Y}_n} B_{\mathbf{t}} \varphi_{\mathbf{t}}(\mathbf{x}) = \kappa_N \rho_N \sum_{\mathbf{t} \in \mathrm{Y}_n} B_{\mathbf{t}} \varphi\left(\frac{\mathbf{x} - \mathbf{t}\tilde{h}_n}{\tilde{h}_n}\right)$$

Under Assumption 3, we have that there exists a constant C such that $E\{m_N^4(\mathbf{X})\} \le C < \infty$ and $m_N(\cdot) \in H_1(\kappa_N \rho_N)$. Since

$$\inf_{m(\cdot) \in H_1(\kappa_N \rho_N)} P\left\{nh_n^{p/2} K^{1/2} T_N(h_n) \ge z_\alpha\right\} \le P\left\{nh_n^{p/2} K^{1/2} T_N(h_n) \ge z_\alpha\right\}$$

for any $m(\cdot) \in H_1(\kappa_N \rho_N)$. The main idea is that if $I\{nh_n^{p/2} K^{1/2} T_N(h_n) \ge z_\alpha\}$ cannot be consistent against alternatives $m_N(\cdot)$ as $\kappa_N \to \infty$, then we can conclude that it also not consistent uniformly against $m_N(\cdot) \in H_1(\kappa_N \rho_N)$ as $\kappa_N \to \infty$.

Based on Lemma 1–3, the test statistic

$$\begin{aligned} nh_n^{p/2} K^{1/2} T_N(h_n) &= nh_n^{p/2} \widehat{\delta}(h_n)^{-1} K^{-1/2} \sum_{k=1}^{K} V_k \\ &= \widehat{\delta}(h_n)^{-1} \tilde{V}_1 - 2nh_n^{p/2} \widehat{\delta}(h_n)^{-1} K^{-1/2} \sum_{k=1} V_{2k} + o_p(1) \\ &= O_p(1) E(\tilde{V}_1) + O_p\left(\sqrt{Var(\tilde{V}_1)}\right) - 2\tilde{V}_2 + o_p(1) \end{aligned}$$

Without loss of generality, we assume that $\mathcal{K}(\cdot)$ has support $[-1,1]^p$ in the following proofs:

(i): For $h_n = a_N\tilde{h}_n$, $a_N \to \infty$.

$$
\begin{aligned}
E(\tilde{V}_1) &= \sqrt{K}nh_n^{p/2}E(V_{1k}) \\
&= \sqrt{K}nh_n^{p/2}E\left(\frac{1}{h_n^p}\mathcal{K}\left(\frac{X_1 - X_2}{h_n}\right)\ell(X_1)\ell(X_2)\right) \\
&= \sqrt{K}nh_n^{p/2}\int_0^1\int_{(0,1)\cap(\mathbf{x}_2-\mathbf{1}h_n,\mathbf{x}_2+\mathbf{1}h_n)}\frac{1}{h_n^p}\mathcal{K}\left(\frac{\mathbf{x}_1-\mathbf{x}_2}{h_n}\right)\ell(\mathbf{x}_1)\ell(\mathbf{x}_2)f(\mathbf{x}_1)f(\mathbf{x}_2)d\mathbf{x}_1d\mathbf{x}_2 \\
&= \sqrt{K}nh_n^{p/2}\kappa_N^2\rho_N^2\frac{1}{h_n^p}\sum_{\mathbf{t}\in\Upsilon_n}\int_{\mathbf{t}\tilde{h}_n}^{(\mathbf{t}+\mathbf{1})\tilde{h}_n}\int_{(\mathbf{t}\tilde{h}_n,(\mathbf{t}+\mathbf{1})\tilde{h}_n)\cap(\mathbf{x}_2-\mathbf{1}h_n,\mathbf{x}_2+\mathbf{1}h_n)} \\
&\quad \mathcal{K}\left(\frac{\mathbf{x}_1-\mathbf{x}_2}{h_n}\right)\varphi\left(\frac{\mathbf{x}_1-\mathbf{t}\tilde{h}_n}{\tilde{h}_n}\right)\varphi\left(\frac{\mathbf{x}_2-\mathbf{t}\tilde{h}_n}{\tilde{h}_n}\right)f(\mathbf{x}_1)f(\mathbf{x}_2)d\mathbf{x}_1d\mathbf{x}_2 \\
&= \sqrt{K}nh_n^{p/2}\kappa_N^2\rho_N^2\frac{1}{h_n^p}\sum_{\mathbf{t}\in\Upsilon_n}\int_{\mathbf{t}\tilde{h}_n}^{(\mathbf{t}+\mathbf{1})\tilde{h}_n}\int_{\mathbf{t}\tilde{h}_n}^{(\mathbf{t}+\mathbf{1})\tilde{h}_n}\mathcal{K}\left(\frac{\mathbf{x}_1-\mathbf{x}_2}{h_n}\right) \\
&\quad \varphi\left(\frac{\mathbf{x}_1-\mathbf{t}\tilde{h}_n}{\tilde{h}_n}\right)\varphi\left(\frac{\mathbf{x}_2-\mathbf{t}\tilde{h}_n}{\tilde{h}_n}\right)f(\mathbf{x}_1)f(\mathbf{x}_2)d\mathbf{x}_1d\mathbf{x}_2 \\
&= \sqrt{K}nh_n^{p/2}\kappa_N^2\rho_N^2\frac{\tilde{h}_n^{2p}}{h_n^p}\sum_{\mathbf{t}\in\Upsilon_n}\int_0^1\int_0^1\mathcal{K}\left(\frac{(\mathbf{u}-\mathbf{v})\tilde{h}_n}{h_n}\right)\varphi(\mathbf{u})\varphi(\mathbf{v}) \\
&\quad f(\mathbf{u}\tilde{h}_n+\mathbf{t}\tilde{h}_n)f(\mathbf{v}\tilde{h}_n+\mathbf{t}\tilde{h}_n)d\mathbf{u}d\mathbf{v} \\
&= \sqrt{K}nh_n^{p/2}\kappa_N^2\rho_N^2\frac{\tilde{h}_n^{2p}}{h_n^p}\sum_{\mathbf{t}\in\Upsilon_n}\int_0^1\int_0^1\mathcal{K}\left(\frac{\mathbf{u}-\mathbf{v}}{a_N}\right)\varphi(\mathbf{u})\varphi(\mathbf{v}) \\
&\quad f(\mathbf{u}\tilde{h}_n+\mathbf{t}\tilde{h}_n)f(\mathbf{v}\tilde{h}_n+\mathbf{t}\tilde{h}_n)d\mathbf{u}d\mathbf{v} \\
&= \sqrt{K}nh_n^{p/2}\kappa_N^2\rho_N^2\frac{\tilde{h}_n^{p}}{h_n^p}(\tilde{h}_n\gamma_n)^p\left[\int_0^1\varphi(\mathbf{u})f(\mathbf{u}\tilde{h}_n+\mathbf{t}\tilde{h}_n)d\mathbf{u}\right]^2 \\
&= O\left(\frac{\kappa_N^2}{K^{1/2}a_N^{p/2}}\right)
\end{aligned}
$$

(ii): For $h_n = \tilde{h}_n/a_N$, $a_N \to \infty$.

$$
\begin{aligned}
E(\tilde{V}_1) &= \sqrt{K}nh_n^{p/2}E(V_{1k}) \\
&= \sqrt{K}nh_n^{p/2}\int_0^1\int_{(0,1)\cap(\mathbf{x}_2-\mathbf{1}h_n,\mathbf{x}_2+\mathbf{1}h_n)}\frac{1}{h_n^p}\mathcal{K}\left(\frac{\mathbf{x}_1-\mathbf{x}_2}{h_n}\right)\ell(\mathbf{x}_1)\ell(\mathbf{x}_2)f(\mathbf{x}_1)f(\mathbf{x}_2)d\mathbf{x}_1d\mathbf{x}_2 \\
&= \sqrt{K}nh_n^{p/2}\kappa_N^2\rho_N^2\frac{1}{h_n^p}\sum_{\mathbf{t}\in\Upsilon_n}\int_{\mathbf{t}\tilde{h}_n}^{(\mathbf{t}+\mathbf{1})\tilde{h}_n}\int_{(\mathbf{t}\tilde{h}_n,(\mathbf{t}+\mathbf{1})\tilde{h}_n)\cap(\mathbf{x}_2-\mathbf{1}h_n,\mathbf{x}_2+\mathbf{1}h_n)} \\
&\quad \mathcal{K}\left(\frac{\mathbf{x}_1-\mathbf{x}_2}{h_n}\right)\varphi\left(\frac{\mathbf{x}_1-\mathbf{t}\tilde{h}_n}{\tilde{h}_n}\right)\varphi\left(\frac{\mathbf{x}_2-\mathbf{t}\tilde{h}_n}{\tilde{h}_n}\right)f(\mathbf{x}_1)f(\mathbf{x}_2)d\mathbf{x}_1d\mathbf{x}_2 \\
&\leq \sqrt{K}nh_n^{p/2}\kappa_N^2\rho_N^2\tilde{h}_n^p\sum_{\mathbf{t}\in\Upsilon_n}\int_0^1\int_{-1}^1\mathcal{K}(u)\varphi\left(\mathbf{u}\cdot\frac{h_n}{\tilde{h}_n}+\mathbf{v}\right)\varphi(\mathbf{v}) \\
&\quad f(\mathbf{u}h_n+\mathbf{t}\tilde{h}_n+\mathbf{v}\tilde{h}_n)f(\mathbf{v}\tilde{h}_n+\mathbf{t}\tilde{h}_n)d\mathbf{u}d\mathbf{v} \\
&= \sqrt{K}nh_n^{p/2}\kappa_N^2\rho_N^2(\tilde{h}_n\gamma_n)^p\int_0^1\int_{-1}^1\mathcal{K}(u)\varphi\left(\mathbf{u}\cdot\frac{h_n}{\tilde{h}_n}+\mathbf{v}\right)\varphi(\mathbf{v}) \\
&\quad f(\mathbf{u}h_n+\mathbf{t}\tilde{h}_n+\mathbf{v}\tilde{h}_n)f(\mathbf{v}\tilde{h}_n+\mathbf{t}\tilde{h}_n)d\mathbf{u}d\mathbf{v} \\
&= \sqrt{K}nh_n^{p/2}\kappa_N^2\rho_N^2 \\
&= O\left(\frac{\kappa_N^2}{K^{1/2}a_N^{p/2}}\right)
\end{aligned}
$$

Through tedious calculation, we can also get $\sqrt{Var(\tilde{V}_1)} = O(1)$ and $\tilde{V}_2 = o_p(1)$ as $h_n \to 0$ for above two cases. Therefore, for any a_N, there exists κ_N such that $nh_n^{p/2}K^{1/2}T_N(h_n) = O_p(1)$ as $h_n \to 0$. Therefore, we cannot get $P\left\{nh_n^{p/2}K^{1/2}T_N(h_n) \geq z_\alpha\right\} \to 1$. We obtain the same conclusion for $\inf_{m(\cdot)\in H_1(\kappa_N\rho_N)} P\left\{nh_n^{p/2}K^{1/2}T_N(h_n) \geq z_\alpha\right\}$. Thus, the theorem is proved. □

Author Contributions: Conceptualization, Y.Z.; methodology, Y.Z.; formal analysis, P.L. and Y.Z.; investigation, Y.Z. and L.X.; writing—original draft preparation, P.L. and Y.Z.; writing—review and editing, P.L., Y.Z. and L.X.; visualization, P.L., Y.Z. and T.W.; supervision, Y.Z. All authors have read and agreed to the published version of the manuscript.

Funding: This study was supported by the National Natural Science Foundation of China (12201351) and the Natural Science Foundation of Shandong Province (ZR2022QA013), as well as the Natural Science Foundation of the Jiangsu Higher Education Institutions of China (24KJB110024) the Qinglan Project of Jiangsu Province of China [2022], and the Huai'an City Science and Technology Project (HAB202357).

Institutional Review Board Statement: Not applicable.

Data Availability Statement: No new data were created or analyzed in this study. Data sharing is not applicable to this article.

Conflicts of Interest: The authors declare no conflicts of interest. The funders had no role in the design of the study; in the collection, analyses, or interpretation of data; in the writing of the manuscript; or in the decision to publish the results.

References

1. Zaremba, W.; Gretton, A.; Blaschko, M. B-test: A Non-parametric, Low Variance Kernel Two-sample Test. *Adv. Neural Inf. Process. Syst.* **2013**, *26*, 755–763.
2. Chen, X.Y.; Xie, M.G. A split-and-conquer approach for analysis of extraordinarily large data. *Stat. Sin.* **2014**, *24*, 1655–1684.
3. Battey, H.; Fan, J.; Liu, H.; Lu, J.; Zhu, Z. Distributed Estimation and Inference with Statistical Guarantees. *arXiv* **2015**, arXiv:1509.05457.
4. Fan, J.; Han, F.; Liu, H. Challenges of Big Data analysis. *Natl. Sci. Rev.* **2014**, *1*, 293–314. [CrossRef] [PubMed]
5. Hardle, W.; Mammen, E. Comparing nonparametric versus parametric regression fits. *Ann. Statist.* **1993**, *21*, 1926–1947. [CrossRef]
6. Neumeyer, N.; Van Keilegom, I. Estimating the error distribution in nonparametric multiple regression with applications to model testing. *J. Multivar. Anal.* **2010**, *101*, 1067–1078. [CrossRef]
7. González-Manteiga, W.; Crujeiras, R.M. An updated review of Goodness-of-Fit tests for regression models. *Test* **2013**, *22*, 361–411. [CrossRef] [PubMed]
8. Delgado, M. Testing the equality of nonparametric regression curves. *Stat. Probab. Lett.* **1993**, *17*, 199–204. [CrossRef]
9. Bierens, H.J. A consistent conditional moment test of functional form. *Econometrica* **1990**, *58*, 1443–1458. [CrossRef]
10. Hart, J.D. *Nonparametric Smoothing and Lack-of-Fit Tests*, 1st ed.; Springer: New York, NY, USA, 1997.
11. Ingster, Y.I. Minimax nonparametric detection of signals in white Gaussian noise. *Probl. Inf. Transm.* **1982**, *18*, 130–140.
12. Ingster, Y.I. Asymptotically minimax hypothesis testing for nonparametric alternatives I, II, III. *Math. Methods Stat.* **1993**, *2*, 85–114.
13. Guerre, E.; Lavergne, P. Optimal minimax rates for nonparametric specification testing in regression models. *Econom. Theory* **2002**, *18*, 1139–1171. [CrossRef]
14. Cai, L.; Guo, X.; Zhong, W. Test and Measure for Partial Mean Dependence Based on Machine Learning Methods. *J. Am. Stat. Assoc.* **2024**, 1–13.. [CrossRef]
15. Tan, F.; Zhu, L. Adaptive-to-model checking for regressions with diverging number of predictors. *Ann. Stat.* **2019**, *47*, 1960–1994. [CrossRef]
16. Han, Y.; Ma, P.; Ren, H.; Wang, Z. Model checking in large-scale data set via structure-adaptive-sampling. *Stat. Sin.* **2023**, *33*, 303–329.
17. Zheng, J.X. A consistent test of functional form via nonparametric estimation techniques. *J. Econom.* **1996**, *75*, 263–289. [CrossRef]

18. Zhao, Y.; Zou, C.; Wang, Z. A scalable nonparametric specification testing for massive data. *J. Stat. Plan. Inference* **2019**, *200*, 161–175. [CrossRef]
19. Zhao, Y.; Zou, C.; Wang, Z. An adaptive lack of fit test for big data. *Stat. Theory Relat. Fields* **2017**, *1*, 59–68. [CrossRef]
20. Ibragimov, I.A.; Khasminski, R.Z. *Statistical Estimation: Asymptotic Theory*, 1st ed.; Springer: Berlin/Heidelberg, Germany, 1981.
21. Horowitz, J.; Spokoiny, V. An adaptive, rate-optimal test of parametric mean-regression model against a nonparametric alternative. *Econometrica* **2001**, *69*, 599–631. [CrossRef]
22. Guerre, E.; Lavergne, P. Data-driven rate-optimal specification testing in regression models. *Ann. Stat.* **2005**, *33*, 840–870. [CrossRef]

axioms

MDPI

Article

Modified Bimodal Exponential Distribution with Applications

Jimmy Reyes [1], Barry C. Arnold [2], Yolanda M. Gómez [3], Osvaldo Venegas [4,*] and Héctor W. Gómez [1]

[1] Departamento de Estadística y Ciencia de Datos, Facultad de Ciencias Básicas, Universidad de Antofagasta, Antofagasta 1240000, Chile; jimmy.reyes@uantof.cl (J.R.); hector.gomez@uantof.cl (H.W.G.)
[2] Department of Statistics, University of California, Riverside, CA 92521, USA; barry.arnold@ucr.edu
[3] Departamento de Estadística, Facultad de Ciencias, Universidad del Bío-Bío, Concepción 4081112, Chile; ygomez@ubiobio.cl
[4] Departamento de Ciencias Matemáticas y Físicas, Facultad de Ingeniería, Universidad Católica de Temuco, Temuco 4780000, Chile
* Correspondence: ovenegas@uct.cl

Abstract: In this paper, we introduce a new distribution for modeling bimodal data supported on non-negative real numbers and particularly suited with an excess of very small values. This family of distributions is derived by multiplying the exponential distribution by a fourth-degree polynomial, resulting in a model that better fits the shape of the second mode of the empirical distribution of the data. We study the general density of this new family of distributions, along with its properties, moments, and skewness and kurtosis coefficients. A simulation study is performed to estimate parameters by the maximum likelihood method. Additionally, we present two applications to real-world datasets, demonstrating that the new distribution provides a better fit than the bimodal exponential distribution.

Keywords: bimodal; exponential distribution; maximum likelihood

MSC: 62E15; 62F10; 62P99

1. Introduction

Weighted distributions frequently occur in research related to survival analysis, analysis of intervention data, ecology and biomedicine, and other areas. Fisher [1] and Rao [2] introduced the concept of weighted distributions to improve the fit of appropriate statistical models; this idea has been used to select an appropriate model for the data observed (see Rao [3]). A random variable Y follows the weighted distribution if its probability density function (pdf) is given by

$$f_Y(y) = \frac{w(y)f(y)}{E(w(Y))}, \tag{1}$$

where f is a density function, and w is a positive function. Analysis and applications using this methodology can be found in Patil and Ord [4], Patil and Rao [5], Gupta and Kirmani [6], Gupta and Tripathi [7], Gupta and Akman [8], Gupta and Kundu [9], Reyes et al. [10], Hassan and Hijazi [11], Gómez-Déniz et al. [12], Chesneau et al. [13], Alzaghal et al. [14], Cortés et al. [15], and others.

Reyes et al. [10] considered the exponential model, $f(y) = \alpha e^{-\alpha y}$, and the weight function $w(y) = \left(1 - q\alpha\left(y - \frac{1}{\alpha}\right)\right)^2 + 1$; using (1) they constructed and study the bimodal exponential (BE) distribution, the pdf of which is given by

$$f_Y(y;\alpha,q) = \frac{\alpha}{2+q^2}\left[\left(1 - q\alpha\left(y - \frac{1}{\alpha}\right)\right)^2 + 1\right]e^{-\alpha y}, \quad y \geq 0, \tag{2}$$

with $\alpha > 0$ and $q \in \mathbb{R}$. It is denoted by $Y \sim BE(\alpha,q)$. The BE distribution is bimodal and is an extension of the exponential distribution. Furthermore, it can be used to fit datasets containing zeroes and/or very small values. The motivation for studying these families of bimodal distributions stems from the lack of alternative models that can effectively replace mixture distributions, which—as is well known—present estimation problems when using classical approaches like Bayesian methods (see McLachan and Peel [16]; Marin et al. [17]).

The object of the present work is to modify the BE distribution considering a new function $w(\cdot)$ which increases the flexibility of the second mode. We thus obtain a modified bimodal exponential (MBE) distribution, which we denote by $Y \sim MBE(\alpha,q)$. We study its properties, estimating the parameters, and compare it with the BE distribution using a real dataset.

The work is organized as follows. In Section 2, we present the pdf of the MBE distribution and study some of its properties. In Section 3, we study the inferential statistics of the MBE distribution, in particular the moments estimators and maximum likelihood (ML) estimators, and present a simulation study. In Section 4, we present two applications to real-world datasets. Finally, Section 5 provides concluding remarks.

2. Density and Properties

In this section, we present the pdf of the MBE distribution and some of its properties.

Proposition 1. *Let $Y \sim MBE(\alpha,q)$. Then, the density function of Y is given by*

$$f_Y(y) = \frac{\alpha}{1+9q}\left(1 + q\alpha^4\left(y - \frac{1}{\alpha}\right)^4\right)e^{-\alpha y}, \quad y \geq 0, \tag{3}$$

with $\alpha > 0$ defining the rate parameter and $q \geq 0$ defining the shape parameter.

Proof. Considering $f(y) = \alpha e^{-\alpha y}$, $w(y) = 1 + q\alpha^4\left(y - \frac{1}{\alpha}\right)^4$, and using (1), we obtain the result. □

Below, we illustrate graphically the behavior of the density function of the MBE distribution, comparing it with the BE distribution.

Remark 1. *We observe that the MBE can be used to model datasets with an excess of zeroes or very small values, as its support includes zero, and it possesses a mode at zero. We likewise observe that when the parameter $q = 0$, the exponential distribution is obtained as a particular case.*

Proposition 2. *Let $Y \sim MBE(\alpha,q)$. The solutions of*

$$q(\alpha y - 1)^4 - 4q(\alpha y - 1)^3 + 1 = 0, \tag{4}$$

correspond to the anti-mode and the non-zero mode of the distribution of Y.

Proof. This follows directly from analyzing the first derivative of (1) with respect to y. □

The quartic equation in (4) can be solved analytically using the Cardano–Ferrari formulas (for details, see Abramowitz and Stegun [18]). For numerical solutions, the

WolframAlpha computational platform (https://www.wolframalpha.com/) provides an efficient alternative; for more details we refer the reader to Weisstein [19].

Let $Z \sim BE(\alpha, q)$, and let $Y \sim MBE(\alpha, q)$. Table 1 shows the values of the modes for the BE and MBE distributions with the same parameter values as in Figure 1.

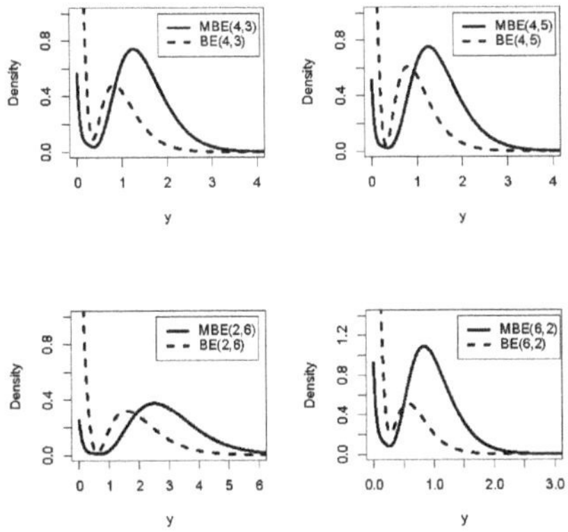

Figure 1. Density function for the MBE and BE distributions for values of α and q.

Table 1. Values of the second modes of the BE and MBE distributions.

α	q	**Modes**
4	3	$M_0(Z) \approx 0.8190$ $M_0(Y) \approx 1.2487$
4	5	$M_0(Z) \approx 0.7950$ $M_0(Y) \approx 1.2492$
2	6	$M_0(Z) \approx 1.5763$ $M_0(Y) \approx 2.4987$
6	2	$M_0(Z) \approx 0.5610$ $M_0(Y) \approx 0.8320$

Proposition 3. *Let $Y \sim MBE(\alpha, q)$ and $Z \sim BE(\alpha, q)$. Then, the height of the second mode of Y is greater than the height of the second mode of Z for $1 \leq q \leq 25.34$, where the second mode of Y is between $\frac{4}{\alpha}$ and $\frac{5}{\alpha}$, and Z becomes $M_0(Z) = \frac{1+2q+\sqrt{q^2-1}}{\alpha q}$.*

Proof. For $q \geq 1$, the second mode of Z is given by $M_0(Z) = \frac{1+2q+\sqrt{q^2-1}}{\alpha q}$ (see Reyes et al. [10]). The first derivative of $f_Y(y)$ is given by

$$f'_Y(y) = -\frac{\alpha^2}{1+9q}(q(\alpha y-1)^4 - 4q(\alpha y-1)^3 + 1)e^{-\alpha y}.$$

Evaluating this at $y = \frac{4}{\alpha}$ and $y = \frac{5}{\alpha}$ yields

$$f'_Y(\frac{4}{\alpha}) = -\frac{\alpha^2}{1+9q}(1-27q)e^{-4} > 0 \quad \text{and} \quad f'_Y(\frac{5}{\alpha}) = -\frac{\alpha^2}{1+9q}e^{-5} < 0.$$

Thus, $\frac{4}{\alpha} < M_0(Y) < \frac{5}{\alpha}$, which implies that the height of the second mode of Y is greater than $f_Z(\frac{5}{\alpha})$. Furthermore, we calculate

$$f_Z(\frac{3}{\alpha}) = \alpha\frac{2-4q+4q^2}{2+q^2}e^{-3} \quad \text{and} \quad f_Y(\frac{5}{\alpha}) = \frac{\alpha}{1+9q}(1+256q)e^{-5}.$$

The inequality $f_Y(\frac{5}{\alpha}) \geq f_Z(\frac{3}{\alpha})$ holds for $1 \leq q \leq 25.34$, as established by solving

$$(256e^{-2} - 36)q^3 + (e^{-2} + 32)q^2 + (512e^{-2} - 14)q + 2(e^{-2} - 1) \geq 0.$$

Since $f_Y(M_0(Y)) > f_Y(\frac{5}{\alpha})$, the proof is complete. □

Proposition 4. *Let $Y \sim MBE(\alpha, q)$. Then, the cumulative distribution function (cdf) of Y is given by*

$$F_Y(y) \;=\; 1 - \frac{e^{-\alpha y}}{1+9q}\Big[\alpha q y(\alpha^3 y^3 + 6\alpha y + 8) + (1+9q)\Big]. \tag{5}$$

Proof. Calculating directly from the definition of the cdf, we have

$$F_Y(y) = \int_0^y f_Y(u)du = \int_0^y \frac{\alpha}{1+9q}\left(1 + q\alpha^4\left(u - \frac{1}{\alpha}\right)^4\right)e^{-\alpha u}du,$$

and the result is obtained by developing the integral. □

Remark 2. *The BE distribution has a unique mode at zero when $q < 1$ (see Reyes et al. [10]); otherwise, like the MBE distribution, it has two modes, as shown in Figure 2. The MBE distribution always has two modes: one at zero and another at a point $x_0 > 0$, with the latter having a greater height.*

Below, we illustrate graphically the behavior of the pdf and cdf of the MBE distribution.

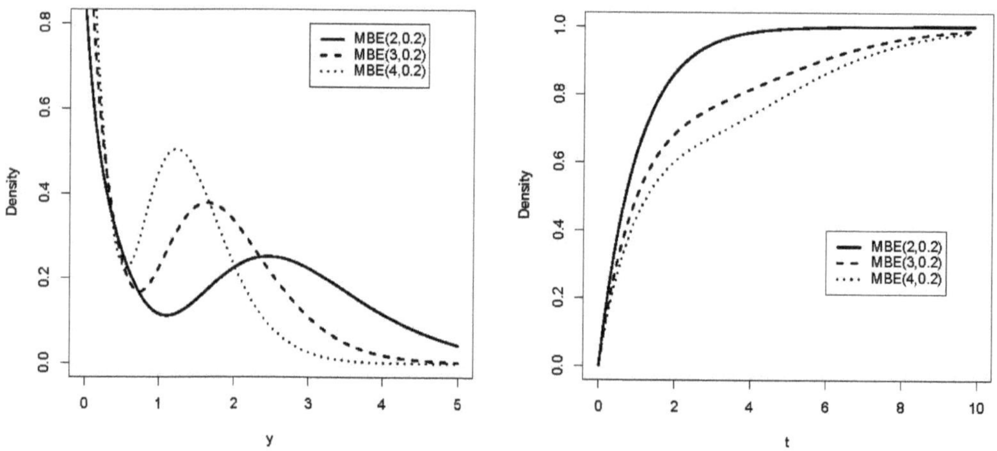

Figure 2. Pdf and cdf for the MBE distribution for values of α and q.

2.1. Order Statistics

Let $Y_1, \ldots, Y_n$ be a random sample of the random variable $Y \sim MBE(\alpha, q)$; let us denote by $Y_{(j)}$ the jth−order statistics $j \in \{1, \ldots, n\}$.

Proposition 5. *The pdf of $Y_{(j)}$ is*

$$\begin{aligned} f_{Y_{(j)}}(y) \;=\; & \frac{n!\alpha(1+q(\alpha y-1)^4)e^{-\alpha y(n-j+1)}}{(j-1)!(n-j)!(1+9q)^n}\{1+9q - e^{-\alpha y}(\alpha q y(\alpha^3 y^3 + 6\alpha y + 8) + 1 + 9q)\}^{j-1} \\ & \times\{\alpha q y(\alpha^3 y^3 + 6\alpha y + 8) + 1 + 9q\}^{n-j}, \quad y > 0. \end{aligned}$$

In particular, the pdf of the minimum, $Y_{(1)}$, is

$$f_{Y_{(1)}}(y) = \frac{n\alpha(1+q(\alpha y-1)^4)e^{-n\alpha y}}{(1+9q)^n}\left\{\alpha q y(\alpha^3 y^3+6\alpha y+8)+1+9q\right\}^{n-1}, \quad y>0.$$

and the pdf of the maximum, $Y_{(n)}$, is

$$f_{Y_{(n)}}(y) = \frac{n\alpha(1+q(\alpha y-1)^4)e^{-\alpha y}}{(1+9q)^n}\left\{1+9q-e^{-\alpha y}\left(\alpha q y(\alpha^3 y^3+6\alpha y+8)+1+9q\right)\right\}^{n-1}, \quad y>0.$$

Proof. Since we are dealing with an absolutely continuous model, the pdf of the $jth-$order statistics is obtained by applying

$$f_{Y_{(j)}}(y) = \frac{n!}{(j-1)!(n-j)!}\, f(y)\, [F(y)]^{j-1}\, [1-F(y)]^{n-j}, \quad j \in \{1,\ldots,n\}$$

where F and f denote the cdf and pdf of the parent distribution, $Y \sim MBE(\alpha, q)$, in this case. More precisely, substituting Equations (3) and (5) yields the result. □

2.2. The Reliability and Hazard Rate Functions

Two important reliability measures are the reliability function and the hazard (failure) rate function. The reliability function of a random variable Y is defined by $R_Y(t) = 1 - F_Y(t)$, where F_Y denotes the cdf of Y. The hazard rate function is defined by $h_Y(t) = f_Y(t)/(1 - F_Y(t))$. For the BE distribution, as a direct consequence of Proposition 1 and Proposition 2, both reliability measures can be expressed in closed form. The corresponding expressions are obtained in a straightforward manner.

Proposition 6. *Let $Y \sim MBE(\alpha, q)$. Then, the hazard function of Y is given by*

$$h(t) = \frac{\alpha\left[1+q(\alpha t-1)^4\right]}{\alpha q t(\alpha^3 t^3+6\alpha t+8)+1+9q}. \quad (6)$$

Proof. By definition of the hazard function, we have

$$h_Y(t) = f_Y(t)/(1-F_Y(t)),$$

and then by replacing $f_Y(t)$ and $F_Y(t)$, the result is obtained. □

To prove the following proposition, we will use the theorem in Glaser [20], together with the idea that to study the behavior of the harzard function $h(t)$, we can examine the function $\eta(t)$ defined by $\eta(t) = -f'(t)/f(t)$, where $f(t)$ is the pdf given in (1).

Proposition 7. *Let $T \sim MBE(\alpha, q)$. Then, the hazard function of T has a bathtub shape.*

Proof. Using item c) of Glaser's Theorem [20], we define the functions

$$\eta(t) = \alpha - \frac{4\alpha q(\alpha t-1)^3}{1+q(\alpha t-1)^4},$$

and the function $g(t) = 1/h(t)$. Their first derivatives are, respectively,

$$\eta'(t) = \frac{4\alpha^2 q(\alpha t-1)^2(q(\alpha t-1)^4-3)}{(1+q(\alpha t-1)^4)^2}, \quad \text{and} \quad g'(t) = \eta(t)/h(t) - 1.$$

If $q \leq 3$, we obtain the following: $\eta'(t) < 0$ in $t \in (0, t_0)$, $\eta'(t_0) = 0$, and $\eta'(t) > 0$ for all $t > t_0$ when $t_0 = \frac{1}{\alpha}\left(1 + \sqrt[4]{\frac{3}{q}}\right)$.

On the other hand, we observe that as $t \to 0^+$, $h(t) \to \alpha(1+q)/(1+9q)$, and $\eta(t) \to \alpha(1+5q)/(1+q)$, which implies that $\eta(t) > h(t)$ as $t \to 0^+$. Additionally, evaluating these functions at t_0, we have

$$h(t_0) = \frac{\alpha}{6\sqrt[4]{3q^3} + \sqrt[4]{27q} + 3\sqrt{3q} + 6q + 1} \quad \text{and} \quad \eta(t_0) = \alpha(1 - \sqrt[4]{27q}),$$

yielding $\eta(t_0) < h(t_0)$. Since $\eta - h$ is a continuous function for all t, there exists $y_0 < t_0$ such that $\eta(y_0) = h(y_0)$. Consequently, $g'(y_0) = 0$; by applying item $c)$ of Glaser's Theorem [20], the result follows.

If $q > 3$, η' is null at three points:

$$t_1 = \frac{1}{\alpha}\left(1 - \sqrt[4]{\frac{3}{q}}\right), \quad t_2 = \frac{1}{\alpha} \quad \text{and} \quad t_3 = \frac{1}{\alpha}\left(1 + \sqrt[4]{\frac{3}{q}}\right).$$

This is because

$$\eta''(t_3) = 3\alpha\sqrt[4]{3q^3} > 0.$$

Since $\eta(t)$ has a local minimum at t_3, the hazard function also attains a local minimum at t_3, resulting in a bathtub-shaped hazard function. □

Figure 3 presents the hazard rate function of the MBE distribution for various parameter configurations. Notably, the hazard function exhibits the characteristic bathtub shape, a feature frequently encountered in reliability and survival analysis.

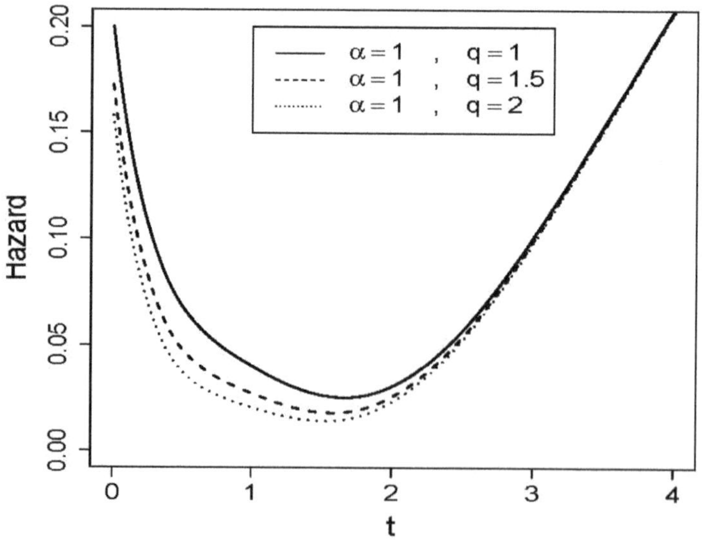

Figure 3. The hazard rate functions for the MBE distribution.

2.3. Moments

The moments of a random variable with modified bimodal exponential distribution are given in the following proposition.

Proposition 8. *If $Y \sim MEB(\alpha, q)$, the r-th moment of Y is given by*

$$\mu_r = \mathbb{E}[Y^r] \quad = \quad \frac{r!}{\alpha^r(1+9q)}[1 + q(r^4 + 6r^3 + 17r^2 + 20r + 9)]. \tag{7}$$

Proof. Calculating directly from the definition, we have

$$\mu_r = \mathbb{E}[Y^r] = \int_0^\infty \frac{y^r}{1+9q}\left(1 + q(\alpha y - 1)^4\right)\alpha e^{-\alpha y} dy.$$

The result is obtained by developing the integral. □

Corollary 1. *Let $Y \sim MEB(\alpha, q)$; then,*

$$\mu_1 = \mathbb{E}(Y) = \frac{1}{\alpha(1+9q)}(1+53q), \quad \mu_2 = \mathbb{E}(Y^2) = \frac{2}{\alpha^2(1+9q)}(1+181q),$$

$$\mu_3 = \mathbb{E}\left(Y^3\right) = \frac{6}{\alpha^3(1+9q)}(1+465q), \quad \mu_4 = \mathbb{E}(Y^4) = \frac{24}{\alpha^4(1+9q)}(1+1001q).$$

Proof. This is an immediate consequence of the previous proposition. □

Corollary 2. *Let $Y \sim MBE(\alpha, q)$; then, the expectation and the variance of Y are given by*

$$\mathbb{E}(Y) = \frac{1}{\alpha(1+9q)}(1+53q), \quad and \quad Var(Y) = \frac{1}{\alpha^2(9q+1)^2}\left(449q^2 + 274q + 1\right).$$

Corollary 3. *Let $Y \sim MBE(\alpha, q)$; then, the asymmetry coefficient (β_1) and the kurtosis coefficient (β_2) of Y are given by*

$$\beta_1 = \frac{5722q^3 - 2634q^2 + 1758q + 2}{(449q^2 + 274q + 1)^{\frac{3}{2}}}, \quad and \quad \beta_2 = \frac{842{,}505q^4 + 891{,}780q^3 + 81{,}654q^2 + 14{,}724q + 9}{(449q^2 + 274q + 1)^2},$$

respectively.

Proof. Using the expressions obtained in the previous corollary and the following equations, the result is obtained as

$$\beta_1 = \frac{\mathbb{E}[Y - \mathbb{E}(Y)]^3}{[\text{Var}(Y)]^{3/2}} = \frac{\mu_3 - 3\mu_2\mu_1 + 2\mu_1^3}{(\mu_2 - \mu_1^2)^{3/2}},$$

and

$$\beta_2 = \frac{\mathbb{E}[Y - \mathbb{E}(Y)]^4}{[\text{Var}(Y)]^2} = \frac{\mu_4 - 4\mu_1\mu_3 + 6\mu_1^2\mu_2 - 3\mu_1^4}{(\mu_2 - \mu_1^2)^2},$$

respectively. □

Figure 4 shows the skewness and kurtosis coefficients as a function of the parameter q for the MBE model.

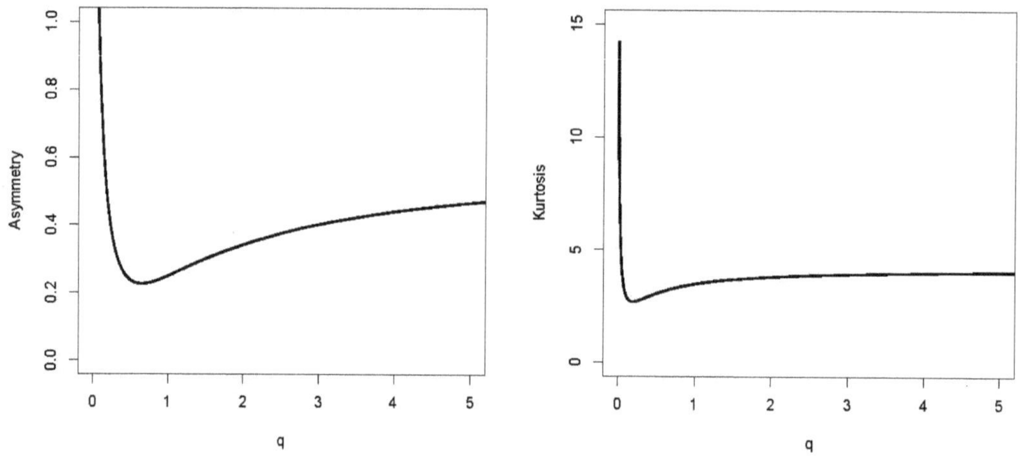

Figure 4. Plots of the asymmetry (**left**) and kurtosis (**right**) coefficients of the MBE distribution.

Proposition 9. *Let $Y \sim MBE(\alpha, q)$. Then, the moment generating function for $\alpha > t$ is given by*

$$M_Y(t) = \frac{\alpha}{1+9q}\left\{(\alpha-t)^{-1} + q\left[(\alpha-t)^{-1} - 4\alpha(\alpha-t)^{-2} + 12\alpha^2(\alpha-t)^{-3} + 24\alpha^3 t(\alpha-t)^{-5}\right]\right\}$$

Proof. Calculating directly from the definition, we have

$$M_Y(t) = \mathbb{E}(e^{tY}) = \frac{\alpha}{1+9q}\int_0^{\infty}\left(1+q(\alpha y-1)^4\right)e^{-(\alpha-t)y}dy,$$

and then, the result is obtained by calculating the integral for $\alpha > t$. □

3. Inference

In this section, we discuss statistical inferences from the moment estimators and maximum likelihood estimators.

3.1. Moment Estimators

Proposition 10. *Let $Y_1, \ldots, Y_n$ be a random distributed sample defined as $Y \sim MBE(\alpha, q)$. Then, the moment estimators $(\hat{\alpha}_M, \hat{q}_M)$ of (α, q) are as follows:*

$$\hat{\alpha}_M = \frac{1+53\hat{q}_M}{\overline{Y}(1+9\hat{q}_M)}, \tag{8}$$

$$\hat{q}_M = \frac{190\overline{Y}^2 - 53\overline{Y^2} + 4\overline{Y}\sqrt{1849\overline{Y}^2 - 704\overline{Y^2}}}{2809\overline{Y^2} - 3258\overline{Y}^2}, \tag{9}$$

where $1849\overline{Y}^2 \geq 704\overline{Y^2}$, the value of $\hat{q}_M$ found is replaced in (8), and $\hat{\alpha}_M$ is obtained.

Proof. From Proposition 8 and using the first two equations and following the moments method, we have

$$\overline{Y} = \frac{1+53q}{\alpha(1+9q)}, \quad \overline{Y^2} = \frac{2(1+181q)}{\alpha^2(1+9q)},$$

solving the first equation above for α, we obtain $\hat{\alpha}_M$ given in (8). Substituting $\hat{\alpha}_M$ in the second equation above, we obtain the result given in (9). □

3.2. ML Estimation

We now discuss ML estimation. Given a random sample $Y_1, \ldots, Y_n$ from the distribution of MBE(α, q), the log likelihood function can be written as

$$l(\alpha, q) = n\log(\alpha) - n\log(1+9q) - \alpha\sum_{i=1}^{n} y_i + \sum_{i=1}^{n}\log\left(1 + q(\alpha y_i - 1)^4\right), \tag{10}$$

and hence, the ML equations are given by

$$\frac{n}{\alpha} + 4q\sum_{i=1}^{n}\frac{y_i(\alpha y_i - 1)^3}{1+q(\alpha y_i - 1)^4} = \sum_{i=1}^{n} y_i \tag{11}$$

$$\sum_{i=1}^{n}\frac{(\alpha y_i - 1)^4}{1+q(\alpha y_i - 1)^4} = \frac{9n}{1+9q} \tag{12}$$

Solutions for Equations (11) and (12) can be obtained using numerical procedures such as the Newton–Raphson procedure. Alternatively, these estimates can be found by directly maximizing the log-likelihood surface given by (10) and using the `optim` subroutine in the R software (version 4.3.2) [21].

3.2.1. Regularity Conditions

To establish the consistency and asymptotic normality of the ML estimators of the parameters (α, q) in the MBE(α, q) distribution, it is necessary to verify a set of regularity conditions commonly used in likelihood theory (see [22]).

We verify the following regularity conditions:

C1. Identifiability: The mapping $(\alpha, q) \mapsto f_Y(y; \alpha, q)$ is identifiable. That is, if $f_Y(y; \alpha_1, q_1) = f_Y(y; \alpha_2, q_2)$ for all $y \geq 0$, then $(\alpha_1, q_1) = (\alpha_2, q_2)$. This holds because the parameters appear uniquely in both the exponential decay and the quartic polynomial term.

C2. Parameter space: The parameter space $\Theta = \{(\alpha, q) \in \mathbb{R}^2 : \alpha > 0, q > 0\}$ is an open subset of $\mathbb{R}^2$.

C3. Differentiability: The log-likelihood function $\ell_n(\alpha, q)$ is three times continuously differentiable with respect to both parameters in the interior of Θ.

C4. Dominated convergence: There exists an integrable function $g(y)$ such that the partial derivatives of $\log f_Y(y; \alpha, q)$ are uniformly dominated by $g(y)$ in a neighborhood of the true parameter value (α_0, q_0). This condition ensures the validity of interchanging integration and differentiation—a key requirement for establishing consistency and asymptotic normality.

The partial derivatives of the log-likelihood with respect to α and q involve polynomial terms up to degree four in y multiplied by an exponentially decaying function. A suitable dominating function is

$$g(y) = C(1+y^4)e^{-\alpha' y},$$

for some $\alpha' < \alpha_0$ and $C > 0$. Since

$$\int_0^\infty (1+y^4)e^{-\alpha' y}\,dy < \infty,$$

this function is integrable over $\mathbb{R}^+$, thus satisfying condition C4.

C5. Fisher information: The Fisher information matrix $I(\alpha, q)$ is positive definite in a neighborhood of the true parameter values. This is supported empirically via simulations and numerically through the computation of the observed Fisher information matrix.

Given that conditions C1–C5 are satisfied, we conclude that the MLEs of (α, q) are consistent and asymptotically normal:

$$\sqrt{n}\begin{pmatrix}\hat{\alpha}_n - \alpha \\ \hat{q}_n - q\end{pmatrix} \xrightarrow{d} \mathcal{N}\left(\mathbf{0}, I^{-1}(\alpha, q)\right), \quad \text{as } n \to \infty.$$

Remark 3. *The fulfillment of these conditions was also supported empirically through simulation studies and real data applications, where profile log-likelihood plots confirmed the existence of a unique maximum for the likelihood function. Specifically, the profile likelihood plots for parameters α and q (presented in the Applications section) demonstrate the uniqueness of the MLE, thereby supporting the theoretical assumptions.*

3.2.2. Fisher Information Matrix

Let random variable $Y \sim MBE(\alpha, q)$. For a single observation y, the log-likelihood function for $\boldsymbol{\theta} = (\alpha, q)$ is

$$\log f_Y(\boldsymbol{\theta}; y) = n\log(\alpha) - n\log(1+9q) + \sum_{i=1}^{n}\log(1+q(\alpha y_i - 1)^4) - \alpha\sum_{i=1}^{n} y_i.$$

The first derivatives of $\log f_Y(\boldsymbol{\theta}, y)$ are

$$\begin{aligned}\frac{\partial \log f_Y(\boldsymbol{\theta}; y)}{\partial \alpha} &= \frac{1}{\alpha} + \frac{4qy(\alpha y - 1)^3}{1+q(\alpha y - 1)^4} - y, \\ \frac{\partial \log f_Y(\boldsymbol{\theta}; y)}{\partial q} &= -\frac{9}{1+9q} + \frac{(\alpha y - 1)^4}{1+q(\alpha y - 1)^4}.\end{aligned}$$

The second derivatives of $\log f_Y(\boldsymbol{\theta}, y)$ are

$$\begin{aligned}\frac{\partial^2 \log f_Y(\boldsymbol{\theta}; y)}{\partial \alpha^2} &= -\frac{1}{\alpha^2} + \frac{4qy^2(\alpha y - 1)^2(3 - q(\alpha y - 1)^4)}{(1+q(\alpha y - 1)^4)^2}, \\ \frac{\partial^2 \log f_Y(\boldsymbol{\theta}; y)}{\partial q^2} &= -\frac{81}{(1+9q)^2} - \frac{(\alpha y - 1)^8}{(1+q(\alpha y - 1)^4)^2}, \\ \frac{\partial^2 \log f_Y(\boldsymbol{\theta}; y)}{\partial \alpha \partial q} &= \frac{4y(\alpha y - 1)^3}{(1+q(\alpha y - 1)^4)^2}.\end{aligned}$$

It can be shown that the Fisher information matrix for the MBE distribution is given by

$$I_F(\alpha, q) = \begin{pmatrix} I_{\alpha\alpha} & I_{\alpha q} \\ I_{q\alpha} & I_{qq}\end{pmatrix}$$

with the following elements:

$$I_{\alpha\alpha} = \frac{1}{\alpha^2} - 4q(3a_{22} + qa_{26}), \quad I_{q\alpha} = I_{\alpha q} = -4a_{13}, \text{ and } \quad I_{qq} = -\frac{81}{(1+9q)^2} + a_{08},$$

where $a_{ij} = E\left[\frac{Y^i(\alpha Y - 1)^j}{(1+q(\alpha y - 1)^4)^2}\right]$, for $i = 0, 1, 2, j = 2, 3, 6, 8$, must be computed numerically.

3.2.3. Simulation Study

We used the acceptance or rejection algorithm to generate random realizations of a variable with the MBE (α, q) distribution. The simulation results appear in Table 2, illustrating the behavior of the ML estimators for 1000 generated samples of sizes 50, 100, 150, and 200 from a population with MBE (α, q) distribution. For each sample generated, ML estimators were computed numerically using the Newton–Raphson procedure. The means of the estimations, the standard deviations (SDs), and the empirical coverage probabilities for 95%, C(·) (in percentages) are presented in Table 2. We observe that, in general, the standard deviation of the estimations diminished when the sample size was increased, suggesting that the ML estimators are consistent. The empirical coverage probabilities approached the nominal level of 95%. The results shown in Table 2 suggest that the ML estimators of α and q show good behavior in small samples.

Table 2. Simulation of 1000 iterations of the MBE (α, q) model.

n	α	q	$\widehat{\alpha}$	$SD(\widehat{\alpha})$	$C(\widehat{\alpha})$	$\widehat{q}$	$SD(\widehat{q})$	$C(\widehat{q})$
50	1.0	0.2	1.0101	0.0762	94.8	0.2210	0.0777	93.8
100	1.0	0.2	1.0059	0.0534	95.3	0.2120	0.0513	94.7
150	1.0	0.2	1.0002	0.0435	95.9	0.2059	0.0404	94.3
200	1.0	0.2	1.0022	0.0378	95.7	0.2033	0.0344	94.6
50	1.0	0.3	1.0099	0.0697	95.4	0.3388	0.1332	93.1
100	1.0	0.3	1.0022	0.0487	93.6	0.3193	0.0848	95.1
150	1.0	0.3	0.9981	0.0397	95.7	0.3110	0.0664	94.7
200	1.0	0.3	0.9996	0.0344	95.5	0.3079	0.0566	95.8
50	1.0	0.4	1.0092	0.0659	95.6	0.4746	0.2131	94.1
100	1.0	0.4	1.0019	0.0462	94.4	0.4275	0.1239	95.0
150	1.0	0.4	0.9990	0.0377	94.0	0.4191	0.0981	94.3
200	1.0	0.4	1.0011	0.0327	94.9	0.4147	0.0833	95.0
50	2.0	0.2	1.9941	0.1514	94.0	0.2141	0.0747	93.4
100	2.0	0.2	2.0014	0.1068	94.6	0.2094	0.0507	95.0
150	2.0	0.2	2.0011	0.0870	95.7	0.2056	0.0403	95.0
200	2.0	0.2	2.0017	0.0755	94.8	0.2041	0.0346	93.9
50	2.0	0.3	1.9994	0.1382	95.9	0.3312	0.1284	93.5
100	2.0	0.3	2.0028	0.0977	94.7	0.3154	0.0834	95.0
150	2.0	0.3	2.0036	0.0795	95.2	0.3157	0.0678	94.4
200	2.0	0.3	2.0018	0.0690	93.2	0.3066	0.0564	94.4
50	2.0	0.4	2.0014	0.1317	94.9	0.4565	0.2009	92.4
100	2.0	0.4	2.0017	0.0926	93.8	0.4347	0.1276	93.7
150	2.0	0.4	2.0036	0.0756	96.0	0.4203	0.0983	95.0
200	2.0	0.4	2.0018	0.0655	93.6	0.4117	0.0824	94.9
50	3.0	0.2	3.0045	0.2267	95.0	0.2239	0.0789	94.5
100	3.0	0.2	2.9987	0.1599	94.8	0.2107	0.0510	95.1
150	3.0	0.2	2.9968	0.1298	94.4	0.2110	0.0415	96.0
200	3.0	0.2	2.9998	0.1130	95.9	0.2061	0.0349	95.7
50	3.0	0.3	2.9995	0.2077	94.9	0.3365	0.1327	91.5
100	3.0	0.3	3.0024	0.1460	95.4	0.3187	0.0845	95.3
150	3.0	0.3	3.0012	0.1191	94.8	0.3140	0.0672	95.1
200	3.0	0.3	3.0025	0.1033	94.3	0.3089	0.0569	94.2
50	3.0	0.4	3.0110	0.1977	95.3	0.4761	0.2182	91.8
100	3.0	0.4	2.9897	0.1382	94.7	0.4274	0.1242	94.8
150	3.0	0.4	3.0018	0.1133	95.3	0.4201	0.0983	94.3
200	3.0	0.4	3.0004	0.0981	95.1	0.4152	0.0834	94.0

3.2.4. Algorithm

To implement the algorithm for generating random values from the MBE (α, q) distribution (presented in Algorithm 1), we first define the required parameters and random variables:

1. n: Size of the output vector (i.e., number of values to be generated).
2. Y: A random variable following the MBE (α, q) distribution.
3. $f_Y(y)$: The probability density function (pdf) of the MBE distribution defined for $y > 0$.

4. l_1: The lower bound used to define the sampling interval for Y; must satisfy $l_1 > 0$.
5. l_2: The upper bound for the pdf $f_Y(M_0(Y)) \approx \left(\frac{1+256q}{1+9q}\right)\alpha e^{-5}$; it must satisfy $l_2 > 0$.
6. $U_1 \sim U(-l_1, l_1)$: A uniform random variable on the interval $(-l_1, l_1)$ used to propose candidate values for Y.
7. $U_2 \sim U(0, l_2)$: A uniform random variable on the interval $(0, l_2)$, which is used in the acceptance/rejection step.

Given parameters $\alpha > 0$ and $q > 0$, we generate a vector of size n with values from the MBE (α, q) distribution using the acceptance or rejection method.

Algorithm 1: Random generation from MBE (α, q) distribution

Input: $n, \alpha > 0, q > 0, l_1 > 0, l_2 > 0$

Output: Vector V of n independent MBE(α, q) random variables

Initialize an empty vector $V \leftarrow [\,]$;

while *length(V)* $< n$ **do**

  Generate $U_1 \sim \mathcal{U}(-l_1, l_1)$;

  Generate $U_2 \sim \mathcal{U}(0, l_2)$;

  if $U_2 < \frac{\alpha}{1+9q}\left(1 + q\alpha^4\left(U_1 - \frac{1}{\alpha}\right)^4\right)e^{-\alpha U_1}$ **then**

    Append U_1 to V;

return V

4. Applications

In this section, we analyze two real-world datasets, comparing the fit of the MBE and BE distributions.

4.1. Application to Vanadium Data

The dataset used was collected by the Mining Department of the University of Atacama, Chile, and represents the vanadium measured in 86 ore samples. The data are shown in Table 3.

Table 3. Vanadium data.

47	37	79	32	24	9	11	63	24	4
14	24	11	33	11	81	9	22	93	188
94	186	238	186	323	263	297	318	190	201
209	131	206	121	105	50	69	167	204	121
152	188	267	212	258	230	232	178	318	212
209	351	24	1	37	53	4	77	92	217
178	110	63	232	29	71	289	142	459	222
111	289	243	180	118	93	47	318	27	6
166	46	157	22	16	65				

The descriptive statistics of these data are shown in Table 4, where γ_1 is the coefficient of asymmetry of the sample, and γ_2 is the coefficient of kurtosis of the sample.

Table 4. Descriptive statistics for vanadium data.

n	Median	Mean	Variance	γ_1	γ_2
86	114.50	133.8	10,912.66	0.60	2.64

Using results from Section 3.1, the method of moments estimators was computed, leading to the following values: $\widehat{\alpha}_M = 0.030$ and $\widehat{q}_M = 0.171$; these were used as initial estimates for the maximum likelihood approach.

Table 5 shows the ML estimates (with (SE) indicating standard error) for the parameter of the MBE and BE models, as well as the values of the AIC and BIC criteria for each model. For each model, we report the values the Akaike information criterion (AIC) introduced by Akaike [23] and the Bayesian information criterion (BIC) proposed by Schwarz [24].

Table 5. Vanadium data: model, ML estimates, AIC values, and BIC values.

Model	ML Estimates	AIC	BIC
MBE(α, q)	$\widehat{\alpha} = 0.028\,(0.002)$, $\widehat{q} = 0.134\,(0.035)$	1007.190	1012.099
BE(α, q)	$\widehat{\alpha} = 0.020\,(0.002)$, $\widehat{q} = 3.308\,(0.814)$	1046.494	1051.402

We observe that the smaller values of the AIC and BIC criteria correspond to the MBE model, indicating that the MBE model fits the data better than the BE model.

In Figure 5 (left), we present a histogram of the vanadium data, as well as the estimated pdfs of the MBE and BE distributions. We observe a good fit between the histogram of the vanadium data and the estimated pdf of the MBE distribution. Figure 5 (right) shows the empirical cdfs with the estimated cdfs of the MBE and BE distributions, which also indicated a good fit between the vanadium data and the BME model.

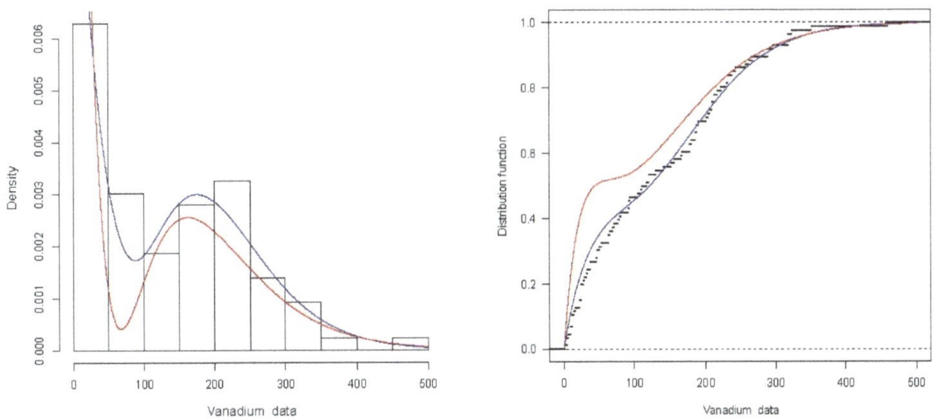

Figure 5. Left: Histogram of the vanadium data, with estimated MBE pdf (blue) and estimated BE pdf (red). **Right**: Plots of the empirical cdf, with estimated MBE cdf (blue), estimated BE cdf (red), and empirical cdf (black).

In Figure 6, the log-likelihood profiles for α and q show a single clear peak, indicating the uniqueness of the maximum likelihood estimator. The well-defined maxima suggest that the optimization converges to a unique solution. This supports the identifiability and stability of the parameter estimates.

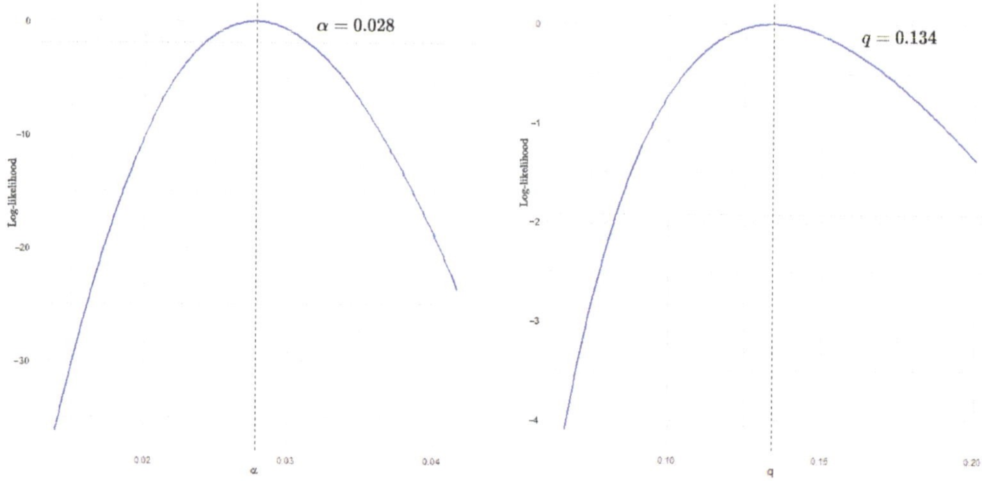

Figure 6. Log-likelihood profiles with estimated parameter values α (**left**) and q (**right**) for vanadium data.

We calculated the quantile residuals (QRs) for the MBE and BE distributions. If the model is appropriate for the data, the QR should be a sample of the standard normal model (see Dunn and Smyth [25]). This assumption can be validated with traditional normality tests, like the Anderson–Darling (AD), Cramér–von Mises (CVM), and Shapiro–Wilk (SW) tests. Figure 7 displays the quantile residuals (QRs) for each distribution. The associated p-values from the Anderson–Darling (AD), Cramér–von Mises (CVM), and Shapiro–Wilk (SW) normality tests are reported in parentheses to assess whether the QRs follow a standard normal distribution. As shown in the Figure 7, all three tests support the hypothesis that the QRs from the MBE distribution follow a standard normal distribution. In contrast, the CVM test rejects this hypothesis for the BE distribution, suggesting that the BE model does not provide an adequate fit to the vanadium data.

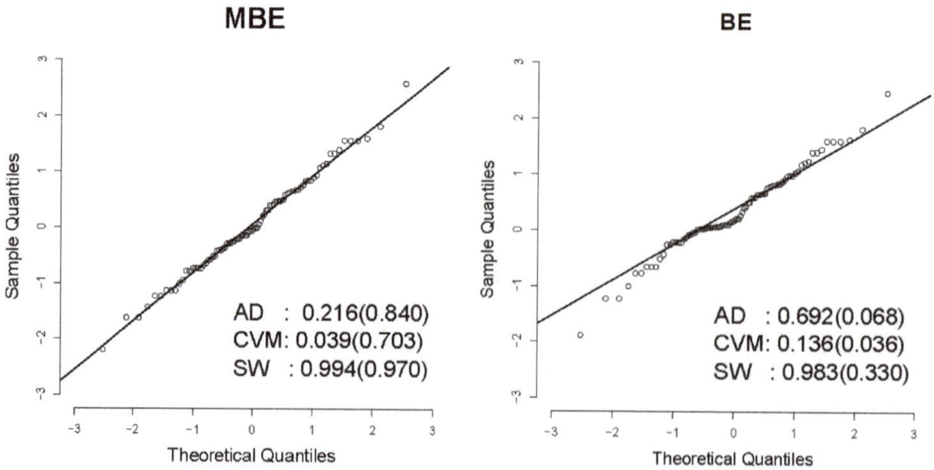

Figure 7. Left: Q–Q plots of the QRs for MBE distribution. **Right:** Q–Q plots of the QRs for BE distribution.

4.2. Application to Exceedances of Flood Peaks Data

The data correspond to the exceedances of flood peaks (in m^3/s) of the Wheaton River near Carcross in Yukon Territory, Canada. The data consist of 72 exceedances for the years 1958–1984, rounded to one decimal place, and are listed in Table 6. Table 7 presents descriptive statistics. In it, we compare the fit of the BE distribution with that of the MBE distribution.

Table 6. Data on exceedances of Wheaton River floods.

1.7	2.2	14.4	1.1	0.4	20.6	5.3	0.7	1.9	13.0	12.0	9.3
1.4	18.7	8.5	25.5	11.6	14.1	22.1	1.1	2.5	14.4	1.7	37.6
0.6	2.2	39.0	0.3	15.0	11.0	7.3	22.9	1.7	0.1	1.1	0.6
9.0	1.7	7.0	20.1	0.4	2.8	14.1	9.9	10.4	10.7	30.0	3.6
5.6	30.8	13.3	4.2	25.5	3.4	11.9	21.5	27.6	36.4	2.7	64.0
1.5	2.5	27.4	1.0	27.1	20.2	16.8	5.3	9.7	27.5	2.5	27.0

Table 7. Descriptive statistics for exceedances of flood peaks data.

n	Median	Mean	Variance	γ_1	γ_2
72	9.5	12.204	151.216	1.473	5.890

Using results from Section 3.1, the method of moments estimators was computed, leading to the following values: $\widehat{\alpha}_M = 0.238$ and $\widehat{q}_M = 0.071$; these were used as initial estimates for the maximum likelihood approach. Table 8 presents the ML estimates for the MBE and BE model parameters, along with their corresponding AIC and BIC values.

Table 8. Exceedances of flood peaks data: model, ML estimates, AIC values, and BIC values.

Model	ML Estimate	AIC	BIC
MBE(α, q)	$\widehat{\alpha} = 0.261(0.028), \widehat{q} = 0.087(0.029)$	504.803	509.356
BE(α, q)	$\widehat{\alpha} = 0.205(0.014), \widehat{q} = 3.411(0.763)$	514.616	519.170

The MBE model demonstrates superior fit to the data, as evidenced by its consistently lower AIC and BIC values compared to the BE model.

In Figure 8 (left), we plot the histogram of the flood peak exceedances data overlayed with the estimated pdfs of the MBE and BE distributions. We observe strong agreement between the histogram of flood peak exceedances and the estimated pdf of the MBE distribution. In Figure 8 (right), we plot the empirical cdf along with the estimated cdfs of the MBE and BE distributions, which further demonstrate the good fit between the MBE model and the flood peak exceedances data.

Figures 9 and 10 show the QRs for each distribution. The p-values for the normality tests (AD, CVM, and SW) are shown in parentheses to verify whether the QRs have a standard normal distribution. In Figure 9, we observe that all three tests indicate that the MBE distribution's QRs follow a standard normal distribution. This is not the case for the BE distribution, as Figure 10 shows that all three tests reject the null hypothesis that the QRs come from a standard normal distribution, indicating that the BE distribution does not fit the flood peak exceedances data well.

Figure 11 demonstrates the ML estimates of α and q, as evidenced by their log-likelihood profiles exhibiting a dominant, isolated peak. The absence of local optima or flat regions confirms that the numerical optimization procedure reliably attains a single, globally optimal solution. These results underscore both the statistical identifiability of the model parameters and the robustness of their estimation.

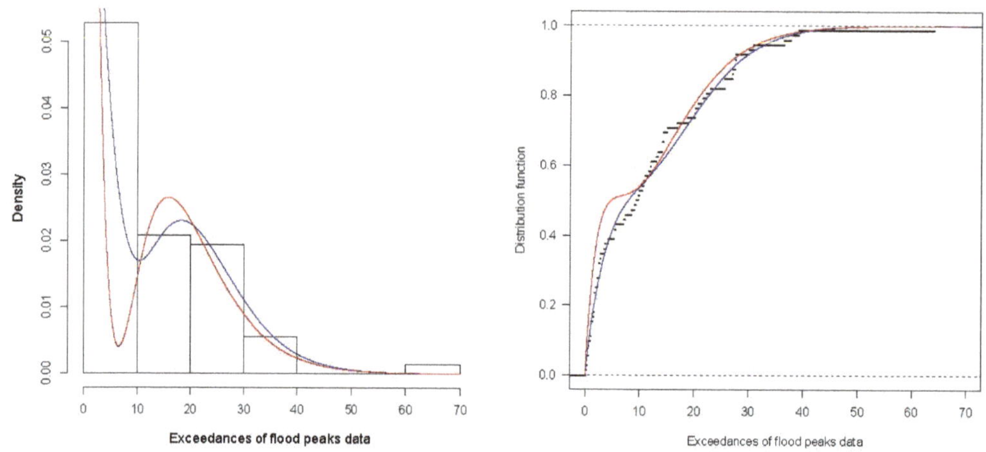

Figure 8. Left side: histogram of the exceedances of flood peaks data with estimated MBE pdf (blue) and estimated BE pdf (red). **Right side:** plots of the empirical cdf with estimated MBE cdf (blue), estimated BE cdf (red) models, and empirical cdf (black).

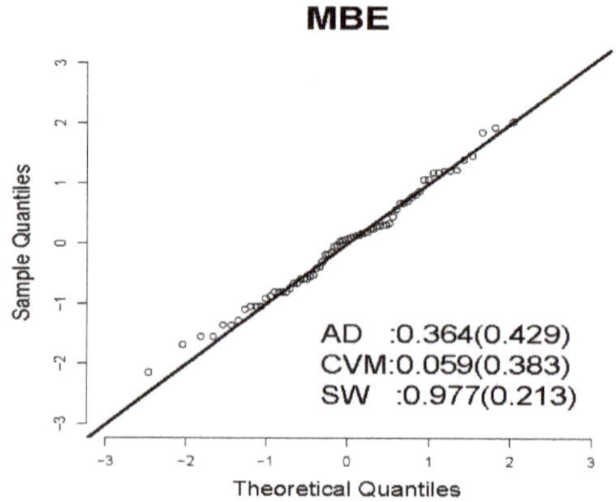

Figure 9. Q–Q plots of the QRs for MBE distribution.

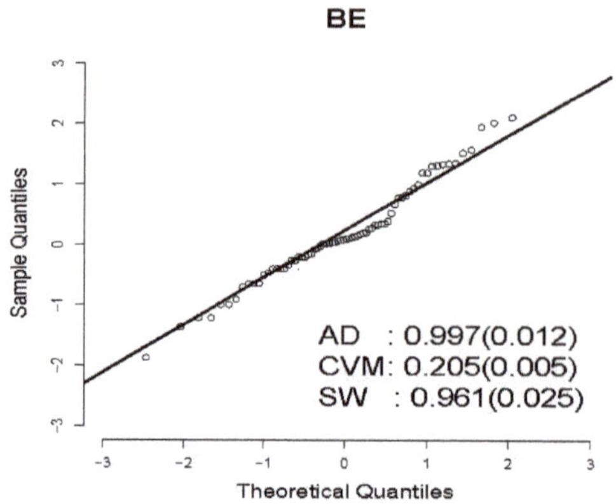

Figure 10. Q–Q plots of the QRs for BE distribution.

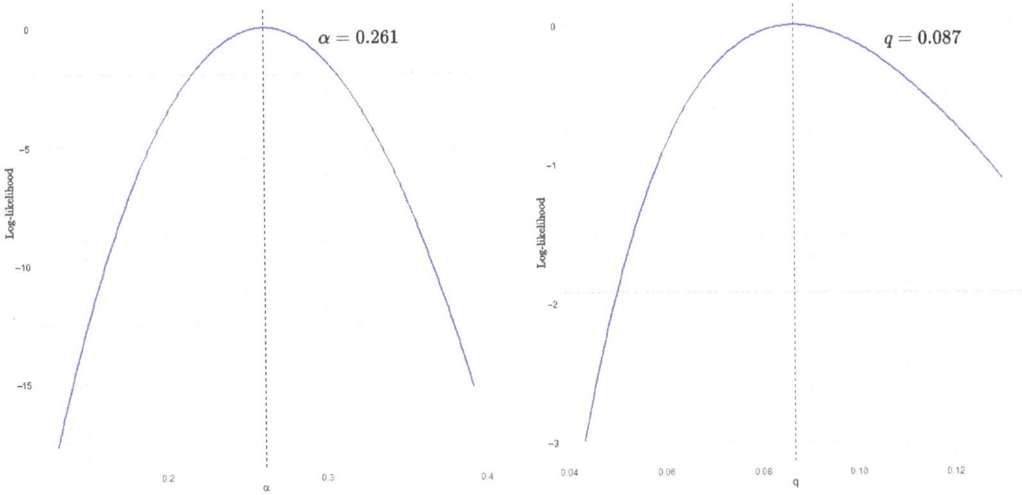

Figure 11. The log-likelihood profiles with estimated parameter values α (**left**) and q (**right**) for flood peak exceedance data.

5. Discussion

Using the methodology introduced by Reyes et al. [10] to generate bimodal distributions with positive support, we employed a new weight function to increase the height of the second mode. We retained the exponential distribution to enable comparison with the BE distribution. The key characteristics of the MBE distribution are as follows:

- The MBE distribution is an extension of the exponential distribution.
- The second mode of the MBE distribution is higher in height than that of the BE distribution.
- The cdf, survival function, hazard function, and moment-generating function are explicit and are represented by simple functions.
- The hazard function is bathtub-shaped.
- The simulation study shows that the ML estimators present good behavior with relatively small sample sizes.
- The two applications demonstrate that the MBE distribution possesses distinct characteristics, including a second mode that is both higher in height and more flexible than that of the BE distribution. Furthermore, the AIC and BIC selection criteria indicate that the MBE distribution provides a better fit for both datasets compared to the BE distribution. This conclusion was further confirmed through a comparison of the QRs of each distribution.
- Finally, exploring new models by substituting the exponential distribution with alternative distributions will be the aim of our future work.

Author Contributions: Conceptualization, J.R. and B.C.A.; methodology, Y.M.G. and H.W.G.; software, Y.M.G.; validation, J.R., Y.M.G. and B.C.A.; formal analysis, Y.M.G. and O.V.; investigation, O.V.; writing—original draft preparation, J.R. and Y.M.G.; writing—review and editing, O.V. and B.C.A.; funding acquisition, H.W.G. and O.V. All authors have read and agreed to the published version of the manuscript.

Funding: This research received no external funding.

Institutional Review Board Statement: Not applicable.

Informed Consent Statement: Not applicable.

Data Availability Statement: The data used are available in Tables 3 and 6.

Conflicts of Interest: The authors declare no conflicts of interest.

References

1. Fisher, R.A. The effects of methods of ascertainment upon the estimation of frequencies. *Ann. Eugen.* **1934**, *6*, 13–25. [CrossRef]
2. Rao, C.R. On discrete distributions arising out of methods of ascertainment. In *Classical and Contagious Discrete Distributions*; Patil, G.P., Ed.; Calcutta Statist. Publ. Soc.: Calcutta, India, 1965; pp. 320–333. Reprinted in *Sankhya A 27*, 311–324.
3. Rao, C.R. Weighted Distributions Arising Out of Methods of Ascertainment: What Population Does a Sample Represent? In *A Celebration of Statistics*; Atkinson, A.C., Fienberg, S.E., Eds.; Springer: New York, NY, USA, 1985.
4. Patil, G.P.; Ord, J.K. On size biased sampling and related form invariant weighted distribution. *Indian J. Stat.* **1976**, *39*, 48–61.
5. Patil, G.P.; Rao, C.R. Weighted distributions and size-biased sampling with applications to wildlife populations and human families. *Biometrics* **1978**, *34*, 179–189. [CrossRef]
6. Gupta, R.C.; Kirmani, S.N. The role of weighted distributions in stochastic modeling. *Commun. Stat. Theory Methods* **1990**, *19*, 3147–3162. [CrossRef]
7. Gupta A.K.; Tripathi, R.C. Weighted bivariate logarithmic series distributions. *Commun. Stat. Theory Methods* **1996**, *25*, 1099–1117. [CrossRef]
8. Gupta, R.C.; Akman, H.O. On the reliability studies of a weighted inverse Gaussian model. *J. Stat. Plan. Inference* **1998**, *48*, 69–83. [CrossRef]
9. Gupta, R.D.; Kundu, D.A. New class of weighted exponential distribution. *Statistics* **2009**, *43*, 621–634. [CrossRef]
10. Reyes, J.; Gómez-Déniz, E.; Gómez, H.W.; Calderín-Ojeda, E. A Bimodal Extension of the Exponential Distribution with Applications in Risk Theory. *Symmetry* **2021**, *13*, 679. [CrossRef]
11. Hassan, M.Y.; Hijazi, R.H. A bimodal exponential power distribution. *Pak. J. Stat.* **2010**, *26*, 379–396.
12. Gómez-Déniz, E.; Sarabia, J.M.; Calderín-Ojeda, E. Bimodal normal distribution: Extensions and applications. *J. Comput. Appl. Math.* **2021**, *388* , 113292. [CrossRef]
13. Chesneau, C.; Kumar, V.; Khetan, M.; Arshad, M. On a Modified Weighted Exponential Distribution with Applications. *Math. Comput. Appl.* **2022**, *27*, 17. [CrossRef]
14. Alzaghal, A.; Aldeni, M. ; Al-Aqtash, R. A New Class of Exponentiated Exponential Distributions: Bimodality, Regression, and Application. *J. Stat. Theory Pract.* **2023**, *52*, 52. [CrossRef]
15. Cortés, I.E.; Venegas, O.; Gómez, H.W. A Symmetric/Asymmetric Bimodal Extension Based on the Logistic Distribution: Properties, Simulation and Applications. *Mathematics* **2022**, *10*, 1968. [CrossRef]
16. McLachan, G.; Peel, D. *Mixture Models: Inference and Applications to Clustering*; Marcel Dekker: New York, NY, USA, 2000.
17. Marin, J.M.; Mengersen, K.; Robert, C. Bayesian modeling and inference on mixtures of distributions. *Handb. Stat.* **2005**, *25*, 459–503.
18. Abramowitz, M.; Stegun, I.A. *Handbook of Mathematical Functions with Formulas, Graphs, and Mathematical Tables*, 9th ed.; National Bureau of Standards: Gaithersburg, MD, USA, 1968.
19. Weisstein, E.W. Quartic Equation. From MathWorld—A Wolfram Web Resource. Available online: https://mathworld.wolfram.com/QuarticEquation.html (accessed on 8 June 2024).
20. Glaser, R.E. Bathtub and Related Failure Rate Characterizations. *J. Am. Stat. Assoc.* **1980**, *75*, 667–672. [CrossRef]
21. R Core Team. *R: A Language and Environment for Statistical Computing*; R Foundation for Statistical Computing: Vienna, Austria, 2023. Available online: https://www.R-project.org/ (accessed on 28 June 2024).
22. Casella, G.; Berger, R.L. *Statistical Inference*, 2nd ed.; Duxbury: North Scituate, MA, USA, 2002.
23. Akaike, H. A new look at the statistical model identification. *IEEE Trans. Autom. Control* **1974** *19*, 716–723. [CrossRef]
24. Schwarz, G. Estimating the dimension of a model. *Ann. Stat.* **1978**, *6*, 461–464. [CrossRef]
25. Dunn, P.K.; Smyth, G.K. Randomized Quantile Residuals. *J. Comput. Graph. Stat.* **1996**, *5*, 236–244. [CrossRef]

axioms

MDPI

Article

Modal Regression Estimation by Local Linear Approach in High-Dimensional Data Case

Fatimah A. Almulhim [1], Mohammed B. Alamari [2,*], Ali Laksaci [2] and Zoulikha Kaid [2]

[1] Department of Mathematical Sciences, College of Science, Princess Nourah bint Abdulrahman University, P.O. Box 84428, Riyadh 11671, Saudi Arabia; faalmulhim@pnu.edu.sa

[2] Department of Mathematics, College of Science, King Khalid University, Abha 62223, Saudi Arabia; alikfa@kku.edu.sa (A.L.); zqayd@kku.edu.sa (Z.K.)

* Correspondence: malamari@kku.edu.sa

Abstract: This paper introduces a new nonparametric estimator for detecting the conditional mode in the functional input variable setting. The estimator integrates a local linear approach with an L^1-robust algorithm and treats the modal regression as the minimizer of the quantile derivative. As an asymptotic result, we derive the theoretical properties of the estimator by analyzing its convergence rate under the almost complete consistency framework. The result is stated under standard conditions, characterizing both the functional structure of the data and the local linear approximation properties of the model. Moreover, the expression of the convergence rate retains the usual form of the stochastic convergence rate in functional statistics. Simulations and real-data applications demonstrate the algorithm's effectiveness, showing its advantage over existing methods in high-dimensional prediction tasks.

Keywords: functional statistics; conditional mode; smoothing approach; L^1 method; spectrometry processing; robust estimator; quantile regression

MSC: 62G08; 62G10; 62G35; 62G07; 62G32; 62G30; 62H12

1. Introduction

In the last decade, interest in the statistical analysis of functional data has grown significantly, driven by its wide range of applications in various domains. The foundational work in this field was first established by [1,2], as pioneer works, and [3] or [4] for recent results and references. Within this field, nonparametric statistics have proven to be highly effective in modeling functional data, particularly when it comes to predicting using conditional mode and conditional quantiles. However, most of the existing nonparametric functional quantiles or mode estimators heavily depend on traditional kernel methods. In this paper, we improve the accuracy and robustness of the previous estimators using the L^1-local linear estimation (LLE) method.

Modal and quantile regression are popular tools in nonparametric statistics for making predictions. They present an alternative approach to traditional regression, which is based on conditional expectation. Unlike the conventional approaches, the proposed predictors often impart deeper insights, especially when the data have asymmetric or multimodal conditional densities, or when the white noise shows a heavy-tailed distribution (refer to [5] for the limitation of the conditional expectation). The latter demonstrated that the conditional mode outperforms the conditional mean. Based on this, Ref. [6] created a prediction model that uses the derivative of the conditional density for multivariate data. Theoretical progress was made by [7], who established the asymptotic distribution of modal regression estimators for independent data. Ref. [8] extended the last result to the dependent cases. Further advancements in the conditional mode prediction are comprehensively covered in [9,10]. While the cited works concern the kernel estimator of the conditional mode (CM) in finite-dimensional cases, the Nadaraya–Watson (NW) estimator was extended for functional data by [11]. They estimated this regression model by maximizing the conditional density and proved its almost complete consistency. This result has been generalized to the functional time series case by [12]. The asymptotic distribution of the NW estimator of the conditional mode was explored for the independent case in [13] and for the strongly mixing case by [14]. There were also significant theoretical advancements made by [15], who determined L^p-convergence rates for NW-based functional CM estimators. For an alternative functional time series, Ref. [16] established stochastic consistency for ergodic functional time series data containing missing at random. Further theoretical and practical contributions in the field of functional CM estimation can be found in [17] and the references therein.

On the other hand, quantile regression has gained increasing interest in nonparametric data analysis. It is worth noting that the quantile regression function is also one of the most well-studied models in nonparametric vector statistics. Earlier foundational works in multivariate statistics go back to [18], and were popularized by [19,20]. Once again in functional statistics, quantile regression has received considerable attention. This high level of flexibility justifies the approach, as it can be treated as a linear, semiparametric, or nonparametric model. The functional linear modeling of the conditional quantile was considered by [21,22], which provides comprehensive overviews of the latest developments. While the semiparametric estimation was developed by [23]. Concerning nonparametric estimation, quantile regression is estimated using the functional version of the NW estimator by [11]. They proved the Borel–Cantelli of the constructed estimator. Ref. [24] has stated the moment integrability of the functional NW estimator. We return to [25,26] for recent results.

The main novelty of this work is the estimation by the LLE method. This approach provides an important advantage compared to the NW estimator. In particular, it permits increasing the efficiency of the estimation by reducing bias. This statement has been observed by [27] in the multivariate case and expanded into functional statistics by [28]. From a bibliographical perspective, the LLE technique has been thoroughly explored in functional statistics by many authors. For example, Ref. [29] demonstrated L_2 consistency of the LLE estimator when estimating the regression operator in Hilbert spaces. Ref. [30] proposes a more general estimator allowing coverage of a wider range of functional covariates, while [31] developed an alternative estimator based on the inverse local covariance operator. Ref. [32] introduced functional LLE-fitting for nonparametric conditional models, establishing pointwise and uniform almost-complete (a.co.) consistency for the conditional density mode. The first results on the LLE-estimation of the quantile function were stated by [33]. Their estimation is obtained by inverting the cumulative distribution function (CDF) estimator introduced by [32]. An alternative was recently considered by [34] based on the M-estimation of the quantile regression.

While most current methods focus on estimating the conditional mode by optimizing a kernel-based conditional density estimator, this paper introduces a new LLE approach based on quantile regression. Unlike traditional methods, our estimator accumulates the robustness of L_1-regression and the performance of the LLE-estimation, which enhances its resistance to outliers and extends its accuracy as a predictor or classifier in functional statistics. Theoretically, we demonstrate the almost complete convergence of the estimator under standard conditions, with precision in the convergence rate. This new estimator's benefits are also emphasized by comparing it to the standard one using a simulated and real data example. Our empirical analysis shows that the new estimator not only outperforms the accuracy of the previous estimators but also remains robust across a wide range of scenarios. Additionally, to demonstrate its practical value, we apply our method to predict the chemical composition of cocoa using spectrometry data. Typically, we have focused on the prediction of fat and moisture content using near-infrared spectroscopy data as functional regressors. It is well documented that near-infrared spectroscopy is a powerful, non-destructive tool for rapidly quantifying cocoa quality, allowing real-time quality control in production. Thus, combining this spectrometry processing with the proposed functional model can help chocolate producers to maintain good flavor and texture in their products, ensuring quality at every step.

The paper is organized as follows. In the next Section, we introduce the conditional mode based on the L^1 rule and explain its LLE estimator. Section 3 covers the principal assumptions and the main theoretical findings. In Section 4 We outline the principal features of our approach and provide a comparative analysis with existing methods. The finite-sample performance of our proposed estimator is examined in Section 5, using both simulation studies and real-world data applications. The detailed proofs of the intermediate results are presented in the Appendix Section A.

2. The L^1 Conditional Mode and Its Local Linear Estimator

Let $\{(F_i, R_i)\}_{i=1}^n$ be an independent and identically distributed (i.i.d.) sample from the random pair (F, R), where F is functional input variable taking values in a semi-metric space $(\mathcal{H}, m)$ (m being the semi-metric) and R is the output real variable. Next, fix $\mathfrak{F} \in \mathcal{H}$ and consider a neighborhood $\mathcal{N}_{\mathfrak{F}}$ of $\mathfrak{F}$. We assume the existence of the regular conditional distribution function $D(\cdot|\mathfrak{F})$ of R given $F = \mathfrak{F}$, which is strictly increasing and has a continuous density $d(\cdot|\mathfrak{F})$ with respect to Lebesgue measure on $\mathbb{R}$. The standard conditional mode is usually defined as the maximizer of this conditional density over a compact set S:

$$MR(\mathfrak{F}) = \arg\max_{y \in S} d(y|\mathfrak{F}). \tag{1}$$

However, in order to introduce a more robust definition of the conditional mode, we reformulate this definition and we relate the modal regression to the quantile derivatives. Indeed, for $q \in D^{-1}(S|\mathfrak{F}) = [a_{\mathfrak{F}}, b_{\mathfrak{F}}] \subset (0,1)$, let $QR_q(\mathfrak{F})$ denote the conditional quantile of order q given $F = \mathfrak{F}$. Following similar ideas to [35] in the linear case, we assume $QR_{\cdot}(\mathfrak{F})$ is continuously differentiable (C^1) with $D(QR_q(\mathfrak{F})|\mathfrak{F}) > 0$, yielding:

$$QR'_q(\mathfrak{F}) = \frac{\partial QR_q(\mathfrak{F})}{\partial q} = \frac{1}{D(QR_q(\mathfrak{F})|\mathfrak{F})}. \tag{2}$$

It follows that the conditional mode can be expressed as:

$$MR(\mathfrak{F}) = QR_{q_{MR}}(\mathfrak{F}), \quad \text{where} \quad q_{MR} = \arg\min_{q \in [a_{\mathfrak{F}}, b_{\mathfrak{F}}]} QR'_q(\mathfrak{F}). \tag{3}$$

Recall that the theoretical conditional quantile $QR_q(\mathfrak{F})$ is robustly defined as M-regression with respect to the following score function

$$\min_t \mathbb{E}\left[L_q(R-t) \mid F = \mathfrak{F}\right], \tag{4}$$

where $L_q(y) = y(q - \mathbb{I}_{\{y<0\}})$ is the quantile loss function. Thus, the LLE estimator of the conditional mode is strongly linked to the LLE estimator of the quantile regression.

For this last point, we adopt the fast LLE approach of [30], approximating $QR_q(\cdot)$ in a neighborhood $\mathcal{N}_{\mathfrak{F}}$ by:

$$QR_q(\mathfrak{Z}) \approx A + Bm(\mathfrak{F},\mathfrak{Z}) \quad \forall \mathfrak{Z} \in \mathcal{N}_{\mathfrak{F}}, \tag{5}$$

and estimate the coefficients (A, B) as solutions of

$$\min_{(A,B)\in\mathbb{R}^2} \sum_{i=1}^{n} L_q(R_i - A - Bm(F_i,\mathfrak{F}))\mathbf{F}\left(\frac{m(\mathfrak{F},F_i)}{f_n}\right), \tag{6}$$

where $\mathbf{F}$ is a kernel function, f_n is a bandwidth sequence. The conditional quantile estimator is then $\widehat{QR}_q(\mathfrak{F}) = \widehat{a}$. Consequently, the LLE estimator of the conditional mode is

$$\widehat{MR}(\mathfrak{F}) = \widehat{QR}(\widehat{q}_M R|\mathfrak{F}) \quad \text{where} \quad \widehat{q}_M R = \arg\min_{q\in[a_{\mathfrak{F}},b_{\mathfrak{F}}]} \widehat{QR}'(q|\mathfrak{F}), \tag{7}$$

with $\widehat{QR}'$ being the estimator of the derivative of the conditional quantile defined by

$$\widehat{QR}'(q|\mathfrak{F}) = \frac{\widehat{QR}(q+b_n|\mathfrak{F}) - \widehat{QR}(q-b_n|\mathfrak{F})}{2b_n}, \tag{8}$$

where b_n is a positive bandwidth-like sequence.

We point out that the functional NW estimator studied by [17] is a particular case of this study; it corresponds to $B = 0$. Next, let us clarify that the existence and uniqueness of $MR(\mathfrak{F})$ are guaranteed by the continuity and strict monotonicity of $D(\cdot|\mathfrak{F})$, while $\widehat{MR}(\mathfrak{F})$ may not be unique. In what follows, $\widehat{MR}(\mathfrak{F})$ refers to any minimizer in (6). Furthermore, the primary contribution of this work is to establish asymptotic properties of $\widehat{MR}(\mathfrak{F})$ when $\mathfrak{F}$ takes values in the semi-metric space $\mathcal{F}_{\mathcal{N}}$. To our knowledge, this is the first study to employ this estimation strategy for the conditional mode, even in multivariate settings. Note that the finite-dimensional case ($\mathcal{F}_{\mathcal{N}} = \mathbb{R}^p$) emerges as a special case, highlighting the generality of our approach.

3. Main Results

All along the paper, when no confusion is possible, we will denote by C or C' some strictly positive generic constants, and we set $B(\mathfrak{F}, f) = \{\mathfrak{F}' \in \mathcal{F} \,:\, m(\mathfrak{F}',\mathfrak{F}) < f\}$. Now, we list some required conditions that are necessary in deriving the almost complete convergence of $\widehat{MR}(\mathfrak{F})$ of $MR(\mathfrak{F})$.

(B1) For any $r > 0$, $\alpha_{\mathfrak{F}}(f) := \alpha_{\mathfrak{F}}(-f, f) > 0$ and there exists a function $\beta_{\mathfrak{F}}(\cdot)$ such that:

$$\text{for all } t \in (-1,1), \ \lim_{f\to 0} \frac{\alpha_{\mathfrak{F}}(tf_n, f_n)}{\alpha_{\mathfrak{F}}(f_n)} = \beta_{\mathfrak{F}}(t)$$

(B2) The functions $QR(\cdot|\mathfrak{F})$ is of class $C^3([a_{\mathfrak{F}}, b_{\mathfrak{F}}])$ and $D(\cdot|\mathfrak{F})$ satisfies the following Lipschitz condition:

$$\text{for all } (\mathfrak{F}_1,\mathfrak{F}_2) \in N_{\mathfrak{F}}, \ |D(t|\mathfrak{F}_1) - D(t|\mathfrak{F}_2)| \le Cd^b(\mathfrak{F}_1,\mathfrak{F}_2) \text{ for some } b > 0,$$

where $N_{\mathfrak{F}}$ denotes a neighborhood of $\mathfrak{F}$.

(B3) The kernel $\mathbf{F}$ is a positive and differentiable function which is supported within $(-1, 1)$, and such that:

$$\begin{pmatrix} \mathbf{F}(1) - \int_{-1}^{1} \mathbf{F}'(t)\beta_{\mathfrak{F}}(t)dt & \mathbf{F}(1) - \int_{-1}^{1} (t\mathbf{F}(t))'\beta_{\mathfrak{F}}(t)dt \\ \mathbf{F}(1) - \int_{-1}^{1} (t\mathbf{F}(t))'\beta_{\mathfrak{F}}(t)dt & \mathbf{F}(1) - \int_{-1}^{1} (t^2\mathbf{F}(t))'\beta_{\mathfrak{F}}(t)dt \end{pmatrix}$$

is a positive definite matrix.

(B4) The bandwidth f_n satisfies:

$$\lim_{n\to\infty} \frac{\log n}{n b_n \alpha_{\mathfrak{F}}(f_n)} = 0$$

The assumed conditions are not very restrictive. They allow us to analyze various aspects of our subject, such as model structure, data framework, and convergence rates. Considering the complexity of our proposed local linear algorithm and the strength of the Borel–Cantelli (BC) consistency, these assumptions offer a good compromise between generality and analytical feasibility. Specifically, each element of the subject is explored through a distinct assumption. For instance, (B1) is particularly essential in NFDA. Specifically, Condition (B1) is indispensable in NFDA, and the function $\alpha_{\mathfrak{F}}(.)$ can be explicitly given for several continuous processes (see [11]). While the regularity conditions are necessary to explore the functional space of the nonparametric path under study, this assumption significantly impacts the bias term in the convergence rate of $\widehat{MR}(\mathfrak{F})$. Finally, conditions (B3)–(B4) relate to the kernel $\mathbf{F}$ and the bandwidths f_n and b_n, which cover the technical aspects of the estimator $\widehat{MR}(\mathfrak{F})$. These conditions are less restrictive than the usual technical requirements in conditional mode estimation. Unlike the conditional density approach, which relies on two kernels, our method requires only one. It is important to recall that these conditions are necessary to determine the convergence rate of the kernel estimator under the Borel–Cantelli mode. Typically, a weaker form of consistency—distinct from BC consistency—can be established for the estimator under more restrictive assumptions. The latter is obtained by evaluating the expectation and variance of the estimator. Although this probability consistency is weaker than Borel–Cantelli consistency, it remains sufficient to justify the estimator's practical applicability. Nevertheless, because this paper aims to demonstrate both the theoretical generality of the model and its practical viability, we have chosen to emphasize the stronger consistency result, which implies the weaker.

The following theorem establishes the almost-complete convergence (cf. [2] for details), (a.co.), of $\widehat{MR}(\mathfrak{F})$. This kind of convergence implies both almost sure convergence and convergence in probability.

Theorem 1. *Under assumptions (B1)-(B4) and if* $\inf_{q\in(0,1)} \dfrac{\partial^3 QR_q(\mathfrak{F})}{\partial q} > 0$ *we have:*

$$\widehat{MR}(\mathfrak{F}) - MR(\mathfrak{F}) = O(f_n^{b/2}) + O(b_n^{1/2}) + O\left(\left(\frac{\log n}{n\, b_n^2 \alpha_{\mathfrak{F}}(f_n)}\right)^{\frac{1}{4}}\right) \qquad a.co.$$

Proof of Theorem 1. The proof is based on some standard analytical arguments. Indeed, we write

$$\widehat{MR}(\mathfrak{F}) - MR(\mathfrak{F}) = \widehat{QR}_{\widehat{q_{MR}}}(\mathfrak{F}) - QR_{\widehat{q_{MR}}}(\mathfrak{F}) + QR_{\widehat{q_{MR}}}(\mathfrak{F}) - QR_{q_{MR}}(\mathfrak{F})$$

Trivially,

$$\widehat{MR}(\mathfrak{F}) - MR(\mathfrak{F}) \leq \sup_{q\in[a_{\mathfrak{F}},b_{\mathfrak{F}}]} |\widehat{QR}(q|\mathfrak{F}) - t(q|\mathfrak{F})| + QR_{\widehat{q_{MR}}}(\mathfrak{F}) - QR_{q_{MR}}(\mathfrak{F})$$

By Taylor expansion,

$$QR_{\widehat{q_{MR}}}(\mathfrak{F}) - QR_{q_{MR}}(\mathfrak{F}) = (\widehat{q_{MR}} - q_{MR}) QR'_{q^*_{MR}}(\mathfrak{F}), \quad q^*_{MR} \text{ being in } \quad (\widehat{q_{MR}}, \quad q_{MR}). \quad (9)$$

Since q_{MR} is minimizer of $QR'_{\cdot}(\mathfrak{F})$,

$$QR'_{\widehat{q_{MR}}}(\mathfrak{F}) - QR'_{q_{MR}}(\mathfrak{F}) = (\widehat{q_{MR}} - q_{MR})^2 QR'''_{q^{**}_{MR}}(\mathfrak{F}), \text{ where } \quad q^{**}_{MR} \in (\widehat{q_{MR}}, \quad q_{MR}). \tag{10}$$

In addition,

$$\begin{aligned} QR'_{\widehat{q_{MR}}}(\mathfrak{F}) - QR'_{q_{MR}}(\mathfrak{F}) &= QR'_{\widehat{q_{MR}}}(\mathfrak{F}) - \widehat{QR'}_{\widehat{q_{MR}}}(\mathfrak{F}) + \widehat{QR'}_{\widehat{q_{MR}}}(\mathfrak{F}) - QR_{q_{MR}}(\mathfrak{F}) \\ &\leq |QR'_{\widehat{q_{MR}}}(\mathfrak{F}) - \widehat{QR'}_{\widehat{q_{MR}}}(\mathfrak{F})| + |\min_q \widehat{QR'}_q(\mathfrak{F}) - \min_q QR'_q(\mathfrak{F})| \\ &\leq 2\sup_{q\in[a_{\mathfrak{F}},b_{\mathfrak{F}}]} |\widehat{QR'}_q(\mathfrak{F}) - QR'_q(\mathfrak{F})| \end{aligned} \tag{11}$$

Thus,

$$|\widehat{MR}(\mathfrak{F}) - MR(\mathfrak{F})| \leq C\left(\sup_{q\in[a_{\mathfrak{F}},b_{\mathfrak{F}}]} |\widehat{QR}_q(\mathfrak{F}) - QR_q(\mathfrak{F})| + \sqrt{\sup_{q\in[a_{\mathfrak{F}},b_{\mathfrak{F}}]} |\widehat{QR'}_q(\mathfrak{F}) - QR'_q(\mathfrak{F})|}\right).$$

Now, for a large enough n

$$\begin{aligned} \widehat{QR'}_q(\mathfrak{F}) - QR'_q(\mathfrak{F}) &= \frac{\widehat{QR}_{q+b_n}(\mathfrak{F}) - QR_{q+b_n}(\mathfrak{F}) + QR_{q-b_n}(\mathfrak{F}) - \widehat{QR}_{q-b_n}(\mathfrak{F})}{2b_n} \\ &+ \frac{QR_{q+b_n}(\mathfrak{F}) - QR_q(\mathfrak{F}) + QR_q(\mathfrak{F}) - QR_{q-b_n}(\mathfrak{F}) - 2b_n QR'_q(\mathfrak{F})}{2b_n} \\ &\leq Cb_n^{-1} \sup_{q\in(a_{\mathfrak{F}}-b_n, b_{\mathfrak{F}}+b_n)} |\widehat{QR}_q(\mathfrak{F}) - QR_q(\mathfrak{F})| + O(b_n) \end{aligned}$$

Thus, it suffices to evaluate, for a large enough n

$$\sup_{q\in[0,1]} |\widehat{QR}_q(\mathfrak{F}) - QR_q(\mathfrak{F})|.$$

Thus, Theorem 1 is a consequence of the following proposition. □

Proposition 1. *Under assumptions of Theorem 1, we have*

$$\sup_{q\in(0,1)} |\widehat{QR}_q(\mathfrak{F}) - QR_q(\mathfrak{F})| = O(f_n^b) + O_{a.co.}\left(\left(\frac{\log n}{n\,\alpha_{\mathfrak{F}}(f_n)}\right)^{\frac{1}{2}}\right)$$

The proof of this proposition is based on the Bahadur representation of the conditional quantile. The latter is a consequence of the following lemmas.

Lemma 1. *Let Π_n be a sequence of decreasing real random functions and Υ_n be a random real sequence such that*

$$\Upsilon_n = o_{a.co.}(1) \quad \text{and} \quad \sup_{|v|\leq M} |\Pi_n(v) + \lambda v - \Upsilon_n| = o_{a.co.}(1) \quad \text{for certain constants} \quad \lambda, M > 0.$$

Then, for any real sequence v_n such that $\Pi_n(v_n) = o_{a.co.}(1)$, we have:

$$\sum_{n=1}^{\infty} \mathbb{P}\{|v_n| \geq M\} < \infty.$$

4. On the Potential Impact of the Contribution

- **Comparison with existing approaches**
  In an earlier contribution [36], we have investigated robust mode estimation under a functional single-index structure, employing the local constant method. Alternatively, in this study, we examine local linear estimation for the same model under a general functional framework. Firstly, observe that the topic of the present contribution can be viewed as a generalization of [36], in the sense that the local constant constitutes a particular case of the local linear approach, and the functional single index structure is a special case of the general functional structure. Moreover, it is well documented (see, for instance, [27]) that the local linear method has many advantages over the Nadaraya–Watson (the local constant method). Particularly, the local linear estimation is usually used to reduce the bias and the boundary effect of the Nadaraya–Watson method. So, the use of the local linear method instead of the standard kernel method substantially improves the prediction accuracy. On the other hand, it is widely recognized that the single-index model reduces analytical complexity by projecting functional covariates onto a univariate index. Thus, it transforms the functional data analysis problem into a one-dimensional real data issue. This oversimplification is unusual in practice, as it ignores potentially influential higher-dimensional interactions. Our generalized framework of this contribution circumvents this limitation. From a practical point of view, the kernel estimator assumes that the nonparametric model is flat within the neighborhood of the location point, which leads to suboptimal prediction. In contrast, the local linear method assumes that the model has a linear approximation in the neighborhood of the location point, which is more realistic and improves the prediction results.
- **On the bias reduction**
  As mentioned in the previous comment, the behavior of the bias term is one of the main reasons for adopting the local linear method. Although the asymptotic behavior of the bias term is usually linked to the smoothness assumptions of the nonparametric model, this term can be significantly improved in the local linear approach. This beneficial characteristic is related to the weighting functions in the local linear estimator (see [27] in the non-functional case). A similar statement can be deduced in the functional case. Specifically, under standard conditions, the local linear approach offers a better bias term compared to the Nadaraya–Watson [36]. Indeed, this improvement is also due to the specific weighting functions implemented in $\widehat{QR}_q(\mathfrak{F})$. It is clear that the leading term of the Bahadur representation of $\widehat{QR}_q(\mathfrak{F})$ such that

  $$\mathbb{E}\Big[\mathbf{D}_i(A_3\mathbf{F}_i - A_2 f_n^{-1}\mathbf{D}_i\mathbf{F}_i)\Big] = 0$$

  where

  $$\mathbf{F}_i = \mathbf{F}(f_n^{-1}m(\mathfrak{F}, F_i)), \quad \text{and} \quad \mathbf{D}_i = m(F_i, \mathfrak{F})$$

  and

  $$A_j = \alpha_{\mathfrak{F}}^{-1}(f_n) f_n^{1-j}\mathbb{E}[\mathbf{D}_i^{j-1}\mathbf{F}_i]; \; j = 2, 3.$$

  Using the same analytical arguments as in [37], we prove that the first part of the bias term can be reduced to $o(f_n^{b/2})$. In conclusion, although the local linear and the Nadaraya–Watson (NW) estimators share similar asymptotic properties, the local linearity of the model and the weighting functions of the LLE method allow us to improve the bias term in certain situations.
- **On the applicability of the estimator**

Of course, the simple use of the estimator greatly depends on choosing its parameters easily. Since the estimator is derived from quantile regression, there are multiple cross-validation methods available for selecting the parameters, particularly the bandwidth parameters associated with the functional component. First, for a given subset H_n of real positive numbers, we consider the cross-validation criterion used by [38].

$$\arg\min_{f_n\in H_n} \frac{1}{n}\sum_{i=1}^{n}\Big(Q_p^L(F_i) - \widehat{Q}_p^{-i}(F_i)\Big)^2,$$

where $Q_p^L(X_i)$ denotes a local empirical quantile and $\widehat{Q}_p^{-i}$ is the conditional quantile estimator at F_i after excluding this observation from the sample. Secondly, we apply the cross-validation approach that was utilized by [39]

$$\arg\min_{f_n\in H_n} \frac{1}{n}\sum_{i=1}^{n} L_p\Big(R_i - \widehat{Q}_p^{-i}(F_i)\Big).$$

Additionally, various other methods can be utilized, such as the least squares cross-validation technique suggested by [6]:

$$\arg\min_{f_n\in H_n} \frac{1}{n}\sum_{i=1}^{n}\Big[R_i - \widehat{MR}(F_i)\Big]^2.$$

Of course, the diversity of selection methods makes the estimator easier to implement in practice.

5. Computational Part

5.1. Simulation Study

In this section, we demonstrate the practical effectiveness of our theoretical development through some simulation experiments. Our principal goal is to show the easy insertion of the estimator in practice and to emphasize clear benefits of the proposed estimator over its competitors, such as the kernel conditional mode and the conditional density-based LLE-mode. In order to cover many practical situations, we generate data from different scenarios. Indeed, we consider two different nonparametric functional models that are:

$$\begin{aligned}
\textit{heteroscedastic (Het.) Model}: R_i &= 4\int_0^1 \exp\Big(\frac{1}{3+F_i^3(t)}\Big)\,dt \;+\; \cos\big(3+F_i^3(t)\big)\,\epsilon_i,\\
\textit{homoscedastic (Hom.) Model}: R_i &= 5\int_0^1 \log\Big(\frac{2+F_i^2(t)}{3+F_i^3(t)}\Big)\,dt \;+\; \epsilon_i,
\end{aligned}$$

where ϵ_i and F_i are independent. The functional input variable is also generated in two ways: smoothly and roughly. The smooth way is generated according to the following formula:

$$\textit{Smooth curves}\;\; F_i(t) = a_i \cos(4(b_i - t\pi)) + b_i$$

while the rough way is drawn from the following equation:

$$\textit{rough curves}\;\; F_i(t) = a_i \cos(4(b_i - t\pi)) + b_i + \eta_{i,t}$$

For both cases, b_i is distributed in $N(0, 0.7))$ and a_i is generated according to a $N(3, 4)$ distribution, while the random variables $\eta_{i,t})$ are drawn from $N(0, 2)$. All the input curves F_i's are discretized on the same grid represented by 100 equispaced measurements taken in the interval $(0, 1)$. The resulting functional variables are shown in Figures 1 and 2.

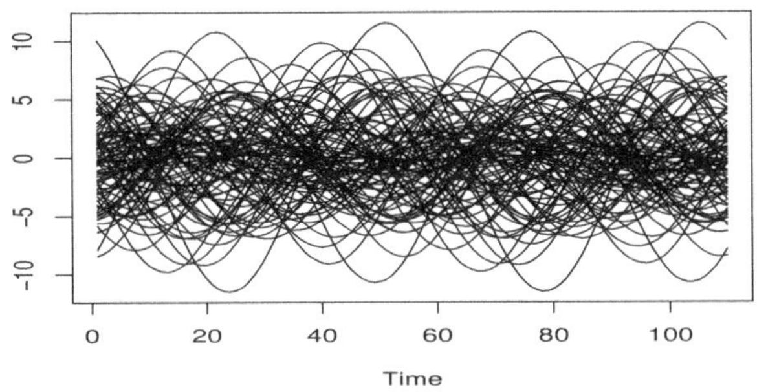

Figure 1. Smooth curves $F_i(t)$ for 100 equispaced measurements t in $(0,1)$, as displayed on the X-axis.

Obviously, choosing various curve forms is essential for evaluating how the data's functional structure affects the accuracy of estimates. Typically, the spline metric is used for modeling smooth curves, while the PCA metric is used for rough curves.

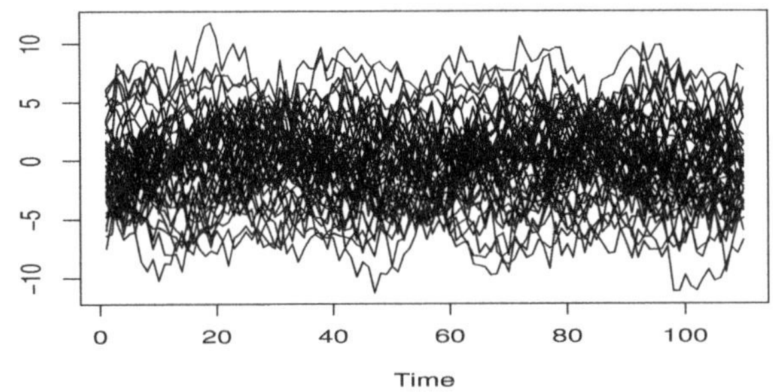

Figure 2. Rough curves $F_i(t)$ for 100 equispaced measurements t in $(0,1)$, as displayed on the X-axis.

This strategy of data sampling is intentional. It allows us to test the robustness of different models and assess how the data functionality affects the estimation accuracy. We also evaluate the nonparametric model using three distributions: Normal, Weibull, and Laplace. These were chosen because they remain consistent under translation and exhibit different levels of heavy-tailed behavior, which helps us to measure how well the estimators handle outliers. In mathematical terms, the two competitors' modal regression estimators are defined by:

$$\text{The NW estimator:} \quad \widetilde{MR}(\mathfrak{F}) = \arg\max_{y} \frac{\sum_{i=1}^{n} \mathbf{F}\big(f_n^{-1} m(\mathfrak{F}, F_i)\big)\, \mathbf{F}\big(b_n^{-1}(y - R_i)\big)}{\sum_{i=1}^{n} b_n\, \mathbf{F}\big(f_n^{-1} m(\mathfrak{F}, F_i)\big)}, \tag{12}$$

$$\text{and the LLEestimator:} \quad \overline{MR}(\mathfrak{F}) = \arg\max_{y} \frac{\sum_{i,j=1}^{n} \mathbf{W}_{ij}\, \mathbf{F}\big(b_n^{-1}(y - R_j)\big)}{\sum_{i,j=1}^{n} b_n\, \mathbf{W}_{ij}}, \tag{13}$$

where $W_{ij}(x) = m(F_i, \mathfrak{F},)\big(m(F_i, \mathfrak{F},) - m(F_j, \mathfrak{F},)\big)\mathbf{F}\big(f_n^{-1} m(\mathfrak{F}, F_i)\big)\mathbf{F}\big(f_n^{-1} m(\mathfrak{F}, F_j)\big)$.

Of course, the behavior of the three estimators, $\widehat{MR}$, $\widetilde{MR}$, and $\overline{MR}$, as well as their straightforward insertion, is influenced by the choice of parameters, metric m, kernel $\mathbf{F}$, and smoothing parameters (f_n, b_n). Evidently, the selection of the metric m is intrinsically linked to the smoothness of the functional curves. Smoother curves are better analyzed by the B-spline metric, which accommodates their regularity, while rougher curves require the PCA-metric to handle their more irregular structure. We refer to [2] for more details on the definitions of these metrics. The choice of kernel is motivated by technical considerations. In order to incorporate the assumption (B3), we have simulated using the quadratic kernel in $(-1,1)$. For the smoothing parameters (f_n, b_n), we have used the cross-validation rule based on the mean square error defined by

$$MSE(\ddot{MR}) = \frac{1}{n}\sum_{i=1}^{n}(R_i - \ddot{MR}(F_i))^2, \tag{14}$$

where $\ddot{MR}$ represents either $\widehat{MR}$, $\overline{MR}$, or $\widetilde{MR}$. It follows that

$$(f^{opt}, b^{opt}) = \arg \min_{f_n \in \mathbf{H}_n, b_n \in \mathbf{B}_n} MSE(\ddot{MR})$$

$\mathbf{H}_n$ (respectively, $\mathbf{B}_n$) is the set of positive real numbers, f_n, such that the ball centered at $\mathfrak{F}$ with radius f_n (respectively, the interval $[y - b_n, y + b_n]$) contains exactly k neighbors of (respectively, y). Typically, the number k is selected from the subset $\{5, 10, 20, \ldots, 0.5 * n\}$. For our goal, we generate $n = 200$ observations of (F_i, R_i), and we examine the robustness and the accuracy of different estimators using the MSE defined in (14). The obtained results are reported in the following table.

The performance of these estimators is strongly influenced by various components of the study, particularly the nature of the functional data and the nonparametric approach. Nevertheless, combining L^1-techniques with the LLE-smoothing method proves highly advantageous in terms of robustness and accuracy. As evidenced by the MSE results in Table 1, the variability in $\widehat{MR}$ is lower than that of the other estimators. This lower variability demonstrates that the L^1-LLE estimator for the conditional mode offers greater robustness and improved accuracy.

Table 1. MSE for different estimators in different scenarios .

Cond. Dist.	Model	CURVES	$\widehat{MR}$	$\overline{MR}$	$\widetilde{MR}$
Normal	Hom.model	Smooth	0.0258	0.0897	0.1672
		Rough	0.1067	0.4676	0.5679
Normal	Het.model	Smooth	0.2672	0.7426	1.0578
		Rough	0.3617	1.2725	1.8811
Laplace	Hom. model	Smooth	0.4257	0.6150	0.6317
		Rough	0.9804	1.0922	1.1788
Laplace	Het. model	Smooth	0.8967	1.6824	1.7088
		Rough	0.9176	2.4521	2.6588
Weibull	Hom. model	Smooth	0.5179	1.5005	1.5446
		Rough	0.8399	2.4873	2.7098
Weibull	Het. model	Smooth	0.7840	1.6253	1.4102
		Rough	0.9705	3.3567	4.3456

5.2. Real Data Application

Spectrometry data analysis is a powerful tool for generating high-frequency functional data. In this study, we focus on food quality as a critical real-world issue. Clearly, ensuring high-quality food is a top priority for both consumers and producers. Traditionally, quality control relies on chemical testing as an effective but destructive, time-consuming, and expensive approach. Instead, we provide a smart solution that combines spectrometry techniques with advanced statistical tools. It permits us to create an efficient, cost-effective, and non-invasive approach to ensure food quality. Specifically, we demonstrate how our new predictor can accurately predict fat and moisture contents in chocolate. Therefore, we evaluate our approach against leading alternatives, including the NW estimator, LLE-conditional expectation, and density-based LLE-mode. This computational study allows us to demonstrate the superiority and practical advantages of $\widehat{MR}$ in robustness as well as in accuracy. We compare these three approaches by testing their predictive performance using the near-infrared spectroscopy curve as functional input F, with the fat (or moisture) quantity as response variable R. The near-infrared data set available on the website (https://data.mendeley.com/datasets/7734j4fd98/1, (accessed on 8 May 2025)). This issue has been considered by many authors using different algorithms (see [40] for a list of references). Formally, in this real data example, we assume that the spectrum curve gives the absorbance of light across wavelengths ranging from 1000 to 2500 nm. These curves are visualized in Figure 3.

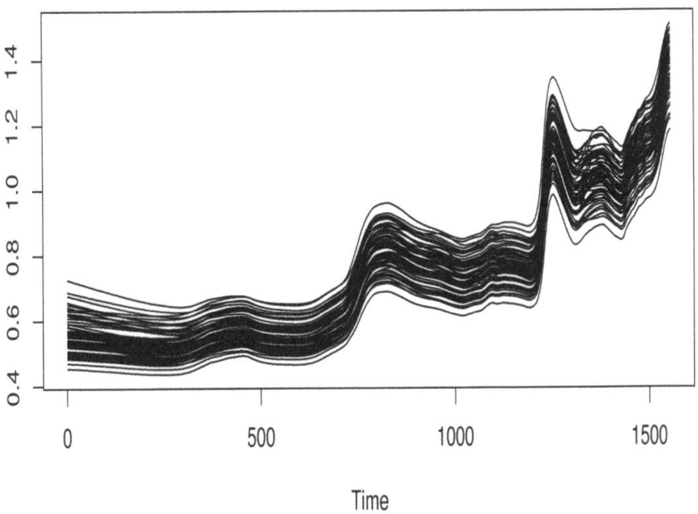

Figure 3. NIR curves.

These curves represent the absorbance spectrum (NIR) in the wavelength range from 1000 to 2500 nm for a total of 72 bulk intact cocoa bean samples. Each bulk amounted to 50 g of intact beans. Recall that the choice of the response variable R is motivated by the fact that the fat or moisture quantities are determinants of cocoa quality. The quality of cocoa beans is the cornerstone of exceptional chocolate production, profoundly influencing the sensory, nutritional, and commercial value of the final product. Thus, precise determination of cocoa contents is essential for compliance with chocolate quality standards, economic valuation, and research in agriculture and nutrition. Consequently, optimizing fat and moisture percentage is primordial to delivering high-quality chocolate products that meet both consumer and industry demands. Now, to put our predictors into action, we need to carefully select the principal parameters that drive our estimator's performance. This step is crucial to ensuring the potential feasibility of the four predictors $\widehat{MR}$, $\widetilde{MR}$, $\overline{MR}$, and

$$\overline{CE} = \frac{\sum_{i,j=1}^{n} \mathbf{W}_{ij} R_j}{\sum_{i,j=1}^{n} b_n \mathbf{W}_{ij}},$$

Based on our earlier discussion, the kernel selection is a direct consequence of assumption (B3), ensuring theoretical consistency. Meanwhile, the metric m plays a crucial role in the quantification of the smoothness of the functional curves F_i, allowing us to better analyze their behavior. Clearly, the curve's shape in Figure 3 shows that the metric of L_2 between the first derivatives of the curves (the curves being regular) is more suitable for this data. Once again, the smoothing parameters (f_n, b_n) according the same strategy as in (14). This latest approach has proven highly effective in our predictive modeling, highlighting the importance of leave-one-out cross-validation data-driven algorithms in functional data analysis. Figures 4 and 5 summarize our statistical predictions for fat and moisture for the 70 observations, comparing each approach's performance by plotting predicted values against the true values.

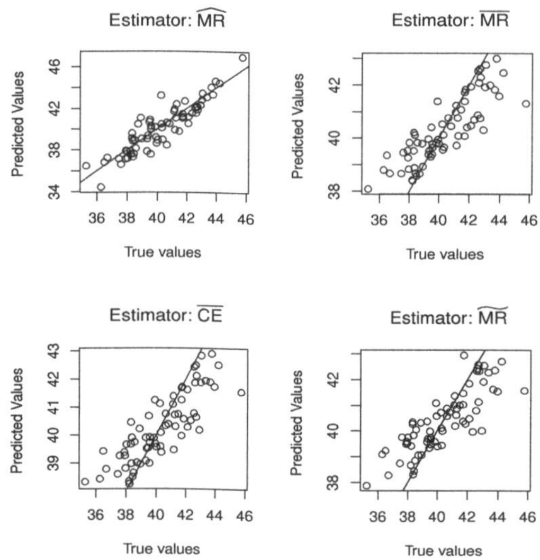

Figure 4. Moisture prediction.

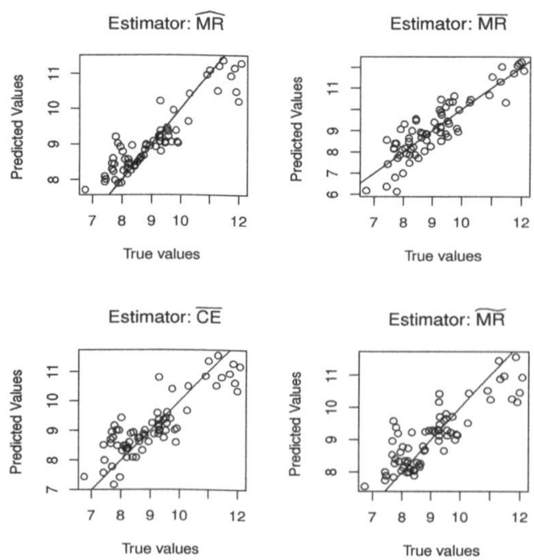

Figure 5. Fat prediction.

We use (MSE) error to assess model performance for the predictiom results. It is defined by

$$MSE(\ddot{\theta}) = \frac{1}{70}\sum_{i=1}^{70}\left(R_i - \ddot{MR}(F_i)\right)^2,$$

where $\ddot{\theta}$ can represent either $\widehat{MR}$, $\overline{MR}$, $\widetilde{MR}$ or $\overline{CE}$. Clearly, the predictor $\widehat{MR}$ outperforms the other predictors in precision. The latter predicts (fat, moisture) with MSE equal, respectively, to $(0.97, 1.06)$. It is the best one compared to the results obtained by the predictors $\overline{MR}$, $\widetilde{MR}$, and $\overline{CE}$. Typically, we record for both components (fat, moisture) $(1.70, 2, 89)$ for $\overline{MR}$, $(4.89, 7.48)$ for $\widetilde{MR}$ and $(3.45, 6.22)$ for $\overline{CE}$.

Author Contributions: The authors contributed approximately equally to this work. Formal analysis, F.A.A.; Validation, M.B.A.; Writing—review & editing, A.L. and Z.K. All authors have read and agreed to the published version of the manuscript.

Funding: This research was funded by Princess Nourah bint Abdulrahman University Researchers; Supporting Project number (PNURSP2025R515); Princess Nourah bint Abdulrahman University, Riyadh, Saudi Arabia; and the Deanship of Scientific Research and Graduate Studies at King Khalid University for funding this work through Small Research Project under grant number RGP1/41/46.

Data Availability Statement: The data used in this study are available through the link https://data.mendeley.com/datasets/7734j4fd98/1 (accessed on 8 May 2025).

Acknowledgments: The authors would like to thank the Editor, the Associate-Editor and two anonymous reviewers for their valuable comments and suggestions which improved substantially the quality of an earlier version of this paper. The authors thank and extend their appreciation to the funders of this work: This work was supported by Princess Nourah bint Abdulrahman University Researchers Supporting Project number (PNURSP2025R515), Princess Nourah bint Abdulrahman University, Riyadh, Saudi Arabia, and the Deanship of Scientific Research and Graduate Studies at King Khalid University for funding this work through Small Research Project under grant number RGP1/41/46.

Conflicts of Interest: The authors declare no conflicts of interest.

Appendix A. Proofs of Intermediate Results

Proof of Proposition 1. We apply Lemma 1 on

$$\nu_n = \begin{pmatrix} \widehat{A} - A \\ f_n(\widehat{B} - B) \end{pmatrix}$$

$$\mathcal{X}_n(\nu) = \frac{1}{n\alpha_{\mathfrak{F}}(\widetilde{F}_n)}\sum_{i=1}^{n}\zeta_q(\nu)\begin{pmatrix} 1 \\ f_n^{-1}\mathbf{D}_i \end{pmatrix}\mathbf{F}_i, \quad \text{for} \quad \nu = \begin{pmatrix} c \\ d \end{pmatrix}$$

and

$$\mathrm{Y}_n = \mathcal{X}_n(\nu_0) \quad \text{with} \quad \nu_0 = \begin{pmatrix} 0 \\ 0 \end{pmatrix}$$

where

$$\zeta_q(\nu) = q - \mathbf{1}_{R_i \leq (c+A) + (f_n^{-1}d + B)\mathbf{D}_i'}, \quad \mathbf{F}_i = \mathbf{F}(f_n^{-1}m(\mathfrak{F}, F_i)), \quad \text{and} \quad \mathbf{D}_i = m(F_i, \mathfrak{F}).$$

So, the main result is a consequence of the following lemmas. □

Lemma A1. *Under assumptions (B1)–(B5), we have*

$$\|Y_n\| = O(f_n^{\min(k_1,k_2)}) + O_{a.co.}\left(\left(\frac{\log n}{n\,\alpha_{\mathfrak{F}}(f_n)}\right)^{1/2}\right).$$

Proof of Lemma A1. Firstly, we set

$$\mathbf{Z}_i^1 = \left(q - \mathbf{1}_{[R_i \leq A + B\mathbf{D}_i]}\right)\mathbf{F}_i - \mathbb{E}\left[\left(q - \mathbf{1}_{[R_i \leq A + B\mathbf{D}_i]}\right)\mathbf{F}_i\right]$$

and

$$\mathbf{Z}_i^2 = \left(q - \mathbf{1}_{[R_i \leq A + B\mathbf{D}_i]}\right)\mathbf{D}_i\mathbf{F}_i - \mathbb{E}\left[\left(q - \mathbf{1}_{[R_i \leq A + B\mathbf{D}_i]}\right)\mathbf{F}_i\right].$$

Then

$$Y_n - \mathbb{E}[Y_n] = \begin{pmatrix} Y_n^1 \\ Y_n^2 \end{pmatrix}$$

where

$$\begin{cases} Y_n^1 = \dfrac{1}{n\alpha_{\mathfrak{F}}(\widetilde{F}_n)} \displaystyle\sum_{i=1}^n \mathbf{Z}_i^1 \\ Y_n^2 = \dfrac{1}{nh\alpha_{\mathfrak{F}}(\widetilde{F}_n)} \displaystyle\sum_{i=1}^n \mathbf{Z}_i^2. \end{cases}$$

Obviously

$$|\mathbf{Z}_i^1| \leq C \quad \text{and} \quad |\mathbf{Z}_i^2| \leq C'h.$$

Moreover,

$$\mathbb{E}\left[\mathbf{Z}_i^1\right]^2 \leq C\alpha_{\mathfrak{F}}(\widetilde{F}_n) \quad \text{and} \quad \mathbb{E}\left[\mathbf{Z}_i^2\right]^2 \leq C' f_n^2 \alpha_{\mathfrak{F}}(\widetilde{F}_n).$$

It follows that

$$Y_n^1 - \mathbb{E}\left[Y_n^1\right] = O_{a.co.}\left(\sqrt{\frac{\log n}{n\alpha_{\mathfrak{F}}(\widetilde{F}_n)}}\right)$$

and

$$Y_n^2 - \mathbb{E}\left[Y_n^2\right] = O_{a.co.}\left(\sqrt{\frac{\log n}{n\alpha_{\mathfrak{F}}(\widetilde{F}_n)}}\right).$$

Next,

$$\begin{aligned} \mathbb{E}\left[Y_n^1\right] &= \frac{1}{\alpha_{\mathfrak{F}}(\widetilde{F}_n)}\mathbb{E}\left[\left(q - \mathbf{1}_{[Y_1 \leq A + B\mathbf{D}_1]}\right)\mathbf{F}_1\right] \\ &\leq \frac{1}{\alpha_{\mathfrak{F}}(f_n)}\mathbb{E}\left|D(QR_q(\mathfrak{F})|\mathfrak{F}) - D((A + B\mathbf{D}_1)\mathbf{F}_1|F)\right| \\ &= O(f_n^{\min(k_1,k_2)}). \end{aligned}$$

Similarly,

$$\begin{aligned} \mathbb{E}\left[Y_n^2\right] &= \frac{1}{h\alpha_{\mathfrak{F}}(\widetilde{F}_n)}\mathbb{E}\left[\left(q - \mathbf{1}_{[Y_1 \leq A + B\mathbf{D}_1]}\right)\mathbf{D}_1\mathbf{F}_1\right] \\ &\leq \frac{1}{h\alpha_{\mathfrak{F}}(f_n)}\mathbb{E}\left|D(QR_q(\mathfrak{F})|\mathfrak{F})) - D((A + B\mathbf{D}_1)\mathbf{D}_1\mathbf{F}_1|F)\right| \\ &= O(f_n^{\min(k_1,k_2)}). \end{aligned}$$

Therefore,

$$\|Y_n\| = O(f_n^{\min(k_1,k_2)}) + O_{a.co.}\left(\left(\frac{\log n}{n\,\alpha_{\mathfrak{F}}(f_n)}\right)^{1/2}\right)$$

□

Lemma A2. *Under assumptions (B1)–(B5), we have*

$$\sup_{\|v\|\leq M} \|\mathcal{X}_n(v) + \lambda_0 D v - \mathrm{Y}_n\| = o_{a.co.}(1)$$

with

$$D = \begin{pmatrix} \mathbf{F}(1) - \int_{-1}^{1} K'(t)\beta_{\mathfrak{F}}(t)dt & \mathbf{F}(1) - \int_{-1}^{1} (t\mathbf{F}(t))'\beta_{\mathfrak{F}}(t)dt \\ \mathbf{F}(1) - \int_{-1}^{1} (t\mathbf{F}(t))'\beta_{\mathfrak{F}}(t)dt & \mathbf{F}(1) - \int_{-1}^{1} (t^2\mathbf{F}(t))'\beta_{\mathfrak{F}}(t)dt \end{pmatrix}$$

and

$$\lambda_0 = d(QR_q(\mathfrak{F})|\mathfrak{F})$$

Proof of Lemma A2. We prove

$$\sup_{\|v\|\leq M} \|\mathcal{X}_n(v) - \mathrm{Y}_n - \mathbb{E}[\mathcal{X}_n(v) - \mathrm{Y}_n]\| = O_{a.co.}\left(\sqrt{\frac{\log n}{n\alpha_{\mathfrak{F}}(\widetilde{F}_n)}}\right) \tag{A1}$$

and

$$\sup_{\|v\|\leq M} \|\mathbb{E}[\mathcal{X}_n(v) - \mathrm{Y}_n] + d(QR_q(\mathfrak{F})|\mathfrak{F}) D v\| = O(f_n^{\min(k_1,k_2)}). \tag{A2}$$

Next, use the compactness of the ball $B(0,M)$ in $\mathbb{R}^2$ and we write

$$B(0,M) \subset \bigcup_{j=1}^{d_n} B(v_j, l_n),\ v_j = \begin{pmatrix} c_j \\ d_j \end{pmatrix} \text{ and } l_n = d_n^{-1} = 1/\sqrt{n}.$$

Taking $j(v) = \arg\min_j |v - v_j|$ and we use the fact that

$$\begin{aligned} &\sup_{\|v\|\leq M} \|\mathcal{X}_n(v) - \mathrm{Y}_n - \mathbb{E}[\mathcal{X}_n(v) - \mathrm{Y}_n]\| \\ &\leq \sup_{\|v\|\leq M} \|\mathcal{X}_n(v) - \mathcal{X}_n(v_j)\| \\ &\quad + \sup_{\|v\|\leq M} \|\mathcal{X}_n(v_j) - \mathrm{Y}_n - \mathbb{E}\left[\mathcal{X}_n(v_j) - \mathrm{Y}_n\right]\| \\ &\quad + \sup_{\|v\|\leq M} \|\mathbb{E}\left[\mathcal{X}_n(v) - \mathcal{X}_n(v_j)\right]. \end{aligned}$$

Since $|\mathbb{1}_{[Y<a]} - \mathbb{1}_{[Y<b]}| \leq \mathbb{1}_{[|Y-b|\leq|a-b|]}$ then

$$\sup_{\|v\|\leq M} \|\mathcal{X}_n(v) - \mathcal{X}_n(v_j)\| \leq \frac{1}{n\alpha_{\mathfrak{F}}(\widetilde{F}_n)} \sum_i Z_i$$

where

$$\Omega_i = \sup_{\|v\|\leq M} \mathbb{1}_{[|R_i - (c_j + A) - (f_n^{-1} d_j + d)\mathbf{D}_i| \leq C l_n]} \left\| \begin{pmatrix} 1 \\ f_n^{-1}\mathbf{D}_i \end{pmatrix} \right\| \mathbf{F}_i.$$

Clearly

$$|\Omega_i| \leq C, \quad \mathbb{E}[\Omega_i] = O(l_n \alpha_{\mathfrak{F}}(\widetilde{F}_n)) \quad \text{and} \quad \mathbb{E}[\Omega_i^2] = O(l_n \alpha_{\mathfrak{F}}(\widetilde{F}_n)).$$

By using the fact that

$$l_n = o\left(\left(\frac{\log n}{n\alpha_{\mathfrak{F}}(\widetilde{F}_n)}\right)^{1/2}\right) \tag{A3}$$

we get

$$\sup_{\|v\|\leq M} \|\mathcal{X}_n(v) - \mathcal{X}_n(v_j)\| = O_{a.co.}\left(\left(\frac{\log n}{n\alpha_{\mathfrak{F}}(\widetilde{F}_n)}\right)^{1/2}\right).$$

For the last term,

$$\sup_{\|v\|\leq M} \|\mathbb{E}[\mathcal{X}_n(v) - \mathcal{X}_n(v_j)]\| \leq \frac{1}{\alpha_{\mathfrak{F}}(\widetilde{F}_n)}\mathbb{E}[\Omega_1] \leq Cl_n$$

then, by (A3) we obtain

$$\sup_{\|v\|\leq M} \|\mathbb{E}[\mathcal{X}_n(v) - \mathcal{X}_n(v_j)]\| = o_{a.co.}\left(\left(\frac{\log n}{n\alpha_{\mathfrak{F}}(\widetilde{F}_n)}\right)^{1/2}\right).$$

Now

$$\sup_{\|v\|\leq M} \|\mathcal{X}_n(v_j) - \mathrm{Y}_n - \mathbb{E}[\mathcal{X}_n(v_j) - \mathrm{Y}_n]\|.$$

For this

$$\mathcal{X}_n(v_j) - \mathrm{Y}_n - \mathbb{E}[\mathcal{X}_n(v_j) - \mathrm{Y}_n] = \begin{pmatrix} \Theta_n^1(v_j) \\ \Theta_n^2(v_j) \end{pmatrix}$$

where

$$\begin{cases} \Theta_n^1(v_j) = \dfrac{1}{n\alpha_{\mathfrak{F}}(f_n)}\displaystyle\sum_{i=1}^{n}\Lambda_i^1 \\ \Theta_n^2(v_j) = \dfrac{1}{nf_n\alpha_{\mathfrak{F}}(f_n)}\displaystyle\sum_{i=1}^{n}\Lambda_i^2 \end{cases}$$

with

$$\Lambda_i^1 = (\zeta_q(v_j) - \zeta_q(v_0))\mathbf{F}_i - \mathbb{E}[(\zeta_q(v_j) - \zeta_q(v_0))\mathbf{F}_i]$$

and

$$\Lambda_i^2 = (\zeta_q(v_j) - \zeta_q(v_0))\mathbf{D}_i\mathbf{F}_i - \mathbb{E}[(\zeta_q(v_j) - \zeta_q(v_0))\mathbf{D}_i\mathbf{F}_i].$$

clearly

$$|\Lambda_i^1| \leq C \quad \text{and} \quad |\Lambda_i^2| \leq C' f_n.$$

Moreover,

$$\mathbb{E}\left[\Lambda_i^1\right]^2 \leq C\alpha_{\mathfrak{F}}(f_n) \quad \text{and} \quad \mathbb{E}\left[\Lambda_i^2\right]^2 \leq C' f_n^2\alpha_{\mathfrak{F}}(f_n).$$

Therefore, there exits $\eta > 0$ such that

$$\begin{aligned} &\sum_n \mathbb{P}\left(\sup_{\|v\|\leq M} \|\mathcal{X}_n(v_j) - \mathrm{Y}_n - \mathbb{E}[\mathcal{X}_n(v_j) - \mathrm{Y}_n]\| \geq \eta\sqrt{\frac{\log n}{n\alpha_{\mathfrak{F}}(f_n)}}\right) \\ &\quad \leq \sum_n d_n \max_j \mathbb{P}\left(\|\mathcal{X}_n(v_j) - \mathrm{Y}_n - \mathbb{E}[\mathcal{X}_n(v_j) - \mathrm{Y}_n]\| \geq \eta\sqrt{\frac{\log n}{n\alpha_{\mathfrak{F}}(f_n)}}\right) < \infty \end{aligned}$$

which complete the proof of (A1).

Concerning (A2) we write

$$\mathcal{X}_n(v) - \mathrm{Y}_n = \begin{pmatrix} \Theta_n^1(v) \\ \Theta_n^2(v) \end{pmatrix}$$

where

$$\Theta_n^1(v) = \frac{1}{n\alpha_{\mathfrak{F}}(f_n)}\sum_{i=1}^{n}(\zeta_q(v) - \zeta_q(v_0))\mathbf{F}_i$$

and

$$\Theta_n^2(\nu) = \frac{1}{nh\alpha_{\mathfrak{F}}(f_n)} \sum_{i=1}^{n} (\zeta_q(\nu) - \zeta_q(\nu_0)) \mathbf{D}_i \mathbf{F}_i$$

On the other hand, we have

$$\begin{aligned}
\mathbb{E}\left[\Theta_n^1(\nu)\right] &= -\frac{1}{\alpha_{\mathfrak{F}}(f_n)} \mathbb{E}\left[\left(\mathbf{1}_{[Y_1 \le (c+A)+(f_n^{-1}d+B)\mathbf{D}_1]} - \mathbf{1}_{[Y_1 \le A+B\mathbf{D}_1]}\right)\mathbf{F}_i\right] \\
&= -\frac{1}{\alpha_{\mathfrak{F}}(f_n)} \mathbb{E}\left[\left(D(((c+A)+(f_n^{-1}d+B)\mathbf{D}_1)|F_1) - D((A+B\mathbf{D}_1)|F_1)\right)\mathbf{F}_1\right] \\
&= -\frac{1}{\alpha_{\mathfrak{F}}(f_n)} \mathbb{E}\left[\left(D((c+A)+(f_n^{-1}d+B)\mathbf{D}_1|\mathfrak{F}) - D(A+B\mathbf{D}_1)|\mathfrak{F}\right)\mathbf{F}_1\right] + O(f_n^{k_1}) \\
&= -\frac{1}{\alpha_{\mathfrak{F}}(f_n)} \mathbb{E}\left[d(A+B\mathbf{D}_1)|\mathfrak{F}\left(1, f_n^{-1}\mathbf{D}_1\right)\nu\mathbf{F}_1\right] + O(f_n^{k_1}) + o(\|\nu\|) \\
&= -d(QR_q(\mathfrak{F})|\mathfrak{F}) \frac{1}{\alpha_{\mathfrak{F}}(f_n)} \left(\mathbb{E}\mathbf{F}_1, f_n^{-1}\mathbb{E}[\mathbf{D}_1\mathbf{F}_1]\right)\nu + O(f_n^{\min(k_1,k_2)}) + o(\|\nu\|)
\end{aligned}$$

Similarly,

$$\mathbb{E}\left[\Theta_n^2(\nu)\right] = -d(QR_q(\mathfrak{F})|\mathfrak{F}) \frac{1}{h\alpha_{\mathfrak{F}}(f_n)} \left(\mathbb{E}\mathbf{D}_1\mathbf{F}_1, f_n^{-1}\mathbb{E}[\mathbf{D}_1^2\mathbf{F}_1]\right)\nu + O(f_n^{\min(k_1,k_2)}) + o(\|\nu\|).$$

Thus

$$\begin{aligned}
\mathbb{E}[\mathcal{X}_n(\nu) - Y_n] &= -d(QR_q(\mathfrak{F})|\mathfrak{F}) \frac{1}{\alpha_{\mathfrak{F}}(f_n)} \begin{pmatrix} \mathbb{E}[\mathbf{F}_i] & \mathbb{E}\left[\mathbf{F}_i f_n^{-1}\mathbf{D}_i\right] \\ \mathbb{E}\left[\mathbf{F}_i f_n^{-1}\mathbf{D}_i\right] & \mathbb{E}\left[f_n^{-2}\mathbf{D}_i^2\mathbf{F}_i\right] \end{pmatrix} \nu \\
&\quad + O(f_n^{\min(k_1,k_2)}) + o(\|\nu\|).
\end{aligned}$$

Obviously

$$f_n^{-a}\mathbb{E}[\mathbf{D}_i^{-a}\mathbf{F}_i^b] = \alpha_{\mathfrak{F}}(f_n)\left(\mathbf{F}^b(1) - \int_{-1}^{1} (u^a\mathbf{F}^b(u))'\mathbf{D}(u)du\right) + o(\alpha_{\mathfrak{F}}(f_n)).$$

Hence,

$$\sup_{\|\nu\| \le M} \|\mathbb{E}[\mathcal{X}_n(\nu) - Y_n] + d(QR_q(\mathfrak{F})|\mathfrak{F})D\nu + o(\|\nu\|)\| = O(f_n^{\min(k_1,k_2)})$$

implying the result (A2). □

Lemma A3. *Under assumptions (B1)–(B5), we have*

$$\sup_{|\nu| \le M} \sup_{q \in [0,1]} |\Pi_n(\nu, q) - \mathbb{E}[\Pi_n(\nu, q)]| = O_{a.co.}\left(\left(\frac{\log n}{n\,\alpha_{\mathfrak{F}}(f_n)}\right)^{1/2}\right).$$

where

$$\Pi_n(\nu, q) = \frac{1}{n\alpha_{\mathfrak{F}}(\widetilde{F}_n)} \sum_{i=1}^{n} \zeta_q(\nu) \begin{pmatrix} 1 \\ f_n^{-1}\mathbf{D}_i \end{pmatrix} \mathbf{F}_i, \quad \text{for} \quad \nu = \begin{pmatrix} c \\ d \end{pmatrix}$$

Proof of Lemma A3. The compactness of $[0,1]$ implies

$$[0,1] \subset \bigcup_{k=1}^{d_n} [q_k - l_n, q_k + l_n], \ \textit{for}\ q_k \in [0,1].$$

Next, for all $q \in [0,1]$ we put $F_q = \arg\min_k |q - q_k|$ and we evaluate the term as function of ν and q. We have,

$$\sup_{|\nu|\le M}\sup_{q\in[0,1]} |\Pi_n(\nu,q) - \mathbb{E}[\Pi_n(\nu,q)]| \le \sup_{|\nu|\le M}\sup_{q\in[0,1]} |\Pi_n(\nu,q) - \Pi_n(\nu_{j(\nu)},q)|$$

$$+ \sup_{|\nu|\le M}\sup_{q\in[0,1]} |\Pi_n(\nu_{j(\nu)},q) - \Pi_n(\nu_{j(\nu)},q_{F_q})|$$

$$+ \sup_{|\nu|\le M}\sup_{q\in[0,1]} |\Pi_n(\nu_{j(\nu)},q_{F_q}) - \mathbb{E}[\Pi_n(\nu_{j(\nu)},q_{F_q})]|$$

$$+ \sup_{|\nu|\le M}\sup_{q\in[0,1]} |\mathbb{E}[\Pi_n(\nu_{j(\nu)},q_{F_q})] - \mathbb{E}[\Pi_n(\nu,q_{F_q})]$$

$$+ \sup_{|\nu|\le M}\sup_{q\in[0,1]} |\mathbb{E}[\Pi_n(\nu,q_{F_q})] - \mathbb{E}[\Pi_n(\nu,q)].$$

Firstly, we write

$$\sup_{|\nu|\le M}\sup_{q\in[0,1]} |\Pi_n(\nu,q) - \Pi_n(\nu_{j(\nu)},q)| \le \frac{1}{n\mathbb{E}[\mathbf{F}_1]}\sum_i \Omega_i^0$$

with

$$\Omega_i^0 = \sup_{|\nu|\le M}\sup_{q\in[0,1]} \mathbb{1}_{[|R_i - \nu_{j(\nu)} - QR(q|\mathfrak{F})|\le Cl_n]}\mathbf{F}_i.$$

As

$$|\Omega_i^0| \le C, \quad \mathbb{E}[\Omega_i^0] = O(l_n\alpha_{\mathfrak{F}}(f_n)) \quad \text{and} \quad \mathbb{E}[\Omega_i^{0^2}] = O(l_n\alpha_{\mathfrak{F}}(f_n))$$

we get

$$\sup_{|\nu|\le M}\sup_{q\in[0,1]} |\Pi_n(\nu,q) - \Pi_n(\nu_{j(\nu)},q) = O_{a.co.}\left(\left(\frac{\log n}{n\alpha_{\mathfrak{F}}(f_n)}\right)^{1/2}\right)$$

and

$$\sup_{|\nu|\le M}\sup_{q\in[0,1]} |\mathbb{E}\left[\Pi_n(\nu,q) - \Pi_n(\nu_{j(\nu)},q)\right] = o\left(\left(\frac{\log n}{n\alpha_{\mathfrak{F}}(f_n)}\right)^{1/2}\right).$$

Similarly,

$$\sup_{|\nu|\le M}\sup_{q\in[0,1]} |\Pi_n(\nu_{j(\nu)},q) - \Pi_n(\nu_{j(\nu)},q_{F_q})| \le \frac{1}{n\mathbb{E}[\mathbf{F}_1]}\sum_i \Omega_i^1$$

with

$$\Omega_i^1 = \sup_{|\nu|\le M}\sup_{q\in[0,1]} \left(\mathbb{1}_{[|R_i - \nu_{j(\nu)} - t(q|\mathfrak{F})|\le Cl_n]} + \mathbb{1}_{[|R_i - t(q_{F_q}|\mathfrak{F})|\le Cl_n]}\right)\mathbf{F}_i.$$

Since

$$|\Omega_i^1| \le C, \quad \mathbb{E}[\Omega_i^1] = O(l_n\alpha_{\mathfrak{F}}(f_n)) \quad \text{and} \quad \mathbb{E}[\Omega_i^{0^1}] = O(l_n\alpha_{\mathfrak{F}}(f_n))$$

we obtain

$$\sup_{|\nu|\le M}\sup_{q\in[0,1]} |\Pi_n(\nu,q) - \Pi_n(\nu_{j(\nu)},q) = O_{a.co.}\left(\left(\frac{\log n}{n\alpha_{\mathfrak{F}}(f_n)}\right)^{1/2}\right)$$

and

$$\sup_{|\nu|\le M}\sup_{q\in[0,1]} |\mathbb{E}\left[\Pi_n(\nu,q) - \Pi_n(\nu_{j(\nu)},q)\right] = o\left(\left(\frac{\log n}{n\alpha_{\mathfrak{F}}(f_n)}\right)^{1/2}\right).$$

By the same manner

$$\Pi_n(\nu_j, q_k) - \mathbb{E}[\Pi_n(\nu_j, q_k)] = \frac{1}{n\mathbb{E}[\mathbf{F}_1]}\sum_{i=1}^{n}\Lambda_i'$$

where

$$\Lambda_i' = \left(\mathbf{1}_{R_i \le t(q_k|\mathfrak{F})} - \mathbf{1}_{R_i \le \nu_j + t(q_k|\mathfrak{F})}\right)\mathbf{F}_i - \mathbb{E}\left[\left(\mathbf{1}_{R_i \le t(q_k|\mathfrak{F})} - \mathbf{1}_{R_i \le \nu_j + t(q_k|\mathfrak{F})}\right)\mathbf{F}_i\right].$$

By Bernstein inequality

$$|\Lambda_i| \le C \quad \text{and} \quad \mathbb{E}[\Lambda_i]^2 \le C\alpha_{\mathfrak{F}}(f_n)$$

to show that there exits $\eta > 0$ such that

$$\sum_n \mathbb{P}\left(\sup_{|\nu|\le M}\sup_{q\in[0,1]} |\Pi_n(\nu_{j(\nu)}, q_{F_q}) - \mathbb{E}[\Pi_n(\nu_{j(\nu)}, q_{F_q})]| \ge \eta\sqrt{\frac{\log n}{n\alpha_{\mathfrak{F}}(f_n)}}\right)$$
$$\le \sum_n d_n^2 \max_j \max_k \mathbb{P}\left(|\Pi_n(\nu_j, q_k) - \mathbb{E}[\Pi_n(\nu_j, q_k)]| \ge \eta\sqrt{\frac{\log n}{n\alpha_{\mathfrak{F}}(f_n)}}\right) < \infty.$$

Therfore,

$$\sup_{q\in[0,1]}\sup_{|\nu|\le M} |\Pi_n(\nu, q) - \Upsilon_n - \mathbb{E}[\Pi_n(\nu, q) - \Upsilon_n]| = O_{a.co.}\left(\sqrt{\frac{\log n}{n\alpha_{\mathfrak{F}}(f_n)}}\right)$$

Obserrve that by the same techniques we prove that

$$\sup_{q\in[0,1]} |\Upsilon_n - \mathbb{E}[\Upsilon_n]| = O_{a.co.}\left(\sqrt{\frac{\log n}{n\alpha_{\mathfrak{F}}(f_n)}}\right)$$

□

References

1. Ramsay, J.O.; Silverman, B.W. *Functional Data Analysis*, 2nd ed.; Springer: New York, NY, USA, 2005.
2. Ferraty, F.; Vieu, P. *Nonparametric Functional Data Analysis. Theory and Practice*; Springer Series in Statistics; Springer: New York, NY, USA, 2006.
3. Xu, Y. Functional Data Analysis. In *Springer Handbook of Engineering Statistics*; Springer: London, UK, 2023; pp. 67–85.
4. Ahmed, M.S.; Frévent, C.; Génin, M. Spatial Scan Statistics for Functional Data. In *Handbook of Scan Statistics*; Springer: New York, NY, USA, 2024; pp. 629–645
5. Collomb, G.; Härdle, W.; Hassani, S. A note on prediction via estimation of the conditional mode function. *J. Stat. Plan. Inference* **1986**, *15*, 227–236. [CrossRef]
6. Quintela-Del-Rio, A.; Vieu, P. A nonparametric conditional mode estimate. *J. Nonparametr. Stat.* **1997**, *8*, 253–266. [CrossRef]
7. Ioannides, D.; Matzner-Løber, E. A note on asymptotic normality of convergent estimates of the conditional mode with errors-in-variables. *J. Nonparametr. Stat.* **2004**, *16*, 515–524. [CrossRef]
8. Louani, D.; Ould-Saïd, E.L.I.A.S. Asymptotic normality of kernel estimators of the conditional mode under strong mixing hypothesis. *J. Nonparametr. Stat.* **1999** *11*, 413–442. [CrossRef]
9. Bouzebda, S.; Khardani, S.; Slaoui, Y. Asymptotic normality of the regression mode in the nonparametric random design model for censored data. *Commun. Stat. Theory Methods* **2023**, *52*, 7069–7093. [CrossRef]
10. Bouzebda, S.; Didi, S. Some results about kernel estimators for function derivatives based on stationary and ergodic continuous time processes with applications. Communications in Statistics. *Theory Methods* **2022**, *51*, 3886–3933. [CrossRef]

11. Ferraty, F.; Laksaci, A.; Vieu, P. Estimating some characteristics of the conditional distribution in nonparametric functional models. *Stat. Inference Stoch. Process.* **2006**, *9*, 47–76. [CrossRef]
12. Bouzebda, S.; Chaouch, M.; Laïb, N. Limiting law results for a class of conditional mode estimates for functional stationary ergodic data. *Math. Methods Stat.* **2016**, *25*, 1066–5307. [CrossRef]
13. Ezzahrioui, M.H.; Ould-Saïd, E. Asymptotic normality of a nonparametric estimator of the conditional mode function for functional data. *J. Nonparametr. Stat.* **2008**, *20*, 3–18. [CrossRef]
14. Ezzahrioui, M.H.; Saïd, E.O. Some asymptotic results of a non-parametric conditional mode estimator for functional time-series data. *Stat. Neerl.* **2010**, *64*, 171–201. [CrossRef]
15. Dabo-Niang, S.; Kaid, Z.; Laksaci, A. Asymptotic properties of the kernel estimate of spatial conditional mode when the regressor is functional. *AStA Adv. Stat. Anal.* **2015**, *99*, 131–160. [CrossRef]
16. Bouanani, O.; Laksaci, A.; Rachdi, M.; Rahmani, S. Asymptotic normality of some conditional nonparametric functional parameters in high-dimensional statistics. *Behaviormetrika* **2019**, *46*, 199–233. [CrossRef]
17. Azzi, A.; Belguerna, A.; Laksaci, A.; Rachdi, M. The scalar-on-function modal regression for functional time series data. *J. Nonparametr. Stat.* **2024**, *36*, 503–526. [CrossRef]
18. Stone, C.J. Consistent nonparametric regression. *Ann. Stat.* **1977**, *5*, 595–620. [CrossRef]
19. Koenker, R.; Zhao, Q. Conditional quantile estimation and inference for ARCH models. *Econom. Theory* **1996**, *12*, 793–813. [CrossRef]
20. Hallin, M.; Lu, Z.; Yu, K. Local linear spatial quantile regression. *Bernoulli* **2009**, *15*, 659–686. [CrossRef]
21. Cardot, H.; Crambes, C.; Sarda, P. Quantile regression when the covariates are functions. *J. Nonparametr. Stat.* **2005**, *17*, 841–856. [CrossRef]
22. Wang, H.; Ma, Y. Optimal subsampling for quantile regression in big data. *Biometrika* **2021**, *108*, 99–112. [CrossRef]
23. Jiang, Z.; Huang, Z. Single-index partially functional linear quantile regression. *Commun. Stat.-Theory Methods* **2024**, *53*, 1838–1850. [CrossRef]
24. Dabo-Niang, S.; Kaid, Z.; Laksaci, A. Spatial conditional quantile regression: Weak consistency of a kernel estimate. *Rev. Roum. Math. Pures Appl.* **2012** *57*, 311–339.
25. Chowdhury, J.; Chaudhuri, P. Nonparametric depth and quantile regression for functional data. *Bernoulli* **2019**, *25*, 395–423. [CrossRef]
26. Mutis, M.; Beyaztas, U.; Karaman, F.; Lin Shang, H. On function-on-function linear quantile regression. *J. Appl. Stat.* **2025**, *52*, 814–840. [CrossRef]
27. Fan, J. *Local Polynomial Modelling and Its Applications: Monographs on Statistics and Applied Probability 66*; Routledge: Abingdon-on-Thames, UK, **2018**.
28. Rachdi, M.; Laksaci, A.; Demongeot, J.; Abdali, A.; Madani, F. Theoretical and practical aspects of the quadratic error in the local linear estimation of the conditional density for functional data. *Comput. Stat. Data Anal.* **2014**, *73*, 53–68. [CrossRef]
29. Baíllo, A.; Grané, A. Local linear regression for functional predictor and scalar response. *J. Multivar. Anal.* **2009**, *100*, 102–111. [CrossRef]
30. Barrientos-Marin, J.; Ferraty, F.; Vieu, P. Locally modelled regression and functional data. *J. Nonparametr. Stat.* **2010**, *22*, 617–632. [CrossRef]
31. Berlinet, A.; Elamine, A.; Mas, A. Local linear regression for functional data. *Ann. Inst. Stat. Math.* **2011**, *63*, 1047–1075. [CrossRef]
32. Demongeot, J.; Laksaci, A.; Madani, F.; Rachdi, M. Functional data: Local linear estimation of the conditional density and its application. *Statistics* **2013**, *47*, 26–44. [CrossRef]
33. Messaci, F.; Nemouchi, N.; Ouassou, I.; Rachdi, M. Local polynomial modelling of the conditional quantile for functional data. *Stat. Methods Appl.* **2015**, *24*, 597–622. [CrossRef]
34. Laksaci, A.; Ould Saïd, E.; Rachdi, M. Uniform consistency in number of neighbors of the k NN estimator of the conditional quantile model. *Metrika* **2021**, *84*, 895–911. [CrossRef]
35. Ota, H.; Kato, K.; Hara, S. Quantile regression approach to conditional mode estimation. *Electron. J. Stat.* **2019**, *13*, 3120–3160. [CrossRef]
36. Almulhim, F.A.; Alamari, M.B.; Bouzebda, S.; Kaid, Z.; Laksaci, A. Robust Estimation of L 1-Modal Regression Under Functional Single-Index Models for Practical Applications. *Mathematics* **2025**, *13*, 602. [CrossRef]
37. Belarbi, F.; Chemikh, S.; Laksaci, A. Local linear estimate of the nonparametric robust regression in functional data. *Stat. Probab. Lett.* **2018**, *134*, 128–133. [CrossRef]
38. Iglesias Pérez, M.D.C. Estimación de la función de distribución condicional en presencia de censura y truncamiento: Una aplicación al estudio de la mortalidad en pacientes diabéticos. *Estad. Esp.* **2003**, *45*, 275–302.

39. Yuan, M. GACV for quantile smoothing splines. *Comput. Stat. Data Anal.* **2006**, *50*, 813–829. [CrossRef]
40. Panchbhai, K.G.; Lanjewar, M.G. Portable system for cocoa bean quality assessment using multi-output learning and augmentation. *Food Control* **2025**, *174*, 111234. [CrossRef]

axioms

Article

Robust Adaptive Lasso via Robust Sample Autocorrelation Coefficient for the Autoregressive Models

Yunlu Jiang [1], Fudong Chen [1] and Xiao Yan [2,*]

[1] School of Economics, Jinan University, Guangzhou 510632, China
[2] School of Public Administration, Jinan University, Guangzhou 510632, China
* Correspondence: xiaoyan@jnu.edu.cn

Abstract: For the autoregressive models, classical estimation methods, including the least squares estimator or the maximum likelihood estimator are not robust to heavy-tailed distributions or outliers in the dataset, and lack sparsity, leading to potentially inaccurate estimation and poor generalization capability. Meanwhile, the existing variable selection methods can not handle the case where the influence of explanatory variables on the dependent variable gradually weakens as the lag order increases. To address these issues, we propose a novel robust adaptive lasso method for the autoregressive models. The proposed method is constructed by using partial autocorrelation coefficients as adaptive penalty weights to promote sparsity in parameter estimation, and by employing a robust autocorrelation estimator based on the FQ_n statistic to enhance resistance to outliers. Numerical simulations and two real data analyses illustrate the promising performance of our proposed approach. The results indicate that our proposed approach exhibits good robustness and sparsity in the presence of outliers in the dataset.

Keywords: autoregressive model; PACF adaptive lasso; robust autocorrelation coefficient

MSC: 62M10; 62F35

1. Introduction

Financial market stability is significantly influenced by the prices of the stock index, which serve as crucial indicators of macroeconomic conditions. However, constructing robust and generalizable prediction models for stock indices presents considerable challenges due to their inherent volatility, a characteristic driven by complex interactions among economic, political, cultural and demographic factors. Among various forecasting approaches, time series analysis models, particularly autoregressive (AR) models, have been widely employed for stock price prediction.

Traditional estimation methods for AR models, such as the ordinary least squares (OLS) estimator and the maximum likelihood estimator, perform adequately under some regular conditions, but become unreliable when financial data contain outliers. Such outliers frequently arise from unexpected events such as policy changes, major accidents, and social phenomena. As demonstrated by Box et al. [1], outliers can severely distort time-series model estimates. Two primary approaches have been developed to address this issue: outlier detection and removal, or robust estimation methods that mitigate outlier effects.

In outlier detection research, Huber [2] pioneered methods for identifying outliers in AR models. Chang et al. [3] subsequently extended these methods to ARIMA models with iterative procedures for innovational outliers (IOs) and additive outliers (AOs).

 https://doi.org/10.3390/axioms14090701

Tsay et al. [4] generalized these approaches to multivariate cases, while McQuarrie and Tsai [5] proposed a detection method that does not require prior knowledge of the order, location, or type of the model. Further developments include techniques by Karioti and Caroni [6] for shorter time series and unequal-length AR models, and continuous detection methods introduced by Louni [7] that demonstrate superior performance for IOs. However, most detection methods rely on specific distributional assumptions that are often unrealistic in practice. To address this limitation, Čampulová et al. [8] proposed a nonparametric approach combining data smoothing with change point analysis of residuals.

Compared to outlier detection, robust estimation methods for time series have received less attention. Notable contributions include Pan et al. [9] application of local least absolute deviation for PARMA models and Jiang [10] introduction of exponential square estimators for AR models with heavy-tailed errors. Recent advances by Callens et al. [11] weighted M-estimators with data-driven parameter selection and Chang and Shi [12] reweighted multivariate least trimmed squares and MM-estimators for VAR models.

Traditional time series estimation methods also suffer from poor generalization due to the lack of sparsity. This issue was addressed by the least absolute shrinkage and selection operator (lasso) method [13], which produces sparse and interpretable models. Subsequent developments include smoothly clipped absolute deviation (SCAD) penalty [14] and adaptive lasso [15] to overcome the bias of the lasso method. For AR models, Audrino and Camponovo [16] investigated adaptive lasso's theoretical properties, Songsiri [17] formulated ℓ_1-regularized least squares problems, and Emmert-Streib and Dehmer [18] proposed a two-step lasso approach for vector autoregression with data-driven feature selection. However, traditional AR model estimation methods are sensitive to outliers and can not deal with the case that the influence of explanatory variables on the dependent variable gradually weakens as the lag order increases. In order to overcome this issue, we propose a novel robust adaptive lasso approach that combines the partial autocorrelation coefficient to construct adaptive penalty weights and uses robust autocorrelation coefficients constructed using the FQ_n statistic. Both extensive numerical simulations and a real data example demonstrate the validity of our proposed method.

The rest of the paper is organized as follows: In Section 2, we first review traditional estimation methods for AR models, and present our proposed robust adaptive lasso method. In Section 3, we evaluate the finite-sample performance of the proposed method through Monte Carlo simulations and compare it with other methods. In Section 4, we employ the proposed method to analyze two distinct time series: the S&P 500 Index and the USD/CNY exchange rate. We conclude with some remarks in Section 5.

2. Robust Adaptive Lasso for AR Models

2.1. Least Squares Method

The autoregressive models with order p, denoted as AR(p), can be expressed as follows:

$$y_t = \beta_0 + \beta_1 y_{t-1} + \cdots + \beta_p y_{t-p} + \varepsilon_t, \tag{1}$$

where y_t is the dependent variable, $y_{t-1}, \ldots, y_{t-p}$ are explanatory variables, $\boldsymbol{\beta} = (\beta_0, \beta_1, \ldots, \beta_p)^T$ are unknown parameters, and ε_t is an independent error term with $E\varepsilon_t = 0$. Given n samples, the coefficients in model (1) can be estimated by minimizing the residual sum of squares:

$$\hat{\boldsymbol{\beta}}_{ols} = \arg\min_{\boldsymbol{\beta}} \sum_{t=p+1}^{n} \left(y_t - \beta_0 - \sum_{k=1}^{p} y_{t-k}\beta_k \right)^2. \tag{2}$$

However, the least squares method is non-robust and incapable of order selection, and cannot yield sparse solutions.

2.2. Lasso and Adaptive Lasso Methods

Tibshirani [13] proposed a lasso method that simultaneously performs variable selection and parameter estimation by introducing a penalty term to the objective function in (2), which is given as follows:

$$\hat{\beta}_{\text{lasso}} = \underset{\beta}{\operatorname{argmin}} \left(\sum_{t=p+1}^{n} \left(y_t - \beta_0 - \sum_{k=1}^{p} y_{t-k}\beta_k \right)^2 + \lambda_1 \sum_{k=1}^{p} |\beta_k| \right), \quad \lambda_1 \geq 0, \tag{3}$$

where λ_1 is nonnegative tuning parameter.

However, the lasso method applies uniform penalty coefficients to all features, which results in biased estimates. To address this limitation, Zou [15] proposed the adaptive lasso method, which assigns smaller penalties to larger coefficients and vice versa. The estimation procedure is introduced as follows:

$$\hat{\beta}_{\text{adl}} = \underset{\beta}{\operatorname{argmin}} \left(\sum_{t=1}^{n} \left(y_t - \beta_0 - \sum_{k=1}^{p} y_{t-k}\beta_k \right)^2 + \lambda_2 \sum_{k=1}^{p} \omega_{k1} |\beta_k| \right), \quad \lambda_2 \geq 0, \tag{4}$$

where λ_2 is a nonnegative penalty parameter, $\omega_{k1} = 1/|\hat{\beta}_k|^{\delta_1}$, δ_1 is a positive constant, and $\hat{\beta}_k$ is the estimated value of β_k.

2.3. Robust Adaptive Lasso for AR Models

Classical estimation approaches such as the least squares method lack robustness. For the AR(p) models, the Yule-Walker equations can be expressed as:

$$\begin{aligned} \rho_1 &= \beta_1\rho_0 + \beta_2\rho_1 + \cdots + \beta_p\rho_{1-p}, \\ \rho_2 &= \beta_1\rho_1 + \beta_2\rho_0 + \cdots + \beta_p\rho_{2-p}, \\ &\vdots \\ \rho_p &= \beta_1\rho_{p-1} + \beta_2\rho_{p-2} + \cdots + \beta_p\rho_0, \end{aligned} \tag{5}$$

where ρ_j denotes the j-th order autocorrelation coefficient.

The Yule–Walker equations form a system of linear equations between the sample autocorrelation function and the coefficients. Clearly, robust coefficients can be obtained by deriving robust autocorrelation functions. However, the expression of the sample autocorrelation function for weakly stationary time series contains the sample mean, which is highly sensitive to outliers, resulting in non-robust $\hat{\rho}_k$. Gnanadesikan and Kettenring [19] proposed an alternative definition of the autocorrelation function, which is defined as follows:

$$\rho = \frac{\text{var}(U) - \text{var}(V)}{\text{var}(U) + \text{var}(V)}, \tag{6}$$

where

$$\begin{aligned} U &= (X/\sigma_1 + Y/\sigma_2)/\sqrt{2}, \\ V &= (X/\sigma_1 - Y/\sigma_2)/\sqrt{2} \end{aligned}$$

with σ_1 and σ_2 being the standard deviations of X and Y, respectively. The correlation coefficient of the sample can be expressed as follows:

$$\hat{\rho} = \frac{\hat{S}^2(U) - \hat{S}^2(V)}{\hat{S}^2(U) + \hat{S}^2(V)}, \tag{7}$$

where $\hat{S}^2(U)$ and $\hat{S}^2(V)$ are the sample variance based on the random sample from U and V, respectively, and are the estimators of $\mathrm{var}(U)$ and $\mathrm{var}(V)$, respectively.

Since $\hat{\rho}$ in (7) involves the sample variance, it inherits non-robustness. Therefore, it is necessary to seek a robust alternative for the estimator of ρ. The median absolute deviation (MAD) is a robust estimator of standard deviation, and has a high breakdown point of 0.5, but at the cost of an efficiency of only 0.37. The breakdown point is a global robustness measure from the perspective of resistance to outliers, referring to the maximum proportion of contaminated data that an estimator can tolerate before becoming meaningless [20]. Refs. [21,22] point out that a 50% breakdown point means that the estimator is insensitive to the corruption made by outliers, provided that the outliers constitute less than 50% of the set. Rousseeuw and Croux [23] proposed another robust estimator, the lower quartile of the absolute pairwise differences (Q_n), which has a maximum breakdown point of 0.5 and an efficiency of 0.82. However, the Q_n estimator suffers from high computational complexity. Subsequently, Smirnov et al. [24] constructed an M-estimator by matching its influence function to that of the Q_n estimator, thereby maintaining the high asymptotic efficiency of Q_n while avoiding its high computational complexity, resulting in a fast Q_n statistic, denoted as FQ_n:

$$FQ_n(x) = 1.483\mathrm{MAD}_n(x)\left(1 - \left(Z_0 - \sqrt{n/\sqrt{2}}\right)/Z_2\right), \tag{8}$$

$$Z_k = \sum_{i=1}^{n} u_i^k e^{-u_i^2/2}, \quad (k = 0, 2;\ i = 1, 2, \cdots, n), \tag{9}$$

where MAD_n is the median absolute deviation and $\mathrm{med}(x)$ is the median.

In (8), by employing the k-step M-estimation approach, the final estimator inherits the breakdown point of the initial estimator (Rousseeuw and Croux [25]). Therefore, when MAD is selected as the initial estimator, the FQ_n also achieves a breakdown point of 0.5. Using FQ_n to estimate the sample standard deviation yields robust sample autocorrelation coefficients:

$$\hat{\rho} = \frac{FQ_n^2(u) - FQ_n^2(v)}{FQ_n^2(u) + FQ_n^2(v)}. \tag{10}$$

The Yule–Walker equations establish the relationship between sample autocorrelation coefficients and parameters to be estimated. By obtaining robust autocorrelation coefficients, we can derive robust parameter estimates through the corresponding algorithms. To achieve both robust and sparse results, these robust correlation coefficients are incorporated into the adaptive lasso method to enhance the model's robustness.

Generally, the influence of explanatory variables on the dependent variable gradually weakens as the lag order increases. We combine the partial autocorrelation coefficient commonly used in time series order determination with the adaptive lasso method to improve the traditional lasso model.

$$\hat{\beta}_{ra} = \underset{\beta}{\mathrm{argmin}}\left(\sum_{t=p+1}^{n}\left(\hat{\rho}_t - \sum_{k=1}^{p}\hat{\rho}_{t-k}\beta_k\right)^2 + \lambda_3\sum_{k=1}^{p}\omega_{k3}|\beta_k|\right), \quad \lambda_3 \geq 0, \tag{11}$$

where

$$\omega_{k3} = \frac{1}{|\hat{\beta}_k|^{\delta_2}|\hat{\phi}_{kk}|^{\delta_3}}, \quad \delta_2, \delta_3 > 0, \tag{12}$$

$\hat{\rho}_t$ is the t-th order robust autocorrelation coefficient, the k-th order sample partial autocorrelation coefficient $\hat{\phi}_{kk}$ is computed recursively as follows:

$$\hat{\phi}_{kk} = \frac{\hat{\rho}_k - \sum_{j=1}^{k-1} \hat{\phi}_{k-1,j}\hat{\rho}_{k-j}}{1 - \sum_{j=1}^{k-1} \hat{\phi}_{k-1,j}\hat{\rho}_j}, \tag{13}$$

where $\hat{\rho}_k$ is the k-th order sample autocorrelation coefficient, $\hat{\phi}_{k-1,j}$ represents the j-th coefficient estimate from the $(k-1)$-th order partial autocorrelation, and the recursion is initialized with $\hat{\phi}_{11} = \hat{\rho}_1$.

3. Simulation Studies

In this section, we investigate the numerical performance of the proposed method using Monte Carlo simulations. We simulated 100 data sets from the following autoregression model (14) with sample sizes $n = 200, 400$.

$$y_t = \beta_1 y_{t-1} + \cdots + \beta_{10} y_{t-10} + \varepsilon_t. \tag{14}$$

The data are generated by the following three scenarios:

- Scenario 1: The coefficients $(\beta_1, \ldots, \beta_5) = (0.45, -0.37, 0.28, 0.20, 0.15)$ with $\beta_j = 0$ for $j > 5$. The error term follows a Gaussian mixture distribution: $\varepsilon_t \sim (1-\varepsilon)N(0,1) + \varepsilon N(0,10)$, where the contamination proportion ε takes values $\{0, 0.10, 0.20\}$.
- Scenario 2: Maintaining the same coefficient as Scenario 1, the error distribution is replaced by $\varepsilon_t \sim (1-\varepsilon)N(0,1) + \varepsilon\text{Cauchy}(0,1)$ with $\varepsilon \in \{0, 0.10, 0.20\}$. The Cauchy component introduces extreme outliers due to its heavy-tailed properties.
- Scenario 3: The coefficients $(\beta_1, \ldots, \beta_5) = (0.85, -0.20, 0.15, 0.10, 0.05)$ with $\beta_j = 0$ for $j > 5$. Characteristic root analysis confirms stationarity with a dominant root modulus of 1.031, inducing strong persistence and slow mean reversion typical of economic time series. The error term follows that of Scenario 1.

To demonstrate the advantage of our proposed method, we compare our proposed method (RA-LASSO) with the traditional adaptive lasso method (LS-LASSO) and the ordinary least squares estimation (OLS). Furthermore, the following four criteria were computed to evaluate the finite sample performance:

1. TP: The average accuracy rate of parameter estimates over 100 repetitions.
2. Size: The average number of non-zero coefficients in the estimation results over 100 repetitions.
3. AE: Mean absolute estimation error: $\sum_{j=1}^{p} |\hat{\beta}_{nj} - \beta_j|$.
4. SE: Root of mean squares estimation error: $\sqrt{\sum_{j=1}^{p} |\hat{\beta}_{nj} - \beta_j|^2}$.

For RA-LASSO and LS-LASSO, we take $\delta_1 = \delta_2 = \delta_3 = 0.5$. Meanwhile, these methods require the selection of initial values $\hat{\beta}_{(k)}$ and the tuning parameters λ_2, λ_3. In this simulation, we use the ordinary least squares estimates as initial values $\hat{\beta}_{(k)}$, and select the tuning parameters λ_2, λ_3 by minimizing the following BIC criterion [26]. The BIC criterion is defined as follows:

$$BIC(\lambda) = \log(SSE(\hat{\beta}_\lambda)) + k\log(n)/n,$$

where $SSE(\hat{\beta}_\lambda) = \sum_{i=1}^{n} (y_i - \hat{y}_i)^2/n$, $\hat{y}_i$ denotes the predicted value of y_i, and k denotes the number of non-zero coefficients in $\hat{\beta}_\lambda$.

The corresponding simulation results are shown in Tables 1–3. These results reveal the following:

1. For Scenario 1, in the absence of contamination ($\varepsilon = 0$), all methods performed well. As the contamination level ε increases to 0.1 and 0.2, the advantage of the robust method became pronounced. RA-LASSO consistently achieves a higher TP and lower AE and SE compared to the other methods under contamination.
2. For Scenario 2, under no contamination ($\varepsilon = 0$), the performance of all methods is similar. However, even a mild contamination ($\varepsilon = 0.1$) drastically degrades the performance of OLS and LS-LASSO. RA-LASSO demonstrates relatively robust performance, outperforming the other two methods. Furthermore, the Size metric reveals that LS-LASSO tends to overfit severely under contamination, whereas RA-LASSO effectively controls model complexity, selecting a model size much closer to the true value.
3. For Scenario 3, RA-LASSO consistently delivers the highest TP and the lowest estimation errors (AE and SE) under contamination. This confirms that the proposed method remains effective in the presence of both persistent serial correlation and outliers in the innovations.

Table 1. Simulation results for Scenario 1.

n	ε	Method	TP	Size	AE	SE
200	0	OLS	0.500	10.00	0.658	0.802
		LS-LASSO	0.820	5.56	0.615	0.768
		RA-LASSO	0.821	5.49	0.665	0.802
	0.1	OLS	0.500	10.00	1.049	1.017
		LS-LASSO	0.752	4.78	1.088	1.040
		RA-LASSO	0.781	5.33	0.889	0.935
	0.2	OLS	0.500	10.00	1.244	1.112
		LS-LASSO	0.674	5.00	1.213	1.100
		RA-LASSO	0.737	5.05	1.029	1.009
400	0	OLS	0.500	10.00	0.447	0.660
		LS-LASSO	0.853	6.35	0.390	0.614
		RA-LASSO	0.922	5.36	0.452	0.655
	0.1	OLS	0.500	10.00	0.982	0.988
		LS-LASSO	0.767	6.43	0.996	0.996
		RA-LASSO	0.856	5.04	0.826	0.902
	0.2	OLS	0.500	10.00	1.148	1.070
		LS-LASSO	0.673	6.81	1.150	1.071
		RA-LASSO	0.804	4.98	0.992	0.993

Table 2. Simulation results for Scenario 2.

n	ε	Method	TP	Size	AE	SE
200	0	OLS	0.500	10.00	0.654	0.798
		LASSO	0.815	5.81	0.606	0.763
		RA-LASSO	0.807	5.73	0.664	0.801
	0.1	OLS	0.500	10.00	1.297	1.130
		LS-LASSO	0.634	6.10	1.283	1.126
		RA-LASSO	0.771	4.69	0.920	0.946
	0.2	OLS	0.500	10.00	1.423	1.189
		LS-LASSO	0.578	7.04	1.407	1.183
		RA-LASSO	0.735	4.39	1.032	1.009
400	0	OLS	0.500	10.00	0.455	0.668
		LS-LASSO	0.856	6.30	0.423	0.639
		RA-LASSO	0.902	5.20	0.541	0.719
	0.1	OLS	0.500	10.00	1.270	1.111
		LS-LASSO	0.671	7.41	1.276	1.115
		RA-LASSO	0.835	4.29	0.910	0.944
	0.2	OLS	0.500	10.00	1.423	1.190
		LS-LASSO	0.550	8.44	1.420	1.189
		RA-LASSO	0.797	3.93	1.041	1.015

Table 3. Simulation results for Scenario 3.

n	ε	Method	TP	Size	AE	SE
200	0	OLS	0.500	10.00	0.706	0.831
		LASSO	0.716	3.76	0.566	0.748
		RA-LASSO	0.656	3.90	0.585	0.759
	0.1	OLS	0.500	10.00	1.224	1.102
		LS-LASSO	0.741	5.99	0.994	0.992
		RA-LASSO	0.672	3.92	0.661	0.807
	0.2	OLS	0.500	10.00	1.329	1.149
		LS-LASSO	0.704	6.76	1.158	1.072
		RA-LASSO	0.660	5.44	0.885	0.931
400	0	OLS	0.500	10.00	0.522	0.712
		LS-LASSO	0.744	4.56	0.477	0.683
		RA-LASSO	0.698	3.10	0.505	0.708
	0.1	OLS	0.500	10.00	1.065	1.030
		LS-LASSO	0.744	6.98	0.929	0.961
		RA-LASSO	0.732	3.82	0.560	0.744
	0.2	OLS	0.500	10.00	1.214	1.101
		LS-LASSO	0.678	7.90	1.122	1.057
		RA-LASSO	0.725	4.57	0.754	0.864

4. Empirical Analysis

4.1. Application to S&P 500 Index

The closing price reflects the final trading price of a stock for the day. It is widely used as a stable indicator to measure stock performance because it accounts for all price movements during the trading session. We select the closing prices of the S&P 500 Index from 24 September 2020 to 18 February 2021 as our research dataset, as this period witnessed significant market volatility and substantial price fluctuations, making it suitable for empirical analysis.

We first plot the closing prices over time in Figure 1, which shows significant fluctuations. To check for stationarity, we performed the augmented Dickey–Fuller (ADF) test. The test results are shown in Table 4. From Table 4, we can observe that p-value is 0.6109, which is greater than 0.05, which implies that the series is non-stationary. To address this issue, we take the first-order difference in the closing prices and plot the differenced series in Figure 2. As shown in Figure 2, the differenced series appears more stable, fluctuating randomly around a constant level. Another ADF test on the differenced series (Table 4) yields a p-value of 0.01, confirming stationarity. Although the differenced series is stationary, pronounced outliers are evident in its time series plot. To rigorously diagnose the presence of outliers, we draw a leverage versus standardized residual plot based on a preliminary AR(p) model in Figure 3, where p was determined by the AIC. We can observe from Figure 3 that the absolute values of standardized residuals for three distinct observations exceed the threshold of 2, some even exceeding 3. These extreme values are likely attributable to transient market shocks, such as unexpected earnings reports, geopolitical events, or abrupt changes in investor sentiment, which can introduce significant short-term volatility not eliminated by differencing. Next, we examine the autocorrelation (ACF) and partial autocorrelation (PACF) plots of the differenced series in Figures 4 and 5. Neither the ACF nor the PACF cuts off sharply. Based on Figures 4 and 5, we proceed to fit an AR(p) model to the differenced series.

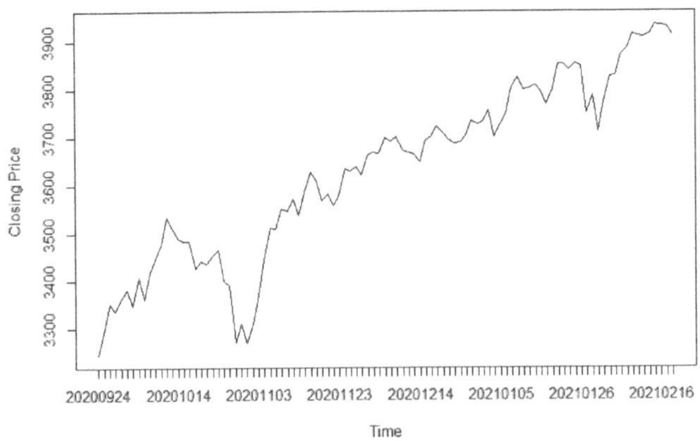

Figure 1. The S&P 500 daily closing price time series plot.

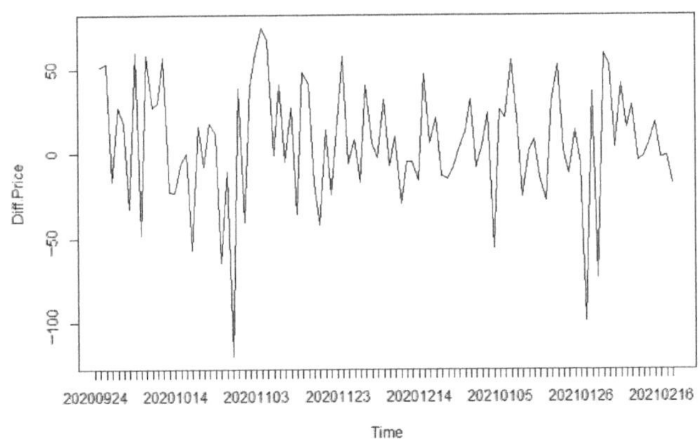

Figure 2. First-Differenced Series of the S&P 500 daily closing prices.

Table 4. ADF test results of the S&P 500 daily closing prices.

ADF Test	S&P 500	The First-Differenced S&P 500
Dickey–Fuller	−1.2007	−6.0134
p-value	0.6109	0.01

We perform first-order differencing on the closing prices of the S&P 500 Index, denoted as y_t, with the p-order lagged differences in daily closing prices denoted as $y_{t-1}, \ldots, y_{t-p}$. Firstly, we apply the Akaike information criterion (AIC) to determine the order p for the AR(p) model. Figure 6 presents the AIC values for different model configurations. The results demonstrate that the AIC value reaches its minimum when the lag order is 12. Therefore, we select $p = 12$ as the optimal order.

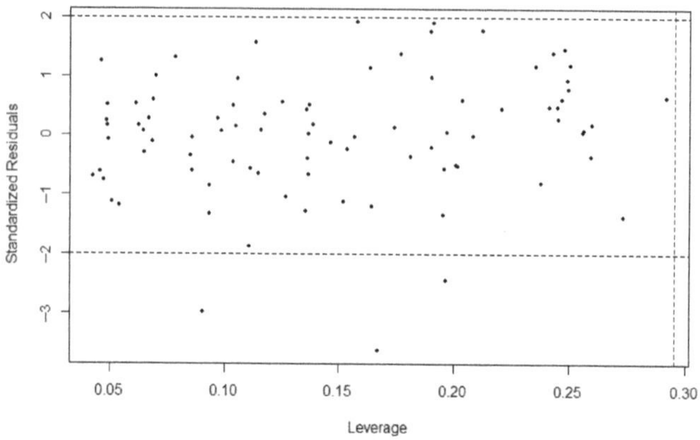

Figure 3. Leverage vs. standardized residuals of the first-differenced S&P 500 daily closing prices. The vertical dashed line indicates the threshold of $2 \times \bar{h}$, and the horizontal dashed line marks the ± 2 standard deviation boundaries.

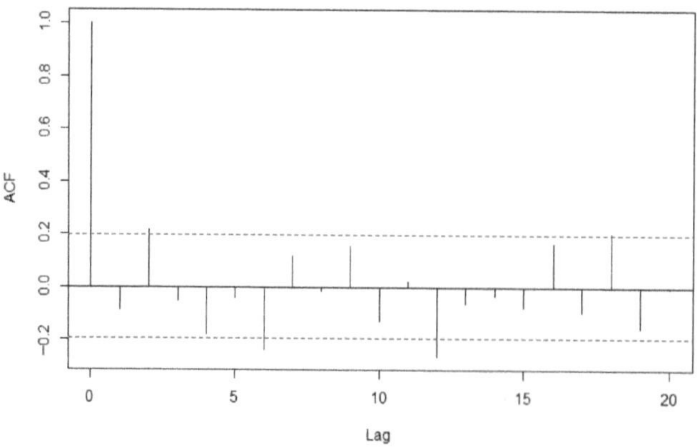

Figure 4. Sample autocorrelation function of the first-differenced S&P 500 daily closing prices. The blue dotted lines represent the approximate 95% confidence interval.

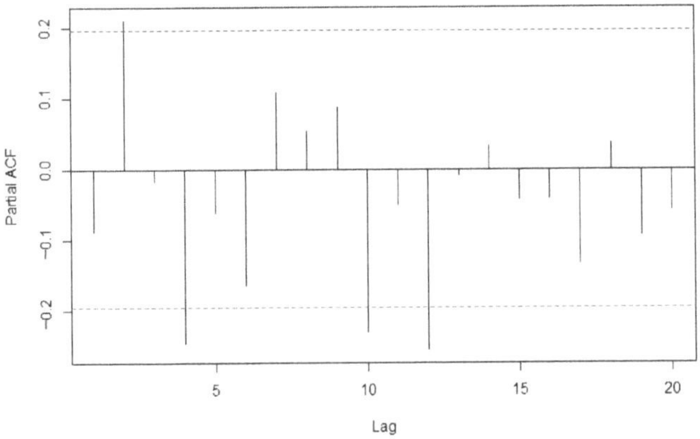

Figure 5. Sample partial autocorrelation function of the first-differenced S&P 500 daily closing prices. The blue dotted lines represent the approximate 95% confidence interval.

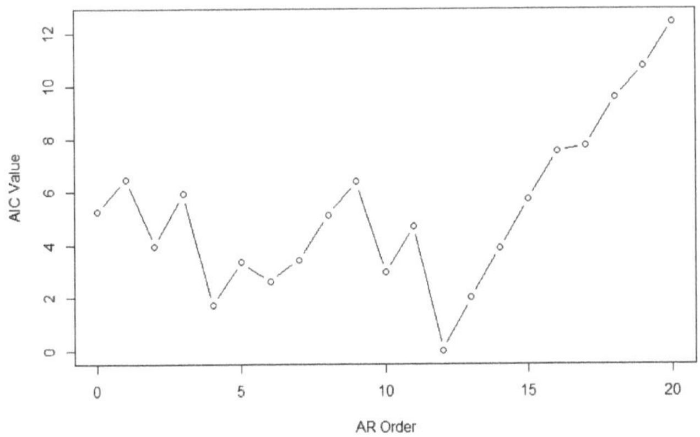

Figure 6. The AIC Values for Different Model Configurations of the First-Differenced S&P 500 Daily Closing Prices.

After determining the lag order, we apply the RA-LASSO method, the LS-LASSO method and the OLS method to fit the AR(12) model. The corresponding estimation results are presented in Table 5. We observe from Table 5 that the number of non-zero elements progressively decreases across the three AR(12) fitted models. The LS-LASSO method selected all lagged days except the $t-5$ day as explanatory variables, the RA-Lasso method selected all lagged days except $t-2$, $t-3$, $t-5$, and $t-8$ days as explanatory variables. Compared with the LS-LASSO method, the RA-Lasso approach demonstrates a faster shrinkage rate and selects fewer variables, indicating superior variable selection performance.

Table 5. Coefficient estimates comparison of the first-differenced S&P 500 daily closing prices.

Method	$t-1$	$t-2$	$t-3$	$t-4$	$t-5$	$t-6$	$t-7$	$t-8$	$t-9$	$t-10$	$t-11$	$t-12$
OLS	−0.03	0.19	0.07	−0.13	−0.09	−0.23	0.11	0.07	0.10	−0.18	−0.05	−0.22
LS-LASSO	−0.14	0.02	0.16	−0.13	0.00	−0.26	0.09	0.06	0.17	−0.21	−0.17	−0.30
RA-Lasso	−0.04	0.00	0.00	−0.17	0.00	−0.20	0.07	0.00	0.06	−0.16	−0.05	−0.22

After obtaining the fitted models using three different methods, we further evaluated their prediction accuracy for stock prices. We apply each model to predict the first-order differenced results of the S&P 500 index. The mean absolute percentage error (MAPE) was calculated for each model, defined as follows:

$$\text{MAPE} = \frac{1}{n}\sum_{i=1}^{n}\left|\frac{\hat{y}_i - y_i}{y_i}\right|, \tag{15}$$

where y_i represents the actual stock price on day i, and $\hat{y}_i$ denotes the predicted price.

The MAPE results of the three methods are presented in Table 6. As shown in Table 6, the proposed RA-LASSO method achieves the smallest MAPE, demonstrating its excellent predictive capability.

Table 6. MAPE comparison of the first-differenced S&P 500 daily closing prices.

Method	Size	MAPE
OLS	12	2.12
LS-LASSO	11	2.28
RA-Lasso	8	1.89

4.2. Application to USD/CNY Exchange Rate

Next, we apply the proposed methodology to analyze the dataset on the exchange rate of the U.S. Dollar against the Chinese Yuan (USD/CNY) from 17 January 2023, to 8 June 2023, sourced from the Federal Reserve Economic Data (FRED) website of the Federal Reserve Bank of St. Louis (fred.stlouisfed.org, accessed on 23 August 2024). During this period, the exchange rate exhibits significant fluctuations. We will utilize these data to compare the robustness of the RA-Lasso method, the LS-Lasso method, and the OLS method. Figure 7 depicts the exchange rate time series, which exhibits considerable variability. An ADF test is conducted to assess stationarity; the results, shown in Table 7, yield a p-value of 0.8908, indicating non-stationarity. First-order differencing is applied to achieve stationarity. The differenced series, plotted in Figure 8, appears stable and fluctuates randomly around a constant level. A follow-up ADF test confirms stationarity with a p-value of 0.01. Despite achieving stationarity, the differenced series contains noticeable outliers, likely attributable to transient market disturbances, such as unexpected macroeconomic announcements, geopolitical tensions, or sudden changes in monetary policy expectations. These factors can introduce short-term volatility that differencing alone cannot eliminate. To rigorously diagnose the presence of any outliers and influential points, we employ a leverage versus standardized residual plot (Figure 9) based on a preliminary AR(p) model, where p was determined by the AIC. The plot reveals two distinct phenomena:

- Numerous high-leverage observations, with leverage values exceeding $2 \times \bar{h}$, where $\bar{h}$ denotes the mean leverage, indicated by the vertical dashed line.
- Several extreme residuals with absolute standardized values surpassing 2.

These high-leverage points, predominantly clustered during periods of exceptional market turbulence, may disproportionately influence parameter estimates. The simultaneous presence of large residuals violates the Gaussian error assumption underlying classical estimation methods. The ACF and PACF of the differenced series are presented in Figures 10 and 11. Neither the ACF nor the PACF cuts off sharply.

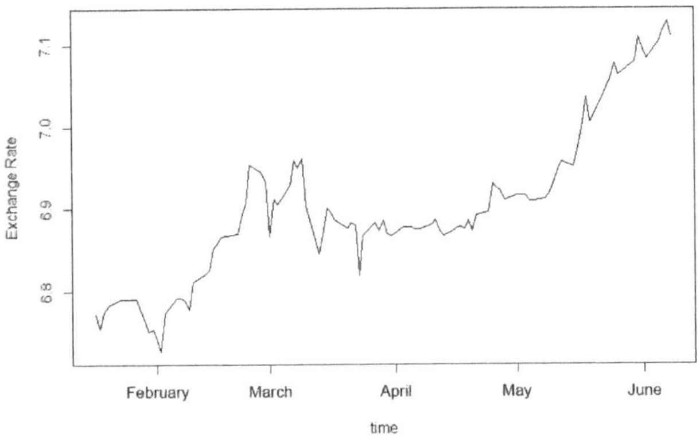

Figure 7. USD/CNY exchange rate time series plot.

Table 7. ADF test results of the USD/CNY exchange rate.

ADF Test	Exchange Rate	The First-Differenced Exchange Rate
Dickey–Fuller	−0.4449	−7.7716
p-value	0.8908	0.01

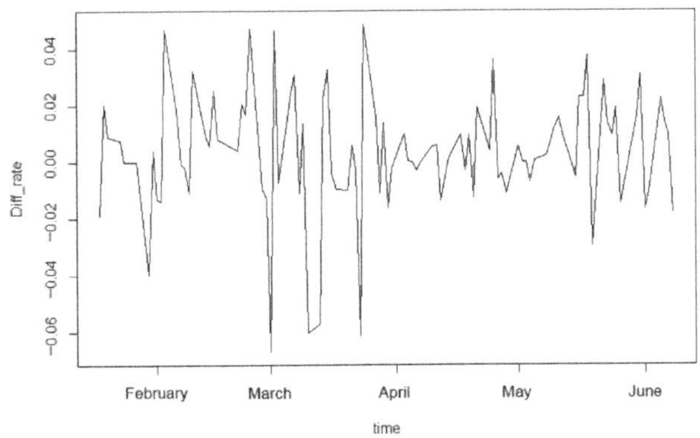

Figure 8. First-differenced USD/CNY exchange rate.

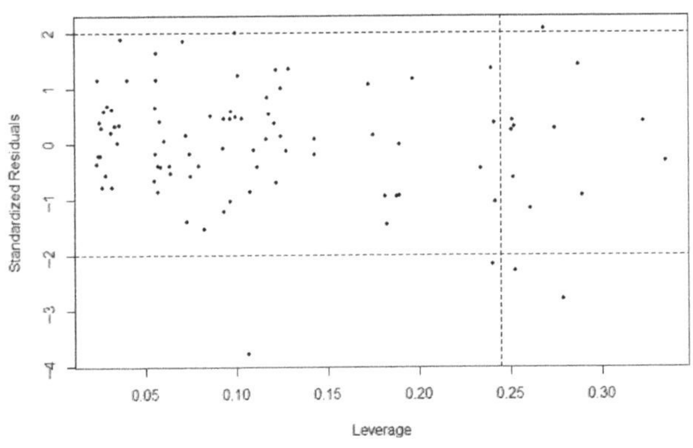

Figure 9. Leverage vs. standardized residuals of the first-differenced USD/CNY exchange rate. The vertical dashed line indicates the threshold of $2 \times \bar{h}$, and the horizontal dashed line marks the ±2 standard deviation boundaries.

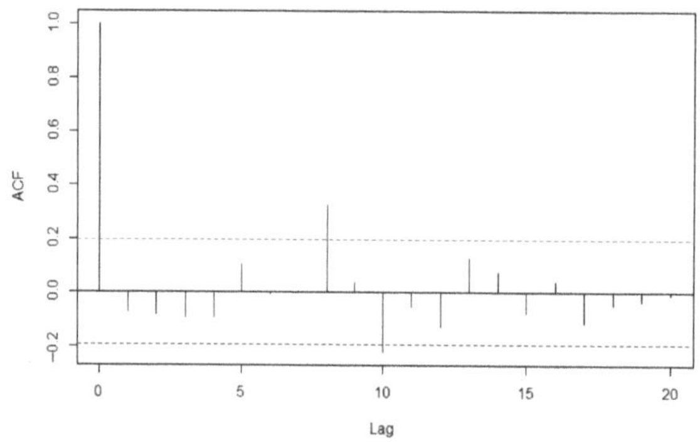

Figure 10. Sample autocorrelation function of the first-differenced USD/CNY exchange rate. The blue dotted lines represent the approximate 95% confidence interval.

Let y_t represent the first-differenced USD/CNY exchange rate, with $y_{t-1}, \ldots, y_{t-p}$ denoting the lagged values. The Akaike Information Criterion (AIC) is used to select the optimal lag order p. As shown in Figure 12, the AIC is minimized at $p = 10$, which is selected as the optimal order. The AR(10) model is estimated using RA-LASSO, LS-LASSO, and OLS. Coefficient estimates are reported in Table 8. The number of non-zero coefficients decreases across methods: LS-LASSO retains all lags, while RA-LASSO further excludes lags $t-1$, $t-7$, and $t-9$. This indicates that RA-LASSO promotes greater sparsity and exhibits a faster shrinkage rate.

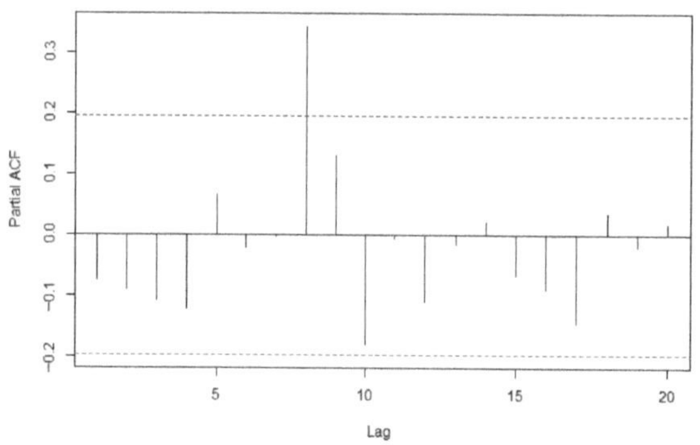

Figure 11. Sample partial autocorrelation function of the first-differenced USD/CNY exchange rate. The blue dotted lines represent the approximate 95% confidence interval.

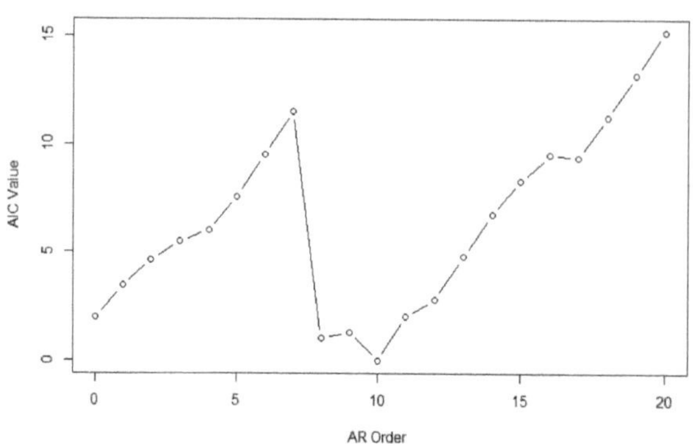

Figure 12. The AIC values of the first-differenced USD/CNY exchange rate.

Table 8. Coefficient estimates comparison of the first-differenced USD/CNY exchange rate.

Method	$t-1$	$t-2$	$t-3$	$t-4$	$t-5$	$t-6$	$t-7$	$t-8$	$t-9$	$t-10$
OLS	−0.095	−0.013	−0.095	−0.047	0.184	0.047	0.055	0.373	0.137	−0.187
Lasso	−0.005	−0.069	−0.026	0.079	0.111	0.120	−0.066	0.161	−0.018	−0.152
RA-Lasso	0.000	−0.063	−0.010	0.058	0.101	0.078	0.000	0.157	0.000	−0.132

Furthermore, the finite sample performance is evaluated using the mean absolute error (MAE) and median absolute deviation (MAD), which are defined as follows:

$$\text{MAE} = \frac{1}{n}\sum_{i=1}^{n}|\hat{y}_i - y_i| \tag{16}$$

$$\text{MAD} = \text{median}(|\hat{y}_i - y_i|) \tag{17}$$

where y_i denotes the actual exchange rate on the i-th day, and $\hat{y}_i$ represents the predicted exchange rate. The results of the three methods are presented in Table 9. The proposed RA-LASSO method achieves lower MAE and MAD values than other two methods.

Table 9. Result of the first-differenced USD/CNY exchange rate.

Method	Size	MAE	MAD
OLS	10	0.0115	0.0150
LS-LASSO	10	0.0114	0.0151
RA-Lasso	7	0.0111	0.0149

5. Discussion

This paper proposed a robust adaptive lasso method for the autoregressive models by combining the partial autocorrelation coefficient and robust autocorrelation coefficients. Simulation studies and two real data analyses demonstrated that the proposed method had better performance than the existing methods.

It is noteworthy that there are further topics to investigate for our proposed method. Firstly, we will investigate the asymptotic properties of the proposed method as future work. Secondly, we further extend the proposed method to tackle other time series models such as the moving average models and the autoregressive moving average models.

Author Contributions: Conceptualization, Y.J.; software, F.C.; data curation, F.C.; writing—original draft preparation, F.C. and X.Y.; writing—review and editing, Y.J. and X.Y.; visualization, F.C. All authors have read and agreed to the published version of the manuscript.

Funding: This research was supported by the National Science Foundation of China under Grant No. 12571284 and Grant No. 12171203, and the Fundamental Research Funds for the Central Universities under Grant No. 23JNQMX21.

Data Availability Statement: Data are contained within the article.

Conflicts of Interest: The authors declare no conflicts of interest.

References

1. Box, G.E.; Jenkins, G.M.; Reinsel, G.C.; Ljung, G.M. *Time Series Analysis: Forecasting and Control*; John Wiley & Sons: Hoboken, NJ, USA, 2015.
2. Huber, P.J. The 1972 wald lecture robust statistics: A review. *Ann. Math. Stat.* **1972**, *43*, 1041–1067. [CrossRef]
3. Chang, I.; Tiao, G.C.; Chen, C. Estimation of time series parameters in the presence of outliers. *Technometrics* **1988**, *30*, 193–204. [CrossRef]
4. Tsay, R.S.; Pena, D.; Pankratz, A.E. Outliers in multivariate time series. *Biometrika* **2000**, *87*, 789–804. [CrossRef]

5. McQuarrie, A.D.; Tsai, C.L. Outlier detections in autoregressive models. *J. Comput. Graph. Stat.* **2003**, *12*, 450–471. [CrossRef]
6. Karioti, V.; Caroni, C. Simple detection of outlying short time series. *Stat. Pap.* **2004**, *45*, 267–278. [CrossRef]
7. Louni, H. Outlier detection in ARMA models. *J. Time Ser. Anal.* **2008**, *29*, 1057–1065. [CrossRef]
8. Čampulová, M.; Michálek, J.; Mikuška, P.; Bokal, D. Nonparametric algorithm for identification of outliers in environmental data. *J. Chemom.* **2018**, *32*, e2997. [CrossRef]
9. Pan, B.; Chen, M.; Wang, Y. Weighted least absolute deviations estimation for periodic ARMA models. *Acta Math. Sin. Engl. Ser.* **2015**, *31*, 1273–1288. [CrossRef]
10. Jiang, Y. An exponential-squared estimator in the autoregressive model with heavy-tailed errors. *Stat. Its Interface* **2016**, *9*, 233–238. [CrossRef]
11. Callens, A.; Wang, Y.G.; Fu, L.; Liquet, B. Robust estimation procedure for autoregressive models with heterogeneity. *Environ. Model. Assess.* **2021**, *26*, 313–323. [CrossRef]
12. Chang, L.; Shi, Y. A discussion on the robust vector autoregressive models: Novel evidence from safe haven assets. *Ann. Oper. Res.* **2024**, *339*, 1725–1755. [CrossRef]
13. Tibshirani, R. Regression shrinkage and selection via the lasso. *J. R. Stat. Soc. Ser. B Stat. Methodol.* **1996**, *58*, 267–288. [CrossRef]
14. Fan, J.; Li, R. Variable selection via nonconcave penalized likelihood and its oracle properties. *J. Am. Stat. Assoc.* **2001**, *96*, 1348–1360. [CrossRef]
15. Zou, H. The adaptive lasso and its oracle properties. *J. Am. Stat. Assoc.* **2006**, *101*, 1418–1429. [CrossRef]
16. Audrino, F.; Camponovo, L. Oracle properties and finite sample inference of the adaptive lasso for time series regression models. *arXiv* **2013**, arXiv:1312.1473. [CrossRef]
17. Songsiri, J. Sparse autoregressive model estimation for learning Granger causality in time series. In Proceedings of the 2013 IEEE International Conference on Acoustics, Speech and Signal Processing, Vancouver, BC, Canada, 26–31 May 2013; pp. 3198–3202.
18. Emmert-Streib, F.; Dehmer, M. High-dimensional LASSO-based computational regression models: Regularization, shrinkage, and selection. *Mach. Learn. Knowl. Extr.* **2019**, *1*, 359–383. [CrossRef]
19. Gnanadesikan, R.; Kettenring, J.R. Robust estimates, residuals, and outlier detection with multiresponse data. *Biometrics* **1972**, *28*, 81–124. [CrossRef]
20. Donoho, D.L.; Huber, P.J. The notion of breakdown point. In *A Festschrift for Erich L. Lehmann*; CRC Press: Boca Raton, FL, USA, 1983; Volume 157184.
21. Amini, M.; Roozbeh, M. Least trimmed squares ridge estimation in partially linear regression models. *J. Stat. Comput. Simul.* **2016**, *86*, 2766–2780. [CrossRef]
22. Rousseeuw, P.; Leroy, A. *Robust Regression and Outlier Detection*; John Wiley & Sons: Hoboken, NJ, USA, 1987.
23. Rousseeuw, P.J.; Croux, C. Alternatives to the median absolute deviation. *J. Am. Stat. Assoc.* **1993**, *88*, 1273–1283. [CrossRef]
24. Smirnov, P.O.; Shevlyakov, G.L.; Smirnov, P.; Smirnov, P.; Shevlyakov, G.; Shevlyakov, G. Approximation of the QN-estimate of scale with the help of fast M-estimates. *Sib. Aerosp. J.* **2010**, *11*, 83–85.
25. Rousseeuw, P.J.; Croux, C. The bias of k-step M-estimators. *Stat. Probab. Lett.* **1994**, *20*, 411–420. [CrossRef]
26. Wang, H.; Li, G.; Jiang, G. Robust regression shrinkage and consistent variable selection through the LAD-Lasso. *J. Bus. Econ. Stat.* **2007**, *25*, 347–355. [CrossRef]

axioms

MDPI

Article

Derivation of a Closed-Form Asymptotic Variance for the Coefficient of Variation Under the Reparameterized Birnbaum–Saunders Distribution

Tossapol Phoophiwfa [1], Piyapatr Busababodhin [1], Andrei Volodin [2] and Sujitta Suraphee [1,*]

1 Department of Mathematics, Mahasarakham University, Maha Sarakham 44150, Thailand; 65010263004@msu.ac.th (T.P.); piyapatr.b@msu.ac.th (P.B.)
2 Department of Mathematics and Statistics, University of Regina, Regina, SK S4S 0A2, Canada; andrei.volodin@uregina.ca
* Correspondence: sujitta.s@msu.ac.th; Tel.: +66-819-414-720

Abstract: This study develops a tractable, closed-form expression for the asymptotic variance of the coefficient of variation (CV) estimator under a reparameterized Birnbaum–Saunders (BirSau) distribution. Using the method of moments, we derive analytical formulas for the mean, variance, and coefficient of variation of $X{\sim}\text{BirSau}(\mu,\lambda)$ and construct a plug-in estimator for the CV. By applying the delta method within this new nonlinear parametrization, we obtain an explicit and compact expression for the asymptotic variance of the CV estimator, thereby extending general asymptotic theory to a distribution-specific setting where higher-order moments lack closed forms under the classical parametrization. Extensive Monte Carlo simulations are conducted to examine the estimator's finite-sample performance under various parameter configurations and sample sizes. The results demonstrate that the estimator exhibits decreasing bias and variance as the sample size increases, with strong convergence to its theoretical asymptotic behavior. A real-data application using rainfall measurements from northeastern Thailand further illustrates the practical utility of the proposed approach in quantifying relative variability across regions. These findings provide a concise analytical foundation for the coefficient of variation under the Birnbaum–Saunders framework, enhancing its theoretical development and facilitating practical implementation in environmental and reliability analyses.

Keywords: Birnbaum-Saunders distribution; method of moments; coefficient of variation; closed-form variance; delta method; reparameterization; simulations

MSC: 62F10; 62F12; 62F25

1. Introduction

The Birnbaum–Saunders (BirSau) distribution, originally introduced by [1], is a flexible model for positively skewed and non-negative data. It has been widely adopted in fields such as reliability engineering, survival analysis, and environmental studies due to its suitability for modeling lifetime and failure-time data [2–4]. To ensure accurate inference and model interpretation under the Birnbaum–Saunders distribution, reliable parameter estimation is essential because the accuracy of estimated parameters directly affects the precision of derived quantities such as the mean, variance, and coefficient of variation, as well as the validity of subsequent statistical inferences.

Among the various estimation techniques, the method of moments estimation stands out for its simplicity and analytical tractability. However, the performance of method of moments estimators can be influenced by factors such as sample size and the underlying parameter values, which may result in biased or highly variable estimates in small-sample scenarios. Therefore, studying the asymptotic properties of the estimators of the distribution parameters, namely the shape and scale parameters obtained through the method of moments, is crucial. Understanding their asymptotic behavior allows for the construction of confidence intervals and supports reliable statistical inference for related quantities such as the coefficient of variation [5].

Beyond parameter estimation, the coefficient of variation, defined as the ratio of the standard deviation to the mean, serves as an important scale-free measure of relative variability. It facilitates meaningful comparisons of dispersion across datasets with differing units or magnitudes, making it especially useful in fields such as hydrology, finance, and materials science. However, despite the Birnbaum–Saunders distribution's extensive applications, the statistical behavior of the CV estimator—particularly under the reparameterized BirSau model—has not been analytically characterized in closed form.

This study addresses this gap by leveraging the reparameterized BirSau model $X \sim \text{BirSau}(\lambda, \mu)$, in which both the mean and variance are expressed as nonlinear yet analytically tractable functions of the parameters. Using the joint asymptotic distribution of the method of moments estimators and the delta method, we derive a closed-form expression for the asymptotic variance of the CV estimator. This derivation not only extends the general delta-method framework but also provides a distribution-specific formulation that reflects the internal parameter relationships of the BirSau family. Through theoretical analysis, simulation, and real-data validation, we demonstrate that this new formulation allows direct analytical inference for CV without relying on numerical approximation of higher moments. The key contribution of this paper is therefore not to re-establish the asymptotic normality of the CV, but to apply and specialize this general principle to the BirSau distribution by deriving an explicit, closed-form formula for the asymptotic variance of the CV estimator. This formulation offers new theoretical insight into how parameter interactions within the BirSau model shape the behavior of variability measures, and it provides practical tools for statistical inference in reliability and environmental applications.

The article is organized as follows. In Section 2, we provide the overview of results presented in articles [6,7] which are important for our investigation. Section 3 presents the main theoretical result on the asymptotic normality of the CV estimator for the BirSau distribution. An intense simulation study is provided in Section 4, and a real-life example for modeling the total rainfall amounts over consecutive rainy days in northeastern region of Thailand is carefully discussed in Section 6. Sections 7 and 8 are devoted to a discussion and concluding remarks, respectively.

2. Methodology

This study focuses on analyzing the asymptotic properties of the CV estimator under the parameterization of the BirSau distribution. The methodological framework consists of the following components:

2.1. Parameterization of the Birnbaum–Saunders Distribution

We say that a random variable follows the BirSau distribution (denoted as $X \sim \text{BirSau}(\mu, \lambda)$, where $\mu > 0$ and $\lambda > 0$ are the parameters), if its probability density function is given by

$$f(x; \mu, \lambda) = \frac{1}{2\sqrt{2\pi}} \left(\frac{\lambda}{x\sqrt{x}} + \frac{\mu}{\sqrt{x}} \right) \exp\left\{ -\frac{1}{2} \left(\frac{\lambda}{\sqrt{x}} - \mu\sqrt{x} \right)^2 \right\}, x > 0.$$

This formulation is referred to as the new parametrization of the BirSau distribution, which differs from the classical parametrization originally introduced by [1]. The advantages of the parametrization are carefully discussed in articles [6,7].

The distribution function for the BirSau(λ, μ) distribution is

$$F(x;\lambda,\mu) = \begin{cases} \Phi\left(\sqrt{\frac{x}{\mu}} - \lambda\sqrt{\frac{\mu}{x}}\right), & x > 0 \\ 0, & x \le 0, \end{cases}$$

where $\Phi(x)$ is the standard normal distribution function. It can be easily shown that the derivative of the distribution function is the density function: $\frac{dF(x)}{dx} = f(x)$.

The survival function for the BirSau(λ, μ) distribution is

$$S(x;\lambda,\mu) = 1 - F(x;\lambda,\mu) = \begin{cases} 1 - \Phi\left(\sqrt{\frac{x}{\mu}} - \lambda\sqrt{\frac{\mu}{x}}\right), & x > 0 \\ 1, & x \le 0. \end{cases}$$

The hazard rate for the BirSau(λ, μ) distribution is

$$h(x) = \frac{f(x;\lambda,\mu)}{S(x;\lambda,\mu)} = \begin{cases} \dfrac{\frac{1}{2\sqrt{2\pi}}\left(\frac{\lambda}{x\sqrt{x}} + \frac{\mu}{\sqrt{x}}\right)\exp\left\{-\frac{1}{2}\left(\frac{\lambda}{\sqrt{x}} - \mu\sqrt{x}\right)^2\right\}}{1-\Phi\left(\sqrt{\frac{x}{\mu}} - \lambda\sqrt{\frac{\mu}{x}}\right)}, & x > 0 \\ 0, & x \le 0. \end{cases}$$

The exact shape of the hazard function (increasing, decreasing, or bathtub-shaped) depends on the values of λ and μ. In reliability theory, an increasing hazard rate implies aging (wear-out), a decreasing hazard implies early failure tendency, and a constant hazard suggests a memoryless property. For modeling the total rainfall amounts over consecutive rainy days, the hazard rate function, $h(x)$, describes the instantaneous risk (or rate) that the total rainfall amount will be around a certain level x, given that it has already exceeded smaller values. An increasing hazard indicates that once a threshold is crossed, the likelihood of even larger rainfall totals becomes greater (heavy-tailed behavior). A decreasing hazard implies that extreme rainfall amounts become less likely as accumulation increases, while a constant hazard suggests that the probability of additional rainfall is independent of the amount already observed. In hydrology, hazard rate functions are often employed to model extreme rainfall events, particularly for assessing flood risk and estimating return periods.

Figures 1 and 2 present the probability density (PDF), cumulative distribution (CDF), survival function (SF), and hazard rate function (HRF) of the Birnbaum–Saunders distribution under different parameter settings, illustrating how variations in λ and μ influence its distributional behavior.

2.2. *Method of Moments Estimation of New Parameters*

The theoretical background for this section follows Propositions 2 and 3 in [6]. For a random variable $X \sim$ BirSau(λ, μ), the mean and variance are given by

$$\mathbb{E}(X) = \frac{2\lambda\mu + 1}{2\mu^2}, \quad \mathrm{Var}(X) = \frac{4\lambda\mu + 5}{4\mu^4}.$$

The moment estimators, obtained using the method of moments, are derived by equating the sample moments to the corresponding theoretical moments, yielding the estimators $\widehat{\lambda}$ and $\widehat{\mu}$ as derived in [6,7] .

Furthermore, as established in Theorem 1 of [6], the MMEs are asymptotically normal with mean vector $(\lambda, \mu)^t$ and covariance matrix Σ; that is,

$$\sqrt{n}\begin{pmatrix} \widehat{\lambda} - \lambda \\ \widehat{\mu} - \mu \end{pmatrix} \longrightarrow N\left(\begin{pmatrix} 0 \\ 0 \end{pmatrix}, \Sigma\right) \quad \text{as } n \to \infty.$$

Full derivations and explicit forms of Σ are presented in [6].

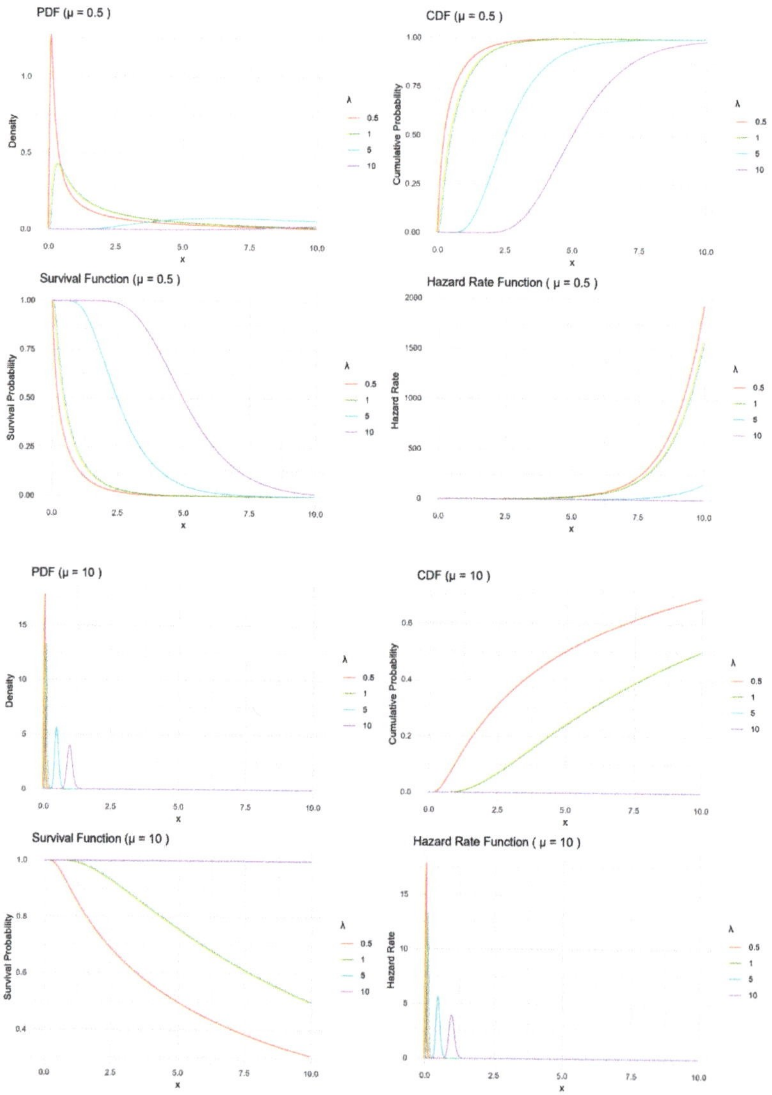

Figure 1. Probability density (PDF), cumulative distribution (CDF), survival function (SF), and hazard rate function (HRF) of the Birnbaum–Saunders distribution under varying $\lambda = (0.5, 1, 5, 10)$, with fixed $\mu = (0.5, 10)$.

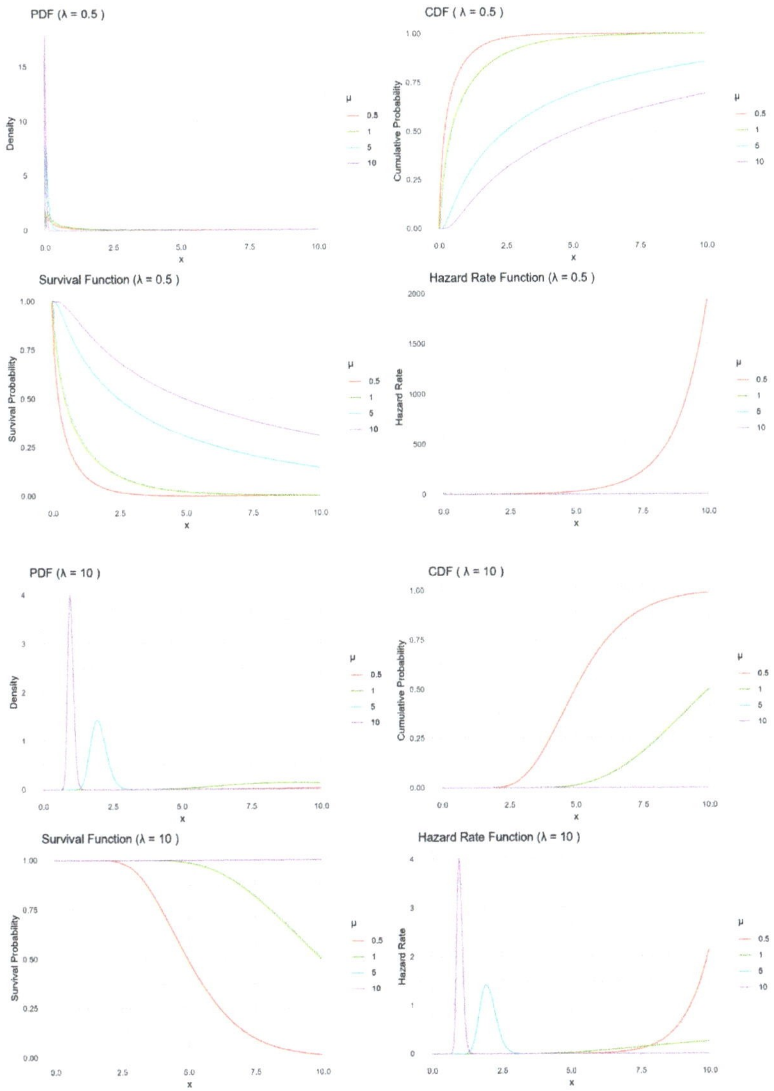

Figure 2. Probability density (PDF), cumulative distribution (CDF), survival function (SF), and hazard rate function (HRF) of the Birnbaum–Saunders distribution under varying $\mu = (0.5, 1, 5, 10)$, with fixed $\lambda = (0.5, 10)$.

3. On the Asymptotic Normality of the CV Estimator for the BirSau Distribution

By the definition, the CV of a random variable X is the ratio of its standard deviation to mathematical expectation $\mathrm{CV} = \frac{\sqrt{\mathrm{Var(X)}}}{\mathbb{E}(\mathrm{X})}$. Taking into consideration the aforementioned formulae for the mean and variance of the BirSau distribution, we establish that if $X \sim \mathrm{BirSau}(\lambda, \mu)$, then the coefficient of variation is $\mathrm{CV} = \frac{\sqrt{4\lambda\mu+5}}{2\lambda\mu+1}$.

Therefore, we suggest the following plug-in estimator of the coefficient of variation:

$$\widehat{\mathrm{CV}} = \frac{\sqrt{4\hat{\lambda}\hat{\mu}+5}}{2\hat{\lambda}\hat{\mu}+1}, \tag{1}$$

where $\hat{\lambda}$ and $\hat{\mu}$ are the moment estimators of the shape and scale parameters of the reparameterized Birnbaum–Saunders distribution, respectively. To find the parameters of the asymptotic normality of the coefficient of variation estimator $\widehat{\mathrm{CV}}$, we apply the famous delta method,; see fundamental monographs [8,9].

Consider two basic statistics $V_1 = \widehat{\lambda}$ and $V_2 = \widehat{\mu}$. As we already mentioned, random vector $(V_1, V_2)^t$ is asymptotically normal with mean $(\lambda, \mu)^t$ and covariance matrix Σ. Consider function $g(v_1, v_2) = \frac{\sqrt{4v_1v_2+5}}{2v_1v_2+1}$. Note that $g(\lambda, \mu) = \mathrm{CV}$ and $g(V_1, V_2) = g(\widehat{\lambda}, \widehat{\mu}) = \widehat{\mathrm{CV}}$.

Partial derivatives of the function and their values at the point (λ, μ) are

$$\frac{\partial g(v_1,v_2)}{\partial v_1} = \frac{8v_2(1-v_1v_2)}{\sqrt{4v_1v_2+5}(2v_1v_2+1)^2}, \quad \frac{\partial g(\lambda,\mu)}{\partial v_1} = \frac{8\mu(1-\lambda\mu)}{\sqrt{4\lambda\mu+5}(2\lambda\mu+1)^2},$$
$$\frac{\partial g(v_1,v_2)}{\partial v_2} = \frac{8v_1(1-v_1v_2)}{\sqrt{4v_1v_2+5}(2v_1v_2+1)^2}, \quad \frac{\partial g(\lambda,\mu)}{\partial v_2} = \frac{8\lambda(1-\lambda\mu)}{\sqrt{4\lambda\mu+5}(2\lambda\mu+1)^2}.$$

Therefore, the Taylor expansion of the function $g(v_1, v_2)$ at the point (λ, μ) up to the linear terms is

$$\begin{aligned} g(v_1,v_2) &= g(\lambda,\mu) + \frac{\partial g(\lambda,\mu)}{\partial v_1}(v_1-\lambda) + \frac{\partial g(\lambda,\mu)}{\partial v_2}(v_2-\mu) + \text{Remainder} \\ &= \mathrm{CV} + \frac{8(1-\lambda\mu)}{\sqrt{4\lambda\mu+5}(2\lambda\mu+1)^2}(\mu(v_1-\lambda)+\lambda(v_2-\mu)) + \text{Remainder}. \end{aligned}$$

Substituting our basic statistics V_1 and V_2 for variables v_1 and v_2, we obtain

$$g(V_1,V_2) = \mathrm{CV} + \frac{8(1-\lambda\mu)}{\sqrt{4\lambda\mu+5}(2\lambda\mu+1)^2}(\mu(V_1-\lambda)+\lambda(V_2-\mu)) + \text{Remainder}.$$

By the delta method, we know that the Remainder converges to zero in probability as the sample size $n \to \infty$. Hence, the estimator $\widehat{\mathrm{CV}}$ has asymptotic mean CV (asymptotically unbiased) and asymptotic variance

$$\begin{aligned} \tau^2 &= \frac{64(1-\lambda\mu)^2}{(4\lambda\mu+5)(2\lambda\mu+1)^4}\left(\mu^2\mathrm{Var}(\widehat{\lambda}) + \lambda^2\mathrm{Var}(\widehat{\mu}) + 2\lambda\mu\mathrm{Cov}(\widehat{\lambda},\widehat{\mu})\right) \\ &= \frac{64(1-\lambda\mu)^2}{(4\lambda\mu+5)(2\lambda\mu+1)^4}\left(\mu^2\frac{\lambda^2(5+12\lambda\mu+8\lambda^2\mu^2)}{4(2\lambda\mu+1)^2} + \lambda^2\frac{\mu^2(5+12\lambda\mu+8\lambda^2\mu^2)}{4(2\lambda\mu+1)^2} \right. \\ &\left. +2\lambda\mu\frac{\lambda\mu(-1+4\lambda\mu+8\lambda^2\mu^2)}{4(2\lambda\mu+1)^2}\right) = \frac{128\lambda^2\mu^2(\lambda\mu-1)^2}{(4\lambda\mu+5)(2\lambda\mu+1)^4}. \end{aligned}$$

We collect our finding in the following proposition:

Proposition 1. *The coefficient of variation estimator* $\widehat{\mathrm{CV}} = \frac{\sqrt{4\hat{\lambda}\hat{\mu}+5}}{2\hat{\lambda}\hat{\mu}+1}$ *is asymptotically normal with mean* $\mathrm{CV} = \frac{\sqrt{4\lambda\mu+5}}{2\lambda\mu+1}$ *and asymptotic variance*

$$\tau^2 = \frac{128\lambda^2\mu^2(\lambda\mu-1)^2}{(4\lambda\mu+5)(2\lambda\mu+1)^4};$$

that is,

$$\sqrt{n}(\widehat{\mathrm{CV}} - \mathrm{CV}) \to N(0, \tau^2)$$

in distribution as $n \to \infty$.

A notable property of this parametrization is its symmetric structure: both parameters λ and μ enter all estimator formulae in an interchangeable manner, such that swapping their roles leaves the expressions unchanged. This elegant symmetry is not preserved in the classical parametrization of the BirSau distribution.

In the following, we consider the following plug-in estimator of the variance τ^2:

$$\hat{\tau}^2 = \frac{128\hat{\lambda}^2\hat{\mu}^2(\hat{\lambda}\hat{\mu} - 1)^2}{(4\hat{\lambda}\hat{\mu} + 5)(2\hat{\lambda}\hat{\mu} + 1)^4}.$$

The asymptotic $(1 - \alpha)$ confidence interval for the CV is $\widehat{\mathrm{CV}} \pm z_{\alpha/2}\frac{\hat{\tau}}{\sqrt{n}}$.

4. Simulation Study

To assess the performance of the proposed estimator of the CV, a Monte Carlo simulation study was conducted. The simulation design is described as follows:

- **Sample sizes:** $n = 10, 30, 50, 100, 200, 500$,
- **Parameter values:** $\mu, \lambda \in \{0.5, 1, 5, 10\}$,
- **Number of replications:** 10,000 for each combination of (μ, λ, n).

The goal is to evaluate the accuracy and reliability of the CV estimator defined by $\widehat{\mathrm{CV}}$. For each simulation setting, the following performance metrics are computed:

- Bias and mean squared error (MSE) of the CV estimator,
- Empirical standard deviation and sampling distribution of the CV estimator,
- Coverage probabilities of nominal 95% confidence intervals for CV.

The generation procedure for BirSau random variates is discussed in Busababodhin et al. (2025) [6] and can be summarized as follows in Algorithm 1.

Algorithm 1: Generating Birnbaum–Saunders Samples

1. Fix n, $\mu > 0$, and $\lambda > 0$.
2. Generate n independent standard normal random variables $y_1, \ldots, y_n$.
3. For each $j = 1, \ldots, n$, compute the BirSau random variate $x_j = \left(\frac{-y_j + \sqrt{y_j^2 + 4\lambda\mu}}{2\mu}\right)^2$.

Simulation Procedure for Estimating CV

We apply the following procedure (see Algorithm 2).

Algorithm 2: CV Estimation via Simulation

1. For each (μ, λ, n), repeat the following for $N = 10,000$ times:
   (a) Generate a sample of size n using Algorithm 1.
   (b) Compute the method of moments estimates $\hat{\mu}_i$, $\hat{\lambda}_i$.
   (c) Calculate the estimated coefficient of variation $\widehat{\mathrm{CV}}_i$ by Equation (1).
2. Compute the following summary statistics over N replications:
   - Bias: $\mathrm{Bias}(\widehat{\mathrm{CV}}) = \frac{1}{N}\sum_{i=1}^{N}\widehat{\mathrm{CV}}_i - \mathrm{CV}_{\mathrm{true}}$.
   - MSE: $\frac{1}{N}\sum_{i=1}^{N}\left(\widehat{\mathrm{CV}}_i - \mathrm{CV}_{\mathrm{true}}\right)^2$.
   - Empirical standard deviation of $\widehat{\mathrm{CV}}$.
   - Coverage probability of the 95% confidence intervals for CV.

This simulation framework enables comprehensive assessment of the estimator's performance, especially in terms of the accuracy and robustness of the CV estimation across a wide range of sample sizes and parameter configurations.

5. Comparing the Simulation and Theoretical Results

This section presents a comparative analysis between simulation-based and theoretical results focusing on the estimation of the CV under the BirSau distribution. The analysis emphasizes the accuracy and consistency of the CV estimator by examining its average, variability, and confidence interval performance across different sample sizes and parameter values. Specifically, we evaluate the estimated mean, standard deviation, bias, and MSE of the CV, along with the empirical coverage probability of the 95% confidence interval. The simulation results are organized into three categories based on sample size: small ($n = 10, 30$), moderate ($n = 50, 100$), and large ($n = 200, 500$). For each category, various combinations of the true parameter values μ and λ are considered to assess the robustness of the estimator under diverse distributional conditions. The results provide insight into how the CV estimator converges to its theoretical properties as the sample size increases and offer practical guidance for using CV in applied statistical analysis, especially when sample sizes are limited.

The simulation results for small sample sizes indicate that the coefficient of variation estimator $\widehat{\text{CV}}$ exhibits considerable bias and variability (Table 1). Specifically, when $n = 10$, the mean estimates of $\widehat{\text{CV}}$ deviate significantly from the true value, and both the bias and MSE are relatively high. These findings suggest that the estimator is not stable or reliable for small samples. Although increasing n from 10 to 30 slightly improves the accuracy, the bias remains non-negligible, and the variance remains substantial. Therefore, $\widehat{\text{CV}}$ should be used cautiously in applications involving small sample sizes.

Table 1. The simulation and theoretical results for small sample sizes.

n	λ	μ	CV	Mean ($\widehat{\text{CV}}$)	Var ($\widehat{\text{CV}}$)	Bias ($\widehat{\text{CV}}$)	MSE ($\widehat{\text{CV}}$)
10	0.5	0.5	1.6330	1.4933	0.0507	−0.1397	0.0702
10	0.5	1	1.3229	1.1914	0.0509	−0.1315	0.0682
10	0.5	5	0.6455	0.5828	0.0202	−0.0627	0.0241
10	0.5	10	0.4545	0.4100	0.0101	−0.0445	0.0121
10	1	0.5	1.3229	1.1930	0.0508	−0.1299	0.0677
10	1	1	1.0000	0.8958	0.0393	−0.1042	0.0502
10	1	5	0.4545	0.4128	0.0102	−0.0418	0.0119
10	1	10	0.3194	0.2898	0.0051	−0.0296	0.0060
10	5	0.5	0.6455	0.5813	0.0198	−0.0642	0.0239
10	5	1	0.4545	0.4114	0.0100	−0.0431	0.0119
10	5	5	0.2009	0.1827	0.0020	−0.0182	0.0023
10	5	10	0.1418	0.1290	0.0010	−0.0127	0.0011
10	10	0.5	0.4545	0.4102	0.0100	−0.0444	0.0120
10	10	1	0.3194	0.2901	0.0050	−0.0294	0.0059
10	10	5	0.1418	0.1282	0.0010	−0.0136	0.0012
10	10	10	0.1001	0.0911	0.0005	−0.0091	0.0006
30	0.5	0.5	1.6330	1.5799	0.0132	−0.0531	0.0161
30	0.5	1	1.3229	1.2705	0.0164	−0.0524	0.0191
30	0.5	5	0.6455	0.6184	0.0069	−0.0271	0.0076
30	0.5	10	0.4545	0.4347	0.0034	−0.0199	0.0038
30	1	0.5	1.3229	1.2705	0.0161	−0.0524	0.0188
30	1	1	1.0000	0.9571	0.0135	−0.0429	0.0154
30	1	5	0.4545	0.4354	0.0034	−0.0191	0.0038
30	1	10	0.3194	0.3062	0.0017	−0.0132	0.0019
30	5	0.5	0.6455	0.6163	0.0070	−0.0292	0.0079
30	5	1	0.4545	0.4347	0.0035	−0.0198	0.0039
30	5	5	0.2009	0.1922	0.0007	−0.0088	0.0007
30	5	10	0.1418	0.1355	0.0003	−0.0063	0.0004
30	10	0.5	0.4545	0.4344	0.0035	−0.0202	0.0039
30	10	1	0.3194	0.3062	0.0017	−0.0133	0.0019
30	10	5	0.1418	0.1357	0.0003	−0.0060	0.0004
30	10	10	0.1001	0.0959	0.0002	−0.0042	0.0002

For moderate sample sizes, the performance of $\widehat{\mathrm{CV}}$ improves considerably (Table 2). The mean estimates become much closer to the true coefficient of variation, and the bias and MSE decrease notably, particularly when $n = 100$. This indicates that the estimator becomes more consistent and unbiased as the sample size increases. The reduced variability and improved precision in this range suggest that moderate sample sizes are generally adequate for reliable inference using $\widehat{\mathrm{CV}}$. These results support the theoretical properties expected from the method of moments under moderate sample conditions.

In large sample settings, the estimator $\widehat{\mathrm{CV}}$ demonstrates excellent performance (Table 3). The mean estimates are nearly identical to the true coefficient of variation, with bias approaching zero, and both variance and MSE substantially reduced across all parameter settings. These results confirm the asymptotic normality and consistency of the estimator. The precision and stability of $\widehat{\mathrm{CV}}$ in large samples make it highly suitable for practical applications, especially in fields requiring robust statistical inference such as environmental modeling, risk assessment, and decision-support systems.

Table 2. The simulation and theoretical results for moderate sample sizes.

n	λ	μ	CV	Mean ($\widehat{\mathrm{CV}}$)	Var ($\widehat{\mathrm{CV}}$)	Bias ($\widehat{\mathrm{CV}}$)	MSE ($\widehat{\mathrm{CV}}$)
50	0.5	0.5	1.6330	1.6114	0.0074	−0.0216	0.0078
50	0.5	1	1.3229	1.3019	0.0095	−0.0210	0.0099
50	0.5	5	0.6455	0.6366	0.0043	−0.0089	0.0043
50	0.5	10	0.4545	0.4473	0.0022	−0.0073	0.0022
50	1	0.5	1.3229	1.3023	0.0094	−0.0205	0.0098
50	1	1	1.0000	0.9842	0.0079	−0.0158	0.0082
50	1	5	0.4545	0.4489	0.0022	−0.0056	0.0022
50	1	10	0.3194	0.3148	0.0010	−0.0046	0.0011
50	5	0.5	0.6455	0.6356	0.0042	−0.0099	0.0043
50	5	1	0.4545	0.4487	0.0022	−0.0058	0.0022
50	5	5	0.2009	0.1983	0.0004	−0.0027	0.0004
50	5	10	0.1418	0.1399	0.0002	−0.0019	0.0002
50	10	0.5	0.4545	0.4478	0.0022	−0.0068	0.0022
50	10	1	0.3194	0.3152	0.0011	−0.0042	0.0011
50	10	5	0.1418	0.1396	0.0002	−0.0021	0.0002
50	10	10	0.1001	0.0987	0.0001	−0.0014	0.0001
100	0.5	0.5	1.6330	1.6232	0.0035	−0.0098	0.0036
100	0.5	1	1.3229	1.3134	0.0047	−0.0095	0.0048
100	0.5	5	0.6455	0.6419	0.0021	−0.0036	0.0021
100	0.5	10	0.4545	0.4523	0.0011	−0.0023	0.0011
100	1	0.5	1.3229	1.3127	0.0046	−0.0102	0.0047
100	1	1	1.0000	0.9921	0.0041	−0.0079	0.0041
100	1	5	0.4545	0.4518	0.0011	−0.0028	0.0011
100	1	10	0.3194	0.3177	0.0005	−0.0017	0.0005
100	5	0.5	0.6455	0.6403	0.0021	−0.0052	0.0022
100	5	1	0.4545	0.4514	0.0011	−0.0031	0.0011
100	5	5	0.2009	0.1999	0.0002	−0.0011	0.0002
100	5	10	0.1418	0.1410	0.0001	−0.0008	0.0001
100	10	0.5	0.4545	0.4516	0.0011	−0.0030	0.0011
100	10	1	0.3194	0.3178	0.0005	−0.0016	0.0005
100	10	5	0.1418	0.1410	0.0001	−0.0008	0.0001
100	10	10	0.1001	0.0995	0.0001	−0.0007	0.0001

Across all sample sizes, the estimator $\widehat{\mathrm{CV}}$ shows a clear improvement in performance as the sample size increases. While it is unreliable for small samples due to high bias and variability, its performance improves significantly for moderate samples and becomes highly accurate in large samples. These findings align well with theoretical expectations and support the use of $\widehat{\text{CV}}$ in applications where sufficiently large datasets are available.

Figure 3 illustrates how the accuracy of the estimated coefficient of variation ($\widehat{\text{CV}}$) improves as the sample size increases. The plot compares theoretical CV values with the corresponding simulation-based mean estimates for six different sample sizes: $n = 10, 30, 50, 100, 200$, and 500. Each line represents a different sample size and reflects the proximity of the estimated values to their theoretical counterparts.

In small samples ($n = 10$ and 30), the estimates exhibit noticeable deviations from the true CV values, revealing substantial bias and variability. As the sample size increases to moderate levels ($n = 50$ and 100), the estimates become more accurate and stable. In large samples ($n = 200$ and 500), the estimated CVs align almost perfectly with the theoretical values, indicating strong consistency and near-unbiasedness of the estimator.

Table 3. The simulation and theoretical results for large sample sizes.

n	λ	μ	CV	Mean ($\widehat{\text{CV}}$)	Var ($\widehat{\text{CV}}$)	Bias ($\widehat{\text{CV}}$)	MSE ($\widehat{\text{CV}}$)
200	0.5	0.5	1.6330	1.6342	0.0017	0.0012	0.0017
200	0.5	1	1.3229	1.3256	0.0023	0.0027	0.0023
200	0.5	5	0.6455	0.6482	0.0011	0.0027	0.0011
200	0.5	10	0.4545	0.4558	0.0005	0.0013	0.0005
200	1	0.5	1.3229	1.3247	0.0023	0.0018	0.0023
200	1	1	1.0000	1.0023	0.0020	0.0023	0.0020
200	1	5	0.4545	0.4563	0.0005	0.0018	0.0005
200	1	10	0.3194	0.3207	0.0003	0.0013	0.0003
200	5	0.5	0.6455	0.6480	0.0011	0.0025	0.0011
200	5	1	0.4545	0.4562	0.0005	0.0017	0.0005
200	5	5	0.2009	0.2017	0.0001	0.0008	0.0001
200	5	10	0.1418	0.1424	0.0001	0.0006	0.0001
200	10	0.5	0.4545	0.4564	0.0006	0.0019	0.0006
200	10	1	0.3194	0.3206	0.0003	0.0012	0.0003
200	10	5	0.1418	0.1423	0.0001	0.0005	0.0001
200	10	10	0.1001	0.1005	0.00003	0.0004	0.0000
500	0.5	0.5	1.6330	1.6294	0.0007	−0.0036	0.0007
500	0.5	1	1.3229	1.3192	0.0009	−0.0037	0.0009
500	0.5	5	0.6455	0.6433	0.0004	−0.0022	0.0004
500	0.5	10	0.4545	0.4529	0.0002	−0.0017	0.0002
500	1	0.5	1.3229	1.3191	0.0009	−0.0038	0.0009
500	1	1	1.0000	0.9969	0.0008	−0.0031	0.0008
500	1	5	0.4545	0.4531	0.0002	−0.0014	0.0002
500	1	10	0.3194	0.3185	0.0001	−0.0010	0.0001
500	5	0.5	0.6455	0.6434	0.0004	−0.0021	0.0004
500	5	1	0.4545	0.4530	0.0002	−0.0015	0.0002
500	5	5	0.2009	0.2003	0.00004	−0.0006	0.00004
500	5	10	0.1418	0.1413	0.00002	−0.0004	0.00002
500	10	0.5	0.4545	0.4533	0.0002	−0.0013	0.0002
500	10	1	0.3194	0.3185	0.0001	−0.0009	0.0001
500	10	5	0.1418	0.1413	0.00002	−0.0004	0.00002
500	10	10	0.1001	0.0999	0.00001	−0.0002	0.00001

Figure 4 further quantifies this performance by summarizing the mean bias and mean squared error of $\widehat{\text{CV}}$ for each sample size. Both measures decline steadily as the sample size increases, reinforcing the theoretical properties of the method of moments and underscoring the critical role of sufficient sample sizes in achieving reliable inference.

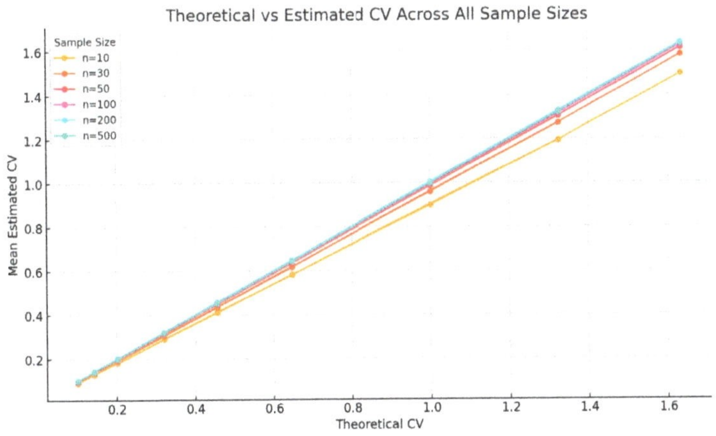

Figure 3. Comparison between theoretical and estimated coefficient of variation ($\widehat{CV}$) across various sample sizes.

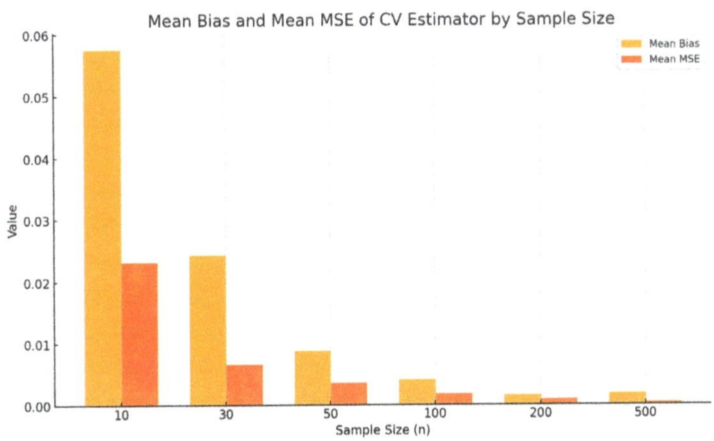

Figure 4. Summary of estimator performance: mean bias and mean MSE of $\widehat{CV}$ by sample size.

6. Real-Life Example

In Section 5 of the article [6], the applicability of the BirSau distribution to model the total rainfall amounts over consecutive rainy days was demonstrated. The rainfall data from 31 meteorological stations in the northeastern region of Thailand was collected, spanning from January 1984 to September 2024. The suitability of the data for the BirSau distribution was assessed using the Kolmogorov–Smirnov test for goodness-of-fit at a significance level of $\alpha = 0.05$. The results indicate that many stations have cumulative rainfall data for consecutive rainy days that align well with the BirSau distribution. Figure 5 presents box plots and density plots for selected stations that passed the goodness-of-fit test for the Birnbaum–Saunders (BirSau) distribution, based on rainfall data aggregated over 2, 4, and 6 consecutive days. Both types of plots reveal that the rainfall distributions are positively skewed, exhibiting pronounced right tails.

CONS-2 to CONS-7 represent different data grouping periods or conditions used in the rainfall analysis, such as time intervals or specific event classifications (Table 4). Each row presents data from meteorological stations located in northeastern Thailand. Variables include Min (minimum), Mean (average), Max (maximum), SD (standard deviation), Skewness (distribution skewness), and Kurtosis (distribution peakedness).

Next, we will apply the theory established in Section 2 for the estimation of the coefficient of variation for the rainfall data. We selected the stations whose total rainfall follows the BirSau distribution and present the asymptotic confidence intervals for the coefficient of variation in Table 5. Non-overlapping confidence intervals suggest statistically significant differences in rainfall variability between stations, while overlapping intervals indicate that the variability may be similar. This approach is particularly useful for identifying regions with unusually high or low relative variability, which is important for hydrological planning and resource management.

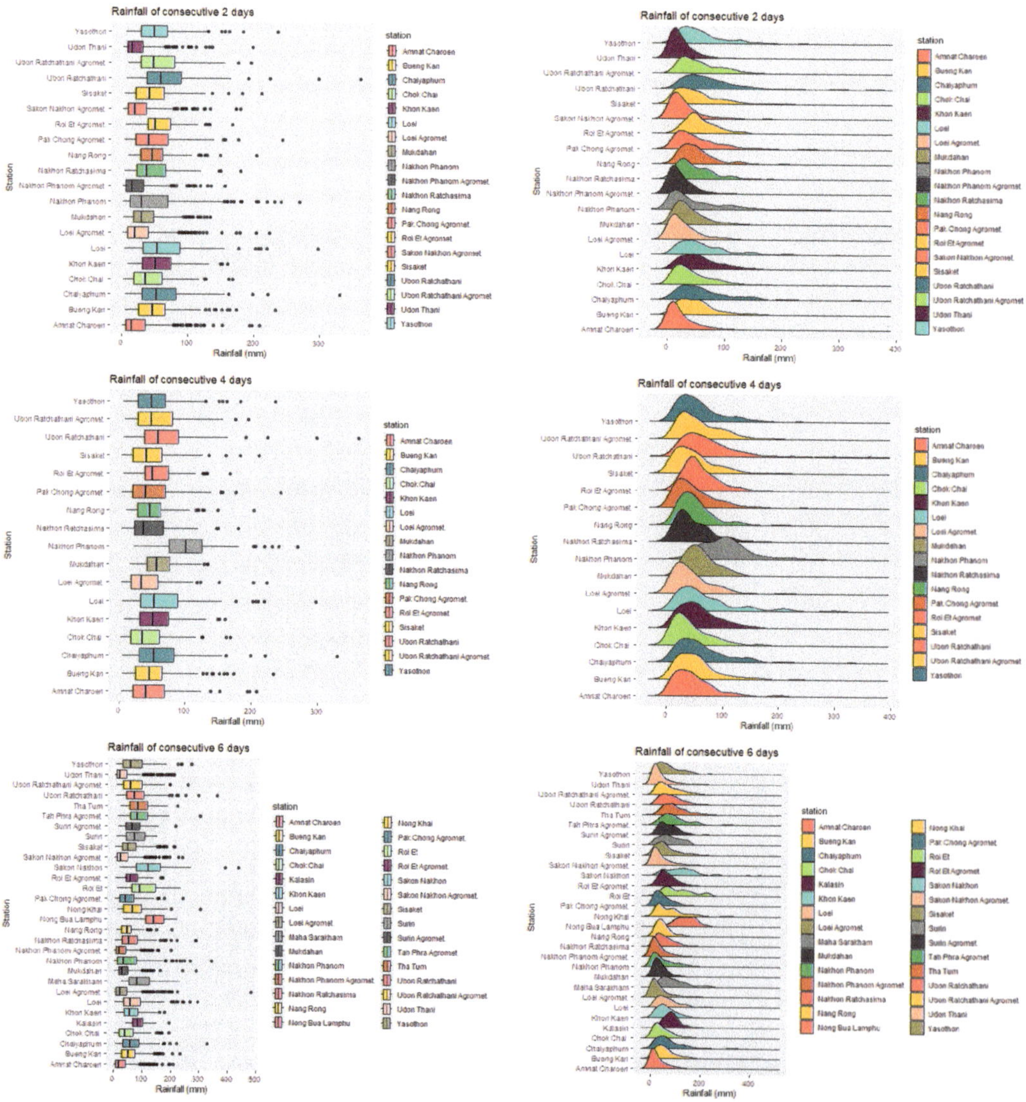

Figure 5. Box plots and density plots for stations that passed the goodness-of-fit test for the BirSau distribution, based on 2, 4, and 6 consecutive days of aggregated data.

Figure 5 displays box plots and density plots for rainfall data collected from selected meteorological stations that fit the Birnbaum–Saunders distribution. The box plots summarize the median, interquartile range, and potential outliers (shown as dots), while the density plots show the probability distribution of rainfall amounts. The results clearly indicate right-skewed rainfall distributions, consistent with the BirSau model's ability to describe positively skewed environmental data.

Table 4. Descriptive statistics of rainfall data by station and CONS period.

Data	Station	Min	Mean	Max	sd	Skewness	Kurtosis
CONS-2	Loei Agromet.	0.4	17.41	129.1	17.75	2.14	9.68
	Udon Thani	0.4	20.78	178.5	23.25	2.81	15.27
	Nakhon Phanom	0.4	27.14	178.4	29.99	2.36	9.84
	Nakhon Ratchasima	0.4	19.78	146.2	21.26	2.05	8.58
	Nong Khai	1.9	40.1	193.8	33.63	1.52	5.61
CONS-3	Nakhon Phanom	1.6	40.47	216.8	36.51	2.05	8.66
	Mukdahan	1	39.86	263.5	37.62	2.18	10.02
	Ubon Ratchathani	2.3	43.29	259.4	38.86	2.21	10.5
	Nakhon Ratchasima	0.9	35.44	173.7	31.94	1.89	7.36
CONS-4	Loei Agromet.	2.5	47	230.4	38.91	1.8	7.08
	Nakhon Phanom	3.6	66.74	297.1	53.61	1.72	6.34
	Mukdahan	7.5	56.12	160.4	34.25	0.9	3.38
	Ubon Ratchathani	5	54.95	234.1	41.02	1.54	5.83
	Nakhon Ratchasima	3.3	48.34	210	38.64	1.5	5.81
CONS-5	Loei Agromet.	5.8	65.06	189.5	41.84	0.91	3.19
	Nakhon Phanom Agromet.	12.7	69.76	177.4	34.58	0.89	3.62
	Bueng Kan	36.5	128.72	302.5	55.65	1.01	3.83
	Amnat Charoen	20.9	68.94	146	28.91	0.68	2.98
	Nakhon Ratchasima	4.7	61.07	238.9	44.81	1.77	7.18
CONS-6	Loei Agromet.	12.8	70.96	300.9	46.49	1.96	10.24
	Nakhon Phanom	21.1	128.51	436	81.07	1.65	6.76
	Mukdahan	26.9	92.81	233.5	53.17	0.98	3.3
	Ubon Ratchathani Agromet.	12.6	101.94	270.5	56.29	0.8	3.66
	Nakhon Ratchasima	15.5	83.13	209	50.42	0.9	2.57
CONS-7	Loei Agromet.	23.7	90.34	271.5	51.72	1.62	6.51
	Nakhon Phanom	18.7	125.9	345.7	71.1	0.97	3.96
	Mukdahan	41.5	104.94	194.7	39.61	0.34	2.49
	Ubon Ratchathani Agromet.	22.5	108.63	250.5	54.09	0.49	2.79
	Nakhon Ratchasima	16.2	69.08	196.2	38.07	1.53	6.53

The analysis of the estimated coefficient of variation ($\widehat{CV}$) for rainfall data, as presented in Table 5 and Figure 6, highlights distinct patterns of rainfall variability across different stations and data groups (CONS-2 to CONS-7). In general, lower CV values were observed in CONS-2, suggesting more stable rainfall distributions over longer periods. In contrast, CV values increased substantially in groups representing more extreme or shorter-duration rainfall events (CONS-4, CONS-6), indicating higher variability and more erratic rainfall behavior. The 95% confidence intervals across all stations remained relatively narrow, reflecting the robustness of the CV estimates. Furthermore, consistent station-level differences emerged, with some locations—such as Loei Agromet. and Nakhon Phanom—exhibiting higher rainfall variability across multiple groups. These findings underscore the importance of accounting for both temporal scale and spatial variability when modeling rainfall and assessing hydrological risks, particularly in the context of extreme events and climate adaptation planning.

Table 5. 95% confidence intervals for the coefficient of variation for the rainfall data.

Data	Station	n	$\widehat{CV}$	L-Limit (CV)	U-limit (CV)
CONS-2	Loei Agromet.	402	0.2864	0.2761	0.2968
	Udon Thani	358	0.2079	0.2008	0.2150
	Nakhon Phanom	332	0.1733	0.1678	0.1787
	Amnat Charoen	372	0.1002	0.0983	0.1022
	Nakhon Ratchasima	439	0.2294	0.2220	0.2368
CONS-3	Nong Khai	207	1.0579	1.0575	1.0583
	Nakhon Phanom	188	1.1007	1.0995	1.1020
	Mukdahan	204	1.0390	1.0388	1.0392
	Ubon Ratchathani	217	1.0421	1.0419	1.0423
	Nakhon Ratchasima	223	1.1202	1.1186	1.1218
CONS-4	Loei Agromet.	136	0.9420	0.9415	0.9425
	Nakhon Phanom	99	0.8918	0.8898	0.8939
	Mukdahan	113	0.7314	0.7205	0.7423
	Ubon Ratchathani	117	0.8228	0.8178	0.8277
	Nakhon Ratchasima	114	0.9841	0.9841	0.9842
CONS-5	Loei Agromet.	93	0.7848	0.7768	0.7929
	Nakhon Phanom Agromet.	76	0.5433	0.5149	0.5717
	Bueng Kan	83	0.4375	0.4073	0.4676
	Amnat Charoen	88	0.4527	0.4234	0.4819
	Nakhon Ratchasima	69	0.8311	0.8252	0.8370
CONS-6	Loei Agromet.	66	0.7201	0.7048	0.7354
	Nakhon Phanom	55	0.6825	0.6618	0.7032
	Mukdahan	51	0.6006	0.5707	0.6305
	Ubon Ratchathani Agromet.	48	0.6973	0.6769	0.7178
	Nakhon Ratchasima	41	0.6256	0.5950	0.6562
CONS-7	Loei Agromet.	27	0.5560	0.5096	0.6024
	Nakhon Phanom	34	0.6510	0.6206	0.6814
	Mukdahan	33	0.4154	0.3679	0.4629
	Ubon Ratchathani Agromet.	35	0.5974	0.5609	0.6338
	Nakhon Ratchasima	23	0.5805	0.5332	0.6278

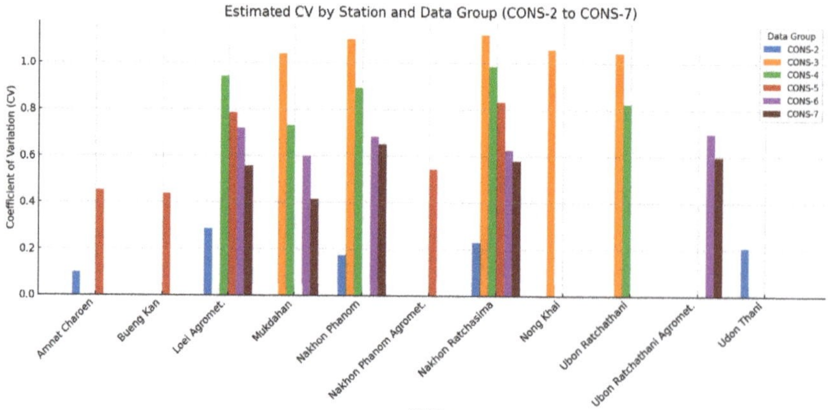

Figure 6. Estimated coefficient of variation ($\widehat{CV}$) with 95% confidence intervals by station for data groups CONS-2 to CONS-7.

7. Discussion

This study provides a comprehensive analysis of the asymptotic properties of the coefficient of variation estimator under the reparameterized Birnbaum–Saunders distribution. Our findings confirm that the method of moments-based CV estimator exhibits strong asymptotic normality properties, consistent with theoretical expectations.

The simulation results reveal clear trends across different sample sizes. In small sample settings ($n = 10$ to 30), the CV estimator exhibits substantial bias and variability, making it less reliable for inference. As sample size increases to moderate levels ($n = 50$ to 100), bias and variance decrease markedly, suggesting that these sample sizes are sufficient for practical applications where robust CV estimates are required. For large samples ($n = 200$ to 500), the CV estimator performs exceptionally well, with minimal bias and variance approaching theoretical limits.

These findings are consistent with prior results on CV estimation in BirSau and other distributions [10,11], and extend the literature by explicitly demonstrating the behavior of the estimator under the reparameterized BirSau model. Moreover, our results complement previous interval estimation work for BirSau parameters [12] and contribute new insights specifically regarding the CV, which is of growing importance in fields such as environmental risk assessment and materials engineering.

The real-data example on rainfall modeling further illustrates the practical value of our approach. The estimated CVs across different stations and aggregation periods highlight significant spatial and temporal variability in rainfall patterns, aligning with findings from related studies on hydrological and meteorological data modeling [13,14]. The relatively narrow confidence intervals in most cases indicate the robustness of the CV estimates under the proposed method.

Taken together, these results reinforce the applicability of the reparameterized Birnbaum–Saunders distribution for modeling positively skewed environmental data and support the use of method of moments-based CV estimators in both research and applied settings.

8. Conclusions

This study rigorously investigated the asymptotic properties of the coefficient of variation estimator for the reparameterized Birnbaum–Saunders distribution using the method of moments framework. Through theoretical derivations and extensive simulation studies, we established that the estimator is asymptotically normal, with its variance converging to the derived theoretical form.

Our findings demonstrate that the estimator performs poorly in small samples but improves rapidly with increasing sample size. For moderate-to-large samples, the estimator exhibits minimal bias and variance, enabling reliable inference. These results align with and extend previous work on CV estimation under the BirSau model and provide practical guidance for its application in real-world scenarios.

The application to rainfall data underscores the practical relevance of our approach, illustrating how CV-based inference can reveal important patterns in environmental variability. The methods presented here can be readily extended to other domains where positively skewed data arise, such as reliability engineering and financial risk analysis.

9. Future Studies

Future studies may focus on enhancing the estimation of the coefficient of variation (CV) in small-sample scenarios, where bias correction techniques or Bayesian approaches could provide improved accuracy. In addition, given the strong asymptotic normality and robustness of the proposed estimator in large samples, a natural extension is the comparison of variability across multiple populations. One particularly promising direction is the development of inference procedures for the ratio of CVs from two independent Birnbaum–Saunders distributions. Furthermore, incorporating the proposed estimator into broader modeling frameworks—such as hierarchical models or spatio-temporal structures—could significantly expand the applicability of the Birnbaum–Saunders distribution in complex and high-dimensional data settings.

Author Contributions: Conceptualization, S.S. and A.V.; methodology, P.B.; software, T.P.; validation, T.P., A.V. and S.S.; formal analysis, P.B.; investigation, S.S.; resources, P.B.; data curation, T.P.; writing—original draft preparation, S.S.; writing—review and editing, P.B., S.S. and A.V.; visualization, S.S.; supervision, A.V.; project administration, P.B. All authors have read and agreed to the published version of the manuscript.

Funding: This research project was financially supported by Mahasarakham University and the Office of the Permanent Secretary of the Ministry of Higher Education, Science, Research and Innovation. Piyapatr and Sujitta's work was also funded by the Agricultural Research Development Agency (Public Organization) of Thailand (ARDA).

Data Availability Statement: Data are contained within the article.

Acknowledgments: The authors are grateful to the reviewers for their valuable and constructive comments. Observational data in the Thailand were provided by Thai Meteorological Department (TMD accessed on 5 September 2024) at https://www.tmd.go.th/.

Conflicts of Interest: The authors declare no potential conflicts of interest.

References

1. Birnbaum, Z.W.; Saunders, S.C. A new family of the life distribution. *J. Appl. Probab.* **1969**, *6*, 319–327. [CrossRef]
2. Balakrishnan, N.; Kundu, D. Birnbaum-Saunders Distribution: A Review of Models, Analysis and Applications. *arXiv* **2018**, arXiv:1805.06730. [CrossRef]
3. Leiva, V.; Santos-Neto, M.; Cysneiros, F.J.A.; Barros, M. Birnbaum–Saunders statistical modelling: A new approach. *Stat. Model.* **2014**, *14*, 21–48. [CrossRef]
4. Reyes, J.; Arrué, J.; Leiva, V.; Martin-Barreiro, C. A New Birnbaum–Saunders Distribution and Its Mathematical Features Applied to Bimodal Real-World Data from Environment and Medicine. *Mathematics* **2021**, *9*, 1891. [CrossRef]
5. Lehmann, E.L.; Casella, G. *Theory of Point Estimation*; Springer: New York, NY, USA, 1998.
6. Busababodhin, P.; Phoophiwfa, T.; Volodin, A.; Suraphee, S. On the Asymptotic Normality of the Method of Moments Estimators for the Birnbaum–Saunders Distribution with a New Parametrization. *Mathematics* **2025**, *13*, 636. [CrossRef]
7. Ahmed, S.E.; Budsaba, K.; Lisawadi, S.; Volodin, A. Parametric estimation for the Birnbaum-Saunders lifetime distribution based on a new parametrization. *Thail. Stat.* **2008**, *6*, 213–240.
8. Cramér, H. *Mathematical Methods of Statistics (PMS-9)*; Princeton University Press: Princeton, NJ, USA, 1946.
9. Lehmann, E. *Elements of Large Sample Theory*; Springer: New York, NY, USA, 2004.
10. Forkman, J. Estimator and Tests for Common Coefficients of Variation in Normal Distributions. *Commun. Stat. Theory Methods* **2009**, *38*, 233–251. [CrossRef]
11. Puggard, W.; Niwitpong, S.A.; Niwitpong, S. Comparison Analysis on the Coefficients of Variation of Two Independent Birnbaum-Saunders Distributions by Constructing Confidence Intervals for the Ratio of Coefficients of Variation. *Sains Malays.* **2022**,*51*, 2265–2281. [CrossRef]
12. Jantakoon, N.; Volodin, A. Interval estimation for the shape and scale parameters of the Birnbaum–Saunders distribution. *Lobachevskii J. Math.* **2019**, *40*, 1164–1177. [CrossRef]
13. Sawlan, Z.; Scavino, M.; Tempone, R. Modeling Metallic Fatigue Data Using the Birnbaum–Saunders Distribution. *Metals* **2024**, *14*, 508. [CrossRef]
14. Suraphee, S.; Busababodhin, P.; Buntao, N. Parameter Estimation on the Asymptotic Distribution of the Maximum Daily Rainfall of Wet Periods in the Northeast Thailand. *Lobachevskii J. Math.* **2024**, *45*, 6415–6428. [CrossRef]

MDPI AG
Grosspeteranlage 5
4052 Basel
Switzerland
Tel.: +41 61 683 77 34

Axioms Editorial Office
E-mail: axioms@mdpi.com
www.mdpi.com/journal/axioms

www.ingramcontent.com/pod-product-compliance
Lightning Source LLC
Chambersburg PA
CBHW061630210926
51850CB00009B/2499
* 9 7 8 3 7 2 5 8 6 8 4 4 5 *